THE STORY OF
Littleborough

THE STORY OF
Littleborough

John Street

Littleborough Civic Trust

Published by Littleborough Civic Trust, 1999

Distributed by George Kelsall,
22 Church Street, Littleborough, Lancashire OL15 9AA
01706 370244

British Library Cataloguing-in-publication data:
A catalogue record for this book is available from The British Library.

ISBN: 0 9536864 0 X Hardback
ISBN: 0 9536864 1 8 Paperback

Design & production by Christopher Lord, Manchester, 0161 953 4007
Printed by Shanleys, Bolton

Cover image © Geoff Butterworth F.R.S.A, B.W.S.
Illustrations by Jane Dodds & Stuart Dawson

CONTENTS

CONTENTS

CONTENTS

CONTENTS

ACKNOWLEDGEMENTS

The whole creation of 'The Story of Littleborough' has been a voluntary effort, the book celebrates generations of Littleborough people who have contributed to the story past and present. Many individuals, groups and societies have helped, willingly providing information, photographs, publications and reminiscences. The generosity of local people has been heart-warming. Indeed: the most difficult decisions have been what information to actually leave out, unfortunately it has been impossible to include everything.

The management group have met regularly over the five years of the projects life, guiding it and contributing to it with all kinds of professional help despite their individually busy lives. There have been many helpers who have assisted with the collation of information and endless proof reading requirements of continually changing chapters affected by new discoveries. All must be heartily thanked.

Particular thanks are due to the Local Studies Department at Rochdale Metropolitan Borough Council, Littleborough Historical and Archaeological Society, The Pennine Township, The Rochdale Observer and Millennium Festival Awards for All, for their help, support and encouragement. We are also indebted to the many Patrons, Sponsors and Subscribers detailed in the book. Without their confidence in the project and willingness to support it we may not have been able to bring the book to the people of Littleborough.

In the creation of the text a special contribution has been made by Peter Cryer whose encyclopaedic store of local knowledge has been freely available. The book would have been much poorer without him and although their contributions are very different, he stands shoulder to shoulder with Fred Jackson, our foremost local historian.

This book started as a very modest project and grew into the publication before you. As Author, I hope that people will enjoy it and see it as a celebration of Littleborough.

JOHN STREET
Chairman, Littleborough Civic Trust

FOREWORD

House of Lords

As Patron of Littleborough Civic Trust and former MP for Littleborough, I am pleased to have this opportunity of commending those involved for many years in the work of the Civic Trust.

It is a wonderful idea to produce a book to provide permanent record of a period from 200,000 BC, up to 2000 AD (the 2nd Millennium). The Littleborough story is one worth recording and I hope this book will prove to be a "Best Seller". It so very much deserves to be for all those involved.

Finally, please allow me to express all good wishes to everyone in Littleborough.

The Rt Hon Lord Barnett

INTRODUCTION

It is possible to ask the question does Littleborough have a story? Bagley's book 'A History of Lancashire' was first published in 1956, and the fifth edition published in 1970 had by then become a self-proclaimed 'classic'. Accepting that its index is comprehensive, it never mentions the Littleborough district once. More evidence can be produced from the writings of one of our most prolific local historians, Henry Fishwick FSA. Apparently by popular demand a century ago, he too wrote a 'History of Lancashire' where Littleborough is mentioned once, but only in an allusion to the dispute about the authenticity of the Roman road.

When the committee of the Littleborough Civic Trust sat down in 1996 to look at our local story, as a fit project to offer to the community for the Millennium, it was imperative to know the boundaries of the story and where to find the material.

For many aspects of this book the geographical scope of Littleborough can be considered as the old Urban District Boundary as illustrated. If you stand on any hill in Littleborough on a clear day you will see that to the north-west, north and round as far as due south the view is limited by the line of the high moorland. The old Urban District Council boundary broadly follows this watershed. Only towards Rochdale does the view open out across a plain. The township sits at the foot of the Pennines and due north there is a great incision in the uplands that is followed by the road, rail and canal to Todmorden and on into Yorkshire.

Fred Jackson, the Littleborough Historian seen here alongside the Roman road on Blackstone Edge; around 1910.

Warland Reservoir

To Todmorden
A6033

White Holme
Reservoir

Great Hill

Warland

Stubley
Cross
Hill

Owler Clough

Light
Hazzle
Reservoir

Turn
Slack
Hill

Cuckoo
Hill

B6138
To Mytholmroyd

Flight Hill

SUMMIT

Blackstone Edge
Reservoir

Higher Stone Pits

CALDERBROOK

Croft

Greenhill
Church

East
Hill

High Lee
Slack

Calderbrook Road

Todmorden Road

A58
To Halifax

Blackstone Edge
Moor

Shore Hall

Shore

Lower
Starring
Farm

Hare Hill
Road

Honresfield

Roman Road

LITTLEBOROUGH

Blackstone Edge Old Road

Blackstone Edge

Whitelees
Road

Parish Church

Birch Hill
Hospital

Falcon

DEARNLEY

Redmires

A58 To
Rochdale

Smithy Bridge Road

SMITHY BRIDGE

THE BOUNDARY OF THE
LITTLEBOROUGH URBAN
DISTRICT COUNCIL

Slippery Moss

M62
JUNCTION
22

Little Clegg

HOLLINGWORTH
LAKE

Owl
Hill

Turnough
Hill

M62

Lower
Eafield

RAKEWOOD

Windy
Hill

To
Milnrow

Heights
Barn

Castle
Hill

Tunshill

Nicholas Pike

Piethorne
Clough

TO
JUNCTION
21

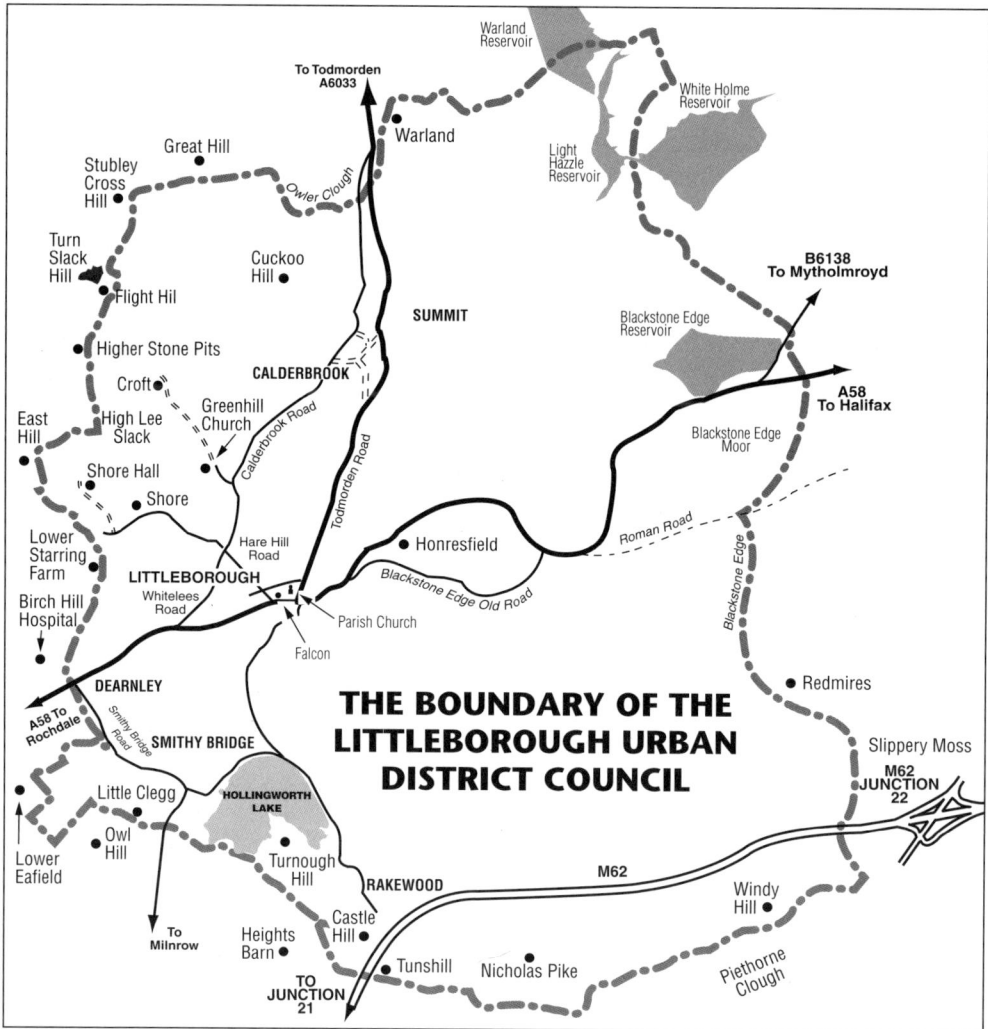

The above description must be qualified since to outline the local history from the Stone Age onwards means that at some times our scope must be all Europe and towards the North Pole in Glacial Times, at others we are part of a Pennine culture which is very distinct from that existing on the plains on both sides. Finally, for a very long period we were part of a district called Honresfeld which stretched from the borders of Rochdale deep into the present Yorkshire. In summary, during most of our story Littleborough has been a collection of small hill communities whose close relations were with similar communities in our part of the Pennines. It is relatively recently that the Littleborough we know today came into existence. The dominance of the hillside communities gave way to a much bigger unit sitting on the floor of the main valley area, straddling the major communication lines.

The project to create this book was inspired by the writings of a local man,

Fred Jackson (1860 - 1943), who wrote a number of papers and articles about Littleborough. The story of Fred Jackson is fascinating in itself, but his writings have become perhaps the most available, accessible story of the life of ordinary people in Littleborough.

This book freely uses the writing of Fred Jackson whenever possible. Broadly this means the chapters in the first half of the book draw on Fred's work extensively. From the 17th Century onwards his contribution is absorbed into a much wider range of reference. We have tried to treat his material with sympathy and respect, if the book is pleasing, it owes a great debt to Fred Jackson. From the 17th Century onwards the material reproduced represents the collection, collation and selection of material from many books, but above all from material provided by people who have lived in, or know about, Littleborough. There have been more than 200 contributors and their work has been filtered through an editorial committee of seven people and a proof reading team of five.

The contributors have given us access to photographs, books, records, letters and given their memories freely for no reward, except the satisfaction of knowing that their part is added to all the others and that they value the outcome. What they have is a story of of the area we know today as Littleborough, a record of much that has happened to the people over the centuries and a sketch of its position at the Millennium. For the help they have all given over a four year period we say thank you, and offer the book as a celebration of their efforts.

It is a story to be read by anyone who lives in or enjoys our area. The story tries to stay within the boundary of known facts, but above all we hope it leads Littleborough people and sympathetic visitors to a greater enjoyment in our local heritage. At the opening of each chapter, we have given a brief summary of contemporary wider national events to set the local story in context. When in 1533 the King's Commissioners seized our local church and bell selling them to someone in London, the chapter opening should give a clue as to why this momentous event came about.

Most stories do not need an index but there is a limited one in this book. This is a 'true' story, with considerable detail, so the index has been provided to give a number of entry points to any chapter, where a topic is given significant space. It would be more detailed were it a history or a text book.

When we set out to make this book we imagined someone picking it up and seeing something of interest. Most of the features discussed in the book are less than two miles from the centre of Littleborough, so after lunch the reader is off 'just to have a look'. If it turns out to really interest you this book cannot answer all your questions so there are further 'associated reading' lists. These sources are listed in the bibliography, within the framework of chapters where they were most useful. A look at some of these sources will open up a world of further available information about our small part of England.

One lesson from this book is that very few families can claim to have lived in Littleborough more than 200 years, yet we can touch and feel history here going back at least, 15,000 years. For anyone who discovers an error or an apparent distortion of events, please let us know and accept our apology in advance. The scope of the book is immense, including much material within living memory so errors are inevitable. This is a 'people's story' to which you all have contributed something.

A NOTE ON MAPS

In preparing this book we have found the Ordnance Survey maps in the Pathfinder Series, at a scale of 1:25000 (2½ inches to a mile), the best for general use. Between them; No 701 SD, 81/91, Bury Rochdale and Littleborough, and No 690, SD 82/92, Rawtenstall & Hebden Bridge give ample coverage. For more detailed investigation on the ground the 6" to one mile sheets are invaluable. However this book is a long story, so the old 6" maps, dated 1850 and 1895, are very helpful when exploring how our area has changed. These can be consulted at the Local Studies library at Rochdale and by arrangement copies of part or all can be provided. If your find your interest grows at a detailed level these maps become indispensible and a section of each is shown in the text. If you want to dig even deeper there are further resources such as Sheet 21 of the first edition of the one-inch O.S. map (1843) which has been re-printed and Littleborough sits right in the middle of the sheet.

In many chapters we have provided diagrams with the modern road lines and other existing features where it seemed helpful. On this framework we have located the names and places discussed in the chapter; many of which have long since gone. Using your diagram in the book and the recommended map you can immediately find to where the name refers on the ground. If you go to look you will realise there is normally no name and frequently little evidence on the ground, beyond some very heavy foundation stones that have proved too arkward to carry away or a great hollow, the remains of the cellars of a tall mill. On a bad day you may find you are standing in a half built 'clump' of new houses.

Much of the property is of course private, so you must exercise some discretion anywhere that is not obviously public space. It sometimes needs patience also, since Clough Head, as described in an account, can quite easily mean somewhere half a mile away from where the O.S map shows it today. As an example, when a new road was opened, like the turnpike from Todmorden to Littleborough, there was quite a rush to exploit the commercial opportunities. A number of communities were formed (eg new Gale) and for their new houses some dismantled their old stone houses and used the material to build the new one. Sometimes they carried the old name with them or simply stuck 'new' in front of it. At other times a community died because of the loss of the trade on which it had been founded. The end of the widespread use of horses caused the decline of many communities with the word 'smithy' somewhere in the title.

Finally it is often useful to have a good street atlas available. It is a comment on the tenacity of names that the vast majority of place names used 200 years ago are still used today, broadly for the same area. However, be cautious, there is no evidence that the name Shakespeare reflects some exciting presence of the bard in 17th century Littleborough.

JOHN STREET

CHAPTER ONE

UP AND DOWN THE VALLEY.
The origins of our scenery

Formation of the millstone grit

One mile north of Littleborough, standing on the bridge at the Green Vale crossing and looking up and down the valley, anyone can see a wonderful variety in the scenery. Up the valley the gaunt rugged masses of millstone grit crop out on either side; the hills are nearly devoid of vegetation and scarcely a tree or bush is to be seen anywhere. Below Green Vale, however, the hills are lower and more rounded, the valley broadens out forming the meadows on Gale Flat, whilst the hillsides are covered with trees and vegetation. Why should one part of the district be so different to another ? How is it that in one area coal was found in good quantities, while in another, separated perhaps by only a few yards, no coal was to be found ?

While it was once a popular belief that the hills and valleys, oceans, seas and rivers are just as they had been from the very beginning of time, the science known as geology proves that quite the contrary is the case. For instance, it is quite evident that the millstone grit rocks (so prominent on the edges of our moors) were deposited, in the form of sediment, along sea shores, and often between low and high water mark, for they contain an abundance of ripple marks, rain pittings, and sun-cracks. The

The prominent outcrop of rocks at Robin Hood's bed on the skyline at Blackstone Edge, high above Littleborough, on the border with Yorkshire.

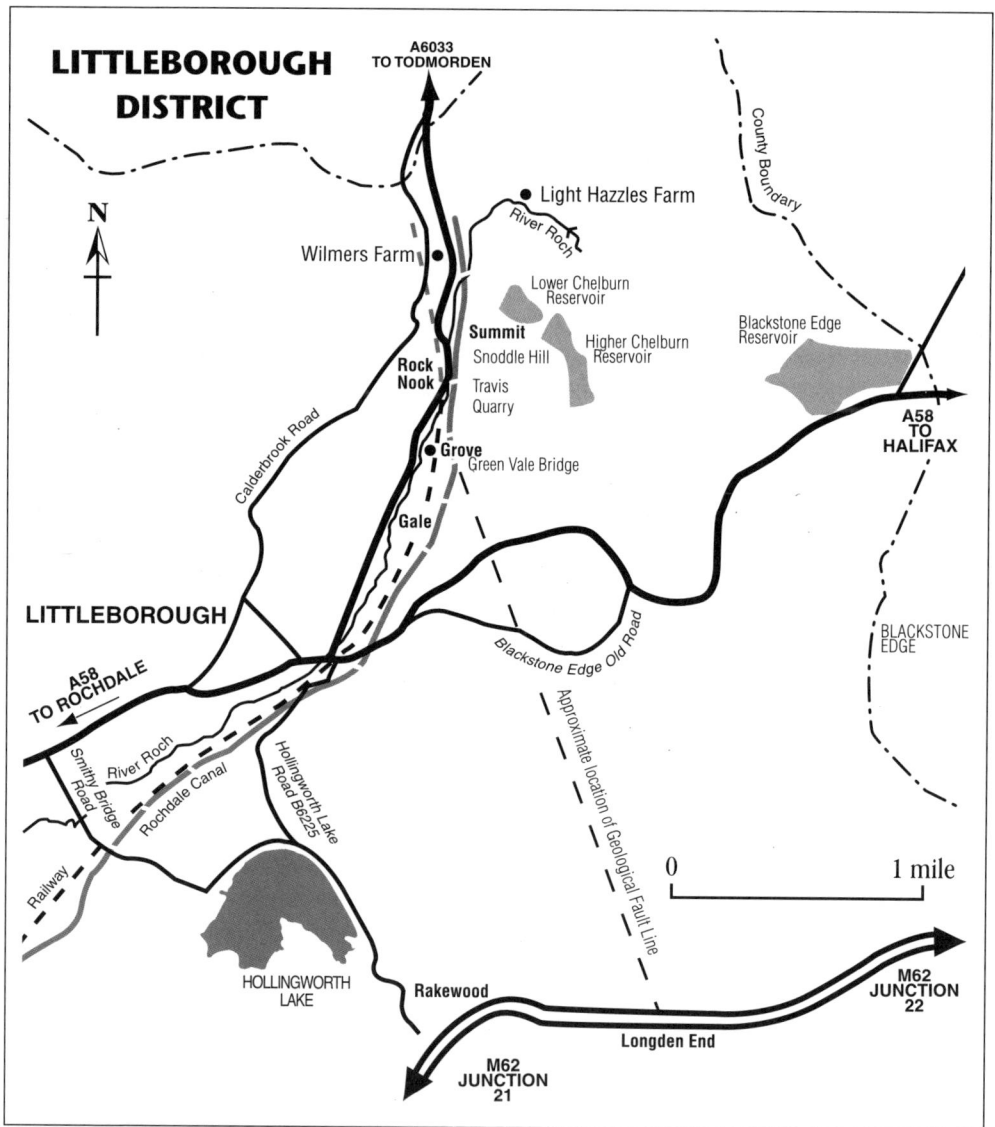

LITTLEBOROUGH DISTRICT

A6033 TO TODMORDEN

N

County Boundary

Light Hazzles Farm

River Roch

Wilmers Farm

Lower Chelburn
Reservoir

Blackstone Edge
Reservoir

Summit
Snoddle Hill

Higher Chelburn
Reservoir

**Rock
Nook**

Travis
Quarry

A58
TO
HALIFAX

Caldebrook Road

● Grove
Green Vale Bridge

Gale

LITTLEBOROUGH

Blackstone Edge Old Road

BLACKSTONE
EDGE

A58
TO ROCHDALE

Smithy Bridge

River Roch

Rochdale Canal

Hollingworth Lake
Road B6225

Approximate location of Geological Fault Line

0   1 mile

Railway

HOLLINGWORTH
LAKE

Rakewood

Longden End

M62
JUNCTION
22

M62
JUNCTION
21

coarseness of many of the grains composing the millstone grit and the absence of shells suggests that it was deposited in turbulent waters. Now as then, large quantities of matter in the form of mud, sand and pebbles are brought down in the brooks to the rivers after every shower of rain. By the rivers they are conveyed to the sea, so that the levelling down of all the hills with the deposition of the material in the seas is merely a matter of time.

Coal occurs in various parts of the district, but very little is found, for example, in the neighbourhood of Summit. After the materials needed to form the millstone grit rocks had been deposited on the sea shores, the land itself sank almost to sea level. The whole of England was converted into immense swamps, upon which forests grew. Later under the pressure of overlying rocks the vegetable matter was converted into coal. After the coal measures had been laid down, great movements gradually altered the arrangements of land and sea. The Pennine range, of which Blackstone Edge forms a part, was lifted bodily up above the surrounding country. In addition to that, the rocks in the immediate neighbourhood of Summit were split up and broken in a remarkable manner. The greatest disturbance, however, occured in a line with Green Vale extending as far as Longden end. Huge masses of rock, from three to four thousand feet in thickness, were split from top to bottom, those on the Summit side being lifted two to three thousand feet higher than those on the other side. This was the cause of the great difference in the scenery between Summit and Littleborough. The hills we see around us today are only the remnants of the mighty ranges existing at the time.

Glacial Period

In the clay pits at Summit and other places is to be found the history of one of the most recent geological periods, the Glacial Period, when ice covered our region. The clay and the boulders it contains being remnants of the time when climatic conditions were similar to those now found in the Polar regions. In the local clay pits there are boulders from Shap Fell, in Cumberland and others from as far north as Galloway and Crifell in Scotland, while in Broadfield Park, Rochdale, there is a boulder from the Cumberland hills, weighing at least seven tons and another example can be seen at Wilmers farm, Summit. Such boulders are called 'glacial erratics'. In the age to which the clay and boulders testify, the Littleborough District, as well as a large part of England, was covered by immense glaciers. At one stage during the ice age, a great glacier flowed down from Scotland and was joined by glaciers from the Lake District and other large ones flowing from Ireland, each portion of the compound glacier thus formed bearing its characteristic boulders. As the ice melted the erratics came to rest far from the area where they originated.

In this district at that period there were mountains thousands of feet in height, covered with ice. In the later glacial period there were also numerous lakes in the valleys stretching from Bacup on the one hand and Oldham on the other, right along to Hebden Bridge. The valley of Littleborough was occupied by one large sheet of water. Water from the lake, escaped by way of Snoddle Hill, carrying huge masses of ice with it along the Walsden valley. Traces of glacial action have been discovered at the top end of Walsden.

There are convincing claims that some of the other local land forms are very directly the result of the immediate post-glacial erosion. For example the Chelburn Reservoirs are said to be sited in a glacial overflow channel worn out by melt water as the ice cap retreated. Similarly looking south-west from Chelburn there are, on the skyline, a series of U-shaped gaps which are said to have been formed in the same way by melt water running along the side of the ice cap during the long periods when it was stable and not retreating. Many such channels can be seen being formed in our high mountain masses today.

Denudation

When any tract of land rises higher than the rest the agents of denudation, rain, frost, wind and snow, begin to act very quickly. The rain cuts channels into the softer ground, carrying the soil to lower levels and a good deal of it eventually to the sea. When the erosion process became the dominant factor in the Summit district, the height of the summits are estimated to have been 2000 to 3000 feet higher than they are today. The waters descending from those mountains would possess enormous force, and had tremendous effect in carving out the river bed. What force must have been required to move along the river bed large stones such as some of those bared in the Grove excavations! At Grove the layer of stones was eight feet deep all across the valley, the individual stones ranged in size from that of an egg, up to some which were 24 inches long by 18 inches deep. All these stones had been brought down from the hills higher up the valley.

There are broadly three stages in the life of a river. First there is the incision into the landscape, which is deepened and widened in time, this is followed by extensive widening and finally the river bed is choked with material in its old age. The little river at Summit has for a long time been in the third stage, and if nothing had been done to deepen the bed, a large part of the valley, especially about Grove, would probably have remained as a marshy waste-land. The level of the valley floor was raised using waste from the railway tunnel and soil cut from the 'hills' of Littleborough (see chapter 15). Grove became the site of a major dye works in the late 19th century and the river was confined to tunnels and a channel which was covered by great stone slabs. The works finally closed and only ruins remained in 1997; the site has since been re-developed as a housing estate.

Built in 1839 the stone and iron aqueduct at Rock Nook, close to Summit Tunnel, still carries the River Roch over the Lancashire-Yorkshire railway line.

The steep valley side at Light Hazzles Fall, rocks and rushing stream make a dramatic setting for this young lady; photographed on a day out with friends around 1900.

Another form of denudation is due to changes in atmospheric temperature which causes expansion and contraction of the rocks. Even the hardest granite rocks readily crack when alternately expanded and contracted by heat and cold. The breaking down of rocks by frost is particularly noticeable at Summit in the winter time and this is especially the case with the shale where constant subsidence has converted a steep cliff into a rounded hillside. A more powerful effect is produced by the freezing of water in cracks and fissures of rocks, which can cause huge blocks to be forced away from a cliff face.

Wind is also a denuding force. In a high wind, dust and sand hurled against the rocks act like a sand blast. On the Todmorden moors there are several remarkable stones that have been shaped by that agency. The Basin Stone at Gaddings Dam, standing in a very exposed position, has been curiously worn and curved by wind.

Between Summit and Littleborough seven distinct strata of geological deposits have been indentified but a general view of the power and complexity of the forces involved can be gained by making an excursion up the river course at a time when there is a good flow of water. The river is today in its old age; above Littleborough it has suffered many indignities; including being diverted into a metal bed to be carried over the railway line, being culverted extensively and being buried many feet below ground in various pipes and tunnels. However it still shows traces of its former activity. Commencing at Gale and walking downhill by the river side, at a point near the bridge leading to Rock Nook and Grove Mills, we can see the river at its work of widening and levelling the valley, cutting the hillside further back at the outside of every curve and depositing fresh material at the inside of each curve - the double process going on at the rate of about one yard in ten years.

Following the river upwards, in the neighbourhood of Light Hazels (Hazzles) Farm, the river forms three pretty little waterfalls. From that point the stream has the characteristics of a mountain torrent. Numerous blocks of stone lie about, one weighing several tons, has completely filled the bed of the stream, causing the water to slightly change its course. The hills on either side of the stream rise to a height of about 100 feet, reminding one of some of the minor passes in North Wales. Nearing the top, just before coming out on the more level portion below Light Hazels Farm, there are two enormous blocks of stone, at least four yards in length and of equal depth. Scattered on the hillside are great quantities of large stones, some bearing marks that proclaim the action of glaciers.

CHAPTER TWO

THE FIRST PEOPLE IN LITTLEBOROUGH

THE STONE AGE
(100,000 BC - 2,500 BC)

It is generally accepted that humans have evolved from some earlier form of life to their present position in the animal world, and that they made their first appearance in Britain during, or immediately after, the last Glacial Period. When piecing together the evidence of life in the Stone Age it is necessary to refer to a wide geographical area. The scope of reference for Littleborough is at least western Europe. The interesting thing is the amount of evidence that the Littleborough area has contributed to the total picture of the earliest *hominids* (men and women and their direct precursors). There is a rich hoard of their flint tools and artefacts buried beneath the peat on our moors.

In the twentieth century we seem to have had little time to look back into the remote days when our ancestors were living as hunters, roaming over the hills and valleys of our immediate neighbourhood, in pursuit of those wild animals they depended on for their daily food and clothing. But our civilization is an evolution from this hunting stage, through pastoral, agricultural and manufacturing stages, to the complex global developments we face today.

In archaeological terms, the latest period is the 'Iron Age' which terminated with Roman rule. This was preceded by an 'Age of Bronze', this by an 'Age of Copper', and this again by an 'Age of Stone'. The implements made and used by humans in the different ages were manufactured from the materials which serve to identify the different periods.

The Stone Age is usually divided into three periods:

The Palaeolithic,	or 'Old Stone Age'
The Mesolithic,	or 'Middle Stone Age'
The Neolithic,	or 'New Stone Age'.

Based on recent research the following spread of dates are considered appropriate for northern England. Palaeolithic 100,000 BC - 12,000 BC, Mesolithic 12000 BC - 4000 BC, Neolithic 4000 BC - 2500 BC.

At the end of the 20th century there is strong evidence of hominids existing at least 2.5 million years ago in Australia and elsewhere. It is enough to say with Sir John Evans, an early archeological enthusiast;

"the mind is almost lost in amazement at the vista of antiquity displayed".

Using this dating framework for the Stone Age, the earliest local finds of flints, relating to humans in the Littleborough area relate to the late Mesolithic / Neolithic period. Radioactive Carbon Dating of charcoal from recently discovered local sites at Waystone Edge, Hassocks (7400 BC) and at Rishworth Drain (4600 BC) confirm this point (see p.11). Of the older Mesolithic or Palaeolithic men we have no positive trace locally and it is reasonable to speculate that either the ice had not retreated far enough to allow habitation or it remains a challenge to find the first authentic site.

Flint scraper.

The Paleolithic Period (100,000 BC - 12,000 BC)

The Geological indications point to a semi tropical climate, with broad marshy rivers and an animal population totally different from the one we have today. England was, at this time, joined to the continent of Europe. The North Sea and the English Channel were then broad valleys, while the Thames meandered lazily over a broad swampy bed several miles wide. The valley on which London is built has been hollowed out by the river since Palaeolithic man chipped his rough tools in its upper gravel beds, where they are found today.

These hominids, who were genetically different from ourselves, inhabited western Europe, including some parts of Britain. They were nomadic hunters, confined to the game grounds of the river valleys, where traces of their camps and the tools of very roughly chipped flints are found, notably in East Anglia, but also in the gravel beds of the Thames, Severn and Hampshire Avon.

The Cave people (30,000 BC) followed the earlier hominids. They improved the process of chipping the flint nodules and were able to manufacture a far larger variety of tools, such as planes, borers, saws, drills, gauges and chisels. They also manufactured lances, harpoons, and picks, from bone and horn; needles, fish hooks, and awls from ivory, clothing from furs and skins; and necklaces and other ornaments from teeth and claws. These cave people also seemed to have some kind of religion, as clearly evidenced by the discoveries of graves in which the dead were ceremoniously buried. Accompanying them were offerings of food and beautifully made implements, together with ornaments and necklaces etc. On the other hand, we have no evidence that they knew about agriculture, kept domestic animals, made pottery, built the crudest kind of dwelling or the clumsiest raft or boat. In 1997 a sample of genetic material was extracted and analysed from a fossil skeleton dated between 100,000 BC and 30,000 BC. The skeleton was discovered in 1856 in the Neander Thal (a valley in Germany). It gave the name 'Neanderthal man' to the hominids thought to be the direct predecessors of ourselves. The analysis proves that this direct relation is not possible and that the origins of existing humans probably lie in Africa not Europe. We are probably the only hominid not to share the planet with others, but 50,000 years ago this was not so.

As the Paleolithic period advanced, the climate cooled and eventually the climatic severity produced an Ice or Glacial Age. The terrific climatic variations which occured during the Glacial Age led to the deterioration of the early hominids. After a long period of fluctuation eventually the climate again changed; the almost lifeless Ice Age came to an end. At the same time the whole configuration of Western Europe altered, for the British Isles and their surrounding seas were formed (6000 BC - 5000 BC). By this time the Cave people with their amazing art and culture had disappeared. They were replaced by other numerous and primitive hominids, from the east, who never equalled them, but who eked out a precarious existence in Western Europe until the arrival, about eight thousand years ago, of the Neolithic Civilization.

Neolithic Period (4000 BC - 2500 BC)

Neolithic man has left widespread evidence of having inhabited the Littleborough district and it is possible to get a glimpse of their mode of life, conditions and customs. The picture was first pieced together by the investigations of men like Sir John Lubbock, Sir John Evans, Sir William Turner, and in our own district by Mr Robert Law, Mr Horsfall, Dr. March and subsequently by many other workers who followed these early pioneers. It is only from the middle of the 19th century that archaeology made headway on the hills and moors of Littleborough, Rochdale and Todmorden. Fred Jackson, as a young man, was an enthusiastic participator and later wrote about the pioneer days.

" I remember the first flint being found in the Rochdale district for I formed one of the party of six persons who were present on that occasion in 1877. Previous to this time a large number of flint chippings had been found, but no arrow heads or other implements.

At that time Mr. Robert Law was a weaver at Ormerod's Mills, Walsden, and he had just begun to teach a Class in Geology under the Science and Art Department at Todmorden, and I was one of his first pupils. It was on a Sunday morning that Mr Law and myself with two other students walked over the hills from Todmorden to Healey, where we were met by Mr. Horsfall and another gentleman who accompanied us to Middle Hill (above Wardle). We spent several hours searching, and at last we were amply rewarded by the finding of a fine example of a flint arrow head by one of the persons present on this occasion.

Littleborough Historical and Archaelogical Society members at work. On the right is Alan Luke, one of the founders and later Chairman of the Society.

I have been on many flint hunting expeditions since then, but not one is so indelibly impressed on my memory as that one. We were like a pack of schoolboys. I well remember Mr. Law throwing his hat into the air and seeming to be as happy as if he had discovered a gold mine. They, and many others who laboured in this particular branch of science, have gone to their long rest, but the result of their labour is seen in the splendid collection of local "flints" which are on view in the Museum at Rochdale."

The museum is being integrated into the Esplanade Arts and Heritage Centre in Rochdale and access to all the existing material is encouraged. In addition the Littleborough Historical and Archaelogical Society (L.H.& A.S.) have one of the finest private collections of 'flints and artefacts' in Britain. Today we have over 100 identified flint sites in the Littleborough district which have been dated by their 'type'. In 1971-72 L.H.&A.S. explored nine of the main flinting sites in our area around Shore Moor and Blackstone Edge.

They collected some 1700 pieces of flint including a fabricator, a scraper, and barbed arrowheads. The sites where these were found are usually at a height of between 1200' and 1300' and the flints are usually washed out of denuded areas of the peat or are in the peat 3" - 4" below the current flat surface. The Society holds records of all these and many other sites. There are no local sources of flint and the bulk of the flints have been identified as chert flint from Derbyshire and pebble flint from the Yorkshire Wolds.

All organic traces of the Neolithic hominids of Lancashire have vanished; only their flint relics and traces of possible earthworks and fires are still to be found on our hills, confirming the resilience of flint to the normal agents of erosion

The evidence that is available gives an outline of the Neolithic people who lived on the hills and moors of our district. We know that they were hunters, from the stone spear heads and arrow heads they have left behind them. They clothed themselves in skins, for the

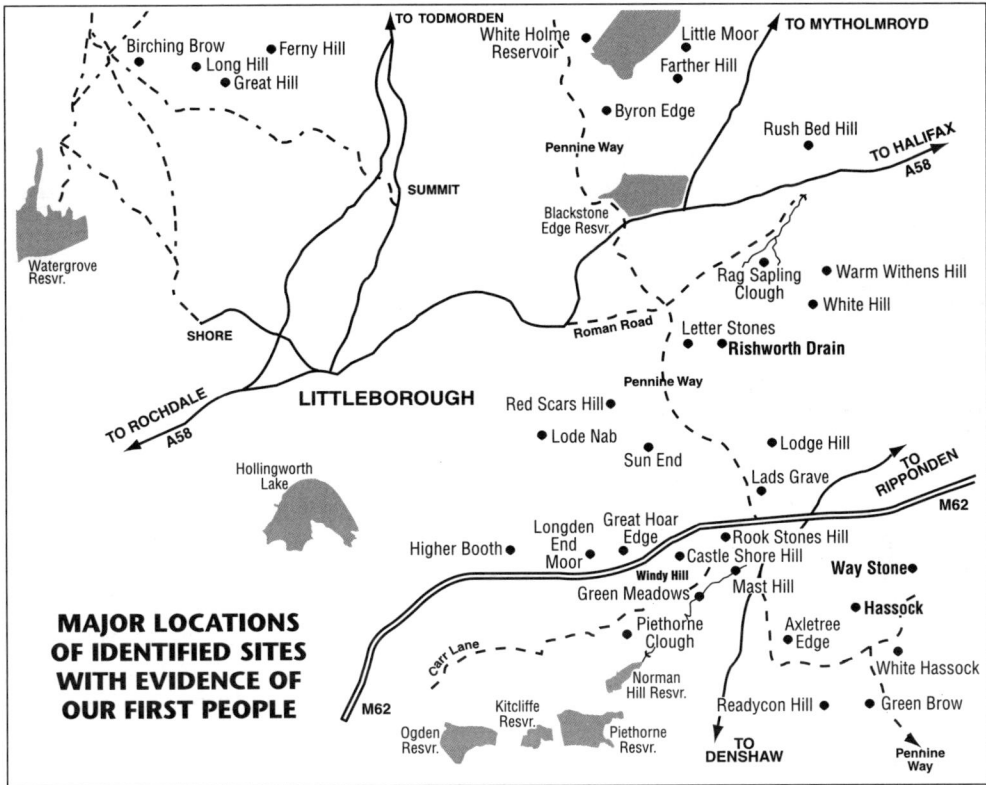

TO TODMORDEN
TO MYTHOLMROYD
Birching Brow • Ferny Hill
White Holme Reservoir
Little Moor
• Long Hill
Farther Hill
• Great Hill
• Byron Edge
Rush Bed Hill
TO HALIFAX
A58
Pennine Way
SUMMIT
Watergrove Resvr.
Blackstone Edge Resvr.
Rag Sapling Clough
• Warm Withens Hill
• White Hill
SHORE
Roman Road
Letter Stones
•Rishworth Drain
Pennine Way
LITTLEBOROUGH
Red Scars Hill•
TO ROCHDALE
A58
• Lode Nab
Sun End
• Lodge Hill
• Lads Grave
TO RIPPONDEN
M62
Hollingworth Lake
Longden End Moor
Great Hoar Edge
•Rook Stones Hill
Higher Booth•
•Castle Shore Hill
Way Stone•
Windy Hill
Green Meadows
Mast Hill
• Hassock
MAJOR LOCATIONS
OF IDENTIFIED SITES
WITH EVIDENCE OF
OUR FIRST PEOPLE
Carr Lane
Piethorne Clough
Axletree • Edge
White Hassock
Norman Hill Resvr.
M62
Kitcliffe Resvr.
Readycon Hill •
• Green Brow
Ogden Resvr.
Piethorne Resvr.
TO DENSHAW
Pennine Way

stone-flaying implements have been found with which they separated the skins from the animals, the stone scrapers with which they removed the fat from the hides, the flint awls which they used to make holes in the skins so that they might tie them with thongs of hide, and the stone perforators used to bore eyes into bone needles with which to make their clothes. There are also graving tools which they used for making ornamentation or perhaps for tattooing and the ruddle (red ochre) and graphite which might have been used for personal adornment. They had saws made from flint, combs and comb-makers, knives and whet-stones and seven or eight different kinds of flint arrow heads, some of them of beautiful design and workmanship. The Neolithic people's food and clothing consisted very largely of the results of their hunting expeditions. In the Littleborough area the only evidence of agriculture is the existence of a rough kind of wheat, called 'spelt'. This was used to make bread in Neolithic times and is still grown in Europe and elsewhere for its distinct flavour.

Although nomadic hunter and gatherers, in winter their dwelling place probably was in caves or in what are known as pit dwellings. Each of them was made by digging a circular hole about 4 feet deep, and 10 or 12ft in diameter, the earth from which was thrown up into a wall around, thus adding another two or three feet to the interior height of the original wall, except where a small gap was left for a door. Then, firmly embedded in the top of the earth wall, poles were sloped upwards and inwards till they met in the centre, where they would be bound together, thus forming the posts of a conical roof. In the smaller dwellings, straight pliable branches were bent over from side to side, like half hoops crossing each other in the centre, to form domed roofs. In either case small branches would then be woven basketwise in and out of the roof posts and the spans between filled in with heather or moss, the whole, as a further protection against the weather, being covered with skins, except for a smoke vent where the roof supports met together in the centre. No convincing remains of pit dwellings have been found in our district, the closest being in the Yorkshire Wolds. The most favourable local sites for the early settlements were on elevated, well drained, south-facing slopes and ledges below the summit level where there was a reliable water supply. These are the sites where the flints are found today around Littleborough.

Palaeolithic man killed the wild dog for food, Neolithic man tamed him and made him his friend in Britain around 7,500 BC, but we have to wait for later times, before such animals as the horse, the ox, and the sheep were tamed. We know very little about this early hominid's religion, but barrows in various parts of the country stand bleak and bare, still witnessing, after thousands of years, Neolithic people's belief in something more than life and death.

What can be learned of the climatic conditions that existed at the end of the Stone Age? Today there are very few trees upon our moors. We know, however, that these hills and moors were once covered with tree life. A search among the peat, which varies in thickness from a few inches to ten feet or more, will reveal the remains of Scotch fir, oak, bush hazel, ash, willow, and Scotch elm, together with a mass of peaty fibre, representing even more ancient undergrowth. All this peat has accumulated since Neolithic man lived and hunted on these hills which then supported a much richer vegetation cover. There is evidence that around 500 BC our climate changed to colder and wetter conditions that led to the spreading of peat and bog wherever vegetation was cleared.

Our story has reached 2500 BC when local conditions were generally becoming more favourable for people to develop new ways of living as traders, farmers and herdsmen.

CHAPTER THREE

THE AGES OF COPPER, BRONZE AND IRON
(2500 BC - 55BC)
THE CELTS

The previous chapter dealt with the advent of humans and the rich hoard of local evidence of the late Mesolithic and Neolithic people who lived in the Littleborough area.

Late Neolithic People (3000 BC)

When people started to settle in one place it represented a great change in human life. Huts were built and villages grew, with the many advantages that stem from living together, such as increased safety and the chance to share labour. The new way of life was brought from the continent of Europe by waves of immigrants who also brought sheep, cattle and corn. New wooden tools were designed, such as ploughs and wooden handles for axes and there is evidence of the first enclosures for stock. The late Neolithic people also developed quite sophisticated tools from bones, such as shovels made from shoulder blades. Dogs, pigs and goats were introduced into farming and the people started to mine for flint. In the same period they started to bury their dead in burial mounds or grave houses. Not only were these people starting to specialise in their activities, but they were also trading over long distances. Flints from our western and northern mountain areas have been discovered throughout Britain and Europe.

Copper (3000 BC) and Bronze (2000 BC) Ages

The next great step was the introduction of the use of metal, first copper then bronze. Britain is rich in copper, tin and gold and it was the 'Beaker People' from the Iberian Peninsula who are thought to have brought working in copper to Britain around 3000 BC. The Copper Age only lasted for a short time and one of the few identified finds discovered locally is a copper arrow head, which is now held by the Esplanade Arts and Heritage Centre at Rochdale.

The Copper age gave way to Bronze, by which time members of the tribes were both skilled craftsmen and experienced traders. Bronze, with a 10% tin content, is easier to work with than pure copper. Bronze tools have been found throughout Britain including harnesses which show the horse was being used (the first evidence of a wheeled cart in Britain is dated 500BC). It is to the increasingly sophisticated

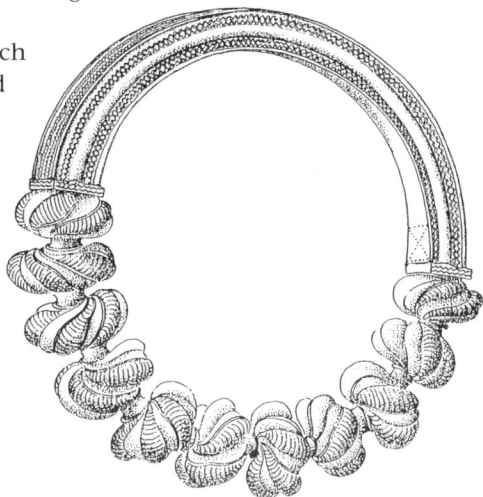

The bronze torque (armlet) discovered in 1831 in a quarry at Mawrode, under a flat stone, by a workman who was rooting out an oak stump.

Bronze Age society that our great stone monuments such as Stonehenge are attributed. Their existence indicates real engineering skills and organised labour. Although there is no evidence that the Bronze Age people could read or write, they clearly had considerable practical ability. A characteristic remnant from the Bronze Age is the long barrow, or burial site. No typical long barrow has been found close to Littleborough, but a round barrow has been found at Hades Hill, Cross Stone (*ref.* 948249), near Todmorden, and what may have been a site of a barrow on Snoddle Hill, Timbercliffe, Summit. A description of the site at Hades Hill and of the various implements that were found there, is included in the museum records at Rochdale. This barrow probably belongs to the early Bronze Age, as round barrows were practically unknown before this time. The site on Snoddle Hill has now virtually disappeared. Fred Jackson records that he spent scores of hours there, seeking evidence of a barrow, before finding anything, but was at last rewarded one morning after unusually heavy rain, by finding a fine specimen of an arrow head, slightly broken, as well as several pieces of ruddle and several pieces of sandstone, showing traces of the action of fire.

It is interesting to compare the above account with the description of another investigation of the same Snoddle Hill site in 1972, which was carried out by the Littleborough Historical & Archaeological Society. First they recognised stones that had clearly been adapted for use by man and others with distinctive chisel marks. Subsequently a number of interesting mounds were explored using an auger to obtain samples. Based on this work trenches were dug into the more promising mounds - including one slightly embarrassing excavation which proved to be a 'tip heap' left from an earlier dig this century! Their persistence paid off because an arrow head was found which the first excavators had missed. Flints and red ochre were also found on the site. Using a model aeroplane, aerial photographs were taken of the site which clearly displayed crop marks on one hillside. Carbon dating techniques were introduced to advance the investigation.

In addition these early inhabitants have left us a few place-names (see Chapter 6) and the remarkable bronze ornaments found elsewhere in 'barrows' (or grave mounds) on our moors and the bronze torque (or armlet) which weighs nearly 1½ pounds, found at Mawrode. A copy and description of the torque is held in the Rochdale Museum archives, the original being in the British Museum. (Mawrode is now renamed Moor Road, midway between Smithy Nook and Temple Chapel). Rochdale Museum Service also has a Bronze Age dagger that was discovered locally.

Earlier we built up a picture of Neolithic man based on the local remains of flints, stone tools and other durable remains that have been discoverd in our area. Recently, in Europe, we have uncovered one of the first examples of the organic remains of a Bronze age man. The corpse was released from an ice field, on the Austro-Italian borde where it was buried for 4000 years. It is very interesting to us because he was someone who lived in an upland region and his bone structure reveals evidence of much hard physical work; just the man we might imagine travelling along our high moorland edges!

The fully dressed corpse revealed a whole new dimension of knowledge about the life in his time and the tools he carried. The most exciting piece of equipment is however the axe that he carried which is a finer example of the axe head that was discovered locally. Another feature is that analysis of hair samples of the man show high concentrations of arsenic and copper which indicate that he had been associated with smelting copper and open-cast mining which are again a similarity with our first evidence of human activity in Littleborough. The man died about age 45 and his last meal was of meat and a form of corn. He died on a 'sheep route' across the Alps which to this day is taken by shepherds. It is very likely that he lost his way and died in a local storm or 'white out'. We have had more than one death in our area for just the same reasons. What is clear after this discovery is that bronze age man was very well adapted to the needs of his environment and had developed considerably since the Neolithic period.

Iron Age (600 BC) and the Celts

Iron is stronger than bronze for weapons, tools and nails but it needs heating to a higher temperature. The appropriate skills arrived in southern England around 600 BC and by the mature Iron Age in northern England smelting and forgeing were carried out both to make utilitarian tools and also for decorative metal working for swords, fittings for carts and personal decoration. The people bringing the skills are commonly referred to as Celts and their language survives today in Scotland, Wales, Ireland and Cornwall. From this language we derive some of our local place names (see Chapter 6).

Only at this stage of our story do we have written descriptions of the people living in Britain, initially from their Roman conquerors. The social structure was one that included priests, chiefs (eg Boadicea), druids and the warriors who are often described as great horsemen. Previous to the coming of the Romans the tribes of Britain inhabiting the south, called the Seganti, like their kinsmen the Brigantes in our part of the country, were already skilled in the methods of warfare of the time. They have left us hill forts some of which were so large they were like small towns. There are few of these 'towns' in Northern England but recent carbon dating of a fort at Mam Tor in Derbyshire suggests that it was constructed during the Bronze age and, as such, is the nearest example to Littleborough. The Belgae were the last Celts to come to Britain only 50 years before Julius Caesar.

Most native people were farmers living in thatched huts. Throughout northern England there is only scant evidence of more than isolated houses or occasionally a loose group. The evidence nevertheless does indicate permanent settlements. The location of the huts indicates that the basis of the farming economy was pastoral especially in the upland areas. The farmers kept cattle and sheep with wheat as the main cultivated crop. They had an iron blade on their plough. The main drinks were barley ale and mead. They were also traders moving all over Europe and large Celtic hoards of silver and gold coin have been found, the later coins imitating the coin of Roman Emperors.

CHAPTER FOUR

THE ROMAN OCCUPATION
(55 B.C. - 420 A.D.)

In the last century B.C. the Roman Empire stretched to the English Channel and the Celts in Britain were helping those in Gaul to fight a young Roman commander called Julius Caesar.

Caesar decided on a reconnaissance into Britain and landed near Deal in 55 B.C. After a month he withdrew to Gaul and returned to England the following year in July. The British resistance collapsed in the face of the Roman war machine, but again Caesar returned to Gaul in the autumn. It was to be ninety years before the Emperor Claudius invaded again in A.D.45 and by A.D. 49 the Romans controlled everything south of a line from the Severn to the Trent. The Romans were in Britain to stay.

The Romans were splendid colonizers. No sooner did they conquer a tract of land, than they set about building a 'castra' or camp for the protection of the inhabitants and as a starting point for further conquests. Fine military roads were made to connect these camps and traders went along these roads as often as the Roman legionaries. In the first century the emperor Agricola made a series of roads in the north and he also built a number of forts. Hadrian, who carried on the work of colonization in the second century, built the first great wall across the country from the Tyne to the Solway. Later, the Emperor Severus built another wall as a protection for the conquered northern territories, against the raids of warlike tribes still further north. This wall went right across the two counties of Northumberland and Cumberland, from Bowness to Wallsend.

The view down the Roman Road with the distinctive line of central stone slabs, the modern day Halifax Road in the background.

The Pennine moorlands stretched as a great barrier for nearly one hundred miles from the region of the Tyne to the Vale of Trent. On the eastern side of these moorlands was the fertile plain of York, where the Romans established the capital of Britain, and on the western side was the less fertile plain of Lancashire and Cheshire. Manchester (Mancunium) and Ribchester, were important Roman centres on the west of the Pennines, connected together by a military road. Littleborough is on a similar line from York to Manchester, but Ribchester, on the river Ribble, has provided the fullest local detail on how Roman forts were built and their likely impact on the surrounding area.

The Ribchester site was first occupied in the Bronze Age and there is evidence that local prosperity declined alongside prevailing climatic conditions. The Romans found an area of simple hill farming when they reached Ribchester. It was a peasant society, that Fred Jackson called the 'Brigantes', but which actually embraced many tribal groupings. It is regrettable that we can only see these early Britons through a haze of Roman prejudice and propaganda as a full picture would also have reflected the conditions that prevailed in the Littleborough area at that time. The fort which dates from A.D. 70 was finally abandoned in A.D. 370. It had a 'model' history starting as a frontier post which developed into a cavalry fort and later became a strategic centre on the road network. It finally grew to be a garrison town far behind the front line. In construction it was a standard Roman fort, which was placed on a low, damp and heavily wooded site for strategic reasons. The life of a timber and turf fort was normally only about 30 years before major works were called for. In its lifetime Ribchester went through phases when stone replaced the wood structures and the isolation of a military outpost was replaced by a co-operative integration into the surrounding environment. In its later years there are signs of an industrial and commercial complex around the fort. The finest object found on the site is the famous 'Ribchester facemask cavalry parade helmet' which is now in the British Museum. A large number of other Roman relics, mainly in stone, which have been found at Ribchester are to be seen in a building provided for the purpose near the old Church.

With this picture in mind we can consider a number of claims for the site of a Roman fort in Littleborough area. Whittaker states, in his History of Whalley:

"Littleborough was a Roman station and the site of the camp was at a place named 'Castle', which is situated about half a mile to the north of the village, at the bottom of the steepest part of the Roman road over Blackstone Edge".

He calls this a subordinate Roman fort. Canon Raines also describes a fort as existing either here or at Windy Bank. John Travis strongly supports the location at Windy Bank based on the likely line of the Roman Road, the geography of the area and the discovery, in the late 1800s, of a number of Roman coins (some dated to Claudius) found at Castle.

Fred Jackson was inclined to agree with Colonel Fishwick who investigated this matter and said,

"there is not a shred of evidence - there is not the slightest trace of either camp or entrenchment, nor has there been found so much as a broken pot or coin, to point to either 'Castle' or 'Windy Bank' as the site of Roman occupation.

Both Town House and Stubley could have greater claim than either of the above to be the site of a fort, as Roman coins and pottery have been found at both these places."

In summary, locally we have no visible remains of a Roman fort. However they were methodical in establishing their defences so there is a strong indication that there would have been a Roman fort in or near Littleborough on the road from Yorkshire to Manchester. With so much excavation and mining in the area it is likely that any signs of it have been destroyed. Apart from Ribchester, within easy travelling distance of Littleborough are the following recognised sites of forts: Melandra Castle (Glossop) and the camps at Mancunium (Castlefield), and Castleshaw (Saddleworth).

Two sides of a coin from the Littleborough Roman Hoard.

The major Roman feature around Littleborough is the 'Roman Road' itself, which is visible from the A 58 where the road bends to ascend the steep portion of Blackstone Edge. The Roman road makes no such compromise and ascends directly up the hillside to the Aiggin Stone (a medieval way-marker) high on the skyline, descending as directly to the A58 again on the other side. The road was scheduled under the Ancient Monuments and Archaelogical Areas Act as an Ancient Monument in 1934. One section of the road is virtually intact and we can only marvel at how horses could pull or carry heavy goods so directly uphill. It is disputed whether the currently visible paving is Roman; however it appears that the line of the road goes to Ilkley and then on to York and is indeed the line of a Roman road.

Despite considerable dispute and scepticism the Blackstone Edge road is seen by many modern authorities as:

"one of the few surviving examples of central ribs, transverse stones attesting gang building and the use of a later loop to an earlier gradient to ease travel."

Hartley and Fitts (1988)

It is also quoted as evidence for the use by the Romans of a 'skid-pan' brake in the steeper gradients.

Frequently associated with the lines of Roman roads are finds of Roman coins, which are often thought to have been hidden and are therefore described as hoards. Three hoards have been found in the Littleborough district but the first two, associated with finds at Stubley Hall and Town House, were never officially documented, although Fishwick refers to them. The third came to light in 1994 when two brothers found coins in the lower Ealees valley. In all they found 76 coins many of which proved to be of good quality silver and some of which were in fine condition. This find along with one other, are the only sites of the 82 recorded in N.W. England where we have a secure date for the last possible dates for them to be hidden; in this case 192 - 222 A.D. The coins were not found in a container but loose near a water course. The value of the coins found equates to about 3 months pay for a medium ranking Roman soldier and the most likely explanation is that they were hidden to be recovered later. Why

The silver arm of the Roman 'statue of victory' dug up in a stone quarry at Tunshill in 1793, near the present M62 motorway. The iron foundry and coalmines nearby were possibly on the site of Roman workings.

and by whom is utterly speculative, but the location is close to the line of a Roman road which had a documented auxiliary Roman fort at the Yorkshire end.

Another outstanding local find of Roman date was made at 'Tunshill in Butterworth'. (Tunshill Farm is at the head of Hollingworth Lake). The right arm of a 'Statue of Victory' was unearthed with a solid cast hand and a hollow arm. Attached to both was an inscribed 'silver plate'. The find is claimed to be part of a statue of the Roman Valerius Rufus.

The rising number of authenticated finds in the 20th century has lead the Greater Manchester Archaeological Unit to recognise the Littleborough Area as having 'a cluster of Roman find spots' which are probably around the junction of two major Roman roads. Amongst these finds are: a piece of Roman bridle harness found close to the Roman Road and the even more exciting discovery in 1998 of a Romano British brooch, 'with late Celtic affinities' near the centre of Littleborough. Made of bronze and iron the brooch has a harp shape and has been identifed as being comparable with two brooches found in a Roman fort in Elslack in Broughton (1908) and two other similar examples in Corbridge and Backworth in Northumberland. With the increasing volume of evidence a project is now being discussed to include a geophysical survey and trial trench excavations not only to look for more finds but to search for the remains of a fort

The Roman rule was operated through local chiefs and by making allies of those people living on the edge of conquered territories. For all the tribal groupings, it was a self-financing, self-government under the watchful eye of a provincial governor. Prosperous cities grew in various parts, but especially in the south of England. By the third century AD the walls around Roman Britain were firm, notwithstanding, most Britons continued to live and work in the countryside and worship their Gods of nature. There were cycles of prosperity and war but by the 5th Century AD the Romans began to withdraw and left the Britons to face the Saxons alone. A life that had existed for 400 years rapidly vanished and the great Roman achievements crumbled with startling rapidity.

The tribes inhabiting the south of Britain, called the Seganti, had enjoyed four hundred years of Roman rule. Civilians were prohibited from acting in a military capacity and they were under the protection of the Roman Empire. They had become law-abiding citizens, who had adopted the civilization and culture of the Romans.

In the northern upland areas, the Brigantes or Britons had never been thoroughly subjugated but were always ready, to pounce out of their strongholds. No doubt many fierce skirmishes took place whenever the Romans were forced to traverse the Blackstone Edge road on the way from York to the camps at Melandra or Manchester.

The latest research modifies the generally war-like view of our local history. For example, for the Brigantes within Hadrian's Wall, which would include our Littleborough people, it has been recently stated that

"there is no evidence that the Third Century or indeed the Fourth Century down to AD 367 was anything but a time of profound peace."

Hartley and Fitts, The Brigantes

In summary, the remains of the Roman Empire in the County of Lancaster tend to be forts which have crumbled into extensive mounds (rather than grown into towns), supplemented by stones, pottery, tiles and hoards of coins, buried long ago, that come to the surface along the trade routes.

This is nothing but a reflection of the general situation: compared with Southern England. We had few 'towns' in the north west, most of the settlements were attached to auxiliary forts. Here civilians, traders and soldiers' families were found in buildings leased from the Legions as at Ribchester. On the west of the Pennines there is a strong impression of low overall density of urban settlement. For example, there are only five recognised villas in all Brigantine territory.

There were probably one and a half million people in Roman Britain, primarily living off the land. In terms of industry there are records of mining for lead, iron ore and stone in bulk during the Roman era. Mining must have been one of the north's biggest industries where the heavy work was often done by slaves. Millstone grit was very important, but there are a great variety of other types of stone in and around the Pennines which were quarried and used. Lime burning was widespread and clay was extracted to be used for the manufacture of pottery and glass for windows. Brick making was first introduced into England by the Romans.

When the legions departed the skills appeared to be lost and it was the late 14th century when brick making was re-introduced into England by Flemish refugees; later the first local bricks were manufactured in Littleborough using their techniques. The first evidence of extensive mining for coal in Britain is dated in the second century A.D. Coal, brick and pottery based industries were to play a very important part in the story of Littleborough

Carpenters, cart makers, tool makers and tanners are identified as established tradesmen at this time. In addition metal workers processed large volumes of gold, silver and bronze to make tools, ornaments and coins. The coins were not only used for payment but also as a form of political propaganda telling the provinces who was in power or favour at the centre of the empire.

The Departure of the Romans

—— AND ——

The Coming of the Saxons

(Paper read before the Beautiful Littleborough Society, February 9th, 1923)

To E. C. Harvey Esq. C. A. F.P.
Christmas 1928.
with the Author's
Very Best Wishes
F. J.

F. Jackson

A personally inscribed copy of one of Fred Jackson's local history papers, 1923.

CHAPTER FIVE

THE COMING OF THE SAXONS
420 A.D. - 1066 A.D.

After occupying Britain for four hundred years the Roman soldiers were compelled to leave the country to defend Rome itself in the year A.D. 420. The Pennines had been to some degree a Celtic (or British) island, surrounded, but never submerged by the influence of Roman civilization. Only with the coming of the Saxons did the civilization of the Celt finally give place to a new one which was very different, both in language and social organisation.

For something like six hundred years after the departure of the Romans, England was the scene of repeated wars owing to invasion or civil unrest. It is easy to realise what the withdrawal of the Roman soldiers would have meant. The immediate effect in our part of the country would have been, that the forts at Manchester, Glossop and Ribchester would have been attacked and destroyed and all the inhabitants who had prospered under the Roman rule would be severely threatened. The walls which had been built across the country in the extreme north and manned by the Roman soldiers, were now stormed by those fierce tribes of Britons of the north and there seemed every chance of civilised Britons being exterminated. In their dire extremity they decided to ask the help of a people from the area we call Germany today. They came from many different tribes but are referred to as 'Saxons'. The remedy proved worse than the disease, for they found to their cost that it was easier inviting Saxons into the country than getting them out again.

No evidence remains that early Saxon tribes settling in Britain could read or write nor is there a contemporary record about them written by a 'romanised' Briton. However, what is usually described as the first English poem, written about 650 AD, is the Anglo-Saxon poem *Beowulf*. There is also earlier material in prose and there follows a short extract, written by a Briton, of what happened after the Romans left. The material is believed to have been recorded about the year 540 AD ie some 120 years after it happened.

The Saxons had come into the country beating back the Picts and Scots; then they began to threaten the British people that unless they fulfilled certain impossible conditions they would break the treaty and plunder the whole island. After a short time they followed up their threats with deeds:

"So that all the columns were levelled to the ground by the battering ram, all the husbandmen routed, together with their bishops, priests and the people, while the sword gleamed, and the flames crackled around them on every side. Lamentable to behold in the midst of the streets lay the tops of lofty towers tumbled to the ground, stones of high walls, holy altars, fragments of human bodies, covered with the livid clots of coagulated blood, looking as if they had been squeezed together in a wine press, and with no chance of being buried, save in the ruins of the houses. Some, therefore, of the miserable remnants being taken in the mountains, were murdered in great numbers, others constrained by famine, came and yielded themselves to be slaves for ever to their foes, running the risk of being instantly slain, ..."

Christianity was practically wiped out and the heathen Saxon gods, Thor and Wodin, were worshipped in its place. The names of these gods are remembered even today in our days of the week. Friday, for example, is from the name of the goddess Frig.

The next period of time is commonly referred to as the 'Dark Ages' because of the lack of credible evidence of any kind. For five or six centuries after the break-up of the Roman Empire we have very little reliable history of our country and less still of the part of the country 'lying between the Ribble and the Mersey' which includes Littleborough. If we look at a map of Saxon times we find this region almost as blank as a map of Central Africa was two hundred years ago. There are only three or four small dots and crosses, which refer to places, in the whole of South Lancashire. The Venerable Bede, the great monk of Jarrow who died in the year A.D. 735, only makes a slight mention in his 'history' of the district between the Ribble and the Mersey. This history is one of the few documents relating to this time.

In the seventh century the great Saxon kingdom of Northumbria (land north of the Humber) dominated northern England and much of Scotland as far north as Edinburgh. In old records we find Manchester referred to as being in Northumbria with its capital at York. The Saxons had become strong enough to extend their conquest through the Pennines and to conquer the Britons of the Lancashire plains. King Ethelfrith crossed into South Lancashire and defeated the Britons at Chester in the year 613. Edwin, the next king of Northumbria in A.D. 617-33, conquered the British in Elmet. This was an enclave which stretched from the southern Lake District to the Pennines and included our district. The Britons in Elmet had remained independent since the Romans withdrew. Edwin built fortresses near Leeds and Huddersfield and then, for more than half a century, the tide of warfare and conquest ebbed and flowed through Yorkshire and Lancashire. It is about this time that the beleaguered Britons created the myth of their saviour Arthur and his Knights of the Round Table who would come to save them as they were driven further north and west or defeated and enslaved. A Saxon king, Oswald, was killed in Lancashire in A.D. 642, and another Saxon king, Pinda, was killed near Leeds in A.D. 655. Following these events comes a period in which practically no mention is made of our region. In the year 937 there was a great fight along the Roman road between Ribchester and York. The Britons had got the help of the Danes in Ireland and the Scots; between them they raised a great army. At last came the decisive battle of Brunanburh, when the northern forces were defeated and "Athelstan the Glorious" became king of all England.

Where Brunanburh was nobody seems to know. Early in the 20th century a Burnley based archaeologist, T.T. Wilkinson, made out a very strong case, claiming the moors south east of that town as the site of the famous battle. Extensive earthworks were identified, which gave every indication that a battle had been fought there at some time. The name Brunanburh can be interpreted as 'the fortified camp on the Brun' and Burnley stands on the River Brun, a tributary of the Lancashire Calder. If that is the case, not more than a dozen miles separated Littleborough from the epoch-making battle, which was fought early in the tenth century.

When the victory was won the Angles and Saxons laid aside their weapons and settled down in this part of the country. It was covered by forests at that time, which would have been felled, camp fires lit, simple huts built and the land made ready for ploughing. The life style was close to that of the Celts previous to the Roman invasion. The basic tribal unit was a family cluster of some 50 people and groups of these families were answerable to a Lord. Saxon society was by no means barbaric. For example the current phrase 'moot point' meaning something that needs debate comes directly from the Saxon word 'moot'. The moot was a gathering where serious local issues could be discussed. Similarly a rich vein of diversity in culture, poetry and language has been recognised.

Elsewhere, another important event had taken place. Augustine and his monks had re-introduced Christianity into Kent in the seventh century (A.D. 670) and converted the Saxon king. Up to this time, whenever the Saxons had beaten the Britons in battle all survivors were killed except the few who managed to escape. After the re-introduction of Christianity wars of extermination ceased and Anglo-Saxons and Britons lived side by side as conquerors and conquered. No doubt many Britons would be left in Lancashire,

The story of the invasion of, and immigration into, our country will never be complete. Neolithic men, Britons, Angles, Saxons and Northmen, encamped in succession on the hills around Littleborough. Thus a mix of peoples and ways of life were already established when the Normans entered Britain.

Equating cultural change with invasion has become unfashionable among modern historians. In addition we now realise that our view of the Anglo-Saxons was based on authorities like Gildas and Bede whose writings have been accepted as historical truth, but really represent clerics writing a theological polemic. The population was probably a mixture of farmers and semi-nomadic herders in a loose tribal structure. When the Romans left, their culture disappeared in a dramatic way and our language changed, but modern genetics provides no support for the idea that a major invasion by Anglo-Saxons triggered the changes. Today, it appears likely the change was a resurgence of the native British, with evidence of the existence of at least two cultures and the existence of extensive bi-lingualism. Similarly, there is growing evidence that the simplistic views about 'Celtic' culture are being displaced by a picture of organic development by a fairly indigenous population. Interestingly the modern genetic work does confirm the outline of a Viking invasion and settlement especially in Cumbria and north Derbyshire. But the migrant and local populations were prepared to integrate and despite conflict, accommodation was the rule. Probably the British never did assimilate the Roman rule and for political reasons the Romans always depicted us as rebellious no-goods. In areas such as ours, the culture of Rome was probably dismantled 'from the inside'.

CHAPTER SIX

THE ROOTS OF OUR LOCAL PLACE NAMES,
NICKNAMES AND DIALECT

In our story we have touched on the waves of invasion and immigration and how these have changed the way people lived. With this background we can look at one of the treasures of our local culture: the inheritance of names, words and dialect that we have from our ancestors. Throughout this chapter a good local Street Atlas will locate many, but not all, of the place names discussed.

The dialect that was spoken in our district was the direct outcome of the languages spoken by the various people who had lived in these hills and valleys during the last two thousand years. In the past, for hundreds of years the old ways of speaking were handed on from one generation to another with few major events to disturb the modest rate of change that will occur in any language. Since the early 1900's, with compulsory attendance at schools and an ever increasing mobility between different districts, dialects have lost their distinct character and only remain among our older people who were born and bred locally.

Around 1920 Fred Jackson wrote:

"I for one should be sorry to see our dialect disappear. To people outside Lancashire, who do not understand it, it may appear rough and uncouth, but our forefathers loved it and I for one hope that I may never be ashamed of it. In times of stress or emotion it always comes to the top with a Lancashire man, however much his education may have striven to cover it up".

This chapter addresses the legacy of 'place names' given by the Saxons to various parts of our district followed by a consideration of the 'nicknames' (Old English: *ekename* an additional name) and 'Lancashire dialect' both still in use in the 20th century and generally accepted as being directly descended from Old English as spoken by the Saxons.

Local Place Names

There is an old rhyme that runs:-

> "In ford, in ham, in ley, and ton
> the most of English surnames run".

Whenever we find any place names with these endings, there is always a sensible case to investigate; to see if it is an area where Saxons had settled.

The Saxons were a nation of squatters. As soon as they occupied a piece of land they began to fell trees, put up fences and build a house. Consequently, they have left more traces of their existence in our area than their predecessors, for it is evident that when they settled at a place, they must give it a name. By the early 11th century from the Domesday Book, we know that the Saxons had been settled on the Yorkshire side of the Pennines for some time. There are other records of their settlements dating back to the latter part of the tenth century; existing evidence suggests that the Saxons expanded westwards into the Littleborough district from Yorkshire.

To illustrate the impact of the Saxons on our area, the two place names Walsden and Walshaw on the Lancashire side of the hill are interesting. Wals, or wealas, to the Saxon meant 'foreigner', den or dean meant 'a little valley', so that Walsden would mean to the Saxons, 'the little valley where the foreigners lived'. Again, with Walshaw, shaw meant 'wood' so the people on that side would be referred to as 'the foreigners who lived in the woods'.

Fred Jackson pictured the Saxons setting out to find new homes on the west side of the Summit Hill.

"It is hardly likely that the Britons gave up without a struggle and many skirmishes probably took place, before they were finally driven out of this country into Wales. But they were no match for the well-trained and well-armed Saxons, with their helmets, two edged daggers, swords and wooden shields."

It is possible to trace the way the Saxons came, at each place on the way which they thought suitable for a settlement, one or more families would be left. These settlements required identification so the Saxons always gave each a name, which not only served as a 'place name', but described it as well (see p.31).

The 'don' or valley was impassable on account of the marshy nature of the ground and they had to take to the hills on each side. One group came by Henshaw, Hollingworth, Bottomley, Deanroyd, Knowl, Calf Lee, Warland Gate and Dean Head. All these are Saxon place names.

On the opposite side of the valley they came by Ramsden, Lower Allerscholes, Higher Allerscholes, to the Reddyshore Scout Gate (or road). At this point there was a branch which went to White Slack on one side and another branch led down into the valley to Deanroyd. About one hundred and seventy years ago, before the present main road was made this branch road crossed the valley on stepping stones. From Higher Allerscholes, still keeping to the Reddyshore Scout Gate, they came to Calf Lee, and another short branch road which led down to Dean Head. From this point to beyond what is now Gale flat, (a modern name) there was marshy ground which was impassable. They had to take to the hill side again and got to Swaindrod (near Handle Hall). A little further on they arrived at Newgate (a recent name). The old Reddyshore Scout road, instead of coming straight down to Caldermoor as it does at present, formerly went down by Town House. Where Town House stands must have been a beautiful spot at that time and there is no wonder that the Saxons decided to stay. The valley at this point is at its widest and it was probably part of the area that had already been cleared by the Britons. It would be an open space of grassland with a river meandering through it. The river would have a far greater volume of water than it does today as many of the contributing streams have been diverted and the remaining water is confined in an open stone drain. Ealees would have stretched down to the river bank, while the hill tops for miles around would be covered with woods.

Herds of deer, strictly protected by game laws, would have grazed in the open spaces of these woods and would have come down to the stream at Ealees to drink.

The first thing the Saxons would do is to clear the land and then enclose it as a protection against the wolves and boars which were common at this time. Once the enclosure was finished they would then build the house within. This would be referred to by the Saxons as the 'Ton House' (or Town House as we call it) for 'ton' meant an enclosure and of course 'Ton House' would be the house within the enclosure.

The brook running through the enclosure (as it does today) would be referred to as the 'Ton Brook'

The following list contains Saxon and other very old names forming the basis for many of our names today.

Acre: an old English word indicating early settlement. The modern 'Whittaker' is first encountered in the thirteenth century as Quit-acre, then Whitiacre and finally Whittaker.

Butterworth: often used to indicate a dairy farm.

Clegg: according to Brierley, is an ancient word for clay.

Clough: meant a cleft in the hill side, so we have Clay Clough, Cloughbottom, Cloughfield, Green Clough, Clough Head, Cloughbank, Long Clough, and Clough Road.

Croft: meant a small field, so we have Croft, Croft Head, Top o th' Croft, Clay Croft.

Don, Den or Dean: meant 'the little valley'. There are the place names such as Ramsden, Longden, Sladen, Dearnley, Dean Head, Whiteley Dean, and Denhurst.

Field: an old English word indicating that the earliest settlements were Anglo-Saxon and so we have Eafield, Greenfield, Cloughfield, Hollowfield, Stoneyfield, Whitfield and Schofield which as a written name does not occur untill 1310.

Gate: the Anglo-Saxon name for road was 'gate' so we have Reddyshore Scout Gate, Lydgate, Moorgate, Gate House, and Newgate. Of course it does not mean that all the above are Saxon place names, but there is no doubt that the majority of them are. Newgate, for instance, is probably fairly recent.

Honresfeld: the general name given to a large district of which we formed a part, and included Wardle, Weurdle, Blatchinsworth, Calderbrook, Wardleworth and parts of Walsden and Todmorden. 'Hundersfeld', unlike any of the similar districts in England, did not give its name to any of the townships comprised within it.

'Windybank' overlooks Littleborough from above Blackstone Edge Old Road. The house dates from the early 14th century; was rebuilt by John Butterworth in 1635 and was also the home of the Lyghtoller Family.

Fishwick says that two sources have been suggested from which the name of Hundersfeld or Honresfeld may have been derived: from a Saxon chief named Honorius, or from its having been the field of some battle, but the evidence for neither of them is satisfactory.

Head: Dean Head, meaning the 'head of the little valley'.

Hurst: meant clumps of trees, so we have Denhurst, Hurstead, Hazelhurst, Hursted Nook. Denhurst according to this interpretation would mean 'the clump of trees in the little valley'.

Knowl: meant a rounded hill, and we have Knowl Farm, Howorth-Knowl, Knowl Top and Knowl Hill.

Leaches: meant a wet area or transient pond, we have Leach pond.

Ley or Lees: There are a number of place names ending in 'ley' or 'lees' such as Dearnley, Stubley, Durn Lea, High Lee, Ealees, Longlees, Buckley, Whitelees, Calf Lee, and Bottomley. 'Ley' meant a pasture so Dearnley would be 'the pasture within the little valley'. Ealees comes from ' Ea' - meaning a stream, so Ealees would mean 'the pasture beside the stream. Buckley, according to Fishwick, would mean 'the field of the male deer'.

Rod or Royd: There are only a few place names ending in 'rod' or 'royd' including Deanroyd, Swaindrod and Mawrode. 'Rod' meant places cleared of woods and made ready for cultivation. So to the Saxons 'Deanroyd' would mean 'The place in the little valley, which had been cleared of woods and made ready for ploughing'.

Shaw: is an old English word indicating early settlement. 'Shaw' meant a wood or sometimes a sheltered place.

Sykes: were small streams.

Ton: Town House is the only place name containing this word 'ton' in the whole of the Littleborough district, though it is common around Rochdale. According to Fishwick this was probably the only substantial dwelling in the whole of what is now the Littleborough district, for nearly three hundred years.

Wood: Place names containing 'wood' suggest early settlement. We have Cleggs Wood, Rake Wood, Lighthazzles Wood, Sladen Wood, Whittaker Wood.

Worth: Of place names ending in 'worth' we have Blatchinworth, Wardleworth, Hollingworth, and Butterworth. The meaning of 'worth' is 'fenced off places' - usually places fenced off from the surrounding woods. The meaning of the prefixes is not quite so clear, though the following have been suggested :- 'Blatchinworth' - from Blacca meaning black. 'Wardleworth' derived the first portion of its name (Wardle) from the word hill. 'Hollingworth' came from the holly bushes that existed there. The bushes were planted to provide feed for cattle and mark boundaries.

There are other place names which have not been mentioned; some of which have been claimed to be of Scandinavian origin. The Scandinavians came from the modern countries of Norway, Denmark and Sweden. In the 9th century they invaded eastern England. By 878 AD they ruled one third of England, the Danelaw, as part of a maritime empire. It is often claimed that the line of these Scandinavian people may be traced in many parts of the Craven district of Yorkshire to this day. Recent work based on genetics has supported this claim. It is unlikely that any Viking place names exist in the Littleborough district.

A list of the more obscure place names which play a part in this book follows (see p.35):

Mawroad, near the site of the Temple Wesleyan School, Calderbrook. Fred Jackson wondered whether there is any connection with this word 'Mawr' and the Welsh (or old British) word 'Mawr' as it occurs in Pen-maen-mawr, Plas Mawr, and other places in Wales (*in modern Welsh mawr means large*?). In the Rochdale Museum there is a drawing and description of a bronze torque or armlet found at this place which Sir John Evans declared to be of Celtic or British origin. Taking these two things together, is it too much to assume that the old Britons had a settlement here, and gave the place its name? If this surmise is correct this place name goes even further back than 'Ton House' and must be close on two thousand years old.

'Steanor Bottom' - S'teaner' - stony, 'Botm' - low lying land (see Chapter Seven).

'Holme' - may simply mean Meadowland.

'Lightowlers' - or as Fishwick gives it, as it occurs in Saxon times, 'Lightolres'. In the thirteenth century a family of the name of Lightolres lived on this site.

'Dog Isles (Hills)' - probably some connection with the public house which used to be at this place before the new road over Summit was made - about one hundred years ago.

'Timbercliffe' - a place name at Summit, the meaning of which is fairly evident, Fred Jackson did not "think it is as old as some of the others". Recent study indicates that in a similar format the name may be very old.

'Pike House' - some authorities say that it probably derived its name from the custom in feudal times, of the owner having to provide a certain number of 'Pikes' when required by the king to do so, for the defence of the country.

'Windy Bank' probably derived its name from a family which resided there, and who may have built the original hall in 1335 and resided there for several generations (see Chapter Seven).

Byenames (Nicknames)

From the same roots that gave us many place names came a convention which was still widely used in the late 19th century: nearly everbody in our community had a byename. There were:-

Shimmy and Shock,

An' 'sich a lot',

And Barney and Block,

And Can and Boll.

The convention was that each individual had a single name and description for identification. It seems to predate our current convention of surname and forename and is widespread elsewhere in the world

There were endless examples including: Jim-o'-Butts and Fan-o'-Butts, John-o'-Fanny's, and Rob-o'-Jamies, and Old Tom Treadlow. There were Old Pibbs and his donkey "Cuddie." There were Billy Segg and Jacky Flap of Allerscholes, Pinkie, Joe, and Jim-o'-Matts. Byenames occur in the following piece of reporting:

In the 1860's Jim-o'-Matts was a hand-loom weaver, but things were very slack and so he had to remove to an area where he could get work. Somebody asked their Betty o'-Watts about him. "Oh", she says, "he's gone to foreign parts." "And where's he gone to ?" "He's gone to Rachda."

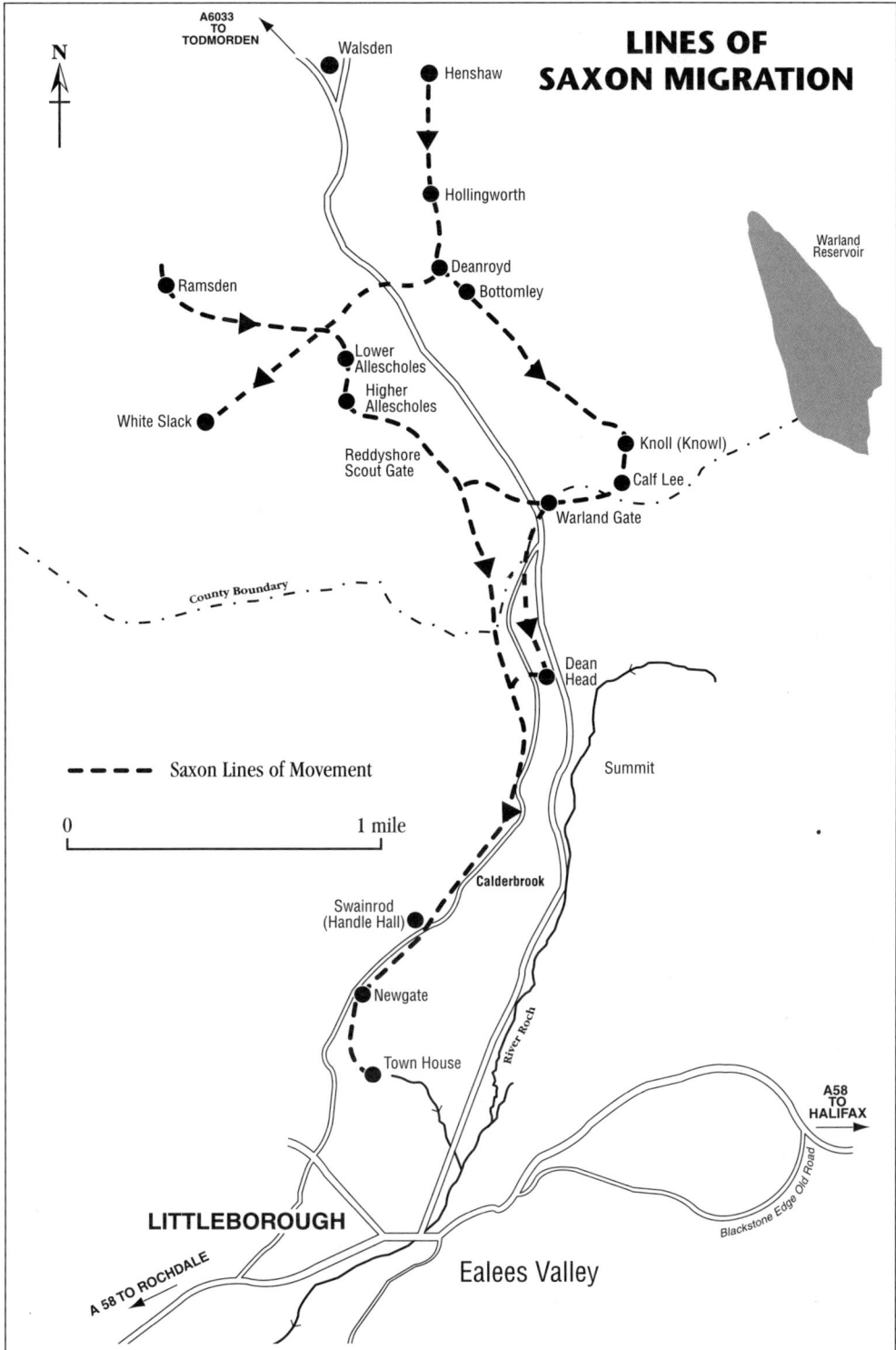

LINES OF SAXON MIGRATION

N

A6033
TO
TODMORDEN

Walsden

Henshaw

Hollingworth

Ramsden

Deanroyd
Bottomley

Warland
Reservoir

Lower
Allescholes

Higher
Allescholes

White Slack

Knoll (Knowl)

Reddyshore
Scout Gate

Calf Lee

Warland Gate

County Boundary

Dean
Head

Summit

- - - Saxon Lines of Movement

0   1 mile

Calderbrook

Swainrod
(Handle Hall)

River Roch

Newgate

Town House

A58
TO
HALIFAX

LITTLEBOROUGH

Blackstone Edge Old Road

A 58 TO ROCHDALE

Ealees Valley

Among the many changes in language that have taken place during the last 150 years, one of the biggest is the the loss of this use of byenames. The practice has died out. Fred Jackson asked a friend to write down those he remembered and was given a list of more than one hundred whom the friend knew personally around 1900. Having looked at the list Fred concluded:

"Some of them seem rather coarse to our ears and would probably hurt the feelings of the descendants of these people if they were published, so that perhaps it is better that they should be forgotten, so I have contented myself with selecting just a few of them. There were Jack of Owd Abs, Jack-o'-Betty's, Tommy-o'-Tummies, Sly Tommy, Towsle, Jack-at-Box, Bill-o'-Bobs, Bonker, Jim-o'-Bumps, Jim Bit, Bob Nit, Crumper, Bill-o'-Dans, Dindy, Ike-o'-Doitches, Dob Double, John-o'-Mary's, Ned-o'-Malleys, Ned-o'-Merrys, Jack-o-'Martins, Tom Flip Snip, Royton Ab, Mildra Dick, Tom-o'-Forrys, Ned-o'-Dicks, Jamie-o'-Flups, Ned Lurries, Ailse-o'-Fussers, Ned-o'th'-Butes, Owd Manton.

Ailse-o'-Fussers was quite a noted character, according to all accounts. She used to drive a string of twelve Galloways (gals) over the moors from Whitworth, carrying coal to the farms in the Littleborough district. Mr. John Magson says he well remembers seeing her 70 years ago. A short squat woman, nearly as far round as she was in height.

Jimmy-o'-Laddies drove a horse and cart carrying coal from Handle Hall Coal pit. He had a white horse which he called "Owd Tommy" and he was very much attached to it. One morning, as Jimmy was going into the stable to give Old Tommy his breakfast, he thought he heard him saying to him "What time is it?" Old Jimmy ran out of the stable up to his master's house, shouting "Come on down to th'stable. Owd Tommy's spokken to me this morning". It turned out that a man who tramped the district had got a free night's lodging in Tommy's stall, and it was he who was asking Owd Jimmy the time of day."

We are likely to smile at these byenames of the past, but like many other old customs they have a meaning and carry us back to the time, nearly a thousand years ago, when our Saxon forefathers came into this part of the country. To distinguish one from another people added these prefixes, suffixes or byenames. Sometimes it would be from some peculiarity in the individual, or sometimes he would be named after his trade. This practice obtained from the King down to the humblest person. Ethelwulf 'The Glorious', Alfred 'The Great', Edward 'Longshanks'. Just in the same way a great number of people would get their names from their occupations. John, who happened to be a shepherd, would be called John the Shepherd. If John the Shepherd had a son called Bill, he would be called Bill-o'-'John's the Shepherd. They would go back like this for several generations. For instance, a man died at the top end of Walsden in the late 19th century and he was referred to by one of his cronies as "Jack-o'-Jonas,-o'-Bills,-o-'Toms,-o-'Johns, o'th Bottoms i' Walsden.

Our dialect

Most languages have dialects, with a distinctive accent, grammmar, vocabulary, and idiom frequently centred on a geographical region. Along with many of the place names in our district and nickname conventions our local dialect dates back to the Saxons.

Fred Jackson was a convinced supporter of the value of our dialect not only as a way of remembering the past but for its power of expression. He makes a strong case in the following paragraphs.

"I was very much amused some little time ago at hearing a word used that I had not heard for some considerable time. I had been off work through illness, and one of our old weavers, who had given up working, was asking another, who was still at work: " How's Fred goin' on?" The answer was: "Oh champion. He's jarting us o' ra -and agean." Now I don't suppose that one out of a hundred of the younger generation know the meaning of the word jart, but I daresay that a large proportion of the older people both knew and felt the meaning of it in their young days (jart; to pull, jerk or throw quickly). When one comes to examine this question of dialect words, it is surprising to find the large number which have dropped out of use, during the last fifty or sixty years (1870 - 1930). But the change has been so gradual as to be barely noticeable. Whether this is all for the good or not I leave for others better qualified to judge. It makes one wonder at times however, whether there is any connection between the decay of the vigorous, blunt, dialect speech, and the decay, shall I say, of the sturdy independent, self-reliant, Lancashire men of a former day. As a recent writer says: 'False ideas of gentility and culture have banished many pure-blooded words of unimpeachable ancestry from polite conversation, and they are now only to be discovered enjoying a healthy but unduly restricted vogue in the confines of provincial dialect.

Would Edwin Waugh's poem *Come whoam to thi childer and me* appeal to a Lancashire man with anything like the force it does if it was written in modern English? Or take the following verses from a poem by Joseph Baron (Tum o' Dick o' Bobs).

SOME FOOAK

There's some fooak are olez on t' chunner
An' there's no'body can tell wet abeawt
An' there's others, as look black as thunner
An as sackless as hens are i' t' meawt
They're young, an ' they're strong, an' they're healthy
They possess every God given sense
But they're not wot they choosets call wealthy
Meeanin' sov'rans, an' shillins an' pence.

Poor Joo's it's for shadows yo're pinin'
An' yo've substance reight under yo'r een
Up aboon yo' God's lamps may be shinin'
As yo rake at yo'r muck heaps so keen
An' yo' rake, an' heeap up an' keep sighin'
An' God's marvels are lost to yo'or seet
An' yo'r brief day on earth here is flyin'
An o' th' sudden (heaw sudden), it's neet.

Oh look on yon breet orb descendin'
In a glory o' crimson an' gowd'
On yon ocean as tempests are rendin'
With a fury sublime to behowd
On each bonny green vale an' each river
On mankind and' on birds, an' on trees
Ay, an' think as yo' thank the Great Giver
Could earth's treasure buy gifts sich as these.

Hev yo' just a green hill top to walk'to
An' a song fro' a linnet or lark ?
Hev ya' just an' owd crony to tawk to
Or a book, when yo've finist yo'r wark ?
Hev yo' wife an' young childer as love yo'
An' mek breeter yo'r life wi' their mirth
Then thank God in His heaven above ye'
For yo're t' blessedest mortal on earth !

And yet some people say that our dialect is vulgar and barbarous and not fit to be referred to; much less the meaning of it taught in our day schools. How much wiser are the Welsh people in having their own language taught in every school in Wales where modern English is taught. One of the results of this is that the average Welsh schoolboy knows far more about the traditions and history of his native village than our Lancashire (or Littleborough) schoolboys do of theirs. I think it is a pity that time is not found in all our schools when giving history lessons for a short account of the history of the place in which we live. How much more interesting it would make it for the children, to know for instance, about the first people who came to our district. The old Neolithic people, who lived and died on our hills and moors long ages before we had any written history, and who have left behind them the flint implements they used in their every day life which we find on our hills and moors today. What a revelation it would be for the children to be taken to see the fine collection of these stone implements - found on local moors - which are to be seen in the collection held in Rochdale. What an added pleasure it would give them on their moorland walks, especially if they themselves were sometimes lucky enough to find some of these 'flints' themselves.

I must confess to a great regard for our Lancashire dialect myself, and in some respects I think it is a pity that it is going out of use, and it would be more pity still if it should be altogether forgotten. It may not sound very refined to some people, and I have even heard it referred to as vulgar, by some super-sensitive individuals. But I wonder do these people ever try to trace it to its origin; if they did I think they would find that our south-east Lancashire dialect is, after all, the nearest approach to the old Saxon, which was the language of the mass of the people of England for hundreds of years. It is far nearer to the language made use of by Chaucer, Spenser, Shakespeare, and Bunyan than the so-called good English spoken and written today. Granted that it is unsuitable for scientific nomenclature, in my opinion it is still a gradely way of expressing the thoughts and ideas of our every day life."

SOME OBSCURE LITTLEBOROUGH PLACE NAMES (Fred Jackson c1920)

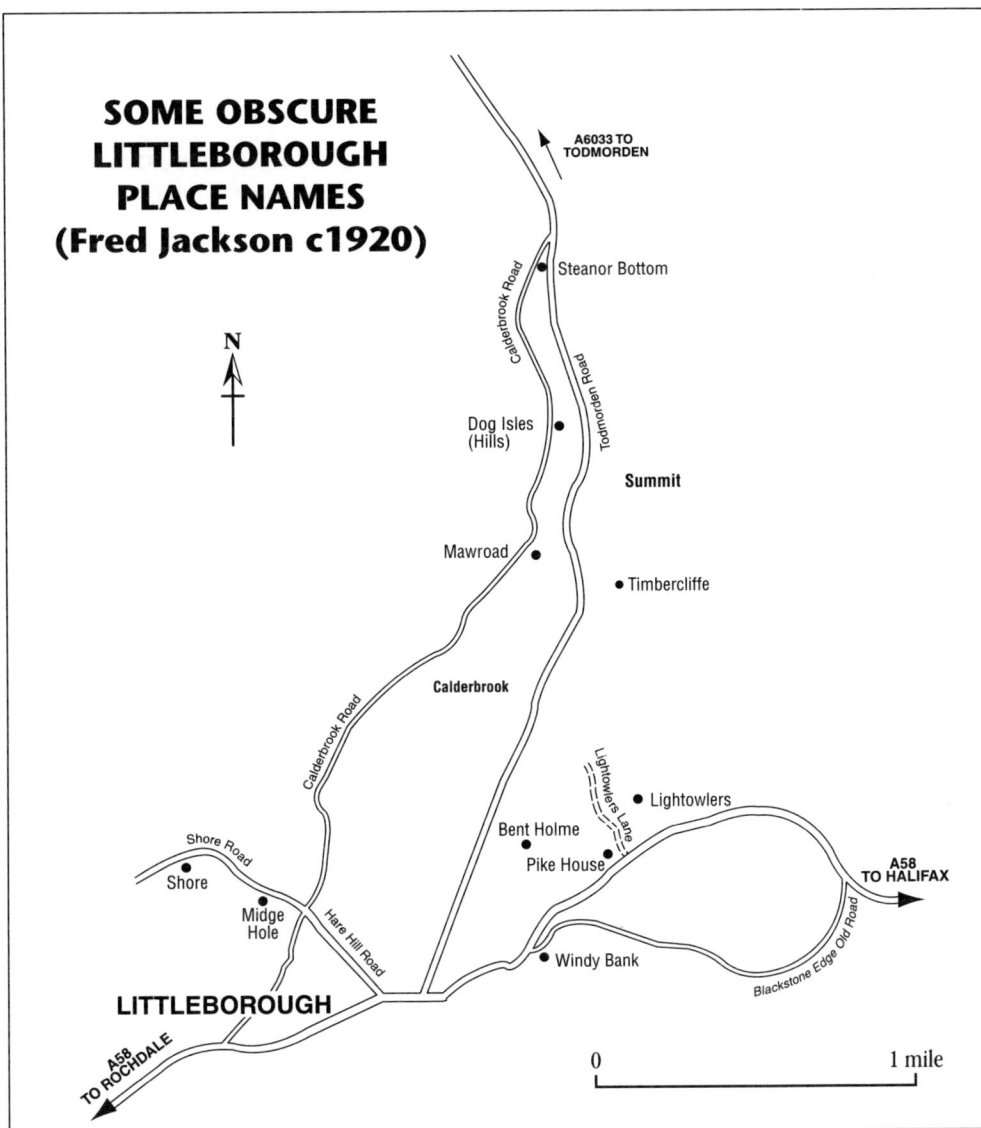

N

A6033 TO TODMORDEN

Steanor Bottom

Calderbrook Road

Todmorden Road

Dog Isles (Hills)

Summit

Mawroad

• Timbercliffe

Calderbrook

Calderbrook Road

Lightowlers Lane

• Lightowlers

Bent Holme

Pike House

A58 TO HALIFAX

Shore Road

Shore

Midge Hole

Hare Hill Road

• Windy Bank

Blackstone Edge Old Road

LITTLEBOROUGH

A58 TO ROCHDALE

0   1 mile

Fred Jackson ends by quoting an accomplished interpreter of our dialect, (Thos. Heywood H. S. A.):

"It is second to none in England, in the vestiges it contains of the tongue of other days....To explain Anglo-Saxon there is no speech so original and important as our own south-east Lancashire dialect. To the ears of strangers who know nothing about it, the sound is often uncouth and barbarous, that it is far from being so, is proved by the use long made of this dialect for lyric poetry and for both racy and pathetic touches. It has a pathos and simplicity that never fails to touch the heart".

Fred gave the following brief list of words that had gone out of use, to illustrate the richness of the local dialect;

35

Addle-	To earn	*Agaate-*	Get going
Ank-	I think	*Arta-*	Are you
Aussin-	Start working	*Ava-cakes*	Oat cakes
To Bagg-	To discharge	*Batch-o-bread-*	a baking of oat cakes
Benk-	A stone shelf	*Berrin-*	Funeral
Baggin-	Tea (Get thi' baggin)	*Beal-*	Pot handle
Steyl-	A brush handle or broom stall	*Tine-*	To shut (tine th' door after thee)
Gradely-	Well, thorough (a gradely sort of chap)	*Fettled it-*	Mended it
		Kneivi-	Mist
Wackered-	Shivered, Shuddered	*Beck-*	A brook
Sper-	To make enquiry	*Feaw-*	In an ugly manner
Syke-	A small riverlet or well	*Cammed-*	Crooked (clog cammed at thi' heel)
Chunner-	To grumble		
Fain-	Glad	*Wick-*	Alive (ar'nt ta fain tha'rt wick)
Nobbut-	Only		
Boose-	Drink	*Brat-*	Child (Tha' little ugly brat)
Brat-	coarse apron		
Chuseheaw-	However it is	*Pow or Powl-*	To have one's hair cut
Skallions-	Young spring onions	*Scawse-*	A blow
Meitherin-	Bothering	*Slutchy-*	Muddy
Capt-	Surprised (A'wm fair capt wi' thi')	*Farrantly looking-*	Comely
		Gate-	Road
Pi'kin-	Picking	*Olez-*	Always
Beawt-	Without	*Nelly-*	Nearly
Caps thi'aule-	Beats the devil	*Awse-*	To offer, attempt
Welly blynt-	Nearly blind	*Sneck bant-*	Band to latch on door
Dree-	Wearily-continuous	*Pottering about-*	Doing something (Always pottering aba-at)
Rooit-	Search, root		
Swaith-	Long grass (Roo'it among swaith and yo'll find it)	*Kist o' drawers-*	Chest of drawers
		beawn-	Going
		Warty-	Weekday
Gaumless-	A bit short	*Gumption-*	All there
Broitched-	Tapping an ale barrel	*Fleyd-*	Frightened.
Hutch-	Shrug	*Jart-*	To jerk or throw quickly.

He continued:

"It is not my intention to write a glossary of our dialect words. I think a much more striking way of showing the change which has taken place, is to take a passage from some writer of the period if possible. We are fortunate in being able to do this. Miss Jessie Fothergill lived at Sladen Wood House, and wrote a good many of her novels there. No doubt she would be in almost daily contact with her father's workpeople (Fothergill and Harvey's) and hear dialect regularly spoken. In her novel 'Healy' she has several humorous passages in the dialect. One of her characters is supposed to represent a typical Summit woman, named Mrs. Holden, and she does it very well indeed. It is worth getting the book from the Free Library for this character alone.

A final example of writing in dialect can be based on events that occurred at the

Holy Trinity Parish Church.

A winter journey, over Ealees Bridge, down to Halifax Road.

The Lock House which dates from the early 1800s alongside the Rochdale Canal at Ealees.

Hare Hill Road with the Wheatsheaf Buildings and the Royal Oak beyond.

The playing fields at Hare Hill.

Hollingworth Fold Cottage restored in the 1970s as a wardens house for the Country Park.

Recent new houses at Whitelees Road, built on the site of the former Whitelees Mill.

The engine from Durn Mill made by Earnshaw and Holt of Rochdale in 1864. A & W Law were spinners and weavers of Scottish Tartans. Working until the 1950s it is now on display at the Museum of Science and Industry in Manchester.

Looking under the motorway viaduct towards Hollingworth Lake.

Since the 1950s the eastern side of Todmorden Road has been developed for industrial and commercial use.

Underneath the arches.

Royal Oak in Littleborough. This inn was often visited by the famous "Tim Bobbin", of Milnrow, not only for the sake of those 'sneakers of punch, which were as good to him as oil to a clock', but for the purpose of selling his pictures to the Yorkshire manufacturers who stayed at the house. This is said to be the house where Tim fixed the scene of 'Tummus's misadventure' and where he so inadvisedly 'Eet like a Yorksharmon un cleart th' stoo,' and lodged for the night declaring that he 'never lee eh sich a bed sin he were kersuat.' It was here too where when he should have settled with the landlady in the morning he says: 'When ot eh soom't grope eh me slop t' pey ur, I'r weandedly glopp'nt, for th' dule a hawp'ny had eh,' and had to leave his 'sneeze hurn,' that he was 'louth' to part with because 'Seroh-o'-Ruchots gaitht him last Kesmus,' and after all, 'broddling fussock look't as feaw as thunner,' where also occurs the scene between Wythen Kibbs and Mezzil Faco, and one gets 'wawtit o'er into th' galker full o' new drink wortching."

(If you read this paragaraph slowly, aloud and exercise imagination you will get the drift of the story !)

This chapter can end with a stout defence from a true enthusiast.

Aw know awm reet broad spocken,
    These fine foak sen it's slang.
But ther's music in a mouthful
    O'gradely Lancashire twang.

It tastes o' th' fields un th' meadows,
    Un smells o' new mown hay.
It warms a man ut's parished,
    Like suppin' rum and tay.

Gi'e me a bowl o' porritch,
    A stake, wi' onions on,
A mess o' broth un' dumplins,
    Just reeching eaut O'pon.

This life's o teaw un' turmoil,
    It's wark to keep o streyght,
But a mon's no need to grumble
    If he gets enugg to heyt.

If a mon does fairly jannock,
    Un tries to do what's reet,
Aw think if there's a Heaven,
    He'll stond a rare good seet.

(anonymous)

Fred's last words on the importance of dialect echo the poem:

"I have tried my best to be 'Jannock' and write in a 'gradely sooart of a way ' about these old times and people, for I am proud of the dialect and prouder still to be a Lancashire mon mysel".

Summary

In the year 2000 place names, like a good many simple things we come across in our everyday life, have a lesson to teach us if we only try to get at the proper meaning of them. They give us an insight into the early life of our district better than any general history of the country can do. The people who settled here and gave the places these names have gone and every vestige of the buildings they built has passed away; but these words still tell us a lot about our Saxon forefathers of a thousand years ago.

Similarly, the convention of a single name and an identification by a nickname is strange to our ears today but has centuries of tradition and when these aspects come together in a rich dialect the preservation of the material becomes worth while and its place in local history undeniable

Finally, we do not know the nicknames of the early pioneers who gave so many of the place names that we use today, but we do know from 'Domesday Book' that a few years later - that is in Edward the Confessor's reign in 1041-66, a Saxon Thane (or lord) held all the land in the Littleborough district direct from the king. With the death of this king we come to the end of the Saxon period. After six hundred years of strife and conquest they were at last masters of all Angle-land, but the time was near when they themselves had to bow their knees to the Conqueror.

CHAPTER SEVEN

THE NORMANS AND THE MEDIEVAL PERIOD
(1066 A.D to 1485)
and THE ORIGINS OF THE OLD FAMILY HOUSES

After the death of Edward the Confessor, William of Normandy laid a claim to the English throne. In this he was supported by some of the English nobles, while others, especially in Northumbria (which included the Pennines), strenuously opposed him. Britain, when the Normans came, was a divided country.

In January 1066, Harold was proclaimed King of the "Angles" and had already successfully fought two great battles to establish his local dominance. However, William of Normandy claimed the throne as Edward the Confessor's nominee and also declared himself to have been chosen by the Pope as the representative of the Church. He landed at Pevensey near Hastings, on September 28th, 1066 A.D. The battle of Hastings took place on October 14th the same year and Harold was slain, along with an enormous number of his followers. William at once marched on London, where he was proclaimed king, and on December 25th, 1066 A.D., he was crowned at Westminster.

The Littleborough District at the time of the Norman conquest.

What was the condition of our local people when the Norman conquest took place? At least three successive invasions and settlements had left their traces, and very probably there were still representatives of the people of each. The earliest was the Neolithic people followed by the Celtic-speaking Britons. The Saxons reached our district late in the 5th century A.D followed by, perhaps, a sprinkling of Norsemen in the 9th century.

In 1066 A.D., Gamel, a Saxon thane, was the most important landowner in the Manor of Pontefract, which included Recedam (Rochdale). His rule also extended far beyond Recedam, for he had under his jurisdiction the townships of Elland, Gretland, Southowram and the surrounding districts. It is thought that he had his castle at Recedam and it is reasonable to speculate that it was one of his retainers who resided at 'Ton House' (Town House). These large houses, or castles, were mainly constructed of wood, which may explain why no part of them has survived.

The common people had their homes at some distance from the Ton House and were probably situated in the various 'worths' such as Blatchinworth, Butterworth, Wardleworth, ('worth' meaning land reclaimed from the forest and palisaded) thus forming tiny villages of not more than ten or fifteen families. Their houses were very primitive, for the most part huts constructed of sticks and mud and thatched with straw. They had no chimneys and the smoke from the wood fires, which were placed in the middle of the room, escaped through a hole in the roof. Glass was not available to them, so another hole in the wall served for a window (the word derives from the Old English 'wind eye'). The earthen floors of these dwellings were sometimes covered

OLD FAMILY HOUSES
(Fred Jackson c1920)

N

The marked locations show the
approximate sites of the buildings.
The following houses have
been demolished.

Lightowlers
Dearnley
Steanor Bottom
Pike House

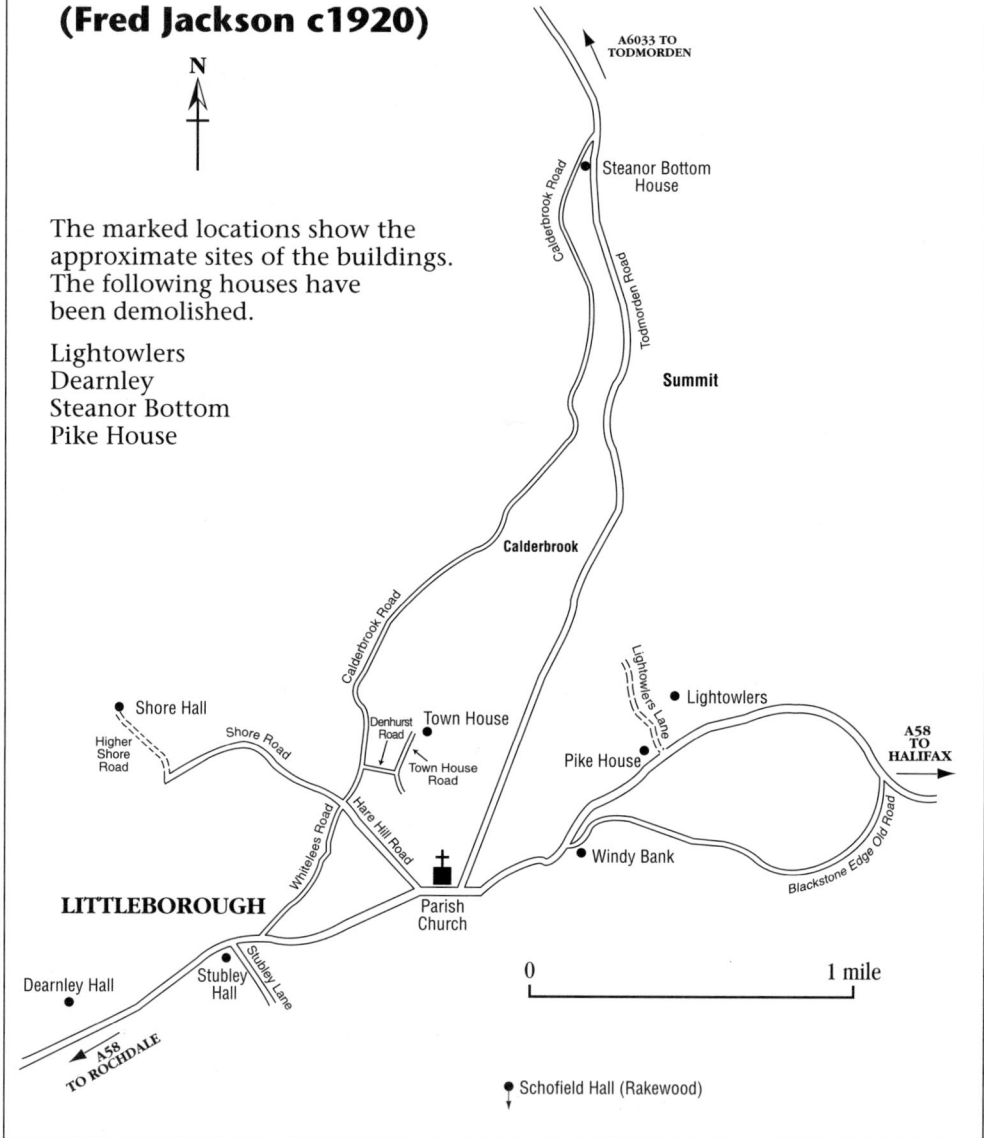

A6033 TO
TODMORDEN

Calderbrook Road

Steanor Bottom
House

Todmorden Road

Summit

Calderbrook

Calderbrook Road

Shore Hall

Higher
Shore
Road

Shore Road

Denhurst
Road

Town House

Town House
Road

Lightowlers Lane

Lightowlers

Pike House

A58
TO
HALIFAX

Whitelees Road

Hare Hill Road

Parish
Church

Windy Bank

Blackstone Edge Old Road

LITTLEBOROUGH

Dearnley Hall

Stubley
Hall

Stubley Lane

0   1 mile

A58
TO ROCHDALE

Schofield Hall (Rakewood)

with rushes. Even the 'rich man in his castle' had no bed or bedclothes; skins served
for blankets and a wood block for a pillow. The only light they had for the long winter
evenings were candles made from rushes which had been steeped in oil or fat, but these
were a luxury, so that it was customary to retire early and rise with the sun. Rye bread,
butter and cheese formed their chief articles of food. The meat they had consisted
chiefly of salted pork and beef. Beer, which was weak but pure, was their chief
beverage. They had no sugar, but wild honey was used in place of it. Root crops, such

as turnips, swedes, beet and potatoes were unknown, so that cattle could not be kept in large numbers during the winter months. They had to kill most of them in the autumn and salt their flesh to provide food during the winter.

The cultivation of the land was on the co-operative principle. It belonged to the whole village and each villager had the right to use strips of land in various parts of this area. The men of the village would hold a meeting to decide what crops they should grow. If they had three fields, the first might be for rye, the second oats or barley, and the third had to be fallow. They would also have a large meadow for hay. The open field was divided into strips about seven yards wide and two hundred yards long, with a length of unploughed land between each to mark the boundary.

The first strip was claimed by the ploughman, the second by the man who provided the plough; the next two strips went to the owners of the principal pair of oxen, next came the driver's turn, and after him the owners of the other oxen, and so on. The same order would be gone through several times until the land was ploughed up, so that each man's strips were scattered up and down the field. This kept the field common, for if a man had been allotted the first four strips instead of, say numbers 1, 13, 29, and 40, he would probably have fenced his strips and made them into a field of his own. In Mankinholes (Todmorden) a remnant of this method of farming still survives; aerial photographs of Snoddle Hill providing some evidence of similar cultivation methods there. The long narrow strips of meadow land at Mankinholes, stretching down towards the mountain stream are a reminder to us of the days of common farming, when an effort was made to give every man a fair share of both good and inferior land.

Each of the small villages was complete in itself, with its own shoemaker, carpenter and blacksmith. Rough skin shoes, harnesses and leather drinking vessels were shaped from hides. The sheep's wool would be washed and carded by the women and the rough yarn would be woven into coarse cloth, to serve as tunic and hose.

Such were the conditions of life of our Saxon ancestors, but the coming of the Normans was to bring about a radical change in the habits and customs of the people.

Norman Colonisation

The first impact of the Norman power on northern Britain was felt in the year 1069 A.D. The Northumbrians (which included the people of the Pennines) revolted against the King, and a battle took place at York in September 1069, when many Normans were slain. William gathered an army together and hastened to Northumbria, and throughout the winter systematically destroyed the area between the Humber and the Tees, with a ferocity and completeness which has seldom been equalled in English history. Then, according to Hilaire Belloc in his book 'Warfare in England', he pushed west over the hills to the western plain, and we know that he came to the edge of our district. Fifteen years after this 'harrying of the Shires', as it was called, there were over 400 Yorkshire manors despoiled and it was claimed that only forty-three human beings remained within their former boundaries, some of the wretched survivors were driven to cannibalism. William of Malmsbury, writing some 60 years later, said: "The land lay waste around York for a breadth of 60 miles."

Gradually the Norman Conquest affected all classes of society. Saxons and their retainers were wholly or partially deprived of their estates, to make room for William the Conqueror's knights and barons. He appropriated some 1,400 to 1,500 manors, with their lands and forests, for the support of the crown, and then distributed the remainder of the country among his followers and relatives.

To his nephew, Hugh de Abrinces, he gave the whole of Cheshire. To his half-brother, Odo, Bishop of Bayeux, he gave 430 manors; to Earl Percy, 119 manors; but what concerns us most is that he gave all the land between the Mersey and the Ribble, including the 'Hundred of Salford' to the Earl of Poictiers. Roger of Poictiers took from Gamel, the Saxon, most of his estates, leaving him with only one sixth of his former possessions and probably built the original Clitheroe Castle. No army could easily pass from the Lancashire plain, through the Pennines, without first subduing this castle. It was also used as a prison for offenders from the surrounding areas including Littleborough, who had committed park and forest offenses.

Hunting and the Forest Law

The Domesday Book records some 250,000 acres of dense wood and forest remaining between the Ribble and the Mersey which title embraces what we now know as Littleborough. In the mediaeval period deer were common in our district and also in the Forest of Sowerby on one side and the Forest of Rossendale on the other. The unlawful killing of them was a serious offence, as the following instance shows:

Nicholas de Werdhyl (Wardle) having slain a fat buck, in the Forest of Rochdale, Lawrence de Knowl, Adam de Grimshaw, and Andrew de Halgh, keepers of the Earl's forest came by night, seized him, and dragged him to Clitheroe Castle, where he was imprisoned until a heavy fine was paid for his release.

The Normans were great hunters and Upper Calderdale provided a sporting estate for the earls of the king's court. They had a deer park in Erringden, from Cragg Vale to Callis Wood while the forest for hunting extended up onto the Sowerby side to share a common boundary with our own district, a little beyond Blackstone Edge. This enclosed park for breeding deer is mentioned several times in 14th century documents.

The large tracts of land, such as the Forests of Rossendale, Sowerby, Pendle and our local deer park, were not really forests in the modern sense. Enclosures within the forests housed cattle breeding stations or 'Vaccaries', as they were called. The vaccary was managed by a Bailiffe, or Instourater, and one of the yearly accounts from such a manager to his master, in relation to the stock of cattle, has been preserved. He had 407 cattle which were looked after by five assistant cowherds, who sheltered in 'Booths' in the forest. (Booth-royd, Booth-hollins, Crawshaw-booth, etc.) The cattle reared were small and oxen were of more value than cows, because they were able to draw the waggons and ploughs. An ox was worth 9s., a cow 7s., a hide 2s. 6d. The cattle were very prone to disease (murrain), but they suffered most from the ravages of wolves, which infested the forest. At each 'booth' it is recorded that cattle had been lost due to attacks by wolves.

In 1370 John by the Water, Thomas del Oldfield, Thomas by the Brokebank, and Richard de Whitelees were ordered to repair the pallisades of our local deer park (which included Littleborough) and which continued to be used for breeding deer until the reign of Henry V1).

In the year 1296 A.D. the Earl's foresters had difficulty in preventing people in our area from poaching in the Forest of Sowerby, so the Earl's chief forester killed a deer and sent it, without the Earl's permission, to the Vicar of Rochdale in the hope that the latter would prevent poachers from the Rochdale Parish coming into the Earl's chase. This secret action was discovered and the forester was tried at Wakefield, but the Court acquitted him.

Not many years later a Vicar of Rochdale was himself fined 20s (a heavy fine in those days) for hunting and killing deer in the Forest of Sowerby.

Smaller fines were inflicted for trespassing or allowing cattle to trespass in the King's forests or parks. In 1296 we find that Richard the Fuller was fined 2d for collecting nuts and John of Midgley was fined 12d for carrying away the Earl's timber. In 1275 Thomas, son of John, son of Hugh de Mancanoles, was fined 6d for allowing pigs to escape into the forest. In the same year Henry de Stodly was fined 2d when four of his calves were found in the forest. In 1277 William de Stodley was fined 12d for a similar offence involving cows with six calves. At the court of Wakefield in 1286, Wilcock de Mancanholes, whose mare escaped into the forest, was fined 6d. These examples could be multiplied almost indefinitely, but they serve to show that the forests were strictly guarded and maintained primarily for the hunting of deer, wolves, wild boars, foxes and other game.

The Normans ruled autocratically inflicting the severest penalties on the conquered Saxons if they disobeyed the new social rules. The King became the sole owner of game throughout the country, and no person might hunt, even on his own property, without his permission. The life of a Saxon was counted of less value than that of a buck or doe, for the punishment of death was awarded to those who killed either illegally. If found taking a boar the unfortunate culprit paid forfeit with his eyes, which were 'pulled out of his head'. The lopping of a limb was a common punishment for illegally hunting the roe or fox, and a fine equivalent to ruin, and loss of entire worldly possessions, was inflicted for taking a hare or other inferior game. With the Forest of Sowerby on one side, and the Forest of Rossendale on the other and a large deer park and hawk sanctuary covering the local area, the temptation to poach locally or in adjacent areas was very great.

The following rhymed oath was imposed on everyone living within the Forest fence who was twelve or more years old -

> You shall true Liegeman be
> Unto the King's Majestie.
> Unto the beasts of the Forest you shall no hurt do.
> Nor to anything that doth belong thereto.
> The offences of others you shall not conceal.
> But the utmost of your powers you shall them reveal.
> Unto the officers of the Forest
> or to them who may see them redrest.
> All these things you shall see done
> So help you God at His Holy doom.
>
> *(Newbigging: written circa 1200 AD).*

For an area like Littleborough it is difficult to adequately represent the importance of the old forest laws, and their impact on the people living in scattered hamlets in such a 'forest'. The overall effect appears to have been an extra and onerous burden on an already difficult life. It is no wonder that the popular myth grew up of Robin Hood flouting the forest laws and protecting the poor.

Land Ownership and the Manorial System

During the Saxon period, each village was practically the owner of the land in its own area, but with the advent of the Normans this changed. Even the name of the little settlement was changed, henceforth it was known as a 'Manor' which is a Norman name meaning 'dwelling place'.

After the Battle of Hastings, William the Conqueror claimed all the land as his own. When he parcelled it out among his followers he laid down very strict rules about the services he required in return for it. He had a very comprehensive survey made of all the lands, goods, chattels and serfs. In the case of the land, he had an inventory made of the amount of forest, agricultural land and what implements existed to work it. Estimates were done of what the various assets were worth in Edward the Confessor's time, and what they were worth when the survey was made.

All these particulars were entered into a set of volumes which he named 'the Domesday Book.' This book has been carefully guarded during all the intervening centuries, and has been a mine of information, from which historians have been able to draw particulars about the condition of the land and life, labour and customs of the people at this early period of our history.

Rochdale (or Recedam, as it was called) was surveyed and the particulars were entered in the Domesday Book. It is described as being in the 'Great Hundred of Salford' and that before the Norman Conquest it belonged to Edward the Confessor (1041 - 1066). It records that there were extensive forests in this Hundred, one of which was 9½ miles long by 5 miles 1 furlong broad, with many enclosures and areas allocated for raising hawks for sport. Littleborough falls within this forest.

When William the Conqueror granted land it was rarely an absolute gift; some service was required in every case. (In theory, even today our sovereign is owner of all the land in England). The services which the King required for the use of the land varied in different parts of the country; briefly it was as follows:

He must be worthy of his 'Book Right', the right confirmed by his 'Book' or 'Charta'. He must do three things for his land: Fyrdfare (military service), Burphete (repairing the King's castles or Borough) and Bridge Work.

In addition, from many land grants a greater service arises, at the King's command. These services include; maintaining the deer hedge at the King's abode, provision of war ships, head ward (guard of the King's person) and providing fish, game and bows and arrows.

Each one who received a grant of land in this way was called a 'Lord of the Manor'. Money was not in general use, so the total revenue of the Crown, for the government of the country, had to be found by the manorial lords. When the lord had received a grant of land he in turn allotted certain portions of estate to various residents. Once more, in return for the allotment, certain specified services had to be rendered, and so long as the services were performed the tenant was secure in his holding. The great majority of the people were tied to their village homes, as they had no choice but to live where they were born, to serve the master upon whose manor they resided. They tilled his ground and looked after his cattle. For this they were paid no wages, but had their cottage and the free use of strips of land to sow or plant for themselves. The land, as previously mentioned, was not all in one place, but scattered among the strips that were held by his fellow villagers. Villagers could not sell the land, leave the manor, give their daughter in marriage, or sell an ox without consulting their masters. Every few months they gathered together in the Manor Court and took part in the election of the manorial officers such as the Reeve, the Woodward and the Ale Taster. They also decided on the kind of crops to be sown on the village lands. By the 20th century most of these customs had lost their significance, but for a long time the Lord of the Manor of Rochdale still held what was called his Court Leet annually. Men were appointed, as in the old days, to such posts as Ale Taster, Woodward and Swineherd, though by that time, there were neither duties nor salaries attached to the posts.

Manor of Rochdale

The Manor of Rochdale, which includes all the land we know as Littleborough, has not changed hands very often during the last 900 years. Before the Conquest it was in the possession of Gamel the Saxon Thane. The Earl of Poictiers received it as a grant from the King. Soon after, it passed to the Lacies, who became Lords of Clitheroe and Pontefract and later Earls of Lincoln. It remained in their possession about 240 years, until the death of the then Earl of Lincoln in 1311 A.D.

From 1311 until the end of the 15th century this Manor was held by the Dukes of Lancaster and the Crown. Then by letters patent dated 2nd July, 1519, Henry V111 granted to Sir John Byron the Office of Stewardship of the Lordship of Rochdale, with all its numbers, together with the conduction of all the King's men and tenants, and to hold the same Office from the Feast of St. Michael for his lifetime. This was confirmed by other letters patent, granted in 1543-4, when it was stated that Byron was to govern the tenants not only in Rochdale, but all its hamlets. Fishwick (History of Rochdale) mentions six Lord Byrons, as Lords of the Manor of Rochdale. The last Lord Byron of Rochdale, who sold the Manor to the Dearden family (1823) for the sum of £30,000, was George Gordon Byron - the poet (1789 - 1824). Since then the Manor has remained in the possession of the Dearden family.

The following extract is taken from 'The Palatine Note Book':

'The Rachdales of Rochdale have long been extinct, but it is supposed that they were the ancient Lords of the Manor. The arms of Rochdale are those of the Rachdale family, differenced, and in addition a woolsack surrounded with a branch of the cotton plant. Rochdale (Recedam) is thought to be anglo-saxon: Racu - flood, and Ham - a dwelling.'

Medieval Remains

The Aiggin Stone

The Aiggin stone is a large 'way cross' or marker on the top of Blackstone Edge on the line of the Roman Road. It is generally agreed to be medieval acting as a guide to travellers crossing the Pennines and also as a resting place, where thanks were given for a safe ascent and very possibly a prayer said for a safe descent. The first record we have of the stone is on a canal map drawn early in the 19th century where it is called the Aiggin Stone. The name may come from the Norman-French 'aigualle' meaning a needle. Another possible derivation is from the military word 'agger' which is an ancient term for a dyke or causeway.

The Aiggin Stone.

The top of the cross has been broken off and the whole is weather worn but it has a number of interesting carvings still visible. The stone has been knocked over on a number of occasions, the latest being in 1997 when it was restored by a voluntary community effort organised by the Littleborough Civic Trust, which included placing a plaque by the stone to discourage further vandalism. The stone deserves preservation as ancient reminder of the old roads and our ancestors who travelled them.

It is also interesting that one of our older Littleborough residents, who had responsibility for footpaths and roads under the Urban District Council, located the existence of a second 'ancient cross' on an early footpath map. When subsequently carrying out road repairs close to the entrance to Blackstone Edge Fold farm, a buried plinth was found with a major square hole in the middle (for the cross ?), other holes (for suppports?) and some interesting carving. The plinth was moved out of the road line onto the verge where it can be seen today at the edge of the small car park space. Further enquiry may well establish that this remnant is worth more respect and proper preservation. This prospect has become more exciting as a similar stone plinth has been reported half-buried close to the line of the Roman road where it approaches the Blackstone Edge road on the Yorkshire side of the Pennines.

The 'old' families and family houses in Littleborough.

For a considerable time after the Norman Conquest, very little is known of the history of our district. People lived their lives mainly in agricultural pursuits and for a long period they appear to have been cut off from the more active centres and developments. Communication was difficult and it would be when some traveller, trader or entertainer passed through the small settlements, that they would get any news from the outside world.

For nearly 300 years (says Fishwick), Ton House remained the only house in our district, but in the late thirteenth and the fourteenth centuries, mention is made of several other families, who had settled there:-

Ton House (Town House)	in 970
Stobbligh (Stubley)	in 1277
Shore (Shore Hall)	in 1280
Lightobris (Lightowlers)	in 1280
Dernelegh (Dearnley)	in 1332
Windybonk (Windy Bank)	in 1335
Schofield Hall	in 1340
Steanor Bottom	in 1390
Pike House	in 1561

54

It is from the history of these families and their buildings that something can be learned of our area in the 13th, 14th and 15th centuries. In 1872 a writer commented;

"Probably no part of the country is more thickly studded with old mansions, relics of more barbarous ages, than the neighbourhood of Littleborough."

He went on to itemise, Clegg Hall, Belfield Hall, Wildhouse, Town House, Pike House, Bent House, Foxholes, Butterworth Hall, Stubley Hall and others outside the immediate Littleborough district.

In the brief historical notes that follow, for ease of future reference, the story of each house has been brought up to the year 2000.

TOWN HOUSE (970)

The Saxons had a settlement here in the tenth century and this house was probably the only one in the district and gave its name to a family. It was the seat of Michael, son of William de la Ton as early as 1223. Michael gave certain portions of lands in Hunresfeld, on the south side of Ton-Brook, to the monks of Stanlawe. No payment was to be made, except the prayers for the souls of Nicholas, the donor's brother, and those of his ancestors who had died in the true faith. This charter was witnessed by David del Ton, Hugh de Eland, and others. Another charter dated 1292 mentions Adrew del Ton, and yet another mentions the name of Matilda, the wife of Peter del Tonne in 1336.

The main house appeared to have passed to John de Kyrkshagh (Kershaw) before 1281 and it was extended in 1292. John's son, Mathew de Kyrkshagh, granted lands in

Town House. This photograph probably dates from the early 1900s showing the brothers Gordon and Ernst Harvey.

The old cottages and 'The Warehouse' at Lower Townhouse, recently restored and converted as private dwellings. A datestone records 'L & S N 1752' (Lawrence and Sarah Newall).

Stubley Old Hall, a family group in 1910; used to illustrate Rev. Oakley's book 'Olden Days'.

Honresfield to his son Adam in 1339. He married Margery, daughter of William de Lighttolres. The ancient mansion passed into the possesion of William, son and heir of Lawrence Newall, gentleman, on his marriage in 1452 with Isabella, daughter of Christopher Kyrkshagh of Ton House. From this time it remained in the Newall family for nearly 500 years. Town house was re-built in 1604 and a date stone was inserted over the main door. A branch of the Kyrkshagh family continued to reside at Higher Town House till 1720. Another branch of the same family lived at Caldermoor House opposite the entrance to Denhurst Road. This house (now demolished) carried a date stone of 1611 which was retained by Margaret Newall when she rebuilt it in 1840. Several other members of this branch of the Kershaw family lived at Mawrode (Calderbrook) at this time. On the death of Alexandra Kershaw in 1720 Higher Town House was purchased by Robert Newall. The house was once again extended and altered in 1798: the record states that the old date stone was moved to the servants hall. By the 19th century there were branches of the Newall family in many parts of England, Scotland and Australia. Those who remained around Littleborough thrived and by the end of the century they were occupying a number of mansions, including Hare Hill House, Wellington Lodge and Gale House. Gale house was where the Moleswoths lived (relatives by marriage). After the death of the last Laurence Newall of Town House, the estates descended to his three daughters: Higher Town House going to Mrs. Lomax, Lower Town House, going to Mrs. Molesworth, and the Gale property to Mrs. John Molesworth, who afterwards purchased Lower Town House from her sister. For some little time it was the residence of F.N. Molesworth, Esq. The Hare Hill Estate was sold in 1903 (see Chapter 15) and the Harvey family (Gordon and Ernst) took over the Town House while most of the rest was bought by the Urban District Council. The remaining Newalls and Molesworths left the district. The Harvey family enlarged and modernised Town House during the early 1900s and stayed there until the 1960s when the property was sold and divided into flats.

STOBBLIGH (1277).

In 1277 the name of Nicholas de Stobblegh appears as a witness to a Charter, and in 1307 that of Elia de Stobblegh. It is believed that one of this family sold 'Stobbligh' to John de Holt (Holt: Anglo-Saxon for wood) in 1330. Church records indicate that a Thos, Holt held Church Services at Stubley prior to the building of Holy Trinity in 1471. Thos, Holt of Stubley died there in 1494. Robert Holt his son, who made his will in December 1554, was a Justice of the Peace and seems to have been a wealthy man, who is said to have rebuilt Stubley around 1528. This date was confirmed by a date stone (now lost) which was still on the house in 1851 and was recorded on the government Geological Survey map of that time. At that early date it appears to have been the third house on the site. In his will Robert Holt desired to be buried 'in the channcell', in the Paryisshe Church near where his father was, his feet to 'lye nere wheare' the head of his wife lay. Among other ligaries (*legacies*) he left to Richard Holt 40/-, to Roger Holt 13/4, to his niece Jane, one heffer, Richard Holt a 'satin dublett', Edmund Mylne a 'dublett'. Three of his greatest 'brass pottes', two garnysshe of pewter vessell and four feather beds, were to remain at Stubley as heirlooms. He had considerable property in Hundersfield, Spotland and Middleton, and other places consisting of eighty houses, three water mills, four fulling mills and four thousand acres of land. There was a later Robert Holt living at Stubley in 1561, who made his will in April of that year. The following extract from this will is interesting, on account of its quaint phraseology and the description it gives of the Stubley Hall of that period. He left all his;

'Cartes, waynes, plowes, yokes, harows, and other implements of husbandry, then at Stubley, to his son and heir, Charles Holt, as well all such 'lomes' (heirlooms) as Robert Holt late of Stubley, the elder, did leave by his last will. He left to his brother Holt v.i.s. and v.i.i. i.d. (6/8d) to buy shepe with. To the children of his brother Charles Holt v.i.s. v.i.i.i.d. to be 'wared' (spent) in shepe.'

The inventory mentions the great chamber, my lord's chamber, the new chamber, the chapel chamber, the inner chamber, the hall, the inner parlour, St. Myghell's chamber, and syling timber, that is timber for wainscotting. This Robert Holt was one of the group of local landowners who bought back the Littleborough church after it had been sequestered by the Royal Commissioners. (see Chapter 8)

In the Manor survey of 1626 it was described as 'an ancient mansion called Stubleye Hall, with stables, barns, dove cote, water mill and 110 acres of land'. In 1634 there is a record of a resident 'Chaplaine to the Holts of Stubley'. Early in the eighteenth century the Stubley estate went to the Winstanley family, by a series of marriage arrangements. In 1839 the house was sold to Mr James Schofield of Heybrook who died in 1860. It was his son Joseph who built the large modern hall (New Hall) which was built next to the older one, in 1855. Part of the old hall was left standing. Two sons of Joseph, Arnold and Frank occupied the two houses much of the time until 1920 when the estate passed out of the Schofield family. In 1910 the Reverend G.R. Oakley lived at

Shore Hall at Higher Shore; one of the oldest and best preserved houses in the district.

Stubley for a period and it was there that he wrote the legend of Stubley in his book 'Olden Days' (see *The Dernelighs of Dernelegh later in this chapter*). The new hall was later divided into three separate houses. The Old Hall (claimed to be the one of the first stone buildings in the area to have additions using moulded bricks) was recognised as having architectural and historical value and was designated as a grade 2 listed building. In the 1970s it had a number of occupiers, and in this period parts were restored and the 'cruck beam' construction was uncovered. Later the building was used as a store and office by a building merchant. With the support of local groups it was refurbished as a residential hotel, which in turn was sold and is now used as a restaurant. In the 20th century it has suffered the indignity of being painted as if it was half-timbered and although it is a listed building, it has been much altered.

SHORE FAMILY OF SHORE HALL (1280)

Roger de la Shore, held land in Hundersfield in 1280 and he or another of the same name received other lands from Thomas de Staneringges in 1307.

In 1463 another Roger Shore had lands conveyed to him by Adam Merland, who had received the same from Michael Shore. In 1560 Ralph Shore 'held a messuage' and land in Shore. In 1641 Robert Shore, a yeoman living in Shore 'demised' a house called Shore to Edmund Whitehead of Dearnley. The arrangement was for 99 years subject to 'the life of Dorothy, wife of Jeremy Duerden of Shore'. In 1647 a settlement was made 'in consideration of a marriage about to take place between Thomas, son and heir of Robert Shore, and Elizabeth the daughter of James Bamford'. From this time their descendants continued to live at Shore until the close of the eighteenth century.

In a will dated August, 1775, Robert Shore of Lower Shore, yeoman, left his estate to his two daughters, Mary, wife of Thomas Wolfenden of Lower Shore, and Ann, the wife of James Gibson of Liverpool. In 1796, Thomas Wolfenden of Lower Shore left the property to his son Robert, leaving also other lands in the neighbourhood to his younger sons. None of these family members lived locally so after a period of over 500 years (1280-1796) the Shores' of Shore ceased as a family to live in the district. Some family connection continued until the property and estate was bought by the Cleggs of Shore in the 1920s. Since then the ownership has changed several times and continues to be used as a private residence.

THE LIGHTOLRES OF LIGHTOLRES (1280).

Lightowlers is now the name of a small farm just above Pikehouse, on a site by the Blackstone Edge road. Over 600 years ago there was a fairly large house here, which was the home of a family named Lightolres, who were probably the earliest settlers in the district, after William of the Ton (Town House). They held a considerable amount of land on the opposite side of the valley to Ton House, the river dividing the two estates.

By a deed, without date, William de Lightowlers, granted to his son Roger, the services of his tenants in Hundersfield. In 1280-1, he granted land in Longelgh-heye and Lightolres in Hundersfield to Mathew del Kyrkeschagh (Kershagh) of Ton House. It seems the family had also property in Castleton; in 1304, William the son of Roger de Lightowlers, by Charter dated at the Church of Rochdale, gave to the Abbot of Whalley 'all his right to the Grange of Marland, and in all the 'vill' of Castleton, and all its divisions'. In 1331-2 he was a juryman on an inquisition respecting lands in

Whitworth. In 1340 Mergery the daughter of William de Lightowlers, married Mathew de Kyrkeschagh of Town House, to whose son Henry she released her claim to all her lands in Honresfield.

The Lightowlers gave up their ancestral acres in 1515, when one half went by marriage to the Newalls and Helliwells (the Pike House Estate) and the other to the Chadwick family. However, the family did not leave the neighbourhood. In 1554 Richard Lightolres, yeoman, was living at Windy Bank, and the same or another Richard Lightolres was there in 1592. In 1600 Robert Lightowlers of Windy Bank, yeoman, was appointed tutor to Elizabeth, daughter of Robert Butterworth of Town House. In 1626, Richard Lightowlers held a tenement called Underbank and 'the Knoll', adjoining the road leading to Blackstone Edge, which embraced 101 acres of land. At this time Richard Lightowlers was living at Windy Bank and in 1628 was one of the jury of the Court Leet, held that year at Littleborough. The family seems to have left the district in the next few years. One branch moved to Rochdale and another to Chorley. Their local possessions were mainly absorbed into the Pike House estate and by 1673 Henry Halliwell, brother of Theophilus Halliwell of Pike House and Ealees Mansion, lived at Lightowlers. No remains of the old house called Lightowlers exist today.

DERNELEGH (1332).

Birch Hill Hospital now stands on the estate formerly held by the Derneleghs. The Dernleghs left the district long ago,, but there is abundant evidence that a family of this name lived for several hundred years at Dearnley. The village of Dearnley today is prosaic enough, but the Rev. G.R.Oakley in his book, gives a very pretty legend of love, romance and tragedy which occurred to one of the Dernlegh family in olden days. To quote a few sentences from this legend.

"On a fair lawn, beneath the shade of a great oak tree, on one autumn day in the year 1347, reclined two young girls, who - as is the custom of the sex in all ages - were whiling away the time with gossip anent a thousand matters.

Some fifty yards behind them stood the noble old mansion of the Dernleghs, who since the days when the Conqueror ruled, had, generation after generation, lived the lives of loyalty and honour, which their name and blood demanded. At that very time the heir of the house, Henry de Dernelegh, was in France with his King. He had shared in the glory of Crecy, and had seen the fall of Calais."

As a writer of romantic fiction where fairies, ghosts and humans interact comfortably, the Rev. Oakley was very successful. His legends have provided promotional material, notably for a number of inns and restaurants during the 20th century.

The first recorded Dernelegh is Roger de Dernelegh, who appears in the subsidy roll of 1332 and in the Manor Court Records of 1335 as a witness to a deed in 1334.

At the end of the fourteenth century a Henry de Dernelegh is mentioned as being an outlaw and it is this Henry de Dernelegh around which Mr Oakley has written his legend of love and tragedy. After this time the family is lost sight of, and the Dernelegh estates came into the hands of a family named Whitehead. In 1559 deeds show that one of the Whitehead family was living in the mansion at Dearnley. However, in 1580 a Roger Dernelegh of Glossop in Derbyshire appeared in the Duchy Court, claiming the lands of Dearnley, but failed to get them. In 1626 Arthur Whitehead held Upper and

Lower Dearnley, and in 1626 John Whitehead of Dearnley had a licence granted at Chester to marry Grace Hollas of Rochdale. Since then Dearnley has been sub-divided and passed through several hands.

WINDY BANK (1335)

This is one of the oldest, best preserved and most picturesque-looking houses in the district. It is situated near the old packhorse road leading over Blackstone Edge.

Early in the fourteenth century a Sir Henry de Wyndebonks is a witness to a Charter conveying lands in Whitworth to the Abbot of Whalley Abbey, and the same name occurs in 1335, as does also William de Windebanks.

No further mention of a Wyndebonks family has been discovered. During the next 200 years members of families with the names of Chadwick and Lightowlers have been connected with it. In 1535 Windy Bonk passed into the possession of John Butterworth of Ealees, who left it to his son, Robert Butterworth. The earliest recorded date stone on this property is 1611.

During the next hundred years it had several tenants, but in 1635 it again came into the possession of a John Butterworth, who rebuilt the house. His initials J.B. 1635, are carved on a stone over the doorway. Another Butterworth died in 1703 but it appears that the house was shared at this time and Robert and John Schofield also lived in it during the 17th and 18th centuries. As at Stubley this house, which remains a private dwelling, has been altered and extended on a number of occasions over the years but the main facade is probably much the same as it was when rebuilt 300 years ago.

SCHOFIELD HALL (1340)

The hall is sited above the hamlet at Rakewood and at 700' above sea level must always have been surrounded by open moorland. The Schofield family emerge in records around 1310 with land gifts to the abbot of Whalley. By 1340 there are numerous branches of the family with properties in Rochdale, Burnley, Castleton and elsewhere. The main records available at this time record litigation within the immediate family and between the family and their neighbours. There are some exciting cases of adultery and fleeing couples exiting from windows in the early hours, just ahead of sword wielding husbands and cases of duelling over property. By 1626 the family are the owners of considerable property locally including the Hall, the Round House and Booth Hollins. In 1673 a hard up James Schofield sold the Hall to the Clayton family who subsequently sold it on to Robert Entwistle in 1770. So inter-connected were all these families, it emerges that the Schofields always had an interest in the Hall right up to 1803.

Today Schofield Hall is a truly romantic ruin with a magnificent view over Hollingworth Lake and beyond. In its prime it must have been one of our finest old halls.

STEANOR BOTTOM (1390)

At the northern end of our district is Steanor Botham (as it was formerly named), which was the home of the Clegg family for several centuries.

In 1390-1 John Haworth, chaplain, as trustee for Robert Smith, conveyed the lands at 'Steanor Bottoms' to John, the son of Adam de Clegg and Joan, the daughter of the

Schofield Hall at Rakewood; in fairly good condition in 1900, had suffered serious neglect by the 1920's when this photograph was taken, Today, only low ruins remain.

said Robert Smith, in consideration of a marriage about to take place between John and Joan.

The next document available is the will of Edward Clegg of Steanor Botham dated March, 1594. He had five daughters, to whom he left five pounds each. The will was witnessed by William Grave, curate of Littleborough, and the total inventory amounted to £38-2-6.

A document dated 1613 shows that Ralf Clegg owned the property. In 1626 Ralph Clegg produced the earlier deeds and claimed other lands, which had been either granted to his father Edmund Clegg or acquired in the earlier transactions.

The old house disappeared entirely, to be replaced by a new one built in 1700. Over the door was a quaint inscription, carved in the stonework:-

No man on	By many
earth can te-	strokes the
ll the torment	work is done
that is in el.	that could not be
A.S.E. 1700	performed by one.

The initials refer to the Eastwood family who rebuilt the house.

In 1742 James Clegg, yeoman, left Steanor Bottom to his son James and it remained in the family for several generations.

By the 1840's the house and the adjacent land was owned by the Fielden family and in 1847 Joshua Fielden MP made a will in favour of his illegitimate son Natham Firth and Natham's mother. The will was to be executed by three trustees who were also Fieldens. Joshua died in 1847 and as was allowed by the terms of the will, Nathan created two wills the second being in 1865. In essence he wished the property divided in equal shares between his nine children. Nathan died in 1865 and a dispute commenced between the Firth family and the remaining Fielden trustee. To further complicate matters a claim was lodged that 'under customary tenure the property reverted to the gift of the Lord of the Manor according to 'custom of the Manor'. By 1872 the argument was in court and in 1874 the Chancery Court made a ruling. They judged Nathan's second will to be valid and ordered all the land and buildings to be auctioned, at the same time excluding Nathan's second wife from any share in the money. They instructed the Fieldens to surrender all their rights and then consolidated all the plots of land and declared that when the purchasers were known, they should be issued with 'a good conveyance' over-riding any previous agreements. At the auction John and William Crabtree bought Lot 3 including the house for £1750. They also bought many acres of land. The Crabtrees had a sizeable business run from premises opposite the toll house and owned other land in the area.

There is no record of any money going to either the defendants or the plaintiffs and it appears that the money may have been swallowed up in legal fees.

The house was occupied and in a good state of preservation well into the 20th century but was eventually demolished.

PIKE HOUSE AND THE ESTATE (1561)

For centuries the 'Pike House' was home to the Halliwell family and later the Halliwell-Beswicke Royds. Originally they lived in Yorkshire and in 1343 there is a record of a large estate in Stainland belonging to Nicholas Halliwell. Rather later a member of that family came to live in Littleborough where he built a house at the foot of Ealees. In 1561 the Halliwells, John and James, bought a large area of land including Pike House from the Earl of Derby. At this time James was living in Ealees Hall. It may well be these two had a date stone carved in 1563 which was found centuries later, hidden behind the butler's pantry. The property became known as the Pike House Estate which was generally described by local people as being 'through the Arches' after the railway was built. This family was the closest Littleborough came to having a local Squire of the Manor (the real lord lived in Nottinghamshire).

The first house that the Halliwells lived in was two storeys high and built in stone. It was demolished in the 18th century. In the interim the original purchaser's grandson (John Halliwell) had partially rebuilt Pike House in 1608 - 1609. By 1645 the house was further enhanced and was two storeyed with spacious rooms built on an ambitious scale. The building at this stage was the structure that lasted until the 20th century. For example, Richard Halliwell, who fought on the side of the King in the 17th century, was able to accommodate 10 pikemen in the house.

It was also a branch of the Halliwell family, Theophilus Halliwell (brother to Richard), who founded the 'Free School' in Littleborough. The date stone on his house, often called Ealees Hall or House, was 1602 but the family is recorded as living in Ealees long before that date. The building was apparently a small twin-gabled stone house and it was only demolished in 1837 as it was directly on the proposed line of the railway.

In 1703 the Pike House was updated again and around 1708 the gabled frontage of the house was concealed by a solid parapet, the stone mullions were replaced by sash windows and the front was treated with ashlar. The house was approached through

The family at Pike House around 1890, professionally photographed by A. Brothers of Manchester. The back of the photograph gives the names as Captain Beswicke-Royds, Halliwell Beswicke-Royds, Mrs Beswicke and Mrs Beswicke-Royds.

an ornamental metal gate entrance from the main road, which is the only part of the property that survives today. Old photos suggest this conversion was not entirely successful and the rear view of the house (unconverted) is more pleasing. The interior was much admired for its oaken wainscotting and a staircase that dated back to Elizabethan times. Pike House remained within the Helliwell family until 1771 when another John Helliwell died with no son or heir. The estate was bought by Robert Beswicke, whose grandmother was a Helliwell. The male line terminated in 1842 and the house and estate went to the Royds family by marriage - and they adopted the surname Beswicke-Royds. This family continued until 1918 and the death of Mrs M A G Beswicke-Royds, at which time the total content of the house was auctioned and the family line died out. The house still had a fine glass window, on the staircase landing, which depicted the tenants of Pike House estate setting out to battle armed with 'pikes'. The house, but not the estate, passed from the family and subsequently, it did not have continuous occupancy, suffering fire and vandalism. Despite being a listed building, it was demolished in 1960.

The Pike (Pyke) House Estate was finally auctioned off as 13 lots in July 1945 at the Red Lion Hotel, Rochdale. The diagram shows the location of the lots and the extensive area they occupied.

LOT	NAME	ACRES	OWNERSHIP
1	Higher Swainrod Farm	25	Tenant £31 per annum
2	New Barn Farm	20	Tenant £37 p/a
3	Pike House Farm	24	Tenant £22 p/a
4	Lightowlers Farm and Cottage	30	Tenant £30 p/a
5	Knowl Farm	37	Tenant £32.10 p/a
6	Humber Farm	20	Tenant £20 p/a
7	Fielden Farm	43½	Tenant £38.10 p/a
8	Owlet Hall Farm	4	Tenant £16.16 p/a
9	Lanefoot Farm	24	Tenant £31.10 p/a
10	The Old Duke of York	4½	Tenant £2 p/a
11	Building Land	388 sqr yards	
12	School Yard & No 1 Ealees road	660 sqr yards	
13	Land Ends Farm Milnrow	20	Tenant £58.10 p/a

The old barn at Pike House has been converted into a dwelling and other private houses have been built in the original grounds, the perimeter wall and iron gates remaining.

LITTLEBOROUGH CHURCH (1471)

Although we have used the place name Littleborough in the preceding chapters, up to the 15th century the district had no distinctive name of its own, and places such as Town House, Lightowlers, Ealees and Steanor Bottom etc., were always referred to as being in the Parish of Hundersfield or Honresfield.

There was a Littleborough Church (Little-brucke) long before there was a Littleborough village, so Littleborough Church has the distinction of having given the village its name, and not, as in almost all other cases, the church taking its name from the village.

Up till the year 1471 there was no church in the whole parish of Hundersfield, which extended from Townhead (Rochdale) to Scaitcliffe in the Burnley valley and included Walsden and Todmorden. St. Chad's Rochdale was the nearest and had to serve for the whole district. The nearest churches to the Todmorden end of the district were in Halifax or Heptonstall.

When the first Littleborough Church was built conditions were very different from those we have to-day. The population was small and scattered all over the district. The Roman Catholic religion was supreme and this and the whole region, including St. Chad's Rochdale, was under the control of the Monks of Whalley Abbey. Anyone wishing for favours, either in this world or the world to come, could get them promised if he was prepared to bid high enough for them. It was the custom to make grants of land to the Abbot for these favours (several instances of such in our own district are given in this chapter), and in this way in course of time, the Abbey became very wealthy and powerful. Perhaps this would not have mattered so much if some portion of the wealth had been used for the good of the district, but when all was taken to enrich the Abbey endowments, it became a source of weakness and eventually led to their suppression.

When the inhabitants of Boterworth and Honresfield finally decided on building a Chapel of their own, they had great difficulty in getting the Abbot of Whalley to grant his permission although they were prepared to pay the cost of the building. He was afraid that the revenues of St. Chad's would suffer. When the church was eventually erected in 1471 and the people applied for it to be licensed for worship the Abbot was very careful to lay down the conditions on which he granted the license for the church and a small graveyard. The following is a short extract from the document:-

'The Abbot of Whalley on the Feast of St. Chad's the Bishop (2nd March, 1471):

To the inhabitants of 'Botorworth' and Honresfield that they should have the Chapel within Honresfield, honourably built and newly erected; private masses, celebrated by a proper Chaplain to be licensed by the Bishop; providing that no injury is done to the Mother Church, to which the said Chaplain will pay two tenths of the oblations and other dues.'

The Abbot provided that the Vicar of Rochdale was to be exonerated from instituting or providing of such Chaplain. It was further provided that if any tithes, oblations, or offerings, due to the Mother Church were withheld by the inhabitants the licence was to terminate.

In other words, the Abbot gave the local people the privilege of building the church at their own expense. They could have a chaplain for the church, on condition that they paid for his services themselves and that the chaplain returned two tenths of all the money he received to the Abbot for allowing him to be a chaplain. In addition, if any money or dues, which the people of Butterworth or Honresfeld had been accustomed to pay to St. Chad's when they had no other chuch to go to, were diverted to their own church, the licence was to be taken away. Consequently, until the suppression of the Monasteries in 1553, the people of Littleborough had not only to suppport their own church but help to support St. Chad's as well and in addition to this, the church and all it contained practically belonged to the Abbey of Whalley. Not a bad arrangement from the Abbey's standpoint.

Compared with the position of the present Parish Church the old church was built on a site nearer the river which in the spelling of the time was known as Little-brucke.

Commercial Developments

It is in the Norman period that we see some of the earliest written records we have about our immediate area. For example there is a report about the state of an established track over Blackstone Edge. This is cited in a complaint by Richard Wood to the constables at Sowerby in 1285. Soon after, in 1297, there is a record of the transport of woollen goods over Blackstone Edge, which had attained some importance as a trade route. This indicates that even at this stage Littleborough district was part of a bigger economy.

In the late 15th century when local documentation is scarce there was an important development which later influenced Littleborough greatly. This was associated with clay, which had been used all over Europe for thousands of years in the manufacture of fired clay pots and beakers. During the Roman period they fired bricks for building but the skill was lost and in the 15th century Flemish refugees re-introduced brick making into England. It spread very slowly, based on a simple technology. Where clay existed on building sites, itinerant brickmakers moulded bricks from it. 'Clamp Kilns' were then constructed with these green bricks. Scattered amongst the bricks were small coals which were fired. There is evidence that this same ancient process was well established in Littleborough by the 17th century.

In the medieval period only London grew to be a city; few towns had a population of more than 4000 people. All the houses were built with wood and the danger of fire was enormous. The function of the town was trade, commerce and administration, but so filthy were the conditions that plague and pestilence were an ever-present threat. The Black Death (1349) killed one third of England's population in one year changing forever the balance of power between rulers and the ruled. The acute shortage of labour lead directly to an improvement in working conditions of the reduced labour force.

The aftermath of fire and pestilence was the recognition of the vital importance of hygiene and the advantages of using bricks for housing; the Flemish re-introduced the bricks and local potters realised their skills could be adapted to provide piping for sanitation. Littleborough was very favoured with accessible raw materials which were the basis for these industries. Brick and pipe manufacture were to play a major part in our economic growth in the following centuries.

The end of the Norman Era

What had changed in the living conditions of the local people outlined at the beginning of this chapter, after some 400 years? Nationally, 10,000 Normans had subdued one million English people and left a most public monument in stone castles (fully developed in the 13th century) which only became obsolete with the introduction of gun powder in the 15th century.

A staggering difference grew up between the rich and the poor. Soon after the conquest, three quarters of England's wealth was in the hands of 200 lords (only two were English) and 100 churchmen. We see the local evidence in the great wealth families like the Stobblegh's (Stubley) accumulated between 1277 and 1554 and the despotic power of Whalley Abbey over our local religious development. England was welded onto northern France and for the powerful lords and priests 'life was Norman French', conducted in French. This powerful group soon introduced Norman skills, relating to building and commerce, into England.

For the local population the Normans institutionalised feudalism, which lasted until the Wars of the Roses in the 15th century. The strength of the system was to give some protection to the poor and allow the rich to live in great comfort. As at the beginning so at the end of the Norman period, for the mass of people, life was entirely agricultural and their time was split between working for themselves and their masters, eating and sleeping. It was a tough relentless existence with death around age 45. Priests and the Roman Catholic church were part of the everyday life; they helped the poor, farmed and collected tithes from others who farmed, took a full part in politics and administration and followed a life centred in prayer.

The Norman feudal system collapsed during the hundred years covered by the Wars of the Roses (1399 - 1485). Feudal service gave way to a wage economy, trade expanded greatly and was outside the old framework; gunpowder finally brought down the castle walls.

Norman French was never accepted by the majority of our people and the language of Chaucer was the root of today's English (with many dialects). Printing spread knowledge rapidly to many more people. Finally when Henry VIII died in 1547 he left the church split between Protestants and Catholics and it was clear that many ideas and social structures that had been typical of the Middle Ages were being made obsolete by the rapid changes in the way people thought and lived.

CHAPTER EIGHT

THE SIXTEENTH CENTURY

Henry VII was elected king in 1485 and he took steps to ban private armies and destroy the power base built on local castles. He readily declared his Lords traitors, seized their lands and executed them. As a policy he avoided wars making peace with Scotland and France. Peace brought more royal income and by controlling the administration of justice through his royal judges he further weakened the Barons. When he died in 1509 he had re-established the power of the throne.

In sharp contrast to his predecessor, when Henry VIII became king, he was lavish in expenditure and welcomed war. In 1513 he landed in France where, with the help of Germany, he defeated the French. He then turned on the Scots defeating them at Flodden. The French made peace and supported by Wolsey, a political priest, Henry was in control of his world. In 1520 he met the young King of France - the meeting of the Field of the Cloth of Gold, which proved to be a lavish occasion but solved nothing and by 1522 the two countries were at war again. This war dragged on until 1530 ending in a stalemate. Henry had no son to succeed him and decided to defy the Pope, get rid of his wife, marry Anne Boleyn (who was pregnant) and set up and control a new church. Anne gave birth to Elisabeth (later Elisabeth I) in 1533. The established church had incurred much resentment, of its great wealth and the dissolute conduct of its monks. Wolsey, who acted as the Lord Chancellor of Henry VIII until he was replaced in 1530, was seen as a man whose career was scandalous while the Pope was pictured as a foreign Wolsey. The Catholic Church was seen by some as too damaged to be repaired and the Protestant movement was sweeping westward. The obvious losers were the monks and nuns as they had no protection - yet they owned a quarter of all English farm land. Henry VIII badly needed that wealth and set up an investigation of both monasteries and nunneries. The result was that between 1535 and 1540 Henry destroyed many Christian communities that had served their people for a thousand years. He preserved the monastic schools, however, and allowed the monks to join the new clergy. From 1536 Henry suffered deteriorating health until his death in 1547.

From the 13th century the trading connections of mainland Europe were expanding in all directions and when the Turks cut off the access to the east, the great search began for alternate routes either south or west. The Portugese, Spanish and English were prominent in this endeavour. Others tried to go north east and although this was doomed it did lead to the first regular trade with Russia.

England was becoming more and more a trading nation but the majority of the people continued to live on the land. Between 1500 and 1600 the population is thought to have grown from 2 million to 4½ million people. There was a movement from crop growing to sheep farming; by the end of the century enclosures of the common land were occuring regularly, mainly to the detriment of the poor. The Tudor monarchs opposed the enclosures (where could their archers practice?) and taxed them heavily resulting in a revolt which was bloodily suppressed using German mercenaries. The closing of monasteries and nunneries, which had traditionally offered shelter and food, made the plight of the poor ever more serious. However the clergy and the local squires did try to help the destitute and vagrant by the provision of

The Original Church at Littleborough,
the site being in the same Churchyard as the present structure.
The old edifice was dedicated in 1471, and was taken down
in 1815, during the Incumbency of the Rev. John Rutter.

Opening Ceremony,
SATURDAY, FEBRUARY 5th, 1910.

*The Bazaar will be
opened at 3 p.m. by*

Mrs.

Simpson-Hinchliffe,
OF CRAGG HALL.

Chairman:

A. J. Law, Esq., J.P.

21

A page from the Parish Church Schools 'Grand Floral Bazaar' handbook, February 1910 ; a huge three day fund raising event to meet the cost of the recent school extensions.

almshouses. It was Elisabeth I whose government passed the first Poor Laws in 1601. Overseers were appointed in each area to help the poor; the vicar and the squire who could levy a local rate to pay for it were focal to the initiative. The ill and the elderly were to be cared for, the able-bodied were to be found work and if necessary given places in workhouses. Those who could work, but refused to, were punished with public whipping and placed in houses of correction.

Henry VIII had always seen himself as a loyal Catholic and his break with the Pope simply made him the Head of the English Catholic Church. Only at the end of his life were church services in English allowed. The young Edward VI (1544), guided by a guardian, tried to make the church more Protestant and allowed priests to marry. The reaction went too far and the local landowners looted the churches under the guise of removing 'Popery'. National finances once more fell into chaos and war broke out with the Scots. The young Edward died in 1553 at the age of 16, thereafter the political instability became severe. Lady Jane Grey was both made queen and executed within days and Mary Tudor came to power. She was a devout Catholic and promptly restored the Pope as head of the church but met enormous opposition to restoring the church lands and after a period notable for the suppression of her Protestant enemies she died in 1558 aged 42. The young Queen Elisabeth became queen in 1558 at the age of 25. She came to the throne of a country deeply divided by religious belief with the Scots, the French and the Spanish all having reasons for wishing to depose her. However Elisabeth was well educated, intelligent and a survivor. She insisted that everyone must attend the new Church of England and she had a skilful secretary in Cecil. Cecil negotiated the withdrawal of all French troops out of Scotland by 1560 and made peace with France. The Catholic Spaniards hated the English Protestants and in addition English sea captains were despoiling the Spanish trade in America and the West Indies. In 1585 England was again at war with

Spain. In 1587 Elisabeth reluctantly signed Mary Stuart's death warrant as yet again a plot to replace her as ruler of England failed. The relationships between Protestants and Catholics deteriorated further and in 1588 some 300 Catholics were executed. King Philip of Spain decided to invade England. In July 1588 an armada of 132 ships left Spain but in the fight that ensued the Spanish were routed. The Spanish War dragged on, only to be ended by James the 1st after Elisabeth's death in 1603. It was a new century ...

The affairs of the Queens and Kings and the new commercial developments did not appear to affect our area immediately. For example, the impact of the enclosures of the common land seems to be recorded in court cases some 30 to 50 years later than in the South of England.

Our local records are still about the daily agricultural affairs, watercourses, maintaining walls, fences and especially roads. The roads were often a cause of dispute between townships.

Affrays and bloodshed were a perennial source of litigation but apparently smaller in volume than in the previous century.

The Church

Church affairs are more prominent and here we get a more rapid resonance from the noisy outside world.

We have seen that the first record of a Catholic chapel in our area dates to the 13th/14th Century at Stubley Hall where the Holts had a domestic chapel with a resident priest. This was supplemented by the building of the Holy Trinity Church in 1471. In 1533 there is the record of a gift of money from the Newalls to allow the purchase of a chalice for the church. In 1553 very abruptly, world affairs came to Littleborough. The monastery closures and the assertion of the Supremacy of the Church of England directly affected our religious life.

The Seizure of Littleborough Chapel

In 1553, Littleborough Chapel and one bell there was seized by the King's Commissioners for the use of his Majesty. They were given to one Squire Edward Parker who lived in London. He sold them back to the local 'principal people' viz; Robert Holt of Stubley, Edward Kershaw of Townhouse, Richard Stott of Lightowlers, Thomas Shore, Thomas Hill and others. The bell was returned 'to ye end that it might be used in Littleborough Church as heretofore.'

The sale returning the church was also recorded in an old manuscript in possession of the relatives of a former incumbent of the Church which contained the following: 'In the reign of Edward VI (1544-1553) this Chapel was sold by one of the commissioners belonging to the King, into whose hands it came, for 40/- the inhabitants of this Chapelry and their heirs forever, to solemnize Divine Service therein.'

The last Abbot of Whalley suffered a sad fate at this time. He took part in the 'Pilgrimage of Grace' which was an early example of a protest march. In this case it was against the suppression of the monasteries. The march was brutally repressed and the Abbot was captured and promptly executed

Even at this far off time the Newalls of Town House were connected with the Littleborough Church, for William Newall of Lower Town House in his will dated

March, 1570, acknowledges a debt due to the Reeves of Littleborough Chapel of 8/-. Lawrence Newall of the same place, left by his will dated April, 1557, 3/4d to buy a Chalice or vestment to 'ye Littleborough Chapel', adding that he owed the Chapel 8/- and in wages 12/-. The chaplain at this period would seem to have been maintained by what were termed Chapel Wages, a charge imposed and paid in proportion to the estates and seats of the inhabitants. This Chapel Wage continued to exist until comparatively recent times, when it gradually died out, as an income for the Minister was provided from other sources.

In the great split between Catholicism and Protestantism, despite much of east Lancashire clinging to the old tradition, both Rochdale and Halifax and the upland communities seemed to support the Protestant cause. Already the self-made clothiers were asserting their right to independence, to make their own life and have their own beliefs. Whatever the reasons the Catholic body was to be diminished, fined, crushed by confiscation and persecution. Catholicism only survived in isolated halls and castles with the children being taught their faith abroad in many cases.

The combination of Henry V111 and his officers appear to have eliminated the 'papists' in our area. There was a roll call of 'Recusants', (un-reformed Catholics) in 1671 and none were declared in the Littleborough Area (Spotland and Milnrow were the nearest) and again in 1715 when they listed all non-jurors who would not take the oath of allegiance to King George. It is of course posssible that all the people living in the Littleborough area were too poor to be of any concern. Another census in 1737 showed that the Littleborough area had 182 people who attended the parish church, 4 Presbyterians and Non-conformists and no declared Quakers, Papists, or Baptists.

Although the Relieving Acts (1778 - 1791) generally made things easier for groups not belonging to the established church; it is not until the 19th century that we see the re-establishment of Catholicism in our area.

Apart from the turmoil in the church we have relatively little new local development recorded during the 16th century but what there is relates to the large family houses (see chapter 7), the world of work and the emergence of the name Littleborough.

Local quarrying and mining in the 16th century

In 1579, during the reign of Queen Elizabeth, there is a record relating to Blackstone Edge permitting the quarrying of stone for the purpose of making millstones and also recording 'the existence of divers mynes and mylstones, gryndle stones and ridging stones.'

Farming and the woollen industry are two of the oldest industries in our area but the 16th century brings the first positive mention of the mining industry. In 1582 a lease is recorded between a landlord, a member of the Halliwell family and one of their tenants who occupied a property called Knowle House (Blackstone Edge); granting to the tenant the 'liberty to dig or gett coles for the necessary fuell to be spent on the premises'. Another deed dated 1588 granted Robert Hamer of Lightollers 'one messuage (a dwelling house, outbuildings and adjacent land) called the Lightollers with sev closes & a cole pit'. Robert Hamer's landlord was no less than John Byron, Knight, who was a member of the family who in 1638 became Steward and later Lord of the Manor that embraced Littleborough.

The Name Littleborough

Littleborough has never had the status of a borough and various explanations have been given as to its meaning. Some authorities say that it was a Roman station, others that it owes its origin to a fair or 'brough' which used to be held here. This would give its meaning as little brough or little fair. In the earliest written records the area is shared between the names Blatchinworth and Calderbrook which applied broadly to the areas east and west of the River Roch.

An alternative explanation given by Fishwick has been widely accepted. In his History of the Parish of Rochdale he says:

"The village of Littleborough derived its name from a small estate which in 1563 was described as a freehold tenement and certain acres of land, meadow and pasture, lying in the townships of Hundersfield and Butterworth, within the Parish of Rochdale and commonly called Littleborough".

This small estate was situated between the present Parish Church and the railway station. In 1626 John Belfield, gentleman, held a small tenement called Littleborough. From this evidence the name which embraces the whole district is far more modern than many of the place names previously mentioned. Thus the name 'Ton House' goes back at least nine hundred years, while the name Littleborough only goes back for about four hundred years.

Earlier we learned that the old church was built on the estate by a little brook. This brook was still an open channel in the 19th century and it was crossed by a wooden foot bridge leading to Littleborough Station platform. The line of the brook formed the dividing line between Butterworth and Blatchinworth. In the 15th century it gave its name to a 'parcel' of land in its immediate vicinity, which in a will dated 29th June 1593 was known as Little-brucke. For a long time there was no settled form of spelling; documents speak of Littlebrucke, Littlebrucks, Littleburgh, Littlebrugh, Littlebro, Littlebrough and finally Littleborough. It was not until the church was made into a Parish Church in the 17th century that the area of what now constitutes the Littleborough Parish was clearly defined and the name Littleborough came into general use.

CHAPTER NINE

THE 17TH CENTURY

A WORLD OF AGRICULTURE and LOOMS

The century opened with the death of Queen Elisabeth in 1603 and the accession of James I. He was soon struggling with the political themes that recurred during the century: struggles between King and Parliament over who ruled the country, religious struggles between Protestants and Roman Catholics and finally wars with neighbour countries. The Houses of Parliament only represented about one in every thirty English males and no female at all. The members were rich and powerful but had no private armies or fortified houses and were primarily traders and land owners with enormous economic power.

James I was wily and intelligent - he is still remembered for the King James' version of the Bible which has lasted in daily use in church to this day. He is also remembered as the king who thwarted a Roman Catholic plot to kill him giving England the tradition of Guy Fawkes night and the annual burning of the 'guy'. His problems with Parliament were all about being Scottish, having a Roman Catholic wife and his need to raise money. These were compounded by his personal extravagance on theatre (this is the time when Shakespeare wrote his last plays) and lavish masques. He subsequently ruled without Parliament and the power struggle continued until he died in 1625.

His successor was Charles I who reigned until 1649. Charles took a French Catholic wife whose religious and political influence proved disastrous. He had three expensive failures in terms of raiding expeditions into Europe; his closest supporter, the Duke of Buckingham, was assassinated and as his expenses rose Parliament blocked his demands for more money. In 1629 Charles dismissed Parliament and ruled without it until 1640. He started to purge the Puritans and as a consequence the first group sailed to America in the Mayflower in 1620, in search of a better life. Meanwhile Ireland was becoming a powder keg under the autocratic rule of Charles' minister, Stafford, who rapidly became hated for displacing Catholics by 'imported' Protestants. Charles finally precipitated disaster by his attempts to introduce the English prayer book into Scotland, which had a simple Puritanical faith and a formidable exponent of that faith in John Knox. So violent was the reaction that a Scottish army was raised to oppose Charles, who found that he could not raise enough money to go to war. Charles crumbled and authorised the trial and execution of his closest minister in 1641, followed by the execution of Archbishop Laud. In 1642 Charles, in desperation, marched on his own Parliament with a plan to arrest those members whom he saw as his major enemies. He failed to capture them, making civil war inevitable. The war lasted from 1642 until 1648 involving a number of very wealthy people and armies of modest size but the issue was key - who ruled England? The Royalists were supporting the King; the Roundheads were for Parliament.

On the side of Parliament, Oliver Cromwell emerged as a military leader who developed the first professional army. Effectively the Royalists were defeated by 1646 (at Naseby) and what ensued was a political wrangle with a minor civil war. In 1648 the Army decided to try its own King of England for treason but Parliament compromised with Charles so Cromwell invaded Parliament. Charles was tried and beheaded in January 1649. Cromwell was then

The bottom of Ealees Road around 1900, showing the School House, the school and outbuilding with 'Cromwell Cottage' on the right. The row of houses behind is Taylor Terrace (constructed of the newly developed concrete blocks in 1870) with a mill chimney at Alice Street (now called West View) in the background.

elected as Protector of England. Immediately Holland, France and Spain all declared war on England. By 1652 Cromwell had suppressed the latest Irish rebellion, defeated Scotland and obliged both France and Spain to seek peace. Cromwell became increasingly unpopular but he died in 1658 with his power as Lord Protector unchallenged. His son, who followed him, commanded no respect and abdicated in 1659. A new Parliament was organised which invited Prince Charles to return to his kingdom.

Elections in 1660 restored the Royalists, restored the House of Lords and Charles II was confirmed in power. Cromwell's body was buried in a pauper's grave. Both Puritans and Quakers were persecuted. At the same time the whole argument over taxation broke out again fuelled by the Roundhead's fear that another Roman Catholic dictator was about to emerge. In 1680 the Roundheads were trying to set up a successor to Charles II - who retaliated by dismissing Parliament. After five years of direct rule, in 1685 Charles II died peacefully in bed as a last minute convert to Catholicism.

The successor was James II, who opened a new Parliament in 1685, closed it the following year and never recalled it. When he had a male heir in 1688 a powerful group of politicians asked the protestant William of Holland to invade England. James retreated to France and William and Mary were declared joint rulers; Mary died in 1694 and William ruled until 1701. They established the rule of Parliament and the principle that Kings only ruled subject to agreed policies. Scotland was finally united with England in the Act of Union in 1707.

The power struggle and political activity revolving round London appears unreal when looking at our local situation. We had moved to the periphery of events, the pace of change and the important issues are different. When a history book says that the Middle Ages 'ended' on a date the departures or events marking that event may not have an impact on a remote area like Littleborough for many years.

The Civil War (1642)

Despite the relative remoteness of Littleborough in the 17th century the local people found themselves in the front-line fighting, for a brief period, during the civil war. From the time when the civil war broke out in 1642 until the king was executed, the world of politics came much closer to Littleborough. Trade in the area was badly affected and Rochdale was garrisoned for Parliament. These forces defended Blackstone Edge against Royalist directed from Halifax. In 1643 1200 soldiers were stationed in Rochdale and 800 at the foot of Blackstone Edge. These soldiers built 'light fortifications' on the edge itself. The opposing Royalist forces had a 'stand off' skirmish with the Parliamentarians but then retreated, deciding that the summit area was not a suitable terrain to fight on. Perhaps a quotation from a traveller, Cecilia Fiennes, written 40 years later, will cast some light on this decision:

"Then I came to Blackstone Edge noted all over England for a dismal, high precipice and steep ascent and descent on either end; it's very moorish ground all about and even just to the top, tho so high that you travel on a Causey (causeway) which is very troublesome and it's a moist ground soe as is usual on these high hills: they stagnate the aire and hold mist and raines almost perpetually."

In this period there is a fanciful story of Cromwell visiting our area and resting in a local house, leaving the legacy of a 'Cromwell Cottage' at the bottom of Ealees Road. This story has endured despite its apparent lack of any substance; the site is now a small public garden.

General conditions in the area

Fred Jackson wrote an account of the community around Calderbrook as it would have been early in the 17th century. It is probably typical of conditions throughout the district. The place name 'Calderbrook' is of comparatively recent origin and is said to take its name from the 'Brook of the Calder' which rises on the moors behind the village.

"In 1626, Calderbrook formed part of the Ancient Parish of Hundersfield which was one of the most extensive in England. The boundary ran from Townhead (Rochdale) to a spot behind Scaitcliff (Todmorden) at Beater Clough in the Burnley valley. Its extreme breadth was 5 miles - from Dovelan Stones on Blackstone Edge to the extreme point of Little Wardle, near a place called "Pot Ovens" above Whitworth.

There were only a few farm houses here and there on the uplands, between Walsden and Littleborough. The Old Reddyshore Scout Road which passed behind the present roadside communities, along by Stoneyfield, Clough Head and Stoneyhead, was the main road between Rochdale and Todmorden. It must be remembered that neither the canal nor what we call the 'old road' nor the road through Summit had been made at that time and until the year 1795 Reddyshore Scout Gate continued to be the only road through the district

The slopes of the valley were clothed with woods. These woods extended right along the valley from end to end, and consisted chiefly of oak, ash and fir trees, which attained a very high growth. Today it has a certain beauty of its own, but when the hillsides and valley were covered with trees it must have been beautiful indeed."

When thinking of all this tree life and contrasting it with the bare appearance of today, what brought about its destruction? Fred Jackson concluded that early in the

A646 TODMORDEN
(3½ miles to Cliviger Gorge)

● Gorpley Wood

SOME 17th CENTURY
COMMUNITIES
(Fred Jackson c1919)

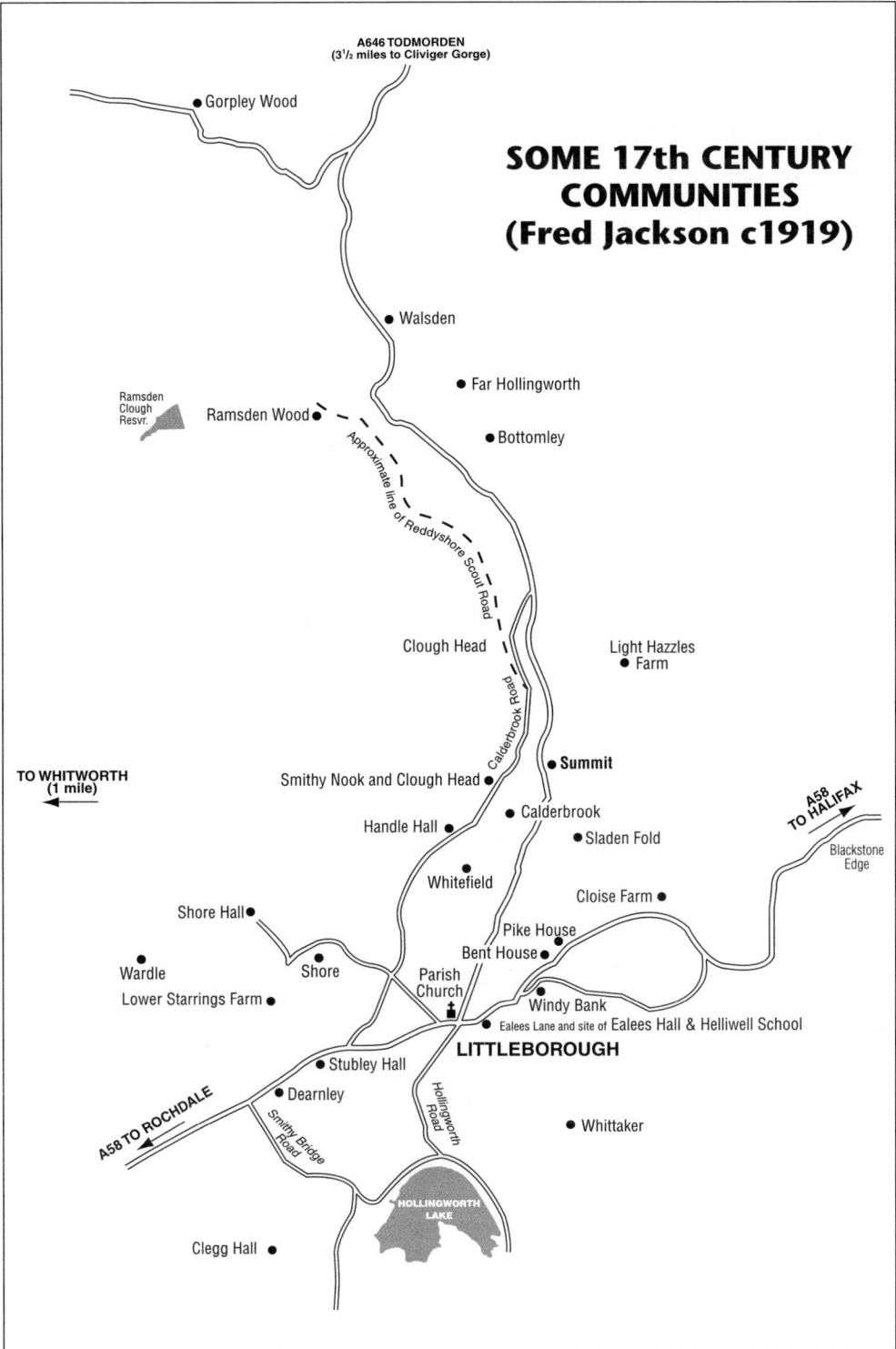

● Walsden

● Far Hollingworth

Ramsden
Clough
Resvr.

Ramsden Wood ●

● Bottomley

Approximate line of Reddyshore Scout Road

Clough Head

Light Hazzles
● Farm

Calderbrook Road

TO WHITWORTH
(1 mile)

Smithy Nook and Clough Head ●

● **Summit**

● Calderbrook

A58
TO HALIFAX

Handle Hall ●

● Sladen Fold

Blackstone
Edge

Whitefield ●

Cloise Farm ●

Shore Hall ●

Pike House ●
Bent House ●

● Wardle

Shore ●

Parish
Church

Lower Starrings Farm ●

Windy Bank ●
Ealees Lane and site of Ealees Hall & Helliwell School

LITTLEBOROUGH

● Stubley Hall

A58 TO ROCHDALE

● Dearnley

Smithy Bridge Road

Hollingworth Road

● Whittaker

HOLLINGWORTH
LAKE

Clegg Hall ●

Queen Ann Inn, Handle Hall.

17th century, our hills and valleys were covered with tree life and that by the year 1777 they had undergone a change. Most of the woods had disappeared and the land was used for agriculture and the pasturage of sheep. The most probable explanation is that the trees were cut down and converted into charcoal, to be used for the smelting of iron ore.

The impact of industry
Bloomeries.

Techniques for extracting iron are dated back to 600 BC but Fishwick provides some material about the earliest records of smelting iron in our area. As early as 1338 there is a record of a legal dispute which arose from the seizure of goods including 300 pieces of iron. The alleged assault, in the Whitworth area, was done by three men carrying bows, arrows and swords. The legal case revolved round who had mineral and extraction rights to the goods. It was an Act in 1563 that forbade the importation of knives and domestic cutlery from Flanders that led to the growth of Sheffield as a major centre of manufacture. Locally there are records of cutlers established around Rochdale in 1581 and 1588.

From very early times each area or parish tried to organise a bloomery and an associated forge locally. Owing to the rudimentary roads and the transport by pack-horses it was essential to avoid carrying heavy goods very far. Thus, as the industry grew there was a very close relationship between the siting of bloomeries and the occurence of shale, coal measures and the 'iron mines'. Similarly the bloomery had to be physically close enough to a fall of water to operate the bellows. Finally we know that up to the time of Dudley's improvements in the smelting of iron, charcoal was the only form of fuel that was used for smelting so the availability of wood was vital.

There is strong evidence to prove that iron-smelting places, or 'bloomeries' as they were called, were widespread in our immediate neighbourhood and major sites have been found in Rossendale, Ramsden wood at Todmorden and Walsden.

About the year 1880 Captain John Aitkin, a local geologist from Bacup read a 'paper' before the members of the Manchester Geological Society on the 'Discovery of an ancient ironstone mine in Cliviger gorge (Riddle Scout) and the remains of ancient bloomeries' to be found in the district. In that paper, at least seven different iron-smelting places were mentioned and the number had risen to more than twenty five by 1994. One was at Bank's Wood near Far Hollingworth, one in Gorpley (above Bottomley) and another in the valley on the site of the present Ramsden Reservoir. Fred Jackson believed that the site at Waterstalls was undoubtedly the most important of them all. It must have been worked on an extensive scale and for a long period of time, for after centuries of erosion by the adjoining stream and large quantities having been used for repairing the road, hundreds of tons of slag and partly melted iron and charcoal still remain.

The first question is where did the iron ore come from? Captain Aitkin referred to a disused iron mine situated at Riddle Scout in Cliviger and concluded that this mine was the source of the raw material for the bloomeries not only in the Littleborough district but also those of Rossendale and others. In the case of the Cliviger mine there is convincing evidence that because of the lack of abundant wood locally much of the ore was taken to Walsden for smelting. The ore would be carried by strings of pack horses over the moors along the old roads to the bloomeries. Later evidence assembled by Titus Thornber details a much wider connection between the Cliviger site and users such as the iron masters in Sheffield. Research has shown there are numerous other sites with varying qualities of iron ore in our area.

For Fred Jackson's theory about the destruction of our woods, research in the 20th century has produced some very interesting evidence. Iron mines were worked on an annual cycle of collecting the raw materials for some 20 weeks (in winter) and operating the bloomery on a 30 week campaign. With a gang of six men 300 tons of iron could be produced by a furnace annually from 1500 tons of ore. To achieve this output takes 6 tons of charcoal daily or 1260 tons for a 30 week campaign. This is a staggering amount of material to be obtained by local felling especially if you consider the average life of a mine was 25 years. In our climate the charcoal had to be kept dry so there had to be huge charcoal barns for storage. Few records exist about where the wood came from but there is evidence of importing wood from distant sites, of legal and physical disputes over the felling of trees and that the iron-masters formed syndicates to protect their supplies of ore and wood.

From this research it appears very likely that the industry in iron had an increasingly severe impact on the local woodland up till the 18th century when Dudley's improvements in the smelting of iron allowed coke to be substituted for charcoal. The needs of the bloomeries may well have stripped our uplands and valleys of trees except where a landowner resisted the chance of quick profit by not selling his timber. This could explain why locally, tree life in the immediate neighbourhood of Smithy Nook and Summit flourished until a considerably later date than 1770's.

There were other significant changes which were to affect the people and the environment.

Coal Mining

A lease dated 1622 gives Alice Wolstenholme of Stansfield a lease to mine coal on Shore Moor. Alice was a widow and the lease was for her life and her assigns for 21 years. She was given 'full power & authoritie to search, myne, digg & drayne for coals'. In addition she was allowed 'the coals to take, draw & carry away, at her or their wills & the same to use and convert to the most profit & advantage the better to enable her for the bringing of the children of the said Henry Bamforth who are manie and meanly provided for'. Her lease is notable for allowing coal extraction for profit whereas other agreements were generally restricted to obtaining coal for local consumption and domestic uses.

In her will of November 1627 Alice bequeathed the profits of the 'sayd Colemynes for the use of the younger children of Henery Bamforth vis Henerie, Maria, Marget and John Bamford'. She also bequeathed to John Wolstenholme 'all the cheins sledds and tools belonginge to the sayd Colemyne'. This bequest indicates that hers was a drift mine, rather than 'Bell Hole' pits of which there is plenty of evidence in the nearby Wardle district. On flat land vertical shafts were driven down to the coal seam and the coal was 'got' from around the shaft bottom until there was danger of the sides collapsing. At this point the pit was abandoned and the spoil from the next shaft used to fill in the old working. In section such pits were shaped like bells; giving them the name 'Bell Pits'.

Woollen Industry and Agriculture.

Between 1530 and 1550 documentary evidence shows signs of increasing wealth and a close connection between this wealth and the growing cloth industry based on wool. Other important factors are the effect of the physical environment and the development of a distinct set of religious and social beliefs. By comparison the political theme of King vs Parliament is a remote echo. Nevertheless it is worth remembering that the financial problems of Charles 1 outlined earlier, led to the sale of the Manor of Rochdale to the Byron family who continued to hold it for generations until Lord Byron (the Poet) finally sold it in 1823.

In the 16th century the collapse of the old system of land tenure, linked to the Norman Period and with much older Medieval roots, had led to widespread illegal enclosure of common land. What occured in the 17th century was the dividing up of common pasture land, as most of the arable fields had already been divided by local agreement. In our area the important moor walls had also become the responsibility of the adjacent land owners. Probably the largest remaining communal responsibility was road / highway maintenance; documentation shows this was a great source of dispute between individuals and communities.

The Yeoman Clothier

Textile manufacture is amongst the oldest of industries. In the Littleborough district, as in much of Britain, the industry was founded on wool. The early manufacture was based on the dual occupation of the farmer/weaver. From early local inventories and wills we find:

1579　James Duerden, Goods inventory: 'a payre of lomes with cards and combs and backstone.'

1614　Dearnley Old Hall, Inventory: 'One pair of looms with all furniture'.

1748　Hill Top Farm, Occupation: 'Wolin - weaver'.

1802　James Travis, farmer at Whittaker: 'to his daughter Ann '£20 and all my Household Goods & Looms.'

The farmer/weavers took the wool from their sheep to be spun by their women (hence the origin of the phrase *on the distaff side*' which today would mean 'womens work', but originated from their responsibility for spinning in one part of the loom room. The farmer would use the hand loom to weave, in another part of the loom room or parlour of their farmhouse. Even at the beginning of the 17th century the Yeomen Clothiers knew that, for their growing wool trade, the bleak, denuded, boggy and acid moorlands were not suitable to provide a basis for anything much larger than supplying local needs. There were some advantages however - such as abundant soft water to wash the wool and to use in the dyeing process and plentiful sites for fulling mills. Thus by the next century (1755) their need for more wool, or prepared woollen weft and warp, was provided for by a 'putter out' such as Isaac and Thomas Lees, who were clothiers in the hamlet of Whittaker. They supplied wool to a number of the surrounding hamlets.

Two extra reasons have been advanced for the industrial growth in our area at this time. The first is the fairly local habit of splitting the assets between male heirs on death, rather than passing them intact to the oldest son on the death of the owner. Thus each son is likely to look for more assets to make a viable living. Obvious possibilities at this time were to clear and cultivate waste land or turn to the loom. For such a life you need land for pasture but also for the tenter frames, which were essential for stretching out the woven cloth to retain its shape during drying. The logical outcome might be to enclose otherwise bleak and high-lying land. The second factor was the availability of large areas of common land which to an entrepreneurial mind, meant the possibility of siting cottages and small holdings close by, to suppport the labour intensive expansion of loom weaving. They could offer an employee a house, a cow and some land. It would protect them all from the fluctuations of market price which sometimes came directly from the political turbulence in the distant south; it would lessen their dependence on one product for their living. Whatever the mix of reasons, here was a people with a Protestant (Puritan) work ethic, enterprise and a long history of struggle and endurance showing great determination to establish a place in the clothing trade.

From the big houses and the small cottages came the same words: 'God, the Loom and Agriculture' - only the scale of property ownership varied. There were Esquires aping their betters and creating something new with their fine stone houses which have, to subsequent generations, become one of the most attractive aspects of their era. Between 1570 and 1750 an enormous number of new houses were built, many surviving into the 20th century. They are built of Millstone Grit, sometimes in clusters as at Bent House, but more often following the edges of the pack- horse roads and reliable spring-water lines, as along Reddyshore Scout Gate. They are fit for their purpose with a porch, mullioned windows, millstone grit walls and low angled roof stones that look like 'grey slates'. We know these houses the moment we see them:

'takkin in steps'

many were built to fill three needs: a house, a parlour and the third was for the' Shop' where they housed the looms. This 'industrial area' within the house was often accessible directly from the outside by the 'takkin in steps'.

A yeoman clothier running three looms might employ 20 or 25 workers, many of these would be out-workers living in their own cottages. The yeoman would need skills in weaving, combing, spinning and finishing cloth. Life was hard and uncomfortable even for quite successful families and many, perhaps most, were illiterate or semi-literate people who only possessed one book - the Bible. What few utensils they possessed were sometimes itemised at death or sale of property, where the bed, the chests (cupboards were uncommon, wardrobes very rare), the long tables and the kitchen and domestic utensils such as pots and pans and farm equipment such as carts were clearly prized.

In the record of their work sheep rarely figure in a major way: cattle, horses, wheeled vehicles, ploughs, harrows, scythes and many references to corn indicate what was important. Authorities suggest that the corn can be interpreted as a hardy variety of oats.

Hand Loom Weaving

There were one or more looms in each house, weaving initially being carried out with short staple wool. The pieces would be about 1 yard wide and perhaps 18 yards long. The steps in this process were broadly as follows:

The wool would be beaten and any alien material, especially burrs, would be removed. All the work would be done by hand and the wool would then be treated with rape oil or butter to make it easier to handle. It would then be carded and be ready to spin. The thread would be drawn out as fine as possible and turned on a wheel to give the twist. It was then wound onto a bobbin. It took 5 or 6 spinners and several carders to keep one weaver working. Woven cloth would go to a local fulling mill, to shrink it and matt the surface fibres. The fulled cloth would then be stretched on tenter frames, to allow drying in the open air and be shrunk to a regular shape. At this stage the piece was dressed, the nap was raised by teazles and then cropped with shears. Finally it was inter-lined with pieces of paper and placed in a press. In the late 17th century worsted manufacture became important: it was based on long staple wool, combing only (not carding) the cloth being finished without fulling.

The dual economy described above, as seen in wills and inventories, went through many changes but was still surviving on the eve of the Industrial Revolution. At its most prosperous it combined independent farming with textile processing, carried on by people who owned their own property. These people were supported by a mass of other people who lived by selling their labour.

The yeoman class were also the administrators of their communities. They appointed their own priests and on a daily basis they answered to no one. They rarely indulged in great ostentation, were often deeply involved in the society around them and left us an incomparable gift in their well built, well proportioned, human scale houses - which 20th century people have bought and adapted to suit the needs of modern living.

The influence of Religion

In this changing world if you wanted a chapel you both built it and paid for the wages of the priest. The church in Littleborough was very poor and a visiting Bishop was advised 'to take a box of tar, for the place is full of scabbed sheep not Holy Lambs.' In the same vein the local Squire, Mr Helliwell of Pike House, had a complaint from the parishoners that the church was very cold. He advised them 'to drink a quart of ale before they come and they won't be cold'. By 1660 the status of the Chapel was raised to that of a Parish, as it served 272 families, of which the earliest remaining legible gravestone is dated 1680.

Religion and school

The first known record of teaching in Littleborough is in a will dated 1688 of Theophilous Halliwell who makes a grant 'for the use of a schoolmaster at the chapel at Littleborough'. In another will of his brother Richard dated 1699 there is a further gift 'towards the maintenance of a schoolmaster to teach children in the school I have recently erected'. What 'recently' means is speculative but 1697 appears reasonable.

The school that Richard had built was in Ealees Lane. It was funded by subscription from the Helliwells who were local landowners and was administered under the wing of the church.

The Helliwell's, at this time, must have been a fairly large and wealthy family, one branch of which lived in a house referred to as Ealees Hall (which was demolished to make room for the railway viaduct). The house was very near to the site where the first school in Littleborough was built at the foot of Ealees road.. The Helliwells came originally from Stainland in Sowerby, where they settled in 1343. Some time after this they migrated into our district and we know that in the year 1561 a John Halliwell was living at Ealees Hall. This John Halliwell, or a descendant of the same name, was still living at Ealees in 1608. The eldest son of this John Halliwell lived here for some time previous to 1661. In 1688 a son of this Halliwell, Theophilous, who was living at Ealees, provided funds to support a school master and for this purpose, 'devised an estate called Crowel Shaws in Sowerby, near Halifax, and a fee farm rent of 20s to do the pleasure of Almighty God and for the use of the school-master of Littleborough.' In the next ten years his brother Richard built the school. It was for boys only and in addition to being a day school it was also open on Sundays for anyone who cared to attend. It could accommodate 10 pupils and the Master lived in two chambers above the classroom. The present 'school house', a private residence, itself over 200 years old, stands along side the site of the original school.

For many years this was the only school between Todmorden and Littleborough; it is a reminder that much of the pioneering work in teaching was done by the churches and monasteries.

There is also little doubt that, because of our isolated geographical position and the demanding physical conditions, there are signs of the growth of a rugged independence of thought about the kind of worship acceptable both in east Lancashire and the adjacent parts of Yorkshire. This was expressed in a leaning towards an extreme of Protestantism, even Puritanism. For example, Rochdale had a Protestant Vicar from 1570 well into the 17th century. It is not difficult to explain why the Protestant / Puritan strain was so attractive to the growing community slowly being built on the prosperity of wool. These people were self-made, independent working people, fiercely defending the virtues of thrift and hard work. In their thinking they came to incorporate their moral position as a great contributor to their success. Since they paid for the church and appointed its ministers they certainly ensured that it reflected and supported their position and beliefs. Thus we find in the early 1600's the great Archbishops were, at a distance, condemning our local priests as 'defaulters'. Our Services were in English as was the Bible and the prescribed Church Services were ignored. The priests were not worshipping according to the established Church Law.

With the defeat of the Royalists (1646 - 1649) the church was re-organised and local groups were set up to appoint new priests and monitor the church activity. Thus the second half of the 17th Century saw the increasing popularity of non-conformist religions only checked by the return of Charles II in 1660. He restored the Anglican clergy, but the sacked dissenting ministers responded by preaching in sympathetic houses or acted as itinerant preachers. Rapidly there grew up large groups of 'illegal' meetings and by 1689 legislation was in place to allow non-conformists (not Catholics) to worship freely. The Quakers were the most 'determined dissenters', with their refusal to pay tithes, bear arms or accept organised religion. They were imprisoned, their goods confiscated and heavy fines imposed. So by the end of the 17th century we find three powerful dissenting sects at the heart of our community: the Independents or Congregationalists, the Quakers and the Baptists. All these groups were disliked and even feared by the Established Church which recognised that these movements, rather than themselves, had won the support of the growing population in areas such as ours.

Some 17th Century Houses

To introduce a review of some of the older houses that still exist in our area a quotation from an old date stone at Pike House is fitting. The datestone was taken from a house at Triangle in Yorkshire which was part of the endowment given to support the school at Ealees.

> 'Forecast as if you will live for ever
> But live as if you will die tomorrow'

Everywhere in the story of Littleborough it emerges that the area was not completely isolated, a quote from a booklet by Wm. F Price illustrates this well:

"During the Stuart dynasty a wonderful improvement took place in the houses of yeomen and farmers. The old cottages of clamp, stave and daub gave way to buildings with stone foundations to the height of two or three feet. The large number of good stone houses and farm houses and buildings which were erected during the 17th century point probably to the division of the large estates and the custom which arose of the greater landlords granting leases which offered tenure of the farms for three generations of the tenant. A man who had such a lease was styled a yeoman and with the security of tenure he expended money upon the improvements of his buildings. Whilst the lord emblazoned his arms and crest upon his mansion or castle the yeoman inscribed over his house door his own and his wife's initials, generally accompanied by the date and some decorative device."

Whitfield and Handle Hall

At Whitfield a substantial part of the the original house is retained in a modern conversion including fine mullioned windows. There is also a ruined barn which in 1997 was offered for sale to be converted into a house. Fred Jackson tells us that "ancestors of The Lord of the Manor of Rochdale lived at Whitfield for several generations, and members of the Dearden family were living there early in the 18th century. A copy of the will of one of the Deardens is dated 1579 *(James of Stoneyheyes)*. He is described as a husbandman. He left to Margaret and Annie Buckley and Thomas Healey six shillings and eightpence each (6/8). To the five children of James Bridge, each a sheep. To Robert Dearden, two shillings (2/-) and to Margaret Dearden 12 pence. To every 'pore' body that came to his funeral one penny each, and to the most poor twenty shillings to be 'wared' (spent) in 'lynen' or woolen clothes. The rest of his goods he left to Isabell, his wife, amongst the items named being "a payre of looms" and a backstone. In total, the value was £59.4s.6d.

The fortunes of the Dearden family must soon after this have improved considerably, for we find that in 1610 Richard Dearden bought some land on Shore Moor (from the Holts of Stubley) and built a house, which he called Warcock Hill, but which afterwards changed to Handle Hall. Here the family lived for several generations before removing to Rochdale. Over the door is a stone inscribed:-

Ricardus Duerden

Strux it

A.D. 1610

This is a relatively modern cutting probably placed when the house was rebuilt in 1829. The oldest date stone is probably that of 1673 which is over the 'shippon' next to the house. The building, called the 'Queen Ann Public House', was used as an inn for many years. Recently it was used as an abattoir but in 1997 the Hall and shippon were converted to become two private houses.

Bent House Community

This group of houses represents some of the oldest buildings in the Littleborough district and like Handle Hall is a visible sign of increasing prosperity. This prosperity was built up to a great degree by the inter-marriage between the prominent local families. The Old Bent House has a datestone 1691 and the core of the building is a long low oblong with pleasing mullioned windows which have been well preserved. The Stotts lived in the Old Bent House and were very active church people during the 17th and 18th centuries. They left a very interesting day book of their lives which covers the cost of food, trading conditions and many aspects of family life. In 1829 the last Stott left Old Bent House and the house went to the Beswickes and later still to the Laws.

Opposite the old building is Bent House which is of a similar age but has had many additions and alterations. There are associated barns, shippons and stables with datestones of 1668, 1704 and 1750. A number of these buildings have been converted into houses. This complex was the original home of the Stott family which achieved prosperity and a coat of arms, which is illustrated in the east window of our parish church.

Brearley Farm.

Old Bent House.

Whittaker House

The Whitacres are recorded as living here since the 13th century. John Travis says that the estate of Whittaker was held by the Schofield family during the second half of the 15th century and George Travis of Inchfield purchased part of it before 1650. The earliest date stone is 1669. The rest of the estate went to James and John Lord in 1802. The Lords rebuilt the house in 1850 and placed a date stone. This part of the Lord family was well known locally for their business in flannel manufacture. The adjacent Whittaker farm was also owned by the Travis family (the earliest date stone is 1720) as was the Sheep Bank farm (1724) close by. Through Whittaker wood a path goes to Hollingworth Fold passing through an interesting group of stone buildings at Brearley Farm.

Other Houses

There are other groups of 17th century houses well worth a visit including Clegg Hall and the Falcon Inn in the Littleborough Square which has a 1657 date stone over the rear door.

Old Farm Houses

Date stones on old farm houses and dwellings include:

Cloise Farm (a short distance off Blackstone Edge Road), 1454.

This date has caused considerable interest from time to time. Ellinore Kyrshagh, the sister of Isabella (see chapter 7, Town House) married Jordan Chadwycke in 1454 and lived at the farm. The stone was cut and placed in its present position as a record of when the Chadwycke family came into the estate. A 1706 datestone on the back of the farm indicates when the 1454 stone was cut and placed. At this date the farm became part of the Sladen estate.

Hollingworth Gate, near Walsden, 1592. Caldermoor House, 1611 (See chapter 7, Town House). Rough Bank Farm, Butterworth, 1616. "Hill Top" Farm, 1638. Higher Hollingworth Fold, 1668. Far Chelburn Farm, 1682. Rake Inn, 1696. Bent Stool Farm, 1702. General Wood Farm, near Walsden, 1704.

Mawroad Farm 1708.

The site of a very ancient house. In 1503 Mowrode was the home of Henry Kershawe and descendants still lived there in 1755. When the porch was dismantled a 1754 date stone was rescued and resited at the back of the house.

Whitfield Farm, 1720. Sladen Fold Farm & Lower Starrings Farm, 1744.

Light Hazzles Farm, 1743.

This is a very ancient site first recorded in the Manor Survey of 1626. The date stone over the kitchen fireplace was described in the early 20th century as very decorative.

Between 1754 and 1780 at least eight more date stones exist locally and they are numerous at later dates.

From the evidence it is clear that by the 17th century a larger and more stable community was increasing in prosperity and could contemplate building solid stone houses. This prosperity was built partly on mineral extraction and quarrying but primarily on textile processing, agriculture, livestock farming and trade. It appears that the local community could face the 18th century with some confidence.

CHAPTER TEN

THE EIGHTEENTH CENTURY (1700 - 1800)

Eighteenth century Britain was governed by rich merchants and country gentlemen. The new royal line (the Hanoverians) did not wish to challenge the power of Parliament as the Stuarts had done. The typical image of the 18th century was to be of a Great House with thousands of acres of land consisting of home farms and areas farmed by people paying rents.

The three-field system of sustainable agriculture with one third fallow gave way to new methods of sowing in straight lines, new techniques of hoeing between crops and protection from predators. Output increased immensely and it was realised that root crops could be grown on fallow soil as they actually helped restore fertility - and provided winter fodder. Suddenly, in exchange for a Christmas slaughter of livestock, continuous breeding was practical. Animals became heavier, fleeces thicker and at the end of the century the farmers had trebled animal body weights. Notably when we were at war with France (1793 - 1815), we needed higher food production and combined with the new methods, farming prospered and many new farms were built. Often the smallest farms were sold to richer men; special Acts of Parliament allowed the farmers to take over village commons, enclosure of land became virtually universal and as ever, the poor lost out.

The estate of a Great House was a virtually self-sufficient world with nobles competing in conspicuous wealth. Alongside this was a growing world of squires and yeoman farmers who modelled themselves on the nobility. The English trading companies were already operating world wide: the wealth that flowed back was used to endow schools, hospitals and support the poor - whilst the owners enjoyed grossly ostentatious personal life styles.

The population of towns was growing very fast although the majority of people still lived in the country. The farmworkers worked on estates belonging to the Great Houses or for the squire. They were tied by their house to one employer and many had a small holding to supplement their food. The squire had cooks, maids and servants; the labourer's wife cooked and worked in the fields. When at home the poor spun and wove textiles.

Many country people, often deprived of their livelihood by the enclosures, left for the growing towns. These towns had no police forces, no sanitation and were centres of poverty and crime with public houses open 24 hours a day. The rich visited spas, followed fashion, and valued manners, style, music and elegance. There was a large contrast between the rich and the poor but the patronage of the rich helped develop craftsmanship in furniture, clocks etc and left the names of Sheraton, Chippendale and Robert Adam to posterity.

Most people still belonged nominally to the Church of England but the appointment of clergymen was in the hands of landowners who were often less than committed to the Church. A village parson may well have continued to help the poor and educate the brighter children but their livings were in the gift of the squire and so the feeling grew that the Church had little care for the increasing mass of poor people. Industry was growing with coal, textiles and tin mining leading the way. It is significant that it was in such communities that a dissatisfied priest, John Wesley, got his first and strongest support. Wesley was, and wanted to remain, a Church of England clergyman but, along with his brother John, felt that the Church had lost touch with the people. He decided to travel the country to revive religious life and when he found himself banned from many churches, thrown into duck ponds and stoned, he simply preached outside. With his brother, who wrote numerous songs, they began to attract huge crowds who openly wept at their direct religious message and spontaneously formed groups to support each other and to 'spread the word'. Wesley realised the importance of this and had been in the habit of talking about organising 'methodically' so the result was that the Methodist Church was born, despite his wishes to remain in the Church of England. When he died in 1791 there were Methodist Churches all over Britain and he had become one of the main Christian influences in Victorian England.

Littleborough on the map

Littleborough as a centre is not recorded on 18th century maps. Rather there is an area with scattered cottages clustered in communities above the valley floor. Calderbrook, for example, is recognisably a separate community. In the valley you can locate a river crossing and near to it a church, a number of cottages and one or two larger buildings. In 1737 it was estimated that there were a 1000 people who were part of the Littleborough community (see p.98).

Conditions locally in the 18th Century

At the end of the 17th century there were rising numbers of stone houses being built either to serve as the nucleus for new farms or to replace the wooden structures on existing properties. The prosperity that this represented was built on a dual economy of trade and agriculture which would continue to thrive up to the time of the Industrial Revolution. By 1750 handloom weaving of 'calico', from cotton weft and warp, was being undertaken in small two-storey cottages in Smithy Nook and Calderbrook with the materials being supplied by a 'putter out' from Todmorden (Fieldens). At the same time Samuel Haslam, of Willow Hall near Halifax, provided warp and weft to weavers at Whitelees. By the end of the century handloom weavers were working from purpose-built, three-storey loomhouses in Smithy Bridge, Dearnley, Stubley, Featherstall, Whitelees and Shore. The first floor 'Takin door' and the full width, narrow, mullioned windows can still be seen today. There is a tendency for books to talk of Yorkshire handling wool and Lancashire cotton but the reality in our upland communities appears to be that they existed comfortably side by side.

The pattern of local life was affected by the existence of counties in England. For instance the counties administered justice in serious cases and provided 'houses of correction'. The correction appeared to combine whipping, exploitation of cheap labour and some industrial training. There were looms and other textile equipment in the 'houses', which were later to become our prisons. Within the county there was a well defined social pyramid with Baronets at the apex, gentlemen in the middle and tenants at the base.

The Littleborough area did not have families with claims beyond that of belonging to the local gentry. They were most familiar with manorial jurisdiction and the administration concerned with local issues on land tenure, rents, farms, mining rights etc. At the bottom level, community issues were handled at twice yearly meetings (tourns) supervised by local copyholders or freeholders. The smallest significant unit was a township which focussed on local concerns and, for example, might adjudicate on communal farming disputes. Officers appointed by the township were answerable

The White House Inn, formerly the Wagon and Horses, at the top of Blackstone Edge seen here before the days of motor travel.

to a combination of the Manor and the Justices of the Peace (a county appointment). Such Officers were appointed on a rotation system from within the ranks of the local landowners. Littleborough was part of the district of Hundersfield and a survey of some of the local officers' duties gives a clear picture of many aspects of the everyday life in a rural economy.

Township Officers

Constable

This officer was responsible for law, order, weights and measures, the local militia, tax collection, vagrants and many other mundane aspects of daily life. At the start of the 18th century his tools were whipping posts, stocks, ducking stools and a prison. The first three of these items were sited within or by the church grounds and were the responsibility of the church warden. The constable also controlled a Pinder who had a stock pen to impound stray animals until the owner paid a fine (an early version of car clamping!). It is clear that the constable was at the heart of local administration.

Churchwarden

This officer maintained the church buildings and furnishings, provided vestments and looked after the church yard including the stocks, pillory and ducking stool. Such officers were nominated, unpaid, but had various gifts and privileges.

The Surveyor of Highways

In our area the responsibility to maintain the highway rested with the owners of the land adjacent to it, which situation continued long after the law changed. The main

Steanor Bottom toll-house built to serve the new Turnpike Road to Littleborough 1824.
This building replaced another further up Calderbrook Road at Dog Isles.

job was the maintenance of the hard wearing 'causeways' built of large rock slabs with smaller stones packed on each side. Some eight feet wide, these were not really suitable for wheeled vehicles because of the steep gradients, so load carrying was mainly by pack horse. The tools for road mending had evocative names viz. Stone Sledge, Badgering Do, Wedges, Iron Crows, Mauls and Picks. To buy these tools a rate would be raised on the local families, or levied as a relief from other communal duties. Depending on the size, responsibility for bridges was split between township and the County. As industry and trade grew, the nature of traffic changed and most passed through communities and did not benefit them. To meet the road maintenance costs of this traffic Turnpike Trusts were formed for main roads and the Trust was authorised to raise an income from tolls. The turnpike was the revolving gate set on a central 'pike' that was opened when the toll was paid. Avoiding these pikes became a major challenge for travellers!

The need for the turnpike roads can be judged from a petition to Parliament in 1734 relating to Blackstone Edge.

'By reason of the nature of the soil and the narrowness of the road in several places and the many heavy carriages frequently passing, it has become so exceeding deep and ruinous that in winter season and often in summer, many parts thereof are impassable for wagons, carts and other wheeled carriages and very dangerous to travellers.'

The Halifax, Blackstone Edge, Rochdale road became a toll road as did the Hebden Bridge, Todmorden, Rochdale road (via Calderbrook).

Before 1766 there was a packhorse road and the Roman road crossing Blackstone Edge and there are graphic descriptions of the hazards in earlier chapters of this book. Post 1766 the Blackstone Edge Old Road supplemented these routes and more recently the present line was developed. Edwin Waugh gives the following picture of 'Crossing Blackstone Edge' in the 18th Century:

"In those early days it was the custom to add two additional horses to the ordinary coach team at Littleborough before attempting the steep ascent, and then unyoking them at the hostelry (now the White House). So great was the traffic, and so famous the baiting place, that the hearth stones were never cold." *(Baiting was a word for food and refreshment at an inn)*

By 1772 there were regular coach services between Leeds and Manchester via Blackstone Edge three times a week and by 1790 there was a stage coach going between Rochdale and Halifax and Leeds. The peak coach traffic came in the early 19th century.

The Todmorden to Rochdale road was interesting as it did not follow an already existing road. It was only authorised in 1760 and two gentlemen and one yeoman (all Quakers) put up the £2000 necessary to start the project. Bridleways were taken over, bridges built and Toll Houses constructed, but the project took years to complete.

We have a fine example of a toll house at Steanor Bottom which was rescued from the threat of being dismantled and taken elsewhere, by the action of the local Civic Trust during the 1970s. An independent trust was formed which converted and extended the derelict toll house to become a private dwelling which could then be safeguarded, by the terms of the trust, from any unsuitable modification.

As the turnpike was extended a charge was levied on all the hillside communities it passed; these charges were bitterly contested because the turnpike was initially of little use to them. Nevertheless heavy, wheeled vehicles could now move along the valley floor and these roads were built with stone, varying from gravel to large blocks, which was needed in large quantities. This gave a huge boost to local quarrying.

(The stimulus represented by the need for turnpike roads led to technical advances in road construction. John McAdam (1756 - 1836), one of the great road builders, experimented surfacing roads with small chips. When these were later rolled and macadamised by the addition of tar to bind the surface it created what is commonly called the 'tarmac road'. Most of the major roads in Littleborough were later surfaced, often over cobbles, using variants of these tarmac techniques.)

The old workhouse at Hollingworth Fold in 1906; demolished about 1940.

The major toll or turnpike roads were usually organised and funded under trust arrangements. In addition there were private toll roads set up by individuals. From the toll house in Littleborough there was such a private road that ran to Ben Healey Bridge and then up to the Fisherman's Inn. It remained a private toll road until it was adopted by the local Board around 1882.

Overseer of the Poor

The records of these officers are a mine of information about the food, clothes, and living conditions of the labouring classes and the poor. Even in the 17th century there were many charities and agencies giving to the poor and overseers levied a 'poor rate' on land and building values. Up to the middle of the 18th century the rate was low but industrial growth, war and the cost of setting up 'work houses' gave very severe increases.

A pauper had to wear a badge or scarf with a large P on it. Payments to the poor were distributed in money and from a stock of blankets, beds and furniture held by the township. The poorest people were lodged with others in separate dwellings or in people's houses. It was 1723 when dedicated Poor Houses were authorised. Hundersfield set up its first Poor House in 1732 and by 1800 most townships had their own. It appears that initially the administration of these houses was benign; it was later, perhaps mainly in the large towns, that the Poor Houses were to become an instrument of oppression hated by the poor.

Locally there was a long established Poor House, known as the Hollingworth Workhouse at Hollingworth Fold. It was there before the 'Lake' was built and in 1785 the rates were 12s.6½d.

The diet of the poor was mainly milk, oatmeal and potatoes. They were under-nourished, living in unhygienic conditions which meant that illness, especially smallpox, was a scourge. Only at the close of the century was there any likelihood of a resident doctor in the area.

The Overseer paid for midwives, christenings, funerals and the meals that went with these events. It can be seen that the whole operation of Poor Law Relief strengthened the connection of local people with their township. This autonomy was part of the fabric of community life which was defended stoutly in the following centuries.

The Industrial Revolution

In the last quarter of the 18th Century the people experienced considerable changes both in prosperity and in the increasing pace of activity which was initiated by causes quite outside their control. What the people living at that time may well not have understood was that their whole way of life was to be transformed by the middle of the 19th century. In England a thinly populated country was to become a crowded one where for the first time more people would live in towns than in the country.

In our area it meant that the centuries old hillside communities would stagnate or contract while the Littleborough hamlet would grow to be a town. On the horizon was an apparently small change which was to become a major feature in our area within 50 years; that was the rapid growth in the canal network. Elsewhere in England by the mid-18th century there was a spate of canal building; for example merchants in Leeds got a Parliamentary Act in 1698 for making and keeping navigable the rivers Aire and Calder. It was 1794 before the Rochdale Canal Company got the go ahead to build a canal that went through the Pennines, between Sowerby Bridge and Manchester, a distance of some 33 miles. On the map submitted in 1794 the Rochdale Canal Company had proposed two reservoirs in the area we know today as Hollingworth Lake. The larger reservoir was to be where Hollingworth Lake is and a smaller one was to be built flooding the area between Hollingworth Fold and Schofield Hall. Nothing came of the smaller reservoir but the larger was to become the basis for the first, and most successful commercial exploitation of Littleborough, based on its potential as a tourist attraction for the surrounding urban areas.

Socially a relatively stable system of living was being altered while the industrial system, in addition to destroying the traditional textile industry, was spawning employment methods that appeared to workers as threatening and seemed to be introducing child slavery into Britain.

It was noted earlier that the County Administration (Lancaster) was starting to affect Littleborough very directly in issues like law enforcement and punishment. A vivid picture emerges from quotations from the 'Orders of General Quarters Sessions: Lancaster, (1779).

'The sole cause of riots, Tumults and Insurrections that have happened in the County of Lancaster is owing to the erection of certain Mills and Engines, for the manufacture of Cotton which in the Idea of the Persons Assembled, tend to depreciate the Price of Labour.'

'It is the opinion of this court that Invention and Introduction of the machines for Carding, Roving, Spinning and Twisting Cotton has been of the greatest utility to the County - affording Labour and Subsistence to the Industrious Poor who have not any pretence (excuse) for committing the late riots from want of work.

The 'Orders' offer thanks to a General and his officers and soldiers, a knight, magistrates and 'gentlemen of the county' for endeavouring to suppress the said riots.

A rather more humane side of the courts is also visible:

'It is highly expedient for the magistrates in this County to refuse their allowance to all indentures of parish apprentices who shall be bound to owners of Cotton Mills or other manufacturies in which children are obliged to work in the night or more than 10 hours in the day.'

From this we can conclude that in the immediate future the main way of earning a living would be in, or associated with, a factory rather than farming.

The Textile Industry

In the 18th century cotton was part of a hand-loom industry based on woollen and linen fibres and mixes. It proved to be very important for future development that there was already an existing network of middlemen who could offer local credit and help the trade expand. They were to grow into merchants and merchant manufacturers. By the late 1700's there were already specialists such as raw cotton merchants at the ports of Liverpool and Hull which were Littleborough's two main outlets when the roads were improved and the canal and railway were built. In addition it was the 1770's when the first banks came into Lancashire; by the 1820's they were a key factor as the main source of short term credit.

Littleborough had other advantages: from the 16th century we were part of an area exempt from the Weavers' Acts, which elsewhere limited the number of apprentices a Master weaver could employ and also from the Calico Acts which limited printing and dyeing capabilities. Especially in the early years the damp climate was a considerable advantage to hand-loom weavers.

The history of textiles runs from fustian (a mixture of cotton and flax/wool) and linen through many other mixes to pure cotton and then artificial fibres. In the 17th century clothes were predominantly woollen or linen.

The estimated UK consumption of raw cotton in the 17th century was:

1720 - 29	14 million lbs
1770 - 79	48 million lbs
1810 - 19	934 million lbs

Thus up till the end of the century cotton consumption was low and our local industry was selling wool and linen products to a 'home' market. As powered looms and factory manufacture started to spread the hand-loom weavers supplied the more complex and better quality yarns and clothes and continued to find a ready and well priced market for their goods.

Brick and Pottery Industry

The most dramatic illustration of the size and speed of the change is that between 1780 and 1850 the population in Britain grew from 13 million to 27 million. With enormous strides in medicine fewer children died at birth while the rapid spread of knowledge about hygiene and cleanliness also meant people lived longer.

The need for a massive increase in new house building stimulated the search for new materials and technology. Fired clay for pots was centuries old, bricks made of clay were re-introduced to England in the 14th century and the need for drainage in house building projects led to the introduction of the earthenware drain pipe in the 1740's. Potters diversified their skills and moved into this new area. In Littleborough amongst the first examples of the new technology in building came in 1758, when bricks were used for internal walls when the stables of the Falcon Inn were converted into cottages. Also during the late 1700's the rear and side walls of the 15th century timber, cruck-framed Stubley Hall were faced in brickwork.

Coal Mining

By 1772 John Stott of Bent House was operating leases giving the right to mine for coal under various parcels of land on the estate. These leases granted the rights and privileges of mining 'coal and cannel' for 35 years to John and William Bamford of Higher Shore, yeoman John Stott of Brown Wardle, Robert Butterworth of Syke, miner, Robert Stott of Wardle Fold, coalminer and Bamforth, coalminer (whose family name appeared in Alice Wolstenholme's will in the 17th century).

The Church and the Evangelical Revival

The Parish Church

Earlier in this book there is some consideration of the growth of religious institutions in our area. In 1700 there was no parson's house in Littleborough to support the parish work, and the parson lived 'where he was welcome'. At that time he had an income of £30 per year and lived with the Stotts family at Bent House. A drawing remains of the Parish Church as it existed in 1770 (on its site nearer to the river). It is clearly in a very poor condition with bleak surroundings. The stocks are prominent in the church yard but there is no picture of the pillory or the ducking stool both of which were also used for punishment. It is interesting that alongside this picture of dereliction the official number of families cared for had fallen to 182, significantly lower than in the 17th century. The graveyard was enlarged in 1793 but in 1800 the Vicar of Rochdale noted that:

'the Littleborough Chapel is in the most wretched of conditions that can be conceived and it is a danger to the people.'

Today we can readily identify the foundations or ruins of former churches and chapels in our community and we have religious buildings which have been converted to other purposes. There remains a spread of churches and chapels which are still active and healthy. To understand the position, we must look at movements that began in the 17th century and flowered in the 18th century.

Non-conformist Religion

The emergence of the Dissenters (Quakers, Baptists and Presbyterians) was noted earlier. In 1737 Littleborough was said to have 182 Church of England and 4 Presbyterian families. The population in total in the district is estimated to have been about 1000. In 1743 a local survey showed that 14% of the families in one community were dissenters while only 11% attended the Church of England. The methodical and vocally appealing religions were clearly gaining acceptance.

The Methodists

The evangelical revival was driven by piety and burning zeal and none more so than the Methodists. In 1747 John and Charles Wesley , preached locally in Wardle and Todmorden to 'Loving simple hearted people' and soon ministers, led by a Mr Grimshaw, were supervising Methodist Societies in our area. In 1748 Wesley was back again and the growth of Methodism continued to accelerate. In October 1749 Wesley visited Rochdale where he recorded that 'as soon as we entered the town we found streets lined with multitudes of people shouting, cursing, blaspheming and gnashing upon us with their teeth.' There is ample confirmation that in the early days the Wesley brothers were more welcome in the 'dark and ignorant' upland communities than in the larger towns. The appeal was that 'he died to save us all' not just the great, the good and the Saints. Wesley was not only a great preacher he could also organise; he believed in the capacity of the ordinary man to preach and teach and proved it by referring to how they ran their townships Lay preachers emerged, some of whom became full time, or itinerant preachers. Wesley was not, however, democratic in the modern sense; he ruled his hierarchy with a rod of iron and punished incompetence as severely as heresy. Both the Wesleys were ordained ministers of the Church of England rejecting the dissenting sects of Baptists and Presbyterians. But they were seen themselves as dissenters by many in the mother church. The Baptists, who had broken away on the issue of 'adult baptism' rather than of the child, now combined with liberal Calvinists so that by the mid-1750's they had created a revitalised Dissenting Sect. Methodists, still eschewing chapels and ordained ministers, had a strong grip on small communities such as Littleborough and Summit. By the 1770's the Anglican Church was more reconciled to the existence of the Methodist movement. In 1788 Wesley was back in Rochdale where he was able to preach in a public 'Methodist House' erected in Toad Lane and say "trouble here is past". All other dissenting groups were badly affected by the evangelical revival, with the exception of the Quakers. In 1784 Wesley broke with the Church of England by ordaining ministers to serve in North America. When he died in 1791 it was claimed that he had preached more than 40,000 sermons. Wesley made visits to Rochdale, Wardle and west Yorkshire but there is no

LITTLEBOROUGH AREA IN THE 18th CENTURY

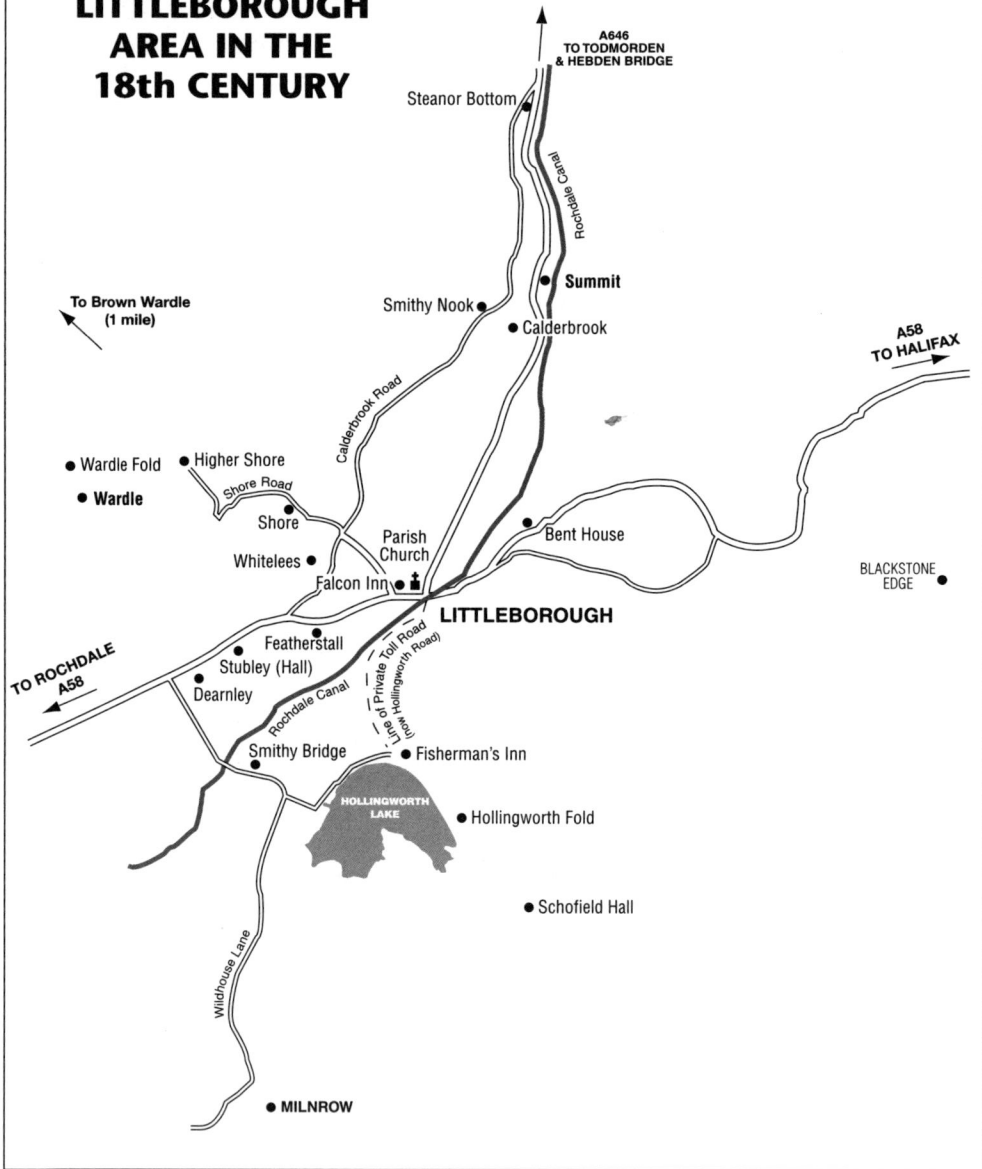

A646
TO TODMORDEN
& HEBDEN BRIDGE

Steanor Bottom

Rochdale Canal

Summit

Smithy Nook

Calderbrook

To Brown Wardle
(1 mile)

A58
TO HALIFAX

Calderbrook Road

Wardle Fold • • Higher Shore

• Wardle

Shore Road

Shore

Whitelees •

Parish
Church

Bent House •

BLACKSTONE
EDGE •

Falcon Inn •

LITTLEBOROUGH

• Featherstall

TO ROCHDALE
A58

Stubley (Hall) •

• Dearnley

Rochdale Canal

Line of Private Toll Road
(now Hollingworth Road)

• Smithy Bridge

• Fisherman's Inn

HOLLINGWORTH
LAKE

• Hollingworth Fold

• Schofield Hall

Wildhouse Lane

• MILNROW

98

record of him visiting Littleborough. However, his impact was so great in the number of followers that he attracted and the chapels and schools that were built that it can be argued that his influence has exceeded that of any other single individual in our area.

The outcome of the evangelical revival was that most people were within easy reach of a place of worship at the end of the 18th Century. For non-conformists the venue was usually a simple 'house' where small groups, often from one community 'met' or 'assembled'. The appeal for ordinary people was that they could be actively involved and it has been argued that this contributed to their industrial achievements. Their thrift, sobriety, persistence and hard work drove them on, Wesley himself portrayed economic distress as a consequence of individual moral failings. Very many successful mill owners were 'active non-conformists', which is the blanket description of Methodists and the older dissenting sects.

The Quakers

The Society of Friends who would tolerate no oaths, carry no arms and pay no tithes was the most persecuted dissenting sect. Denied a career in University or the Law they turned to trade, banking and industry. Their success is documented in families such as the Fieldens (Todmorden), Greenwoods, Brights (Rochdale) and Rowntrees. Such a family did not emerge in the Littleborough area, but the Quakers appear to have used their great wealth from cotton, land and estates, benignly throughout the region. They supported chapels and social structures, as Fred Jackson testified at Summit and funded commercial projects such as the early canal developments and the building of the Toll roads.

Education and local schools

In 1727 yeoman John Hall of Hollingworth founded the 'free' school at Hollingworth Fold. It had an old bell taken from the old Milnrow Chapel which had an inscription with the date 1654. When the school was opened it was used on Sundays for religious services.

At the threshold of the Industrial Revolution we were already a great trading nation helped by the fact that nowhere in Britain is more than 70 miles from the sea. It was a period when Europe was to be the centre of world trade, Britain itself had new canals and improved roads allied to a sympathetic tax system designed to support a social structure which was led by many very rich families. The latter had both the willingness and the ability to spend huge sums of money on inventions and possible improvements. Finally all this coincided with our command of a world-wide Empire providing raw materials. The Empire proved to be flexible and resilient - so for a period any project seemed possible and any problem soluble.

CHAPTER ELEVEN

THE NINETEENTH CENTURY

PART ONE : THE LITTLEBOROUGH AREA IN 1800

ROAD DEVELOPMENT AND THE ARRIVAL OF THE CANAL AND RAILWAY

With the onset of the 19th century it was no longer possible for Littleborough people to think of themselves as a self-contained community, as factors from outside affected every household.

Some important 19th Century events:

Britain entered the 19th century at war with France - a dispute that had started in 1793 and finished in 1815. This was the first British war that really affected the ordinary person with over 15% of the male adult population in the armed forces and well over 200,000 deaths. These soldiers were from the poorest classes, the unemployed and convicted criminals, who very frequently opted to fight as an alternative to prison. After Trafalgar (1805), the British Navy controlled the Channel and took much of France's overseas trade. By 1815 over half the world's trade in manufactured goods was transported on British ships.

The war did mean high prices for farmers but it also stimulated the Industrial Revolution. There was work for armaments' manufacturers, for boot makers and the manufacturers of uniforms. The strains of war accelerated many developments. The cavalry needed enormous amounts of fodder, leading to a shortage at home - as a result the coal industry needed to search for an alternative to the pack-horse, which also needed fodder. It was the ideal environment in which to release the steam engine in 1802 and by 1825 George Stephenson had designed an effective engine called 'Locomotion'. The railway era had begun and it was a group of Lancashire businessmen who saw the opportunity to carry both people and goods, initially between Manchester and Liverpool. It took only 20 years to get all the main lines in Britain laid. In the process great engineers like Brunel emerged, who were supported by 250,000 workmen 'navigators'. The navvies were the highly paid, hard drinking, 'soldiers' of the industrial revolution doing heavy, dangerous work.

The industrial revolution was causing a mass movement of men and women into towns to work in factories - this way of life was to make Britain the wealthiest nation on earth - and possibly amongst the most unhappy. The people were crowded near the factories in the poorest of housing, dark, dingy and ill-lit, in a totally polluted atmosphere. At the beginning of the 19th century child labour was common and very few were educated - boys worked with their fathers and the girls with their mothers. Within a few years children from age six upwards worked and lived in factories many being bought from the 'poor houses' to slave in Lancashire and Derbyshire factories.

Socially Britain was in a period of upheaval. No worker and few manufacturers had a vote: Leeds and Manchester grew to be big cities without a Member of Parliament. By 1815 half a million men were demonstrating - and they included large numbers of ex- fighting men with no work. Luddites smashed machinery and in 1819 came the Peterloo massacre of peaceful

Calderbrook Road, looking north in the 1930's. On the left is Handle Hall Cottage, the tall chimneys opposite appear to be on the site of the old dyeworks.

demonstrators in Manchester. From the 1820's there began the slow and painful process of adapting the law to the new conditions, of tackling the root causes of poverty and disease, of creating a police force and achieving a new political structure. The struggle was between those with wealth and privilege protecting it against those without either. The Victorian workhouses became symbols of fear and hatred: to avoid them you would fight for work and if you were unemployed you would be prepared to emigrate. In 1851 in Manchester and Liverpool the life expectation of an average working man was 25 years as compared to 50 in country districts. Medicine, sanitation, public water supplies and street lighting were the keys to any improvement in health along with nurses' training, anaesthetics and disinfectants, sadly all were lacking.

Between 1815 and 1914 Britain grew to become a great world power, built on world-wide trade. Colonies became a Commonwealth to meet changing challenges. Throughout the 19th century Britain avoided alliances, fought other Empires such as the Turks and Russians and supported Free Trade. Agricultural protection was anathema to our new Free Traders with their commercial and industrial goods. Industry depended on a work force that was too poor to afford anything but cheap food. It was Peel, the son of a Lancashire cotton manufacturer, who repealed the Corn Laws in 1846. By 1872 great changes were coming - voting became secret, education acts started to enforce schooling, a professional Civil Service was created, and the movement for women's suffrage gained importance. Many remained poor but the working classes sensed opportunity by the end of the 19th century. There were trade unions, bicycles, tube trains, holidays and a perception of new horizons. There were also signs that the regular habit of church going was being questioned.

The Littleborough District at 1800

At the start of the 19th century Littleborough was on the edge of an industrial area that was to become one of the largest in the world. An interesting picture of the general condition of our area is found in an old paper entitled 'The Imperial Guide to the Great Post Roads'. It gave an account of a ride on the stage coach from Manchester to Leeds, in1804. Describing the route through Littleborough to Todmorden, the writer says:-

"When we got to Littleborough, we had to take a bye-road as there was no road through the valley. In this short round is a greater succession of natural and artificial beauties than are surveyed in so small a compass in any journey. The shaded streams of the meandering river and the artful lines of the navigation are pleasant guides through this charming glen."

The stage coach went over Calderbrook above Summit, which was typical of the communities that existed then, a vastly different place from what exists today. Until then it was virtually as nature had created it, with gently sloping hills covered with vegetation from the high ground to the valley floor and a stream of clear water from the hills running through the middle of it. This is in striking contrast to the desolate appearance shown in photographs taken in the 1920's.

In 1804 the only houses in what became the village of Summit were three or four farms, one in the valley at the bottom of Grim Wood at the place that is still called Holme Houses (holme meaning meadow land), the others were on the sides of the valley at Chelburn, Sladen and Whitfield. There was no road through the valley at this time, though there were several pack-horse roads crossing the valley from the farms on the Blatchinworth side to the farms on the Calderbrook side. The Walsden to Littleborough road at this time only came as far as Steanor Bottom, where it turned up the hill towards Smithy Nook and Calderbrook and came into the main road again at Featherstall. It was 24 years after this time, in 1828, before the road was carried through Summit to Littleborough.

We still retain the names of the surrounding woods, such as Sladen Wood, Grim Wood, Chelburn Wood, Steanor Bottom Wood, Green Clough (Shop Wood), Light-Hazels Wood and Timbercliffe. Grim Wood really was a fine wood and covered the slopes of the hills below Smithy Nook and extended down to Holme Houses. In the valley there was a farm and a stretch of meadow land, which joined up to the Chelburn Estate and woods. The farm at Holme up to the time of the making of the railway in 1837 was occupied by a family of the name of Grimmey; those of Chelburn by the 'Hamers of Chelburn', who had been owners for generations. A little nearer Summit the woods crossed the valley and covered the opposite hillsides at Light Hazels and right along to Walsden. The trees were mainly oaks and when the road through Summit was made in 1824, it cut through Grim Wood and began the destruction of those trees. The 'Royal Oak' public-house at Summit, now known as the Huntsman, possibly took its name from the oak trees which had to be cut down in Grim Wood. The making of the Summit Tunnel completed the destruction of the woodland, as immense quantities of the debris taken from the tunnel were tipped down the hillsides.

Fred Jackson advanced an interesting theory on the reasons for the decline of the wooded areas close to Smithy Nook.

"The area now known as the 'Dead Forest' (Clough) flourished to a later date still than Grim Wood but by the 1920's it consisted of thousands of dead trees. Nearly 70 years ago Old Ned Lurry lived at th' Forest. At this time all the trees were in vigorous growth and the scholars from Smithy Nook had their annual picnics there. A little further on, near Grimes' Farm (Chelburn) was another smaller wood, called Th'Little Nursery, which was also full of tree life. Considerable discussion has arisen at various times as to what killed all the trees in this part of our district, but I think the most likely theory is that it was owing to the emanation of poisonous gases from the Summit, Rake, Dearnley and Starring potteries, which were all in full work at that time."

Subsequently Fred Jackson was able to write to the editor of the Rochdale Observer as follows:

"Sir, - In a paper of mine which appeared in the Observer some little time ago, it was stated that tree life was practically non-existent to-day, yet previous to 1777 Summit and the hills on both sides of the valley were covered with trees. During the past week rather striking confirmation of this statement has been brought to light. Excavations are being carried out for more houses which are being put up by H.C. Harvey, Esq. on the Timbercliffe estate and a long trench has been cut in the field below the farm. At a depth of about three feet below the present surface the strata for nearly the whole length of the trench was very largely composed of decayed branches of trees, some of the smaller stems still having decayed acorns or nuts clinging to them. In another place are two oak trees crossing the trench and one of them, more than a foot in diameter, has been exposed. Under the trees is a bed of clay, probably the original surface on which the trees grew, while the strata above is composed of loose debris, probably washed down from the higher ground above the farm. Some of the old records are not always reliable and it is very satisfactory to have confirmation of them, as in this instance."

To fill out the picture of our district at the beginning of the 19th century Fred Jackson described what could seen from a viewpoint in Higher Calderbrook:

"Smithy Nook and Higher Calderbrook are pleasantly situated on the higher ground above Summit and command fine views. The old Reddyshore Scout Gate goes through the area and carries us back in imagination 800 or 900 years, or even to the time of the coming of the Saxons. Nestling in the hollow just below Smithy Nook we have Mawroad, the oldest place name in the district, probably dating back to the time of the Ancient Britons. A little to the north is Steanor Bottom, mentioned in deeds of the 14th century, though the present house was not erected earlier than the year 1700 (now demolished). In front of us, across the valley is a fine stretch of moorland and the source of the River Roche, with Robin Hood's Bed, over 1,500 feet above sea level, in the distance. Behind us is fine moorland again and the source of the River Calder. Across the valley, nestling among the trees we see Pike House and Lightowlers. The present house at Lightowlers is quite modern but a family of the name of Lightowlers is mentioned in deeds as living here early in the 12th century. A little farther still is Windy Bank, one of the finest of the old mansions in the district. The present building dates from early in the 17th century, though a Sir Henry de Windybonk is mentioned as living there in the year 1355. Crossing the valley again, we have Whitfield, early 16th century, and Handle Hall, 1610. (Both of these were built by the ancestors of the Dearden family, Lords of the Manor of Rochdale since 1823, and who resided here for several generations).

There is nothing very striking in the long straggling village of Smithy Nook and Higher Calderbrook. The houses are built at all angles and with one or two exceptions are the ordinary type of local stone-built cottages of the period. Most of them have many narrow windows, so as to admit plenty of light to Th' Weaving Chamber. That was a feature of nearly all the country-side houses when hand-loom weaving was

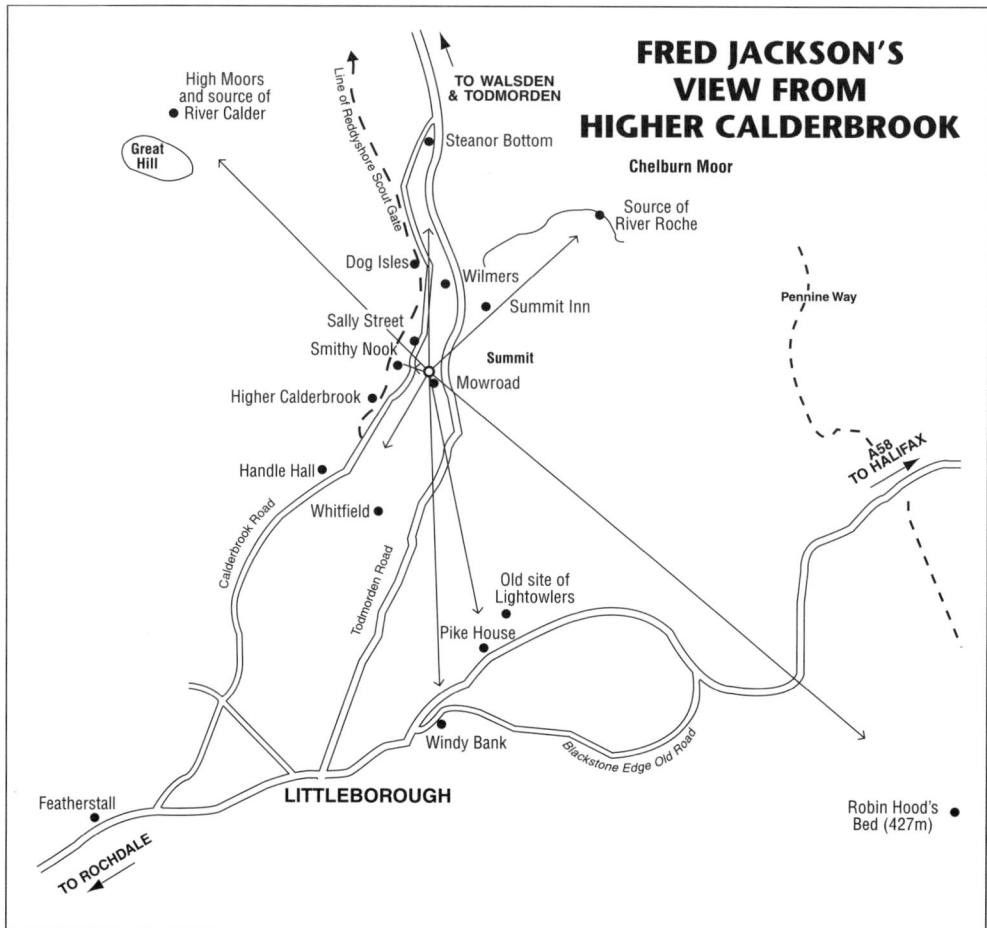

**FRED JACKSON'S
VIEW FROM
HIGHER CALDERBROOK**

Chelburn Moor

general. The houses in Higher Calderbrook are all built on the line of the Old Reddyshore Scout Gate and were probably erected about 1796 -7. The houses at Smithy Nook on the line of the old road from Steanor Bottom to Featherstall were erected about 1799-1800. The houses in Salley Street were built in 1808, the material used being local sandstone from the quarries behind the village. Around 1800 there was a public-house at Dog Isles nearby, kept by a man named 'Th' Butcher of Dog Isles' who had the reputation of being the best pig killer in the district. The pub was called the Bull and Butcher and its landlord was called James Lord. He was born in 1790 died in 1869. He is a strong contender for the distinction of being the longest serving landlord ever in Littleborough and is described as both a publican and a butcher. The public-house was pulled down and the stone was carted down past Wilmers to be used to help re-build the new farmhouse and beer house, the Summit Inn soon after the new road was opened in 1824."

Although the industrial revolution was gathering momentum it is clear that it had not yet had the impact which was to fill the valleys with mills and so pollute the area that even the gritstone edges were discoloured black and many plants died. Also, as a man brought up in a hillside community, Fred Jackson was able to write this description with hardly a reference to a rural hamlet or village and coaching station at the foot of the Pennines called Littleborough. A description is given of its state of development in 1800 in chapter 15.

The Growth of the Road Network

To service primarily the upland communities and the inter-area traffic, over many centuries an extensive network of earth roads and tracks had grown up and was referred to as the 'moorland roads'.

The Old Moorland Roads

The basis of communications in the district in 1800 was four very old moorland roads which can be grouped as two major roads with important branches. These roads remained the main historical lines of communication between Lancashire and Yorkshire which affected the Littleborough area. However, from both counties, new, wider and better maintained roads were being created up the valleys and had reached Littleborough from the west and well beyond Halifax on the east. The easier road access was inevitably bringing new ideas and opportunities to Littleborough.

The Long Causeway - from Cragg Vale to Rochdale

This may well be the oldest of the roads in our area yet it is still used for a great part of its length, by pedestrians, and is known as the Long Causeway. It is not clear when this road was first used, but some parts of it at least carry us back to the time when the Saxons and the Danes inhabited this part of England. Mr Thompson Watkin, in his book,'Roman Lancashire' considers the Reddyshore Scout Gate road, part of the Long Causeway, to be of Roman origin. At any rate this road is considerably over 1800 years old. At that time and for several centuries afterwards, it was the prime means of communication between Rochdale, Todmorden, Halifax and Burnley. Fred Jackson described the section of the road as it comes over the moors and down into Littleborough:

"For a weekend walk that stretch of the road extending from Cragg Vale to Summit would be hard to beat. Starting from Cragg Vale you have the rather steep ascent to Withens and the Withens Clough reservoir. A little beyond this, when the worst part of the ascent is accomplished, the traveller reaches a stone post bearing the words "Te Deum Laudamus" - a thank-offering for having arrived safely at the top of the hill. Soon after this Stoodley Pike is passed on the right and glorious views of the Todmorden and Hebden valleys are now obtained. The Pike itself was built in 1815 to commemorate the conclusion of peace after Waterloo; it fell down on the eve of the declaration of war against Russia and was rebuilt on the signing of the peace in 1856. It stands at a height of 1,307 feet above sea level. From Stoodley Pike a long stretch of the Causeway winds its way down the hill past the village of Mankinholes, a very ancient place dating back to Saxon times and soon reaches the pretty village of Lumbutts. Still keeping to the old road it climbs the hill again to Heyhead and from this point there is a well-defined track over the moors through Shincrack (where there is a very old milestone), Gadden's Dam, Salter Rake Gate, Hollingworth (Walsden), Deanroyd (with a branch causeway to the old

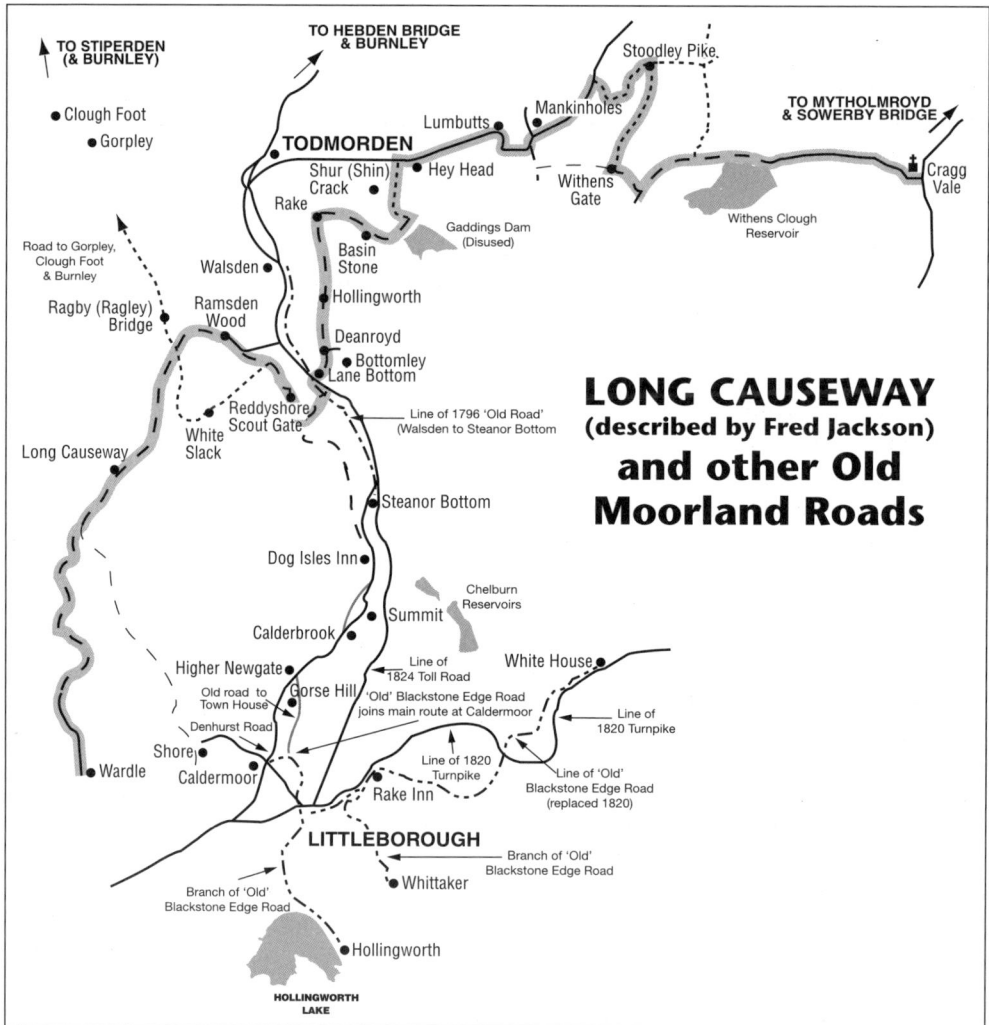

LONG CAUSEWAY
(described by Fred Jackson)
and other Old Moorland Roads

TO STIPERDEN (& BURNLEY)

TO HEBDEN BRIDGE & BURNLEY

Stoodley Pike

TO MYTHOLMROYD & SOWERBY BRIDGE

Clough Foot
Gorpley

Lumbutts
Mankinholes

TODMORDEN

Shur (Shin) Crack
Hey Head

Withens Gate

Cragg Vale

Rake

Gaddings Dam (Disused)

Withens Clough Reservoir

Road to Gorpley, Clough Foot & Burnley

Walsden

Basin Stone

Ragby (Ragley) Bridge

Ramsden Wood

Hollingworth

Deanroyd

Bottomley
Lane Bottom

Reddyshore Scout Gate

Line of 1796 'Old Road'
(Walsden to Steanor Bottom)

Long Causeway

White Slack

Steanor Bottom

Dog Isles Inn

Chelburn Reservoirs

Calderbrook
Summit

White House

Higher Newgate

Line of 1824 Toll Road

Gorse Hill

Old road to Town House

'Old' Blackstone Edge Road joins main route at Caldermoor

Line of 1820 Turnpike

Denhurst Road

Shore

Line of 1820 Turnpike

Wardle
Caldermoor

Line of 'Old' Blackstone Edge Road (replaced 1820)

Rake Inn

LITTLEBOROUGH

Branch of 'Old' Blackstone Edge Road

Branch of 'Old' Blackstone Edge Road

Whittaker

Hollingworth

HOLLINGWORTH LAKE

village of Bottomley), Lanebottom (where the road crosses the valley, probably on stepping stones in the past), then by Top o' Close, Old Guide, on to the Reddyshore Scout Gate road and so over the moors again to Shore, Wardle and Rochdale. All the way from Heyhead to Lanebottom you get glorious views of the valleys of Todmorden, Burnley, Ramsden, and Dulesgate. An important branch road ran by Allerscholes, Old Rake, and Ramsden to the Walsden valley."

Littleborough to Sowerby

Another very old road went from Littleborough by way of Lower Town House, the wood behind, over Gorse Hills by Lower and Higher Calderbrook, then forward over what is now a large stone quarry behind the Musician's Arms (a former public house). Beyond this point the road ran by Dog Isles public-house and thence by Reddyshore

106

Scout Gate, Cragg Vale and Sowerby.

Another branch of this road goes down by White Slack to Ragley bridge, which is still well preserved, then over the hill to Gorpley and Cloughfoot and thence by Scaitcliffe and Stiperden to Burnley. At Stiperden there are the remains of an old cross marking the junction with another road which continued by way of Heptonstall and the Wadsworth uplands to Luddenden.

The use of the old moorland roads

A good number of these roads were paved at one time, as they are today in some places. Where this was not done there was a continuous causeway in the middle of the road for pedestrians and pack horses. From the Middle Ages onwards it was a common sight to see 'fleets' of pack horses, with baskets of coal, wood and textile goods strapped to their backs, accompanied by cattle and sheep, driven by drovers from the farms to the growing markets in the towns. Sometimes the livestock were driven great distances, for example from the border country of Wales to London. Fred Jackson picks up the story:

"It can be readily understood that the roads would be quite unsuitable for vehicular traffic, so pack horses, or rough-haired Scottish Galloways, were employed to do all the carrying between the farms which were scattered over our district. I have at home an old print showing a long string of these pack horses winding their way over the moors. As many as 36 were driven by one man and they used to come over the hill tops, along the road from Clitheroe and Cliviger with bags of coal and lime in their panniers for the farmers of the district. They were all muzzled to prevent them grazing as they passed along the moors. How picturesque it must have been to see these long strings of Galloways threading their way along the moorland roads, the first carrying a bell hung round its neck and the rest sauntering on behind each other to the tinkling of the bell and the carol of the driver.

When the Rochdale Canal was completed, lime was conveyed from Derbyshire at a cheaper rate than previously and better and cheaper coal was imported. The Galloways slowly disappeared; but it is only within my own lifetime, (circa 1900), that they have vanished altogether, for I have a distinct recollection of seeing a very old man, almost as rough-looking as the Galloways which he drove, taking coal to the farms beyond Stoodley Pike and Withens".

They may have been picturesque but the life of a driver was rough and hard. The lime was used on our hill farms to sweeten the acid soils, to make cement and to limewash buildings. Coal was available locally but still had to be taken to the upland farms and small communities. As few people had any reason to move far from where they lived the drivers became a walking newspaper, full of the latest events and scandal. Two of the bells that announced their arrival can be seen in the Rochdale Museum collection. Like the minstrel of the middle ages the drivers could build their own myths. One of the best known was a lady called Ailse o' Fussers. The stories told of her include the claim that she had a 'toy boy' as a partner and was certainly among the last local pack horse drivers.

The old moorland roads are interesting because they represent the only method of travel, by horse or foot, available during most of our story. Only in the 19th century did they start to recede in importance. The Roman road, the mass of farm lanes and

The Rake Inn at the bottom of Blackstone Edge Old Road about 1907.
At that time the landlord was William Feilden serving Massey's Burnley Ales.

minor roads around Littleborough now form a picturesque background to the town and provide interesting walking throughout the area.

The rapid expansion of Littleborough in the 19th century started with very modest steps and to follow the story it is important to understand the sequence of development of the entry routes from the Pennines into the village.

The lines of the old roads entering into Littleborough

As outlined, before 1796 the only means of communication between Rochdale, Littleborough and Todmorden was over the old Reddyshore Scout Gate road. This came down from Higher New Gate, then down by Lower Town House, along Denhurst road to Caldermoor. In 1796, what is called the 'Old Road' was made. This kept to the valley from Walsden to Steanor Bottom, at which point owing to the marshy state of the valley between this point and Littleborough they had to take to the hills again by Calf Lee, Dog Isles, Smithy Nook, to what is now Higher New Gate. Here the road was diverted from Lower Town House and taken straight through Clough and Caldermoor to Featherstall. This continued to be the main coach road through the district till the present road was made in 1824 through Summit and down the valley to Littleborough. With the making of the road the pleasant wooded area between Summit and Littleborough was to be extensively altered. Large numbers of the trees had to be cut down in Grim Wood and Sladen Wood, and this number was largely increased when houses began to be built on the side of the road soon after its completion.

On the opposite side of the valley the old Blackstone Edge Road was still in use until 1820. This old road came down from the White House Inn, at a lower level than the present one, crossed it at the old Toll Bar, and came down by Lydgate, Water Gate,

*Summit, viewed from the higher ground at Temple Lane, before 1905 when tramlines were laid.
Summit brickwork's is seen at the top centre.*

Windy Bank, and the Rake Inn (1696), to Ealees, where it branched off, a by-road going from this point through Cleggs Wood (where the Ealees Colliery operated for over 20 years) to the hamlet of Whittaker. The main road continued down Ealees Road, past Halliwell's School and the so-called Cromwell's cottage, past the Red Lion, and on by the canal wharf to where Littleborough Station is today. Here it divided again, one part going to the old village of Hollingworth, the other main road, coming down by the Old Sheaf Inn, along Church Road, then by the Old Falcon, along a zig-zag road to Denhurst Road and Caldermoor. The house at Caldermoor was built by the Newalls in 1755 but became a pub, the Dog and Partridge in 1818; renamed the Caldermoor in 1968. There was a cinder path with gate and stile from the Royal Oak over Will Hill and across the fields to Caldermoor.

1820 The new turnpike road between Blackstone Edge and Littleborough

Prior to 1820 the road ran up a very uneven gradient taking the line followed by the Blackstone Edge Old Road today. It ascended steeply, from the Rake Inn to level out at upper Lydgate and the site of the old Holehouse Mill. The mill has been demolished and the area is known as High Peak today. Beyond that point it curved round to the foot of the Roman Road and then attacked the steeper ground up to the White House.

The route was considerably improved by not turning up the hill at the Rake Inn but being extended, below Windy Bank, over the sharp sided valley at lower Lydgate. A large quantity of soil was taken from the Littleborough 'hills' to fill this ravine and carry the road. Thus in Travis's words 'the new road went by Pike House, Moorcock Inn and Shepherds Rest, then forward , rounding the hillside, having the great recommendation of one uniform and easy rise until reaching the White House on Th'Edge'.

The realignment was seen as a bold and imaginative piece of road engineering. Incidentally, this road passed the site at 'Water Yate' (later known as the Woodcock beside Sladen mill) which became well known for wedding parties after the couple, or often a number of couples and their guests had done the 7 or 8 mile walk to Rochdale and back to be married.

1824 The new road from Steanor Bottom Toll Bar to Littleborough (the Todmorden Road).
Earlier the 'old road', opened in 1796, extended the valley passage from Walsden to Steanor Bottom and from there rose uphill ultimately to Smithy Nook and down again into Littleborough.

The last road section from Steanor Bottom to Littleborough via Summit was made in 1824. Prior to that date it was little more than a wide footpath going alternatively through light woodland and extensive areas of boggy and flood prone meadow. The possibility of putting a road through this terrain was greatly eased after the construction of the canal succesfully achieved the drainage of the marshy valley bottom.

One John Hartley in Littleborough lost his market gardens between Will and James Hills (see chapter 15) due to this road development and a large part of the surface earth and gravel were taken and deposited on the line of the 'new' road notably between Littleborough and where the Gale Inn now stands (Littleborough Flat). Mr Lawrence Newall was quick to exploit the development, knocking down the old farm house at Gale and erecting 'the Brow' (Gale House), the print works and the Gale Inn. The buildings were then occupied by his servants, workers and dependents.

Coach Travel
In terms of communication after walking and the horse came coach travel. Widespread use of coaches was entirely dependent on the provision of roads with at least a tolerable surface.

At the start of the 19th century we noted that coach and horses were the main method of overland travel. The commercial growth of the stage coach traffic had its roots in the late 17th century. In 1745 it took two weeks to travel from London to Edinburgh, but by 1796 it took two and a half days. In that same period the road system had been revolutionised. In the early 18th century coaches were still very unpopular as they were uncomfortable, slow, expensive and very dangerous. Because of the quality of the roads there were many accidents; the passengers and goods were also vulnerable to highway men. Nevertheless by 1820 there were six coaches daily from Rochdale to Halifax all with attractive names like Defiance, Commerce, High Flier and Shuttle. By the end of the first quarter of the 19th Century conditions had greatly improved as Fred Jackson commented:

"Locally, for example in 1826 a Stage Coach began to run through Summit, mainly for business men going to Manchester market. A man named David Cawthorpe at that time kept the Golden Lion Inn at Todmorden and he and a few other gentlemen formed a Committee to run a Coach through the valley from Halifax to Manchester, twice a week, on Tuesdays and Fridays and back again the same day. This was so successful that later two coaches were run named "Shuttle" and the "Perseverence", and continued till the Railway era (1841), though the narrative adds - a good many of the business men still did the journey on horseback.

At this time it took the Stage Coach Express 9½ hours to go from Manchester to Leeds and about 12 hours to York. The fare from Rochdale to Manchester was 6/-, from Manchester to Liverpool 13/-, and from Manchester to London £4/4/-. We growl about the cost of postage today, but in 1835 the charge for posting a letter from Rochdale to London was 11d, from Rochdale to Liverpool 7d. and from Rochdale to Manchester 4d." (Early in the 19th century a working man may have earned a little over £1 each week.)

Local roads in the second half of the 19th century

In 1843 stage coach services over Blackstone Edge declined under the impact of competition from the railways and canals. However there was still much general traffic and an amusing account exists of a 'chaining' to Blackstone Edge. This describes chaining an extra horse to the normal complement to supplement the pulling power during the ascent of the steep hill. In the bill is an item for 1 gill of gin 'for the horse'.

Also, in the second half of the 19th century much less freight was recorded over the turnpike roads from the time when Pennine rail traffic started to run regularly from Manchester to Sowerby Bridge in 1841.

Probably one of the last attempts at a commercial coach service over Blackstone Edge was staged in 1881. In June that year Hudson's Stage Coach, running a service from Liverpool to York, made its first run over Blackstone Edge. A large crowd of villagers watched the first run and the horses were changed at the Moorcock Inn. The service was terminated in August of the same year and was clearly an ill-advised enterprise.

The use of the major roads continued to decline, pending the arrival of motorised transport which became the great catalyst in the increase of road useage, in the early part of the 20th century.

The impact of the Industrial Revolution

At the beginning of the 19th century, two important developments were to have a great effect on Littleborough; these were the coming of the canal and the railway.

The Rochdale Canal

Lancashire was deeply involved in the development of canals. The Duke of Bridgewater had copious coal supplies on his Bridgewater estate at Worsley and needed a better way than a pack horse to get it to Manchester; his solution was to propose a canal. Between 1759 and 1764 he had the Bridgewater Canal built to connect Manchester to Liverpool. The advantage for business was enormous: one horse pulling a barge could carry more coal than 60 pack horses. The cost of carrying bulk cotton was cut by 83%. By 1770 all the main rivers of Britain were linked by canals which were to enjoy 70 years of prosperity. It was in the middle of the 19th century that the railway began to beat them both in speed and price.

During the 18th century the poor state of cross-Pennine roads in our area was a very persuasive argument for an early canal route in the north to follow that line. Nevertheless it was 1804 before the junction was finally made between Manchester and the Calder and Hebble at Sowerby Bridge to complete the cross-Pennine Rochdale Canal.

The first step towards building it was a major meeting in 1766 when Colonel Beswicke-Royds, of Pike House, Littleborough, strongly promoted the scheme. An

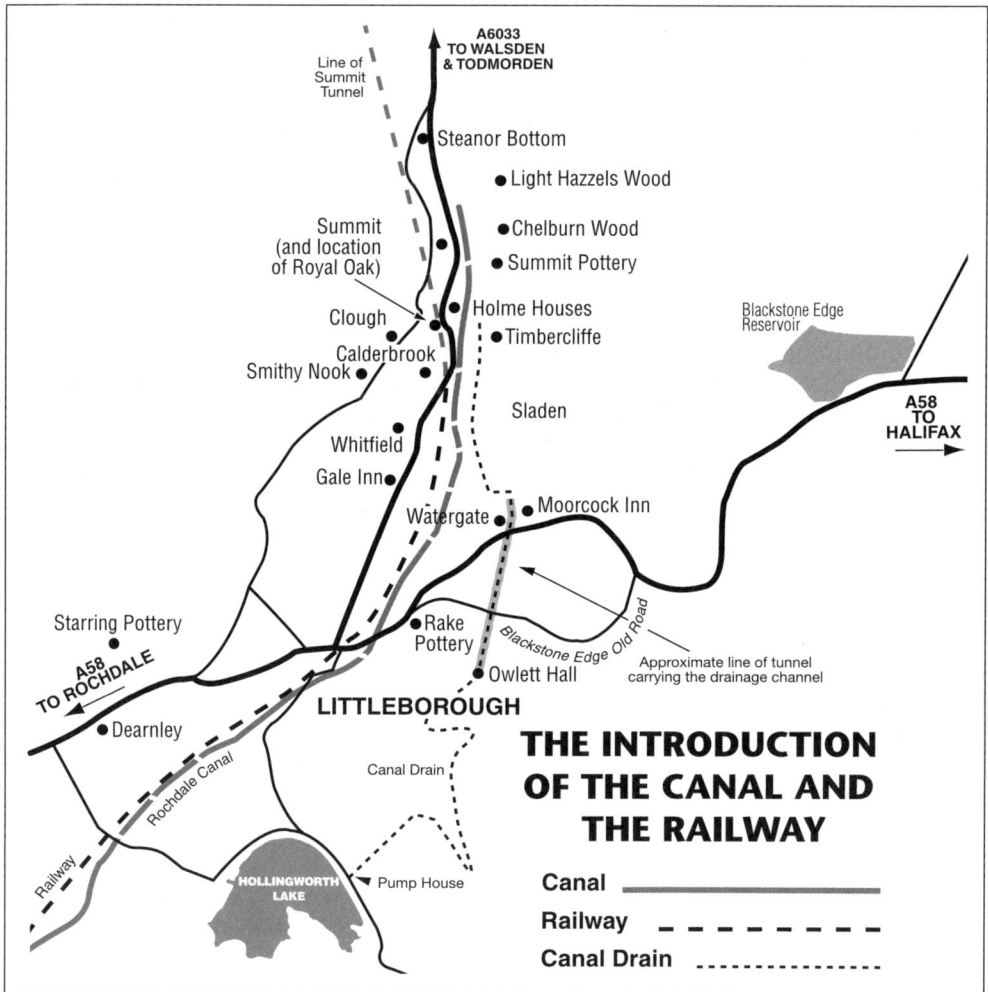

Line of Summit Tunnel

A6033 TO WALSDEN & TODMORDEN

● Steanor Bottom

● Light Hazzels Wood

Summit (and location of Royal Oak)

● Chelburn Wood
● Summit Pottery

Blackstone Edge Reservoir

Clough
Calderbrook
Smithy Nook ●

● Holme Houses
● Timbercliffe

A58 TO HALIFAX

Sladen

Whitfield ●
Gale Inn ●

Watergate ●

● Moorcock Inn

Starring Pottery ●

A58 TO ROCHDALE

● Rake Pottery

Blackstone Edge Old Road

● Owlett Hall

Approximate line of tunnel carrying the drainage channel

● Dearnley

LITTLEBOROUGH

Canal Drain

Rochdale Canal

THE INTRODUCTION OF THE CANAL AND THE RAILWAY

Railway

HOLLINGWORTH LAKE

Pump House

Canal ——————

Railway – – – – – –

Canal Drain ·················

engineering proposal was drawn up by Brindley, the celebrated canal engineer, who had been employed by the Duke of Bridgewater. Brindley was sponsored by Mr Richard Townley of Belfield. It did not go ahead because there was no agreement about the line of the canal and Lord Strange, (a Derby family) frustrated in his plan to take it through Bury, blocked every move in Parliament. He did this in collusion with strong manufacturing interests. It was 1794, and the third Parliamentary Bill, before the new Rochdale Canal Company was given powers to construct the canal, reservoirs and pumping stations. One of the reservoirs was to be sited at Hollingworth and in the original proposal it was only half the size of 'Hollingworth Lake' today.

An important issue about canal building in our area was the direct clash between the business interests involved in the textile industry and the canals, in that they both needed abundant water. The textile industry was already using water supplies, again and again, in chains of mills running down the valleys and they feared the loss of this resource to the canals. To achieve permission to proceed with the canal the Rochdale Canal Company had to create a complex agreement with the mill owners, providing water storage capacity far in excess of the needs of the canal and a contract to supply it to the mills. Similarly the rich mill and property owners soon recognised the potential to make money from the opening of a canal. For this reason there were lengthy delays in even starting the canal building whilst alternate routes were explored by various powerful groups of promoters; one group for example wished the canal to run through Bury. Others started speculative buying of land along the proposed line of the new canal.

Similar issues affected the location of the supply reservoirs. The original plans called for 5 small reservoirs in the Summit area and two in the Hollingworth area. The outcome of the negotiations was a vast complex of reservoirs and feeder channels all over the Pennines around Littleborough. There were eight main reservoirs, White Holme, Warland, Light Hazzles, Upper and Lower Chelburn, Hollingworth, Giddings Dam (Todmorden) and Blackstone Edge Reservoir. There were some 20 miles of feeder channels such as Broadhead and Castle Clough drains connecting them. The Giddings Dam reservoir was built for the sole use of mills.

It is interesting that the final solution to a number of the problems in building this canal became event driven, rather than planned. In all the early plans (1766-93) a tunnel was proposed at Summit, which would have reduced the number of locks by seven. By the final accepted submission, surveyed by Rennie from London, the tunnel had gone and three reservoirs, Blackstone Edge, Chelburn and Hollingworth were stated to be adequate to supply the canal with water. They were to be phased in over a number of years and Hollingworth was only designed to feed into the canal at the lower sector from Littleborough. The canal was open to Rochdale by 1798 and in July/August 1800 a drought stopped all traffic. This confirmed fears that had already been stated and the whole business enterprise was at risk. In a determined response Blackstone Edge reservoir was greatly improved by raising the dam and the completion of Hollingworth was transformed into an immediate priority to be finished within a year. However there were major problems with overflow drains (the coal drain): the embankment had to be raised and a whole new drain created to enable water to reach the Summit level. This had no part in the original plans so there was a hurried search for a pumping engine to raise the water at a new pump station erected on Bear Hill. Even more troublesome was the resistance of local land owners to a surface drain round to the 'summit level' of the canal. This imposed the need to dig a tunnel between Owlett Hall and Water Gate by Lydgate Brook (the N.W. side of Halifax Road). At this end there was still active coal mining which lead to long delays due to the escape of 'bad air' from disused shafts and the need to protect existing mining rights.

Of all the reservoirs associated with the canal the one at Hollingworth was to have the most dramatic effect on the development of Littleborough. In the late 18th century the canal proposals illustrated two reservoirs in the immediate area, but by the time the overall plan was sanctioned the second smaller reservoir had been dropped. The creation of the new Hollingworth reservoir only submerged a few small buildings at Hollingworth and flooded a wide stretch of farmland. To create it needed the building of three dam walls: Hollingworth Bank (Ealees), Fens Bank (Fishermans Hotel to Lower Cleggs Wood Lane, now Heald Lane) and Shaw Moss Bank (near the Sea Cadets Naval

Station). The whole construction was a major project and soon water from the new reservoir was being raised 45 feet by pumping. An open canal drain (part culverted) was constructed to run horizontally, broadly along the 600' contour. The main function was to allow water that was raised up to run round the hillside to enter the canal lock system at Summit. However the engineers anticipated times when the reservoir might need extra water so they arranged the operation of various sluices to channel water from Lydgate Brook into the canal drain and then forced it to flow back to the lake when the water level fell too low. This whole arrangement only ceased around 1910. The reservoir or 'lodge' was also contracted to supply water to mills in the area. When it was completed the announcement stated that it had a holding capacity of 400,000,000 gallons of water. From the 1840s the reservoir was commonly referred to as a 'lake'.

The background to the next development was that the Rochdale Canal Company leased (apart from water rights) the use of the lodge to members of the ubiquitous Newall family, who had a proposal to start pleasure developments based on and around the sheet of water. The principals were Mr Henry Newall, who owned Hare Hill Mills and his engineer Mr Sladen. The original proposals were based on boating and novelty amusements to cater for the tastes of working people whose working week had recently stopped at Saturday lunch time and who were rapidly developing a tradition of an afternoon walk with their families. Despite some serious problems, relating to the extreme cold of the water and the dangerous currents generated by 'drawing off' the water, by the 1850's the lodge was publicised as a 'lake' and had developed into a widely known pleasure resort. It had pubs, a dancing stage in the open air, side shows, photographers, hotels, a steam ferry etc. Captain Webb, of matches fame, publicly practised for his cross-channel swim in the lake. All this grew out of the placing of a feeder reservoir for a canal which always concentrated on the carriage of heavy industrial and commercial cargoes during its active life.

Canal operation

By August 1798 the canal was open from Sowerby Bridge to Todmorden and by December of the same year it was open to Rochdale. By 1804 the canal was navigable to Salford, officially it was 33 miles long, or 35 if you include the branch to Heywood. Built to wide dimensions it could take barges with a beam up to 14' 2". The decision to widen the canal was taken very late in the contracting process leading directly to a major shortfall in the money obtained from subscriptions. The locks were 72' long ie. the canal could handle most types of northern inland trading craft.

The environmental impact of building the canal through the Littleborough area is described by Fred Jackson.

"We have already seen that the building of the canal was a stimulus to the extensive quarrying in the Littleborough area. More seriously, before the canal was made, the meadowland belonging to the farm at Chelburn joined up to the farm land at Holme-Houses. The cutting for the canal about the year 1800 began the desecration of Summit by going through the meadows of Chelburn and Holme and so cutting off their connection with each other. The Woods above the farm at Chelburn and Leach were largely cut down to make room for the reservoirs which supply the canal with water, but on the whole the construction of the canal did not do much to impair the beauty of our district and in some places even enhanced it.

From 1802, when the canal was opened, till 1824, when the road was made through Summit to Littleborough, there was practically no further change, and Summit still retained its woodland beauty, with the river flowing through it."

With hindsight this may be seen as rather a rosy view as a considerable quantity of the water flowing into the river was diverted and the headwaters of the Roch were diverted into an ugly drain alongside the canal. This was probably the first of a number of such unlovely diversions of the river, for example, in the 1850's the river was covered over in part, by Sladen Wood House and a weaving shed.

The building of the canal was a significant engineering achievement and the official opening was a Gala Event. Headed by a yacht there was a procession of vessels which proceeded from Hebden Bridge and Todmorden to Manchester. Thousands of people lined both banks of the canal and cheered them as they passed. It had been the intention to have a real commercial cargo in the procession. However, owing to bad weather it took three attempts to get a barge to London with a cargo of coal, pick up the return cargo and set off for the opening of the canal. Alas the weather turned against them again and the barge did not arrive in time.

For some forty years the canal was the main artery of transport between Lancashire and Yorkshire. It was in 1825 that the railway company was formed despite most strenuous objections from the canal company. They cited:

'The great public advantage afforded by the Rochdale Canal - the serious investment upon that undertaking and the poor return, not 2½% hitherto yielded to the Company, give them sanguine hope that Parliament will, by rejecting the Railway Bill, leave them in undisturbed posession of their property'

Despite these fears, for a long period the railway enjoyed mutually beneficial trading in co-operation with the canal. Thus, contrary to expectation, the canal trade continued to expand alongside the new railway and by the mid-1840's canal operators were competing to lease their canal facilities to a railway company or to amalgamate with one. However, the railway, along with the revival of road transport, later led to the commercial eclipse of the canal.

In 1845 the canal carried an amazing million tons of cargo in the year. Much of this tonnage was 'short haul' off the Bridgewater Canal. In the same year one trader, William Jackson, had more than 30 barges or flats trading on the Rochdale Canal. He also had 120 horses as he specialised in 'fly boats' (express) which required frequent changes of horse. Another trader, Albert Wood, bought two of Jacksons 'fly boats' and continued trading on the Rochdale canal until 1919.

It was 1855 when the Rochdale Canal Company entered into an agreement with the Lancashire and Yorkshire Railway (and others) with a 21 year contract which was actually renewed until 1888. In that year the main cargo was coal, timber and cotton.

Up to 1887 the Rochdale Canal Company was a toll taker but it then became a carrier. The Company, which named its barges after flowers or girls, painted them in a red, white and pale blue livery. Boats were usually worked by two men with a third, a 'horse marine' being hired with the horse. Drivers with horses usually worked 10 mile stages and the barges could carry up to 80 tons each. At this time the Rochdale Canal was claimed to be the most successful trans-Pennine route, comparable to the best

The Shepherd's Rest, Halifax Road about 1910. The pub closed in 1915 and later became a transport café.

canals in the country. This was true despite having no regular passenger traffic to supplement its income (excepting pleasure trips by local groups). The Rochdale Canal Company traded in its own right until July 1921.

The canal was rarely more than 4' deep during the 20th century which limited the maximum cargo per barge to 40 tons. The last complete run of the canal was in 1937 and navigation was abandoned in 1952. The Rochdale Canal Company escaped nationalisation in 1948 and it continued as a property company. There was a period of neglect and doubt over the canal's future when use was reduced to short pleasure outings for Sunday Schools and other casual events. Following this was a new initiative initially promoted by the Civic Trust in the Littleborough area, to re-open the whole length of the canal and re-connect it to the national system. After a period of struggle these objectives have now been embraced into an ambitious proposal: this is a regeneration plan for the Littleborough area which includes the use of the canal for recreational and leisure activities, whilst encouraging any practical commercial use.

The coming of the railway

In the introduction to this chapter the startling speed of the development of the railway network was described in the years 1802 - 1850. The impact of this development, on the mobility of people and the ability to carry bulky and heavy goods was enormous. The incidental effects were to make the canal network obsolete in the long run. In some areas the railway developments caused great environmental degradation. Littleborough district experienced both the major advantages and disadvantages of railway development.

116

Summit Tunnel a mile north of Littleborough is part of the development which was needed to support what was originally called 'The Manchester and Leeds Railway'. The company was formed in 1825 and the Bill to authorise the construction of the railway passed through Parliament in 1835-6. Operations were commenced at once; by 1837 work on the Summit section had begun. In July 1838 George Stephenson travelled behind his own engine to Littleborough where a banquet was held. Littleborough was, at that time, the end of the Manchester to Leeds line; only the Summit pass stood between connection to the line from Yorkshire. The problem was how to go round, over, or as it turned out, through by digging what was at the time the world's longest tunnel. In 1839 the line was officially opened from Manchester to Littleborough. The major tunnel excavations, which started in 1838, took nearly three years to complete.

(*A plaque at Littleborough Station commemorates the start of the first stage of the trans-Pennine journey.*)

By March 1841 there was a regular train service from Manchester to Sowerby Bridge.

The rolling stock and travel arrangements were initially very basic. There were three classes of travel but the cheapest used open trucks with a running board to allow a red-coated official to go along collecting tickets. Littleborough station was made from planks of wood with the booking office beneath the arches of the viaduct. A flight of steep wooden steps led up to the platform. Only later was the office moved up onto the Yorkshire platform, which was lit by a single oil lamp set in the building wall so that it illuminated within and without the area. A level crossing gave access to the canal and the Manchester platform until the 1870's.

Fred Jackson had parents and grandparents who had experienced the opening of the railway and described the impact on the district.

"During the progress of the work a large number of men found accommodation in the villages, but many of the 'navvies' built shanties or huts with sods and stones. They were a primitive type of dwelling, but the men and their families lived in them, making them wind and rainproof with wrought mire and clay and covered them over with a coat of sticks and thatched them with rushes. There was quite a village of rude dwellings at Steanor Bottom Wood. Even in the 1920's there are a few ruins of these primitive dwellings in the woods at Steanor Bottom. The impact of this army of strangers was to have long lasting effects on our area."

One claim is that they introduced the phrase 'living over the brush' into our vocabulary. As many navvies were not inclined to be 'churched' or 'registered', when they decided to live together the man and woman would recite an undertaking to their fellows and seal the union by jumping over a broom handle held horizontally by two others - hence the phrase! Such common law marriages were widely recognised. Mass marriages were also arranged and there is a story of a local vicar who completed such a ceremony on an inspiring note:

 "You are all wed. You know what to do, so get about it".

In 1837 operations were begun on the Summit Tunnel, to which work, more than any other, Summit owes its desolate appearance today.

The tunnel itself is 2,869 yards in length, or nearly 1¾ miles. The height is 21' 6", width 23', and its depth beneath the surface 300'. 23,000,000 bricks and 8.000 tons of Roman cement, together with an enormous amount of sandstone from Smithy Nook and other quarries, were disposed of during its construction. The principal contractor was Mr. John Stephenson, and the resident engineer Mr Bernard Dickenson. It required the labour of 1,000 men for two years and four months and its entire cost amounted to £231,000, being at the rate of £87 per lineal yard. It may be of interest to mention the wages paid at this time to workers on the tunnel. The stonemasons had four shillings per day. Joiners had one pound per week, afterwards increased to twenty-two shillings. Navvies had three shillings per day and ordinary labourers two shillings to half-a-crown.

During the progress of the work, the debris from the tunnel was hauled up the outlets which are now used as ventilating shafts, which dot the hillside on the line of the tunnel.

One of these shafts was at Temple Lane, opposite Holme houses. From the hillside a tramway was built over the present road by wood trestle work covered with planking, and the refuse from the tunnel ran across in waggons to Holme meadows. This accounted for a huge mound of earth which existed there well into the 20th century.

No regard whatever seems to have been taken to preserve the beauty spots or tree life. Wherever they had an outlet from the tunnel the debris was simply dumped down in huge mounds, and hundreds of trees were uprooted or covered up in Steanor Bottom Wood, Grim Wood and Sladen Wood.

Fred Jackson describes the human impact of this disregard for the environment.

"Even the meadow land belonging to the farm at Holme-Houses was used as a dumping ground and the farm rendered useless. At this time the Holme was farmed by a man named Old Crimmy (Crossley), his wife and their three sons. A tale is told that when the contractors for the tunnel began to cut out the sods and remove them from their meadow or Holme, they could hardly believe that anyone would be so degraded as to disturb their "bit o' land", which was sacred in their eyes. However the story was told at the time, that upon the old woman (Mrs Crossley) seeing the men actually cutting and wheeling the sods away to another place, she went back into the house, took to her bed, and died within a few days of a broken heart. The father and sons had to give up the farm and settle down to other work.

Their response is a credit to the resilience and adaptability of the locals at that time. Jimmy, the eldest son, became a hawker of 'flannel and stocking yarn' and spent the next twenty years going round a wide sweep of countryside seeking customers, often visiting the neighbourhood of Todmorden and Langfield, amusing them with his quaint up-dale speech and doing a fair amount of business because he sold at reasonable prices "a bit of as good flannel and stocking yarn as ever ony woman handled". Henry, the next brother, had been a soldier but took work at Stansfield Print Works. Joseph, the youngest, became a loom weaver at home and on Saturdays practised as the village barber and attended at the house of Mr. James Lord (th' old butcher) of Summit Inn, meeting his customers there."

The destruction wrought by the massive works involved in railway construction did not stop with the destruction of forests and the farming land. The railway line obliterated Ealees Manor House in Littleborough and made the oldest chapel in Littleborough, the 'Methodical Piazza' unusable owing to the noise and vibration from the railway (see chapter 15). At present the old chapel site is a scrap yard.

A popular and readable account of life in our locality in the 19th century, including the building of the Summit Tunnel, is to be found in the novel 'The

The entrance to Summit Tunnel portrayed by the artist A F Tait in 1845

World from Rough Stones' by Malcom MacDonald. In 1999 Allen Holt wrote a comprehensive and fascinating account of the construction of the Summit Railway tunnel.

The local people, aware of opportunities that had been opened up, were quick to see the potential of a 1000 or more navvies with a deal of money in their pockets, living in their area. Thus another interesting item of this time was a statement made in regard to the beginning of the co-operative movement. An old Smithy Nook resident (Mr Thomas Staresfield) always maintained that co-operatives started there and not in Rochdale. He said that during the railway era 1837-8, several of them joined together and took a house at Stoney-royd, bought the goods wholesale and sold them out retail to the members. He used to 'wax very indignant' when speaking about it, that Rochdale should claim the honour.

In chapter 15 the first developments leading to the co-operative movement are discussed and it is clear that there were many trials and initiatives years before the cutting of the Summit tunnel. The unique feature of the Rochdale initiative was the combination of objectives, physical organisation, dividend payment, ownership and management that they pioneered. It started as one among many but became the accepted role model for the whole co-operative movement.

CHAPTER TWELVE

THE NINETEENTH CENTURY

PART TWO: THE GROWTH OF NEW INDUSTRIES

Growth of Industry

The major earthworks and building needed to create new transport facilities caused serious damage to our local environment. On the positive side the activity created more jobs and stimulated the growth of a variety of new industries, as well as helping to confirm Littleborough as a suitable area with many advantages to offer to the rapidly expanding textile industry.

Unfortunately many of these new industries used chemicals and produced polluting waste products. With little regard for the future the waste was extensively dumped and the pollution found its way into the atmosphere, peoples homes and the local rivers,

The Stone Quarries

From the time of the Roman occupation there has been a spasmodic demand for the quarrying of local stone. A typical example was the demand for stone as our road system developed with the advent of Turnpike Trusts in the 18th century.

At the start of the 19th century local gritstone and sandstone were already in extensive use for building purposes and during the cutting of the canal in 1801-2 and even down to the time of the making of the Summit Tunnel, large numbers of men were employed.

In 1836 the Manchester to Leeds Railway Co. had begun construction; by 1837 and for a few years afterwards things were very busy. Great quantities of local stone were required for building Summit Tunnel and the quarries of the district were in full production. In addition to this, work was found for a large number of people as labourers. A quotation from Fred Jackson will illustrate the kind of work and the people involved.

"William Haigh, better known as Butty-o'-Reubins, worked one of the stone quarries at Smithy Nook at that time; he also kept a sheep farm at Slack in Calderbrook. He carried on an extensive business for many years, sending the stone by boat to Manchester and other places and had also a number of horses loading coal from Walsden to various firms in the district. He seems to have been a type of man more common in those days than at present. In addition to conducting the sheep farm and the quarry he had a thorough knowledge of cattle and sheep and was a large trader in horses. It may be of interest to mention some of the wages paid when these quarries were first started in the 18th century. The following is a copy of an old account:-

	s.	d.
Paid to John Dawson - 1 day's work	1	0
" " 4 men " " "	4	0
" " 4 men and ale	5	0
" " A Fielden - 3 day's work and horse	4	6
To Samuel Midgley, for hewing a stone trough and setting it	2	2

THE GROWTH OF NEW INDUSTRIES

A6033
TO WALSDEN

Line of Summit Tunnel

Rochdale Canal

Deanhead

Pennine Way

Slack

• Site of Chelburn Brickworks (Summit Brick)
• Snoddle Hill Quarries
Summit
Smithy Nook
• Puncbowl Lock Brick & Tile Works
Timbercliffe
Handle Hall
Calderbrook

A58
TO HALIFAX

White House Inn•

• Rock Nook Mill

Calderbrook Road

• Colliery

• Shore Hall

Halifax Road

• Wardle
Shore •
Colliery •

Pike House

Pennine Way

Gate House Colliery
Lydgate Valley (Water Gate)

Ebor Street

Quarry •

Humber
•High Peak

Red Lion & Taylor Terrace
Ben Healey Canal Bridge

Higher Windy Bank

Paddocks Head Colliery

LITTLEBOROUGH

• Ealees Valley

Dearnley

Cleggswood Colliery
Colliery

A58
TO ROCHDALE

Calliards

• Cleggswood
• Colliery
Whittaker

Smithy Bridge

Hollingworth Road

• Colliery

Brick Works

HOLLINGWORTH LAKE

Rochdale Canal

Wildhouse Lane

Rakewood
• Higher Booth Holtings

M62 JUNCTION 22

TO MILNROW

• Colliery

M62 JUNCTION 21

• Tunshill Colliery

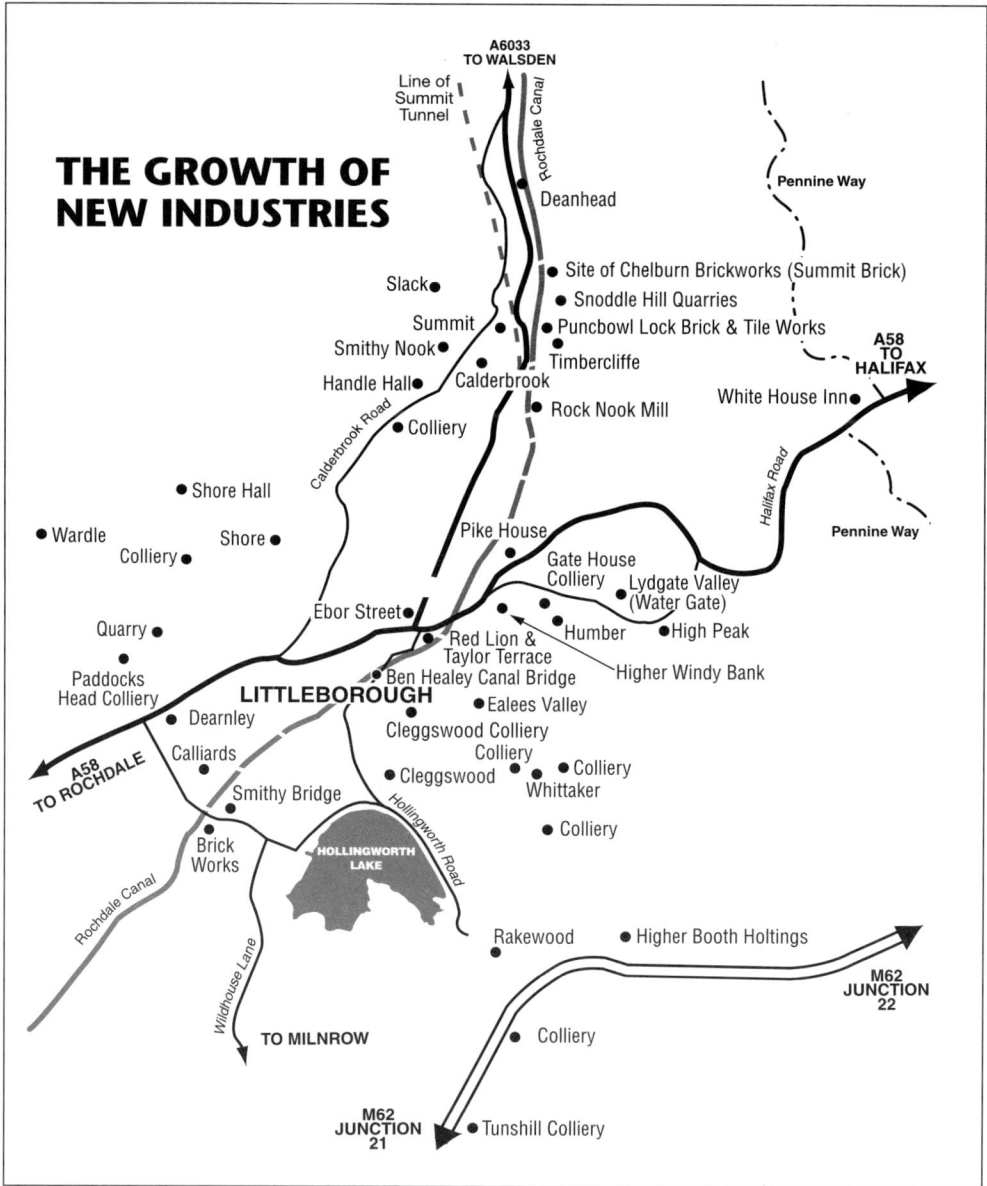

Owing to the widespread acceptance of brick in the building industry, the demand for stone gradually declined and the quarries practically ceased working early in the 20th century. As a result of the widespread quarrying which took place in the district, many quarries can now be found overgrown or re-used in some way.

Brick making and Potteries

In the 18th century we have the first examples of the use of bricks (which have survived) in Littleborough and the start of the diversification of traditional potters into the manufacture of earthenware drain pipes. By the mid-1800s these potters found themselves in an established industry as a result of reports by Poor Law Agencies, Royal Commissions and other enactments. The Sanitary Act (1866) and the Public Health Act (1875) boosted the new pottery activities, just as the brick-making industry had prospered from the increase in house building 50 years earlier. The brickmakers who saw the advantage of the two related trades being under one roof soon engaged the services of potters to expand into a combined business of brickmaking and pipe making, which became a major industry in Littleborough for 120 years.

In the early 1800's sixteen houses were built using clay bricks, on James Hill street. They were built for James Sladen, Clerk to the Church. At much the same time the Royal Oak coaching house and farm, together with their outbuildings, were constructed entirely with clay bricks. Since the first brickworks was established in Littleborough in 1846 it is probable that the bricks were made from clay found on the site and fired by the 'clamp kiln' system using itinerant brickmakers. The use of clay from building sites, to be made into bricks, continued for a considerable time after the establishment of brickworks throughout the Littleborough district.

For example, tenders for making bricks from clay found on building sites were requested by the Calliards Manufacturing Co. Ltd (founded 1859) and the Littleborough Manufacturing Co. Ltd (founded 1860). The Rochdale Property and General Finance Co. Ltd. a building company, in 1866 decided 'to make bricks from clay found on their sites'. In 1879 the trustees of the proposed new Catholic Church to be built at Featherstall requested permission from the local board for 'leave for the making of bricks on their site.'

Long before the first brickworks was established it was common knowledge that shales, clay and fireclay, the basic raw material of the brickmaker and potter, could be found in abundance in the Littleborough area. It was, for example, possible for a local contractor (Messrs Harding and Cropper) to bid for the 'firing of 23,000,000 bricks for the Summit Tunnel' at £47 per yard, 'but if they be allowed to make these bricks at Littleborough then they will deduct £1 per yard from the above prices'. The bid failed and the contract was awarded to John Stephenson.

The basic raw material of each brickmaker was mined in distinct geographical locations, each source supplied a specific brickworks. Snoddle Hill on the Chelburn Estate supplied the Chelburn Brickworks, Lydgate Valley mines supplied the Tetlow's brickworks, Whittaker Moor the Whittaker Fire Clay Works, Cleggswood Hill supplied the Walmsleys and later Hall & Rogers. The brickworks at Rake obtained their clays from under the Higher Windy Bank estate and the Humber Farm estate. The clays were found on the estates of many of the big local landowners, Newalls, Stotts, Peels, Deardens and Beswickes. All these landowners leased the right to mine clay to brickmakers for an annual rental, plus royalties, based on how much clay or minerals were extracted or on the quantity of items the brickmakers produced. The 'getting' of the clay was done by the brickmakers or through sub-contract for them. For example the Chelburn Brickworks, commonly known as Summit Brick Works, paid an annual rental of £76 per annum and royalties on coal, fire bricks, tile tubes, dried clay, ashlar, paving stone and other material. Raw materials were charged by the weight extracted, finished goods by the quantity made. Typical royalties varied from a few pence to 1s.6d for a number or weight of the category, as specified contractually. Some contracts were

The interior of the pipeworks at Starring situated behind Birch Hill Hospital.

much simpler (eg Tetlows, Hall & Rogers) only covering the right to mine the clay, with a rental and a royalty paid on the 'acres of clay extracted'. It was very common for leases to mine clay to be attached in a major lease to extract coal, often limited geographically to such materials found under named fields on the landowner's estate.

A number of different mining techniques were used to extract the shales, clay and fireclay which were found close to the surface in some areas and below the coal measures in others. The 6 feet bed of clay belonging to the Rochdale Property and General Finance Company Ltd. and the 15 feet thick bed of Calliards were extracted by open-cast methods whereas face or quarry methods were used to get the clay and shales from Snoddle Hill. Vertical shafts were driven down to the clay beds at Whittaker, while drift-mining techniques were used at the Lydgate Valley, Higher Windy Bank, Humber and Cleggswood estates.

The mined clay or other materials were usually transported from the workings to the brick or pottery works on small, rimless-wheeled trucks pulled on a tramway by men or horses. After the second World War electricity was introduced at the Chelburn brickworks. The trucks were hauled from the face to the works by an endless cable driven by an electric motor. The Cleggswood clay mines had their trucks lowered down and hauled back up the steep hillside by an endless chain driven by a steam engine. The clay in this case was loaded onto barges from a staith adjoining Ben Healey Canal Bridge and transported to the brickworks at Smithy Bridge about a mile away.

The variety of clay-based goods manufactured covered a full range of bricks including: commons, engineering, facings, stable blocks and glazed bricks for internal and external use. The sanitary-tube makers produced all sizes of drain pipes and plain pipes with butt joints, or later, collared joints, all with a salt-glazed finish. Traps, gullies and other sanitary salt glazed ware were produced along with chimney pots, seating blocks, undertiles, under drains, ventilators, copings and other salt glazed items.

All these products were fired in circular 'bee-hive type' kilns. The walls of the kiln were brick and from 3 to 5 feet thick, the kiln being some 25 feet in diameter. They were bound by strong iron bands to prevent them exploding due to the heat and had a life expectancy of some 25 years.

The 'green' bricks or sanitary goods were carefully stacked into them. The entrance was sealed off and fires lit at various points round their perimeter with the updraft circulating around the kiln. Salt was scattered into the kiln and it vapourised in the heat, causing a glaze to form on the materials being fired.

Hall and Rogers had seven kilns, Tetlows had five, the Whittaker Fire Clay works had only one. Not all the kilns could be in use at any one time as it took time to cool, unload and load again. The number of kilns depended on the type of business and the demand. The Chelburn Works was the exception as it had a twelve chamber Hoffman kiln.

The arrival of specialised 'brickworks' was a response to the enormous demand, the discovery of large beds of clay and the new ability to distribute the fire bricks cheaply to a much larger market, by improved roads, canals and the railway system.

Many of these brickworks have left physical and/or documented evidence of their existence including the following list of major brickworks, with their start dates.

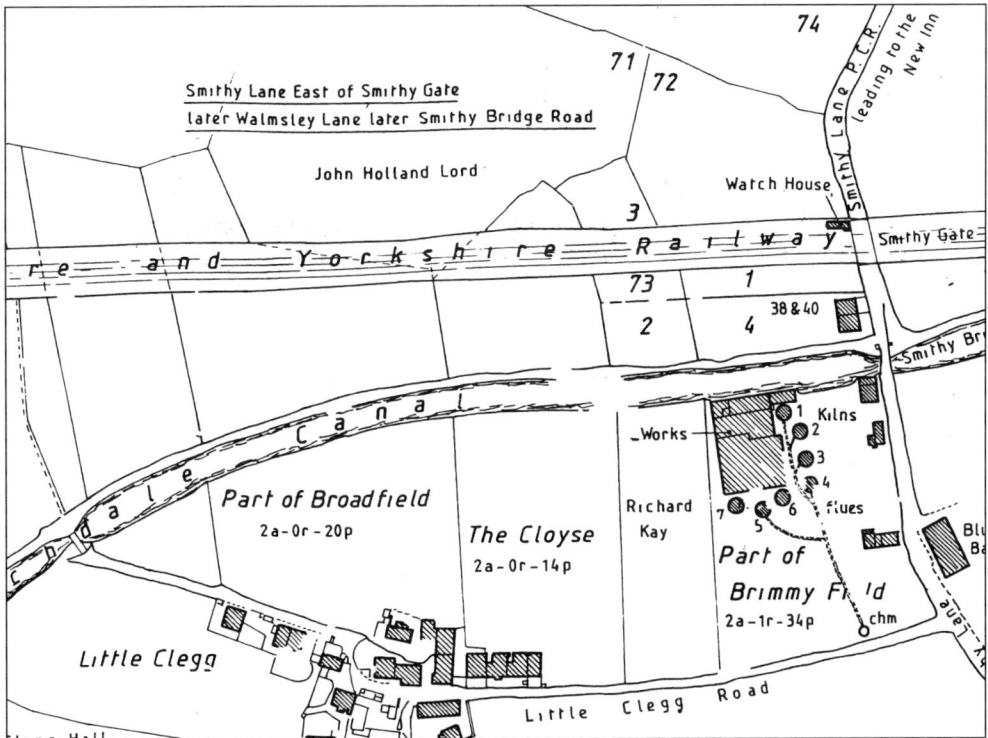

Hall & Rogers land and buildings at Smithy Bridge in 1866

1846. Smithy Bridge Fire Brick and Sanitary Tube works
     (Walmsleys and later Hall and Rogers)
1851. Whittaker Fire Clay works
1852. Punchbowl Lock, Brick and Tile works
     (Honour Mathews and later John Tetlow)
1864. Chelburn Brick works (Summit brick works)
1864. The Rake Brick and Tile works
1864. The Rochdale Property and General Finance Co. Ltd

Others are only known today by a short entry in a trade directory, an advertisement or a notice of auction including:

Smithy Bridge Brick Company
John Hall and Sons, Stubley
Crabtrees, Whitelees
Ireland Buckley & Co., Swainroyd
Dearnley Brick and Tile
John Williams, Whitelees
Robert Leach and Son

(Dearnley Brick and Tile works is interesting as there is ample evidence of its existence on the ground near Birch Hill Hospital, but unfortunately no documentation). Each company has its story but two will illustrate the atmosphere of the time.

Punchbowl Lock, Brick and Tile works.

The founder of this company was Honour Matthews, second son of Robert Matthews, the Engineer to the Rochdale Canal Company. He had previously been employed as a sub-contractor at the New Works Reservoirs, but after these were completed, he settled at Summit. He took a piece of land on the opposite side of the canal to 'King's Shed' on the Timbercliffe estate and began to erect a brick and tile works in 1852. He carried on the business of brick and tile manufacturing with success for five years and then disposed of it in 1857 to Mr. John Tetlow, who under the title of J. Tetlow & Sons, Fire Brick and Sanitary Tube Manufacturer (Castleton) developed the business of drain pipe making and carried it on very successfully for a good many years. He laid a tramway from the works at Summit, skirting the hillside, to the Lower Coal measures at Green Vale and Sladen Mill, worked the under clay for drain pipe making and utilised the coal above it for heating and drying. John Tetlow died in 1883 of 'apoplexy convulsions' and as this was a family business he was replaced by his son John. The business appeared to prosper until in 1898 when John was found guilty of defrauding Manchester City Council of some £5000 over a period of 10 years. He went to jail for 3 years. Again the family stepped in but gradually, as the competition became more keen and probably better controlled, the heavy cost of transporting the clay and coal was cited as the reason for their works being unable to compete with other firms in more favourable circumstances. The business was sold to Fothergill and Harvey in 1911 along with adjoining land, a farm and a house on the Timbercliffe estate.

For a good many years, Mr. Gordon Harvey supported and financed a series of experiments to develop a new material for building purposes. The development work and the machine to make the blocks was, according to his son, the work of William

Gilbody. The resulting material was made into blocks and faced with concrete to make 'clinker building blocks'. Part of the old pottery buildings was pulled down, and the rest were used as places for the making of the new blocks.

Fred Jackson appeared to approve of his patron's achievement, though some might dispute its aesthetic effect today:

"I think it can be claimed that the blocks have been proved to be fairly successful. A good many flats and houses have been and are being erected on the Timbercliffe estate from this material and seem to be withstanding the effects of our rigorous climate very well. They have converted this dismal looking hillside, almost into a thing of beauty, visible from almost every part of the district, the white block showing up very well against the dark background of the hill."

Another initiative supported by Gordon Harvey was the proposed creation of a housing estate at Deanhead, Littleborough, which was to include building on both sides of the Todmorden road. This scheme was never completed and today there are two rows of houses on the canal side. The external walls are constructed of brick with a render finish but the internal walls use the new blocks. The layout and house design was done by architects under the guidance of Harvey; the mullioned windows and some ornate decoration around the doors are seen as an attempt to fit in with local traditional building styles. At the time of the announcement of the new estate the most important innovation claimed was that it would include the construction of bungalows suitable for elderly retired workers.

Another use of the new blocks locally was in a housing development on Blackstone Edge old road. This was financed by Sir Alfred Law who called it High Peak after his parliamentary constituency in Derbyshire. The houses were built by W Gilbody, on the site of the old 'Oil Mill'. The front elevation used the available stone after the mill was demolished, the rear of the houses being built with the new blocks.

It is interesting to note that by the Littleborough Lower Lock near the town centre, off Halifax Road, is a third group of houses called Taylor Terrace. These were built in 1870, by E Taylor and Co. (Ebor Street), a local firm. The man-made blocks used in their construction, at this early date, make these houses pioneer examples of the use of artificial blocks as a building material. This firm appears to have been developed by enterprising people with flair. For example the first car owned in Littleborough was said to have belonged to Edward Taylor. The firm also got the contract to extend Victoria Station, Manchester to give it the fine facade we see today.

The valley viewed from Dean Head.

The original mill buildings on the sites of the present houses at High Peak.

Taylor Terrace, alongside the canal.

The brickwork's quarry at Chelburn.

Chelburn Brickworks

In 1864 the Rochdale Brick and Tile Company Ltd was formed by a party of Rochdale gentlemen and a forty four acre site was acquired at Chelburn, behind the Summit Inn. Their business was fire brick and sanitary tube manufacture. Each brick carried the word 'Summit'.

On this site there was a very large supply of raw material close to hand, suitable for brick making. It was dug from Snoddle Hill, loaded in waggons and carried direct to the works where patent machinery fine ground, shaped and pressed it into the various forms required. In the early days the machinery was driven by a water wheel, but later a steam engine was substituted. When the building trade was brisk, enormous quantities of bricks were made. In 1889 the company went into liquidation and was sold at auction to the Brighouse Brick and Tile Company. This was bought in 1935 by the Rochdale Federated Brick company and thus the brickworks was merged in a much bigger group. Finally it was sold on to T H Halsall and Sons Ltd. of Bury who eventually closed the works in 1973. The 103 manufacturing years at the Chelburn Works is the longest period of brickmaking in one location in Littleborough. The works have now been demolished apart from a few foundations and one small structure said to be part of the gatehouse.

The brickmaking industry has disappeared after a life of 120 years. The aftermath is still visible; the Mathews & Tetlow brickworks are a derelict site on the hillside at Timbercliffe and their canal wharf, fronting the dereliction, can be found on the Timbercliffe side of Punch-bowl Lock. An overgrown quarry can be seen on the hills on the Summit side of Timbercliffe whilst the faint line of the tramway running from the Lydgate Valley to Punchbowl Lock is also visible at the rear of Rock Nook Mill. The huge scar on the side of Snoddle Hill, Chelburn, caused by quarry workings, is the legacy of the brickmaking carried out at the Chelburn Brickworks. Fortunately, apart from mounds of shale, all traces of most of the other brickworks have disappeared, either overgrown by nature or cleaned up during the removal of all the old residues, usually during the levelling of the sites for redevelopment.

Coal Mining

Coal mining had been a 'cottage industry' around Littleborough since Elizabethan times. The moors and hills are riddled with small coal pits and open-cast workings. The coal mining was often carried out by digging into the seams of coal that outcrop along the hillsides and some 300 such sites have been located around Littleborough.

In the early 1800s commercial mining was being undertaken on Cleggswood Hill; by the mid-1800s collieries were producing coal from some 16 sites scattered throughout the district.

Coal Beds in the Littleborough area

There were seven beds, seams or veins of coal worked locally. Each was identified by a special name: The Lower Mountain mine, Inch mine, Six Inch mine, Bullion mine or Upper Foot mine, Bassy mine or the Yard mine or Dirty Yard mine, Lower Foot mine or Little mine and the Upper Foot mine or Mountain mine or Forty Yard mine. There were a number of other names used from time to time.

The thickness and quality of the coal varied. The Inch mine and the Six Inch mine had little economic value but they were mined because they overlaid rich beds of fire clay which had an average thickness of 2 to 3 feet. The Bassy mine at Rakewood comprised coal and coaly shale justifying its name Dirty Yard mine. The Bullion mine, on average 12 inches thick, was worked at Shore and Calderbrook. It was remarkable for 'coal balls' or 'bullions' embedded in the coal seam. The bullions contained perfectly preserved delicate plant tissues which allowed microscopic examination of the plant structure. One bullion obtained from a mine at Shore was several feet in diameter and the estimated weight was nearly two tons.

The most commercially viable seams, with an average thickness of 24 inches to 40 inches, were the Mountain mines and the Foot mines and they were worked from collieries on Whittaker Moor, Hollingworth, Cleggswood, Dearnley Holme, Dearnley, Calderbrook and Lydgate. There were great variations in the depth of the seam below ground level. Some of the seams could be accessed by 'breast eyes' shafts driven into the hillside, others had to be got by vertical shafts. Paddock Head mine-shaft at Dearnley was only 30 feet vertically to reach the Upper Mountain mine but the shaft at the nearby Dearnley Cote went down 252 feet to reach the Lower Mountain mine. By comparison, when the Gatehouse Colliery exhausted the Upper Mountain mine, it went down a further 324 feet to reach the Lower Mountain mine. The extent of the seams in an active mine was enormous. In 1827 the mine under the Cleggswood Estate was offered for sale on the basis of being 500 acres in extent. It was claimed to be producing 30 to 40 tons of coal per day with a potential for 100 tons per day. The mine was on offer for sale again in 1852 and the Mountain mine was said to be over 400 acres in extent and that 'there yet remain to be got about 210 statute acres of this valuable and excellent coal'. In 1852 the Upper Bed or Three Quarters mine was offered for sale by auction. The coal lay under the Hollingworth Estate, a farm and eight fields which were part of the Thornhill Estate and some land that belonged to the Beswicke family. Once again the available coal was measured in hundreds of acres.

The life of a local miner

Sons followed their fathers into mining because of economic reasons. A miner was paid for coal delivered to the pit head. From his wages he had to pay a 'waggoner', a young boy who hauled the coal from the face to the pit head. The cheapest way was to use your own children. In the 1851 census John Whipp, miner, had four sons aged 20, 18, 11 & 9 who were also miners. Of 37 miners in Blatchinworth 29 were aged 15 to 69 and 8 miners were between 10 and 14 years of age. Only ten years before, a survey identified at least three children aged seven or eight working as thrutchers. A thrutcher was a child who pushed at the back of the waggon if it was too heavy to be pulled by one child at the front.

Due to the modest thickness of the seams of coal the miners often had to work in cramped and crowded conditions. In the more substantial seams they could work knelt down on one or both knees with their torso bent forward to pick at the face of the seam. When the seam was only 18 or 20 inches thick the miner had to sit down with one leg tucked under the other, his torso bent fully forward until it rested on his thigh, while he picked at the coal face. Where coal faces were even thinner the miner lay on one side and picked along the face of the seam.

Once down the mine, the miner would stay until the end of a shift or until he had earned enough money; some started at 5 or 6 am and did not come back up until 7 or 8 pm. For months each year some miners never saw daylight during a working day.

To get the coal from the face to the pit head a waggoner was employed to haul the excavated coal in a tub or basket running on wheels or sleds. The tunnel they used for hauling was cut to the minimum height possible. As miners only got paid for good coal they became very adept at extracting coal with a minimum content of clay or stones. A recently exposed mine at Chelburn showed a seam of coal about 2'6" deep, overlaid by rock and sitting on a bed of clay. The miner had extracted the coal only, not an inch above or below.

Miners' pay

In Littleborough the miners were paid by the 'score', which was an agreed number of filled tubs between 20 & 26. The variation was to allow for adjustment, based on the amount of rock and other foreign matter in the tub. If the tubs were 'stone free' the number of tubs the miner needed to fill was lower. A filled tub would weigh about 2 cwt. In 1858 the miners at Gatehouse Colliery went on strike for an increase of 8d per score; they were being paid 7/6 a score for steam coal and 8/6 per score for household coal. In this instance the miners won their increase. In 1874 the Hollingworth Colliery Co. was in dispute with its miners who handed out a broadsheet claiming:

Miner's pay	18/9 per day (cost of candles to be borne by miner)
waggoner	4/0 per day plus 1/- a week for private purposes
Work achieved	20 tubs per day of at least 50 cwt in weight.

At the Whittaker colliery miners were paid 5/- per yard for driving tunnels 2'6" wide and 3' high. An 8' diameter shaft cost 22/- per yard and a 9' diameter shaft 26/- per yard. A vent shaft 5' wide cost 15/- per yard.

Hazards of mining

The miner's life was dangerous and unhealthy. The coal dust, breathing stale air and smoke from the fires lit to circulate the air, all lead to asthma and other respiratory complaints. There was the hazard of working in a confined space with only the flickering flame of a candle. You could be hit by a pick, caught by a blow from a shovel, fingers and feet could be trapped under lumps of coal or under the wheels or sleds of the tubs. One Thomas Dearden had both his legs broken, his face burnt and his fingers nearly severed during his time as a miner. In later life he suffered from fits and had surgery for cancers.

The miner also faced the dangers of roof falls and explosions caused by fire damp. Such accidents were so common-place that they only got a line or two in the newspapers.

Feb. 1860 D. Butterworth aged 13 killed in an explosion at Cleggswood Colliery.

Aug. 1860 Three men burned, one seriously, at Cleggswood Colliery.

Mar. 1862 Five men burned, two seriously, at Cleggswood Colliery.

Nov. 1868 H. Butterworth killed by collapse of unpropped roof at Cleggswood Colliery.

The accidents are reported but there is no follow up or coroner's inquest, neither do there appear to have been any prosecutions for mining accidents, whatever the cause.

The only exception was an accident that occurred in October 1860 at the Gatehouse Colliery. Three men with a boy were descending the deep shaft when the cage caught on a snag and the three men were thrown 200 feet down the shaft. The boy, James Lee, was thrown from the cage into a worked out seam of coal, some 120' below ground level. The three falling to the bottom all died, one instantly the other two soon after. At the inquest the verdict of accidental death was returned and the three miners were buried in a communal grave in the Littleborough Parish Church graveyard.

Leases for coal mining

In the early days mining rights were always contentious though officially they belonged to the Lord of the Manor in most cases. As the medieval principles of rights and duties declined, the power to negotiate mining rights generally lay with the owner of the land.

In March 1845 a typical lease at the time was negotiated by Maria Beswicke of Pike House along with other trustees, for the benefit of her infant daughter. This lease granted to Matthew and John Joblin, coalminers from Cliviger and John Rhodes, a coal miner from Todmorden, the rights and privileges for 14 years to get coal from 'Mine or mines, veins or beds of coal or cannel lying under Pike House, Lightowlers, Kidhills, Swainroyd, Water Gate and Pike House High Field' (Cannel was a dull smoky coal with a bright flame, the name being an abbreviation of candle coal).

In another lease dated July 1854 relatives of the Stotts of Bent House, including a book-keeper, an infant, an agent and a spinster, authorised a lease to a group comprising a Surrey merchant, a Rochdale widow, a cotton manufacturer, a bleacher and a calico printer giving them the rights for 14 years 'of getting coal or cannel of the Mountain or Three Quarter mines worked from Pikehouse Colliery and lying under the land of the Bent House Estate commonly known as the Two Heights and the Back Heights (15 acres).' Under the terms of the lease it was surrendered in July 1859 because the beds of coal at the Pike House Colliery were worked out. The interest here is that the mine was still a viable proposition because of the beds of clay and in 1877 one of the original trustees Edward Chadwick, of Rochdale, an agent, leased essentially the same workings to John Tetlow, Firebrick Maker and Sanitary Tube Manufacturer. The lease was for 15 years to extract coal and clay but was extended and finally terminated by the Tetlows in 1893.

In general the industry developed leases with many standard conditions such as defining the extent of the mining and where coal may not be mined. Such exclusions included specified distances from any building and sometimes a clause relating to land 'under the reservoir, drains, tunnels, banks, lands and works of the Rochdale Canal Company'. Where no such clause existed the canal company found itself having to pay mining companies to shore up areas to avoid subsidence. Other standard conditions related to compensation to farmers for loss of pasturage, sufficient pillars of coal to be left to support the land drains, rivers to be kept clear of contamination, current plans of workings to be kept available, access for the landowner's agent to inspect the workings at any time, permission for 'hovels and shacks' to be built for workmen and staithes and drying bays for materials.

Royalty payments were varied but the annual rental was paid, whether coal or clay was extracted or not. Early royalties were for horse loads and other measures but later contracts revolved round a royalty on the number of tubs of a specified capacity and content that were extracted.

Colliery Railways

In Littleborough colliery railways preceded passenger transport. One example was the line from Tunshill Colliery down to Hollingworth Lake. Cleggs Mill at Shore mined its own coal and Cleggswood Colliery close to Littleborough Station had an endless chain of wagons driven by a steam engine. The tramway ran down the hill between some terraced houses, across a road to reach a wharf and the barges on the Rochdale canal

Decline of the coal industry

By the 1870s the competition from other coal fields in Lancashire and Yorkshire, their better quality coal being brought into Littleborough by the canal and then the railway, was increasing the problem that many local coal seams were exhausted. The result was that by the 1880s local collieries, both large and small, began to close down. The remaining locally-mined coal was poor quality and the lack of a significant financial return made serious mining a marginal operation. By the 1890s, apart from one or two survivors (including Cleggswood colliery), mining for coal in the Littleborough district ceased. An alternative use for one old mine was found when Holme Pit mine was totally flooded. Its water was pumped to the railway to be picked up by passing high-speed trains.

There was the whiff of revival in 1913 when the Alderbank colliery Co of Wardle announced the discovery of a rich new seam near Hollingworth road. They went as far as getting approval for a tramway line from the Littleborough Urban District Council but proceeded no further.

There is relatively little surface evidence of all the local mining activity. For example, there are coal waste tips, now planted over, which remain in the Ealees Valley which are only prominent now in periods of dry weather. The stone waggon way for coal carts can still be seen on the track outside Old Mill cottage at the entrance to the Ealees valley. A walk from above Shore Hall to the White House at Blackstone Edge, or over to Wardle will take you past dozens of old waste heaps left over from drift (breast eye shafts) mining although the shafts have long since collapsed and been overgrown.

Coal Factors and Coal Merchants

The coal industry led to the creation of a number of associated industries including coal merchants who were destined to survive long after coal mining had ceased.

The family business of Emanuel Shackleton Ltd was established in 1869 by Susannah Shackleton of Summit who was a widow with three sons; Emanuel, Benjamin and Ebenezar and a daughter Susannah. The premises were at 2 Halifax Road and consisted of office accommodation, coach house, stables and a large overhead loft for the storage of hay, straw and other materials. The sign on the outside of the building read:

Susannah Shackleton, Dealer in Coal, Coke, Cannel, Hay, Straw etc. Cab Proprietor, Furniture Remover, Wedding Equipages, Dog carts, Wagonettes and Funeral Carriages etc. on hire.

The horse drawn wagonette trips to Hardcastle Craggs at Hebden Bridge were a very popular outing.

Two of the sons and the daughter worked with their mother but Benjamin emigrated to Canada. When the mother died in 1881 she left the business to her son Emanuel and daughter Susannah, the remaining two sons being given the handsome sum of £150 each. The business continued to flourish and Emanuel at the end of the century brought two of Ebenezar's sons into it. These young men were later to become Managing Director and Director Secretary of the company. They built up the wholesale side of the business by obtaining the agency for Carlton Main Quarries in Yorkshire and then supplying coal to various Co-operatives and Coal Merchants throughout Lancashire. By 1930 the company had finished with horse drawn vehicles and the sale of hay and straw. The office had grown and the coach house had become a garage. In 1932 John and Margaret Shackleton joined the company. In 1939 John William Booth who had joined the company in the 1920s as salesman on the wholesale side of the business was made a director and some ten years later became Managing Director. When the Government nationalised the Coal Industry the company lost the agency of the Carlton Main Collieries, the share capital was reduced and the company became Emanuel Shackleton (1950) Ltd.

The company continued in business under John Shackleton with the help of his wife Amy. As Littleborough turned over to smokeless fuel and other forms of heating the business dwindled. In 1986 the two remaining directors being in their late 70s decided to close the company that had been so much a part of the family life. The premises at 2 Halifax Road were later demolished to allow the road to be widened.

Print and Dye Works

The scale of working varied enormously and at any time reflected the general state of the textile industry. For example around 1837 Burgess and Townsend started a print and dye works at Calderbrook. In their day the firm could only print one colour at a time on the machine, so that for every separate figure the copper roller had to be changed and the piece run through again. In those days a duty was levied on the printed piece ranging from four to five shillings, the gauger having to attend and affix the Government stamp on every piece, or in default a heavy fine was inflicted on the printers.

Once again we turn to Fred Jackson to get the human story and a flavour of the local humour at the time.

" Townsend had been living at Summit for some time and had been carrying out the business of dyeing and finishing in a small way, at a house there. Like almost everybody else at that time Townsend had a bye-name, being known as "Pinkie Joe". "Pinkie Joe" was a regular attendant at Smithy Nook Chapel as long as he remained in the village, but he had ambition in life, and after a few years removed to Glasgow, where he became a very successful man. (Similar print and dye works were set up all over our district and the less acceptable side of the story was the frequently very unhealthy working conditions and the degree of pollution of our waterways.)

A tale is told of two Manchester men who came to work at the Calderbrook print works at this time. They lodged in the village with the elderly maiden ladies named 'Moll' and 'Sall', probably Mary and Sarah when they got their Sunday names. One day at breakfast time the lodgers ordered 'frog-i'th-hole pudding' for dinner. When at home they usually had them made with beef steak rolled up inside the pastry wrapped in a cloth and boiled. The sisters not being well acquainted with the art of making such puddings or of town ways, yet without questioning, started off in search of 'frogs' in the meadows behind Handle Hall, but when it was nearly noon they had to go home with only one live frog, which was duly enclosed in the lid and boiled. Then when dinner time came there were great lamentations from the sisters that they had only been able to find one frog. Needless to say the pudding was not eaten.

Another tale told of these two sisters was that they invited a number of friends to a 'tay and coffee do'. Tea and coffee were a rarity in Smithy Nook at this time, but someone had presented them with half a pound of each. This was first brewed and then the liquid was poured down 'th' sink', the tea leaves and coffee grains being set to eat, with salt and pepper, to bread and butter, with milk to drink. Of course, 'cawbruck lasses' are a lot sharper to-day than they were at that time."

Boat Building

From 1820 Job Cogswell and Company were boat masters, repairers and general carriers by water, having graving (graving; to clean and apply a coating of pitch to the bottom of a vessel) docks at Durn and carrying on an extensive business built up after the opening of the canal. At this time they occupied the 'Red Lion' on the Halifax Road, not as a public house or inn, but for the accommodation of the men and horses in their service, the place being convenient for a depot, lying near the Rochdale canal and dockyards. During the time they occupied the house and stabling they had to pay the licence so that the owner, Mr. Beswicke-Royds, would not suffer loss by its lapse in the event of their giving up the premises. Cogswell also used a wharf at Richard Street, Rochdale. He had, at various times, very large debts with the Rochdale Canal Company and many of his 'repairs' appeared to be related to damage caused by his own boats.

There was also a shipwright in Littleborough, called William Banks, who was the licensed publican at the Sloop Inn, Durn (1823-43). Banks had a graving dock at Durn and must have known Cogswell.

Job Cogswell formed a partnership with a man called Thornton in 1824 and he died in 1829. Mrs Cogswell moved to Rochdale, the business declined and in 1843 the Red Lion became a public house again. The first publican to get a licence, in 1843, was William Banks, who continued his boat building at Durn graving dock. This dock is shown on the 1851 O.S. map (surveyed 1847 - 48).

The large boat yards, docks and warehouses were subsequently converted into an iron foundry and yards conducted by Joseph Schofield and Company, under which name it was still trading in the 1930s - although it had been bought by Mr. John O. Hey.

The industrial tradition at Ealees, remarked on earlier, was to continue with its important share in the rise of the textile industry. It is also interesting to observe the growth and viability of a set of well-established small industries which grew up in the relatively remote area of Rakewood, which is much less favoured in size and was for a long time only served by an earth road. From early years it handled textile waste and later flour and other foodstuffs. Small units did various finishing activities in woollens and blankets and later developed into handling modern textile mixes and man-made fibres. It also had a tannery nearby at Booth Hollins. This mixed economy remained viable until the 20th century.

Summary of the environmental effects of development on Littleborough

The canal, the road and the railway, all great advances in their own right, were also the essential infrastructure of an industrial revolution which finally resulted in a huge assault on our environment. In Littleborough, it was brought about by the growth of large-scale factory based manufacture of textiles and a wide range of associated supporting activities, some of which have been covered in this chapter. We must now look at developments which were to have an enormous effect on every aspect of life in Littleborough.

The Canal at Ealees and Durn with Frankfort and Uber Mills about 1905.

CHAPTER THIRTEEN

THE NINETEENTH CENTURY

PART THREE: THE TEXTILE INDUSTRY (1800 - 1850)

This chapter starts to record what is probably the single biggest event in Littleborough's history, the growth of the textile industry. It includes both the woollen industry and the subsequent dominance of cotton as the basic fibre.

Hand Loom Weaving

At the start of the nineteenth century the principal industrial occupation of the local people was hand-loom weaving of wool sometimes combined with agriculture. The grazing of sheep focussed on the upland communities such as Whittaker and the most common sheep breeds were semi-wild Lonks and Gritstones. A large number of the houses were custom built 'loom houses' of the type described in Chapter 12 and they were often part of the system of 'putting out' warp and weft to be woven into cloth. This same work pattern came to be associated with cotton rather later. The dyeing of these goods was done locally.

One location was the site which is now the 'Dyers' Arms' on Whitelees Road. Parts of the old dyeing building can still be seen behind the pub. Travis (1890) gives some

Landlord William Taylor and his horse and cart outside the Dyers Arms dressed for the wartime appeal 1915.

detail not only about the history of this site, but also a rare glimpse of the position of women in a male dominated society. The Dearnley Colliery company had considerable workings beneath Whitelees Road and caused subsidence whilst working for coal. The properties above 'gave way'. Mrs Taylor had inherited these properties and sued for damages and the case must have been uncontestable as the company paid £60 with no defence. Mrs Taylor immediately repaired the buildings and converted two of the dwelling houses 'into six cottages'. The three storey bay of one part of the property had been the place of work of 'a job dyer' so she turned it into a beer house under the name The Dyers Arms'. Travis goes on to record that 'Mrs Taylor went on to improve her wordly advantages greatly for the benefit of her children'.

If any local printing was required, usually on calico (coarse cotton), it would go to Burgess and Townsend's Stansfield Print Works at Calderbrook.

The older communities on the sides of the valleys have nearly always been in the fortunate position that when one staple trade of the district began to decline another took its place. Some little time after the Old Road had been made in 1795, hand-loom cotton weaving was introduced and by the 1820s it had replaced wool as the staple trade of the district.

The introduction of cotton

The spinning and weaving of woollen goods had been carried on for several generations before this time; indeed, every farmhouse of any pretension at all had its spinning wheel and distaff for the women and at least one hand loom for the men. Cotton was an innovation and it was at White Slack farm, lying on the hills between Reddyshore Scout and Allescholes, that cotton was first made into calico on a hand loom in the Littleborough district. It is said that people came in droves to witness the process of making weft and warp into cotton goods. It must have been a very primitive affair, for we are told that the weaver threw the ball of weft between the threads of the warp with one hand and caught it with the other, but improvements were soon made, and hand-loom weaving spread rapidly. One of these improvements was the hand picker (the part of the loom that casts the shuttle), introduced by Mr James Fielden of Walsden, who made the first while sitting at his loom from a flat piece of wood and small pieces of half-tanned leather. These he produced with his pocket knife and a borer of some sort, they were sold in the grocers shops at three half-pence per pair. Under the title of Fielden and Holt this firm was still in existence as picker makers in the 20th century.

Putters out

The chief difficulty of the hand-loom weaver for a long time was the supply of warp and weft, for it took at least six or eight hand spinners to keep one weaver going and considerable time was lost in getting sufficient yarn to keep the loom at work. This led to the introduction of the 'middle men' or 'putters out', as they were called. Fred Jackson picks up the story

"These men made it their business to go around to the various houses where spinning operations were carried on, buy up the spun yarn and then "put it out" to hand-loom weavers to be made into calico, at a price agreed upon between the two. Smithy Nook for example, was very fortunate in this respect, for it was at this time that

Joshua Fielden (which later became the firm of Fielden Bros., of Waterside, Todmorden) began a connection with Smithy Nook, which was to continue for nearly 30 years, until hand-loom weaving was superseded by the power loom.

In 1782 Joshua Fielden and his family were living at Edge End Farm in Todmorden and were part farmers and part cloth-makers, shearing their own sheep, spinning and weaving the wool and keeping one or two hand-looms constantly at work. When the pieces were finished, Old Joshua would set off for Halifax market, carrying his goods on his back. Soon after this time he removed to Laneside (afterwards re-named Waterside) and there occupied three small cottages, in one of which he and his family lived and in the other two he and his sons worked at their spinning and weaving. They carried woollen spinning and weaving on at this place for a few years and then came the era of cotton weaving. No doubt they would be continually hearing the complaints of the cotton weavers about their difficulty in getting sufficient cotton weft and warp to keep the hand looms going. They saw a way of supplying them and profiting themselves at the same time, so they changed from spinning and weaving woollen and in 1787 the first cotton was delivered at Laneside and two pairs of hand mules were installed in one of the cottages. At first the preparation of the cotton and the spinning was still carried on by the family, but as the business expanded he built a small mill close to the cottages. In the new mill there was one willow, two single beater scutchers, ten small carding engines and 49 dozen 'throstles' and 'jennies' and winding and warping for them. He had a steam engine of 16 horse power in addition to a water wheel. He carried this business on, supplying warp and weft to hundreds of hand-loom weavers at Smithy Nook and other local communities, until 1827, when power-looms were introduced. As a 'doffer' at Waterside Mill well over 65 years ago, I remember that we doffers spent many happy hours with these old spinning jennies and 'Bobbin Jones' in the old lumber room at Waterside, when we were supposed to have been better employed.

In 1826, when hand-loom weaving was at its best, the weavers were getting 2s.6d. per cut for weaving 'narrow cally' and in 1837 those few who were still employed in that class of work were only receiving sixpence per cut. The price had gradually dwindled down to this figure in the ten years from 1827, when power looms were introduced. When it was reported that there had been a good market, they were laid on a penny or two pence per cut for a few weeks: then when there was a bad market 'th' pool daan' came on again.

For a good many years after this time a few of the hand-loom weavers kept at their looms, but they had a hard time of it and only managed to eke out a bare existence. They did not take kindly to the power-loom and one can understand what it meant for these men. With his hand-loom in his own home, he had perfect freedom with his weaving. If his work got too monotonous, he could take a turn in his garden, while one of the sons could keep the loom going. He could work either early or late, as he felt inclined and no one could say him nay. No wonder that a new generation of weavers had to spring up before Lancashire people took kindly to mill life.

At the beginning of Joshua and Thomas Fielden's connection with Smithy Nook and for a number of years afterwards they had a cottage opposite Smithy Nook Chapel, where the weft and warp brought from Waterside was given out to the hand-loom weavers each week and the 'cally cuts' which had been woven were received at the same place. For many years, it is said, Thomas Fielden carried the yarn from Waterside to Smithy Nook, received the 'cally' and carried it forward to Manchester Market. Then a man named John Schofield used to fetch the yarn and take the cally in a small hand truck to Waterside, but afterwards, as the business increased, they took the old three-storeyed house at Calf Holes and installed a man called Bob-o'-Jamies' to receive the cloth (finished calico) and give out the warp and weft for them.

During the thirty years the Fielden family were connected with Smithy Nook, many tales were told of their generous acts to their employees and their help in various ways for the improvement of the conditions under which they lived. Not the least of these was the help and encouragement given in the building of Smithy Nook Chapel."

(John Fielden with his three brothers made the largest fortune achieved in the cotton industry before the American Civil war (circa £700,000). From 1824 they shifted their capital from manufacturing to the export/import trade with north and south America.)

The whole 'putting out' system worked because the rudimentary raw material was not very valuable, demand for the processed product was relatively stable and there was abundant labour. The theft of cloth and finished material was always a serious problem in outwork and figured in the argument for factory production.

Hand-loom weaving was still very good in 1824 (when the new road was built) and continued so till 1837. The houses put up along the new roads were all of the traditional type that is, with a large number of narrow windows, to give plenty of light in the weaving chamber. These houses are easily recognised in the older parts of our area owing to a large number of these windows having been walled up to turn weaving chambers into bedrooms. It is appropriate that Fred should sum up the hand-loom weavers, as the last generation were the same age as his parents and their friends and he knew them well:

" On the whole these hand-loom weavers were a fine body of men. Hard times and coarse food fell to their lot pretty frequently. When trade was bad in these days there was no Lloyd George or unemployment insurances and no benevolent funds to fall back on. Only occasionally could they afford to buy a newspaper and with the exception of the Bible or Bunyan's 'Pilgrims Progress', very few books came their way, and yet we owe a good many of the liberties, both in religious and political matters which we possess today, to the work of these men. Many of them rose to distinction as botanists and geologists, for a good many of them were great lovers of nature. They were of the gradely, self-reliant, independent type of Lancashire man."

Power-loom weaving

The first use of power came from harnessing horses but the first large factories ran on water power and as more cotton came available so the textile industry seemed to expand effortlessly. The invention of the Flying Shuttle and the Spinning Jenny had already doubled the output of the home-based, hand-loom spinners and weavers. Now great factories were built which used these principles on new machines that were driven by water power. The first water-powered spinning factory was that which Richard Arkwright opened in 1771 at Cromford near Derby. Close behind this development came the first application of steam power. Steam power had already been harnessed for other applications and the invention by James Watts in the 1760's built on much previous history. The success of the principle can be measured very easily since by 1800 you would find a

Boulton and Watt steam engine being used to power any factory whose owner could buy coal cheaply.

In the Littleborough area the first wave of development was helped by the building of the turnpike roads over Blackstone Edge and to Todmorden and also by the completion of the canal. Littleborough became a location with relatively easy access to Liverpool and Hull. The cost of transporting both raw materials and finished goods was slashed and the cheap transport of coal allowed the exploitation of steam power. Our area in the early 1820s was poised once again to exploit its position at one end of an important trans-Pennine route.

Fred Jackson picks up the story again:

"From 1827, power-loom weaving and the Spinning Jenny began to come into general use and there was an enormous development of the cotton trade in all parts of Lancashire. Our district was well adapted for the weaving of cotton goods, its moist atmosphere and sheltered position being in its favour. Added to this, very large numbers of people who had been employed as hand-loom weavers and spinners and who were now out of work, gave a nucleus of workpeople already partly trained in the industry".

1827 may be seen as the time when a whole way of life based on self reliance and employment was undermined by the demands made by the ever more efficient machines. First they caused the unemployment and then sucked the population into very poor working conditions which were to prevail for some 70 years. It was said that sitting on the top of Blackstone Edge you could count hundreds of mill chimneys by the end of the 19th century.

To meet the commercial needs of an empire only the modern mills could provide the volume production. It led to great social change for the cotton workers.

The growth of the factory-based textile industry in Littleborough

After the introduction of power looms the picture of growth becomes complex, the population increased and the range of manufacturing opportunities widened. Such was the pace of development that in relatively short periods of time mills changed their use for a variety of reasons; many new mills were also built. The development of the power loom was closely linked to that of steam power itself. For example it was more difficult to mechanise weaving than spinning and for a period the hand-loom weavers continued to compete with the power loom on the basis of their cheap labour and their ability to meet exactly a customer's requirements. Power looms were only suitable for coarse cloths until the 1840's and the better quality and more fancy materials had to wait until the 1850's. In a similar way hand block printing lasted until 1850. The industry did seem to focus on minimising costs to maintain profitability rather than maximising revenue.

An apt symbol of the changes that were coming could be seen in 1824 when a large block of stone, 23 feet in length, 3 feet 6 inches in width and 2 feet 6 inches in depth was laboriously carted down from a quarry on Blackstone Edge to form the engine bed for a new steam engine at Schofield's woollen mill at 'Top of Croft' mill (Townhouse). This steam engine and an earlier engine at Whitelees Mill, were both installed to supplement the power of an existing water wheel. The generated power was applied to the driving shafts and pulleys of spinning frames and 'power looms'. The spinning

Tait's lithograph showing the valley view in the 1840's from what is now Timbercliffe.

frames rapidly developed the capacity to control hundreds of spindles worked by one individual, and a man or woman could control four of the power looms. The power looms that were installed at Schofield's were constructed by Edmund Leach 'mechanic' at the old mill at the bottom of Long Clough. These developments can be seen as marking the time when we moved locally, from the cottage industry and the yeoman farmer, to the new factory-based textile industry.

In the next 25 years the speed of change and development was awesome. The infant cotton industry was first represented by the Gale Cotton Factory and it claimed the first steam engine, when it was installed in 1820. A survey in 1814 showed that there was a cotton spinning mill at Rakewood, two fulling mills (compressing and beating cloth) at Stubley and Townhouse (Bottom Mill) and one woollen mill at Hare Hill, all driven by water. In 1827 Townhouse, now driven by steam, changed from woollen to cotton. The hand of the Newall Family was everywhere during the next 100 years. It was said that they and their children occupied every substantial house between Calderbrook and the Roch and that they were represented or consulted over most matters. By 1848 there were mills at Booth Hollins, Rakewood, Smithy Bridge, Dearnley, Stubley, Featherstall, Whitelees, Higher and Lower Shore (fulling), Clough, Calderbrook, Sladen and High Peak. Each fulling mill had a tenter field where pieces, mainly red flannel were spread.

The Sladen mill set in the bottom part of Lydgate Clough, was one of the earliest of the water-powered mills. It grew to be a handsome multi-storey building overlooked by the owner's house on the hill above. The Woodcock Inn nestled close beside it. The mill was later destroyed by fire and although it was rebuilt and dyeing and finishing continued, it was finally bought by Courtaulds, who closed it in 1980. Higher up Lydgate Clough was Lydgate Mill, another early site, eventually owned by the Laws of

Sladen Mill with the Woodcock Inn and the Mill Owners House on the hillside.

Durn. Again there was a pub beside the mill which faced onto the Blackstone Edge 'old road' or turnpike. This mill closed in 1970 and in the 90's became the framework for a small housing development. The Gate was the name of the pub and it was in competition with the Falcon and the Rake to be labelled as holding the oldest known licence in the Littleborough area. There was a claim that during the excavation of the old kitchen floor some 'Roman tiling' was unearthed. It closed in 1943 and was opened again in 1975 as the Lydgate. When the mill was converted the pub was changed into a private house.

The Gale cotton mill, a mile out of Littleborough, acquired some notoriety because its owner had installed his son in a shop opposite the mill gates. This being before the Truck Acts, wages were paid in chits and exchanged for goods in the shop. This became a source of great resentment for all except the owner and his family.

In a survey of the Littleborough district (1847 - 48) it was recorded that there were 26 premises using water wheels, steam engines or a combination of both. The power was harnessed to drive looms, spinning frames and other machines all used in the preparation, manufacture and finishing of woollen and cotton goods. The analysis of the premises in the Littleborough district by function and number was as follows:

Woollen Mills	14
Cotton Mills	4
Fulling Mills	5
Print Mills	2
Bleach Works	1

It is perhaps a surprise to see the numerical domination by the woollen industry even at this stage and the speed with which the hand-loom weaver was reduced to being an extra resource at busy periods.

THE MILLS IN LITTLEBOROUGH

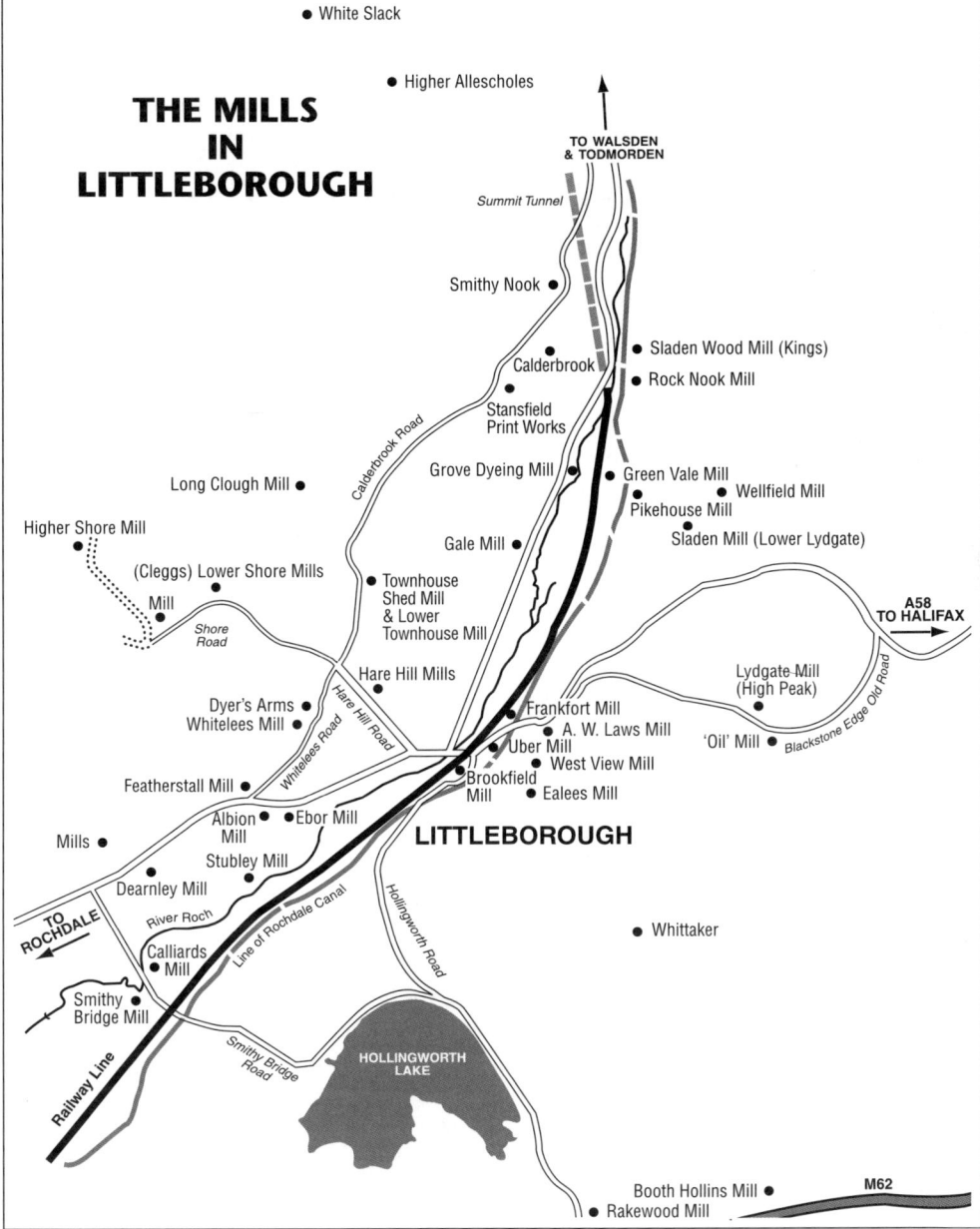

• White Slack

• Higher Allescholes

TO WALSDEN & TODMORDEN

Summit Tunnel

Smithy Nook •

• Sladen Wood Mill (Kings)

Calderbrook •

• Rock Nook Mill

Stansfield Print Works

Grove Dyeing Mill •

• Green Vale Mill

• Wellfield Mill

Pikehouse Mill

Long Clough Mill •

Calderbrook Road

Gale Mill •

Sladen Mill (Lower Lydgate)

Higher Shore Mill •

(Cleggs) Lower Shore Mills

Townhouse Shed Mill & Lower Townhouse Mill

A58 TO HALIFAX

Mill

Shore Road

Hare Hill Mills

Lydgate Mill (High Peak)

Dyer's Arms
Whitelees Mill •

Hare Hill Road

Frankfort Mill

• A. W. Laws Mill

'Oil' Mill

Blackstone Edge Old Road

Whitelees Road

Uber Mill

• West View Mill

Featherstall Mill •

Brookfield Mill

• Ealees Mill

Albion Mill • Ebor Mill

LITTLEBOROUGH

Mills •

Stubley Mill •

Dearnley Mill •

River Roch

TO ROCHDALE

• Whittaker

Line of Rochdale Canal

Hollingworth Road

Calliards Mill •

Smithy Bridge Mill

Smithy Bridge Road

HOLLINGWORTH LAKE

Railway Line

Booth Hollins Mill •

M62

• Rakewood Mill

143

With explosive growth in the textile industry, gone were the charming landscape, the quiet village and the clear streams. However for many, hardship, hunger and hazard also started to decline as the factory replaced living off the land and the modest returns and physical dangers of the existing small scale industries. There was a flood of migrants into Littleborough in response to the opportunities in textiles that were opening up.

The textile industry was always characterised by good years (eg. the 1820's) and years of depression (eg. 1831-32). The constant improvement in spinning and weaving technology reduced the production costs and lessened the need for human skill and at each stage the outcome was social misery and poverty. The atmosphere of development and change also threw up many opportunities.

In retrospect it was clear to Fred Jackson that one such opportunity occurred in 1845.

"The subsequent direction of our local textile industry was enormously influenced by a takeover in 1845 by Messrs. Leach & Clegg and Consterdine & Kershaw, of a mill, erected by Mr Bomford on Lower Shore, to manufacture fustian. This takeover was to become the progenitor of 'massive spinning mills and weaving sheds with handsome residential houses, gardens, ponds and water lodges.' The small beginning was in a room over the Whitelees Factory where a spinning mule was erected, cotton was bought and the twist and weft were moved about by wheel barrow. Messrs. Consterdine and Kershaw soon left to initiate the Brookfield Mill; Consterdine moved again to Featherstall.

A small weaving shed was built in the 'backing hole' of the Sladen Wood estate around 1850 and in the early 50s Messers. Shackleton and Co. appear to have taken a lease on this shed which expired in the early 70s leading to the auction of machinery in February 1872. Fothergills purchased the mill in 1877 and over a period transformed it into Rock Nook mill.

A Mr Holt also operated a weaving shed on the Sladen Wood estate known as the Kings Shed until in 1859 it was also taken over by Fothergill and Harvey."

Associated Industries

As the cotton industry grew so did the supporting infra-structure of textile machine manufacture and maintenance with the associated improvements and the need for regular replacements. Spinning machines needed bobbins, flyers and spindles and looms needed shuttles, heralds and reeds: local suppliers grew to meet these needs and sometimes they were actively encouraged by the larger firms. Some of the associate industries were mentioned in chapter 12.

Other notable associated industries were:

Sizing of cotton:

With flour and china clay to strengthen the warps.

Local textile engineering:

There was a continuous process of local machinery design followed by modification and improvement to achieve reliability, speed and of course reduced costs.

Bobbin making:

This was perhaps the biggest ancillary trade. For example Fieldens were said to control 100,000 spindles which would need a stock of a million bobbins at any one time.

Chemical manufacture:

This can be seen mainly as growing in response to the demands of the dyeing industry.

Some major aspects of the new textile manufacturing industry
Sheds and mills

As the industry developed weaving of cotton or wool was generally undertaken in single storey 'weaving sheds' but there were exceptions where weaving was carried out in multi-storey premises, as at Uber, West View, Rock Nook, A.W. Laws' mills and one small section at Cleggs of Shore.

Warp and Weft, Scutching and Carding

The preparation of wool or cotton warp and weft was undertaken in multi-storey 'mills'. Warp is yarn prepared in a suitable quality to be used lengthways on a loom. Weft is yarn suitable for use across the width of the loom.

The scutching machine (designed to separate out the fibre from associated woody material prior to spinning) posed a serious fire hazard and if it was not in a separate single storey building it was located in a semi-basement or ground floor room (the blowing room). This room would be separated, by a fire-proof floor, from the upper storeys occupied by carding and spinning frames.

After scutching, the disentangled fibres are carded into manageable groups drawn out and twisted into a continuous thread that can be wound onto a bobbin or spindle.

Traditionally carding and spinning was women's work, men prepared warp thread and wove cloth. All these activities were intensive and time consuming when done manually.

Lighting

Early sheds such as Townhouse, Whitelees, Featherstall, Brookfield had evenly pitched roofs, fully slated with a scattering of roof lights for natural lighting. The later sheds had 'saw-toothed' profiled northern light, with one face slated and the other face fully glazed.

Further natural light was obtained by windows in all four walls. The five storey Frankfort Mill (Littleborough Manufacturing Co. Ltd), had 44 windows on each floor. E.T.Lord's four storey Uber Mill had 24 windows to each floor. This mill was totally destroyed by fire in 1916.

Artificial light, prior to cheaper gas being obtained from the Littleborough Gas Co. Ltd, was provided by individual mill plant. In 1847 mills at Whitelees, Calliards, Hare Hill, and Clegg Hall all had their own gas retorts and gasometers. In 1866 Consterdine and Kershaw's Brookfield Mill had a retort house and gasometer (20' by 15') supplied by Baldwin's of Rochdale. In 1867 James Pilling's Featherstall Mill had two gas retorts and a gasometer (15' by 10') supplying gas to

139 jets in the weaving shed. In the late 1870's Hambrose Veevers offered to sell gas for street lighting from his Green Vale Mill gas plant to the local board at a cheaper price than the Littleborough Gas Co.

Electric lighting was first available in 1891 when one or two mills started to use it; the bulk of the firms followed in 1900 when district lighting was introduced.

Size and number of mills

The size of mills varied enormously. The Uber Mill in William Steet was modest in size. Elsewhere, a local man George Shepherd, raised enough money to rent the second floor of the three storey Dearnley Mill to set up a spinning room. In contrast: the Land Lake Mills of Cleggs of Shore occupied 17 acres. Amongst the biggest local enterprises was the Sladen Mill Co. Ltd. which included Sladen Wood, Green Vale, and Rock Nook (proprietors Fothergill and Harvey). They also owned the Alma Mill, Walsden (1910) for some 30 years, the Harvester Mill, St Helens (1954 - 64) and the Grove Dyeing Co. Ltd

The manufacturing and marketing process in textiles
Manufacturing

The process started with bales of raw cotton or wool which was commonly processed to a finished product in a single mill which had its own spinning and weaving departments. There were exceptions such as the Broadfield Mill, Smithy Bridge (Broadfield Spinning Co. Ltd) and Consterdine Brothers' Albion Mill, Featherstall which specialised in spinning cotton.

Cotton and Woollen Products

The cotton and woollen looms produced a wide and varied range of goods over the years, which reflected the demands and fashions dictated by market forces from both home and abroad.

Early products had a coarse warp and weft producing heavy calico and Rochdale flannels. With finer yarns being spun a wider range of products were made available: fustians, corduroys, imitation Welsh and Lancashire flannels, woollen and union blankets. There were also specialised lines such as an Anti - Rheumatic Blanket manufactured by the Hare Hill Mills of the Lancashire and Yorkshire Productivity Co. Ltd. in 1892.

Other products had a limited life span, then ceased production. Examples are: plain split, jaconets, oxfords, velveteens, drills and plaids.

Markets for the products

In addition to the home market many of the goods found a market abroad. Lawrence Newall of Hare Hill Mills sold flannels and blankets and other woollen goods to the Russian market. Clegg and Leach of Shore Mills, between 1852 - 1857 exported their cotton products through their agent at Liverpool (A.W. Laws). Before the First World War they shipped woollen goods to Australia in two ships that they owned, called the 'Lydgate' and the 'Honresfeld' (which was later lost at sea). The ships returned laden with Australian wool. Their trade mark on goods was an oak tree with the wording 'While I Live I Grow'. They also exported to South Africa.

Cleggs' of Shore produced a very successful product, the world famous 'Shore Sheets'. The Hare Hill Mills of the C.W.S. Ltd. produced and exported the 'Dorma Blankets' which were hem-stitched at the former Whitelees bleach works.

Despite technical, administrative and marketing advances the slump and boom cycles of the textile industry continued with another depression (1839 - 42) called the 'hungry forties' and following this period industry boomed again between 1842 and 1844. The Littleborough district was totally involved in the trade cycles of the cotton industry and some mills went bankrupt, but it was the hand-loom weavers who were the hardest hit in the first half of the century. By the 1840's they were facing subsistence living and real poverty with few options other than to work in the mills.

The impact of railway development

In the middle of all this change and development centred around textiles, the railways arrived to challenge the dominance of road and canal. With the completion of the Summit Tunnel (1840) and the termination of the 'road coach' section of the railway around the tunnel in 1841 there were, within a year, some 10 daily trains running in each direction between Leeds and Manchester and the journey only took 3 hours. There were three classes of travel all expensive initially. A second class ticket, Leeds to Manchester return, cost £1 which was a week's wage for a male textile worker. A third class ticket meant travelling in an open truck like cattle and in the long Summit Tunnel the hot ash spewed out by the train burnt holes in your clothing!

On the railways, in the early 1840s with cotton booming, the tonnage of goods carried per annum doubled and the number of passengers increased by some 200,000 to 1,350,000 per year on our main line.

In July 1847 the Manchester and Leeds became the Lancashire and Yorkshire Railway. In the next 80 years this company was to earn a reputation of being a 'journeyman' operation. It concentrated on freight movement and passenger traffic was always treated as a lower priority. In the early years working conditions on the railway were as hard as those of the cotton workers, with weekly shifts for some workers of 75 and 90 hours in alternate weeks. The railway grew by amalgamation with other entities and finally became part of the L.M.S.R. (London, Midland and Scottish Railway) in 1922 - 23.

The pattern of work in the Littleborough area in 1850

In 1841 70% of people employed nationally in the cotton industry were in Lancashire employed by some 1100 firms. In the same year there were 127 calico printing works mostly in north east Lancashire and it was estimated one third of all Lancashires working population was in cotton.

To quantify the local outcome of the enormous changes that took place in the first half of the 19th century the following analysis was taken from the 1851 Census. Included with it is a summary of a similar analysis done for a part of the Todmorden district, which acts as an illustration of the similarity between the cotton towns in our area at this time and also as a marker to ensure some consistency in the known difficulties of extracting data from this census material. Todmorden includes Walsden, Littleborough includes Blatchinworth and Calderbrook:

Township	Population	Hand-loom weavers	Power-loom weavers	Weavers (unspecified)	Total
Todmorden (Totals only)	7700	106	713	111	930
Littleborough	4500				
Weavers					
Cotton		54	365	55	
Woollen				137	
Fustian				11	
					622
Spinners & Piecers etc.					
Cotton				162	
Woollen				121	
Un-defined				29	
					312
Mill hands					
Cotton				40	
Woollen				5	
Un-defined				8	
					53
Fullers				130	130
Slubbers				6	6
Totals	4500	54	365	704	1123

The 'unspecified' weavers were probably hand-loom weavers and for every weaver it can be seen that there was another worker in an associated job in the factory or home. Of the total number of weavers 329 were women ie. more than half.

In addition to the total of 1123 directly employed with skills in textiles, other workers in the suppport, commercial and manufacturing aspects of the textile industry viz. warehousemen, managers, loom jobbers, loom overlookers can be added. Beyond these workers are all those in the associated industries which made textile machines, or bobbins in millions, or repaired existing equipment. Overall a fairly consistent picture can be derived from many studies that have been done. In the Littleborough district (as elsewhere in Lancashire and the South Pennines) at least 25% of the total population were working in the textile industry and were directly affected by its periods of boom and recession. Of the potential working population (ie. over 10 years old but excluding the elderly) the percentage jumps to 45%. If you add in the less directly employed it is not hard to see how the general conclusion is that the 'reasonable estimate' escalates to 60% of the working population being 'dependent on textiles'. Expressed in terms of families this means practically every family had one or more workers in textiles. The family connection was very strong in the Littleborough area and most recruitment was done through the families and community sources. It is believed this pattern of employment also ensured women got more parity in pay than existed in much of Lancashire. On the other side there was sometimes bitter feuding between families about who supplied labour to various sections and departments.

Lancashire had developed a single county industry and our local area was an extreme example of that dedication.

One example, of many, will show the reality which lies behind the statistics outlined above.

The Butterworths living at Durn (1850)

Mary Butterworth, Head of Household, 34 years old, pauper

William Butterworth, Son 14 years old, collier

Margaret Butterworth, Daughter, 8 years old, piecer at a woollen mill (piecer: ties up breaks in the yarns, a fault that held back large scale mechanisation for many years.

Betty Butterworth, daughter, 4 years old

John Butterworth, son, 1 year old

A fourteen year old boy and an eight year old girl were the bread winners for the family and they worked in coal mining and textiles.

The use of batches of children, sometimes brought from London and elsewhere not only provided labour but reduced the parish costs. The practice of using children peaked in the early 1800s when 'parish apprentices' made up one third of the cotton work force in Lancashire. Littleborough probably had a larger proportion of family children in the mills than this figure suggests. When the power source was water the small, single process mills were dispersed to find adequate supplies but by the 1820s the industry was firmly based on urban sites. In Littleborough in 1838 the average employees per mill were around 70 compared with 216 in Manchester.

As well as the hard times, endemic poverty and dangerous work, there were many interesting and new opportunities also opening up in the Littleborough district.

The firm of architects, Russell and Whittaker, illustrate the growth potential and business prospects that existed in the textile industry. The partnership were architects for West View, A.& W. Laws, Uber and the Albion mills They were also the architects for mills elsewhere such as John Bright's mills. Diversifying, they acted as architects to mill owners to build fine new stone residences, mill worker's housing estates, and gasometer sites for the mills. They also designed a group of houses for the co-op on Bare Hill, the new Littleborough Police Station on the Todmorden Road and a number of chapels in the area.

The birth of Fothergill and Harvey's Group of companies

For Littleborough one of the most important events in the second half of the 19th century took place in Manchester, when in 1848 Alexander Cummins Harvey entered a partnership with Mr Fothergill 'to conduct a yarn and cloth business'. Alexander was brought up in some luxury but his father dissipated a fortune and at 18 (through connections with Gladstone and other emininent families) he entered a cotton firm (Swainson & Clayton) in Manchester. These were the 'hungry forties' and he was horrified at the poverty and starvation around him and became a life long radical.

These attitudes he passed on to his children including Gordon and Ernst. For six years he worked long days and spent much time trying to lessen the horror of Manchester's slums

The Fothergill and Harvey partnership purchased Sladen Wood Mill in 1859 to enter textile manufacture and 20 years later Alexander's eldest son Gordon was taken out of Owens College (Manchester) at age 21, to become the manager there. Alexander's action was forced on him by the death of his business partner, Fothergill. By 1886 Alexander had all 5 sons in the business.

Gordon Harvey set up home in Sladen Wood House next to the mill and spent the weekends with his family in Cheshire. This was the beginning of a relationship between Littleborough, Gordon Harvey and the Fothergill and Harvey Group that continued throughout and beyond Gordon Harvey's lifetime and provided the single largest employer in Littleborough for a period of some 150 years.

Fred Jackson took up employment as a weaver at the Sladen Wood Mill in 1881. In 1886 Ernst Harvey, the youngest of Alexander's sons, abandoned his career in medicine and joined his older brother, Gordon to work in the textile industry. In the years to come Ernst directed the companies' development in terms of their use of machinery and processing systems in the production area. In 1903 Gordon (a bachelor) and Ernst (recently married) moved to Townhouse which had previously been the home of the Newalls. To support their dispersed business they installed the new miracle, a telephone system. Their personal numbers were 2X and 2Y and the mill number was 8. Such developments later helped Gordon to move into politics where he became a national figure. In 1889 he was elected to Lancashire County Council, with a special focus on education. In 1894 he became the Chairman of the new School Board in Littleborough.

In their great years the financial and commercial centre of Fothergill and Harvey was in Manchester but the manufacturing capabilities were firmly anchored in Littleborough. By 1907 Alexander and two of his sons were dead, Gordon was deeply involved in politics (elected to Parliament in 1906) and the head of his company. He and Ernst supervised manufacturing operations in Littleborough and Henry looked after the Manchester operation.

Fred Jackson provided brief histories of three of the main mills. This material is summarised below. Each mill still exists and can be seen today. It is not hard to conjure up a picture of the hundreds of people who used to work in them even though the nature of the business has changed. Sladen Wood Mill for example is now used to manufacture furniture.

Green Vale Mill

This mill was the among the first to be erected in our district. A little time after the railway was opened for traffic, a Mr. Chadwick, who had been employed as a manager at a cotton-spinning mill at Burnage, near High Crompton, came over to Littleborough, took land from Colonel Chadwick the owner and soon after began to erect Green Vale Mill for the spinning and weaving of cotton goods. The construction of the mill was uneventful and in due course it was filled with textile machinery and commenced with a fair prospect of success. Mr Chadwick carried on the business for a few years but due to a run of adverse circumstances the business had to be sold. It was bought by Messrs.

Part of the Fothergill and Harvey group of mills at Summit.

John Veevers & Sons of Todmorden (1861 census), who afterwards built a row of cottages near the Mill. Gas for lighting purposes had not yet been introduced locally, so a small gas-making plant was installed to supply gas to the mill and the houses at Green Vale. It was a good many years after this time before the Littleborough Gas Company extended their mains to Summit. John Veevers & Sons carried on the concern very successfully until their deaths, after which the property was sold to Messrs. Joseph Schofield and Co. who carried on the business until the end of 1893, when it was purchased by Messrs. Fothergill and Harvey. It was greatly improved to become one of the most up-to-date mills in the country. Gordon Harvey made it a model mill in regard to smoke emission, long before other people began to consider that it was possible for a mill to consume its own smoke, instead of being a nuisance to everybody in its vicinity.

Backing Hole or 'Back in Hole' (Rock Nook Mill)

   Backing Hole is a name which has practically died out, but which the older residents in the late 19th century would have recognised; the younger generations knew it as Rock Nook shed and mill. Not far from Green Vale on the opposite side of the canal, it was formerly a disused stone quarry. Soon after Green Vale Mill was built, a weaving shed was erected in this quarry, which was commonly called 'Backing Hole'. The quarry had been used for getting sand and rough stone for interior walls of buildings and other jobs which needed 'backing'. The shed was very small and could hold about 200 looms. For some years it was worked by Messrs. John Shackleton & Co. (1861 census) but about the year 1877 it was purchased by Messrs. Fothergill and Harvey, who, from these small beginnings raised the large, well equipped, up-to-date mills and sheds which would make cloth for the next hundred years.

In 1886-7 the mill was greatly extended to include spinning as well as weaving. In 1892 ground was purchased to allow the warehouse to be extended. In 1896 the the spinning department was extended and new Engine & Boiler Houses were built. The old boiler houses were converted into the canteen & dining rooms for the workpeople. In 1905 ground was purchased for the New Shed, which was originally used for slashing and winding and finally became in 1912-14 the Northrop Shed with 356 Northrop looms. At the same time, further extensions took place and new Winding, Beaming and Slashing departments were erected.

Sladen Wood Shed (Kings)

The continued great demand for cotton goods in the 1840's stimulated further building operations and about the year 1850 Mr Thomas Holt, Manager for Messrs. Fielden Bros. of Todmorden purchased some rough pieces of land on the Sladen Wood Estate, lying between the new roadway and the canal. This had been used as a dumping ground for the refuse from the new roadway and railway, but Mr Holt had it levelled up from one of the dumps left on Holme Farm (Old Crimmy's). The river Roch ran through the area and it was confined to a stone channel which was then covered with massive stone slabs. Mr Holt then proceeded to build a weaving shed and a large house and garden near it. He lived to see the building completed, but died before the shed was filled with machinery. It was afterwards let to James King & Co. and Thomas & Robert Walmsley and Henry Ashworth & Bros. all manufacturers of cotton goods. They equipped the shed and carried on business with varying success for some years. Later Mr Walmsley departed and the place was carried on under the title of Messrs. King & Co. until it was taken over in 1859 by, Messrs. Fothergill & Harvey, though it was still referred to as 'King's Shed' by a generation of local people.

Work in a mill

A vivid description of what it was like to work in a weaving shed during the second half of the 19th century was written by Fred Jackson. It is however, disputed whether he refers to the Sladen Wood mill as stated in the official Harvey memoirs, or more likely Rock Nook No. 1 Shed.

"The shed I am about to describe was neither the worst nor the best in its class. It was filled with ordinary Lancashire looms, all simple weaves, three and four shafts, with both men and women weavers running three or four looms each. In those days the looms were so closely packed together you could hardly pass between them. The general average of pay was four shillings and sixpence per loom per week. Some weavers could earn five shillings weekly, on each loom or £1 per week on four. The working week was 5½ days 6.00 am to 5.30 pm with one hour for lunch. The speed of the looms averaged about 190 picks per minute. All sweeping, cleaning, pulling off-cuts, fetching weft etc. had to be done by the weaver. There was no heating or planned ventilation in the mill and in winter the temperature was near freezing. When steam was introduced into the shed to make the warps weave better, the condensed water dropped all over the place. Humidity was introduced in the summer when 'degging' or water cans were employed to moisten the floor of the shed and keep the atmosphere humid.

Provision for the comforts of the workers was meagre. To warm their food they placed it on the boiler. Later the place was lit with gas and when that had to be kept burning all day, as happened many times during the winter months, for whole days together, the carbon dioxide nearly knocked you down when you came in from the fresh air."

Indoctrinated by their father, the brothers Gordon and Ernst Harvey started to tackle these problems early in their careers. The condition of all workers but especially children were a lifelong concern. They recognised that mill work changed healthy moorland farm children into pale, dull listless adults. They also knew this mill fodder was asked to work in very dangerous conditions. At Rock Nook Mill they had all the machines re-set with broader 'alley ways' between them to lessen the danger from moving belts and shuttles. They saw the results of loss of concentration due to fatigue and in 1893 introduced regular breaks in the operating routines and snacks. They were deeply concerned about the health of their workers and for example, from 1890 they made a hot drink/milk service available to all workers for a token payment and it was free for child workers. They improved the overall conditions, introduced pioneering corrections to the atmosphere humidification and provided heated cloakrooms and canteen facilities. In later life, as a politician, Gordon Harvey fought for similar provisions to be imposed on the whole industry by law.

The brothers also achieved improvement through smoke abatement. Smoke had so polluted the area that it even turned the gritstone outcrops on Blackstone Edge literally black with grime. The mills that they controlled were among the first to 'consume their own smoke'. In 1912 Gordon Harvey introduced a bill to Parliament to compel all industry to do the same but it was unsuccessful at the time. Britain had to wait longer for the Clean Air acts.

Uber Mill at Durn, destroyed by fire in 1916.

CHAPTER FOURTEEN

THE NINETEENTH CENTURY

PART FOUR: THE TEXTILE INDUSTRY (1850 - 2000)

(For mill locations see diagram in Chapter 13)

The Textile Industry 1850 - 1900

Introduction

The old communities created along the hillsides were under pressure as roads were opened up in the valley bottom and work gravitated into the mills. One milepost was passed when in 1861 Fielden Brothers of Todmorden, a giant among our South Pennine textile firms, pensioned off their last handloom weaver. By this time nearly all processes from the new fibre to finished cloth happened in a factory environment. Workers had specific jobs deeply influenced by age and gender, women had low status, were poorly paid and often recruited by the overlookers. They had little control over their own lives. The men began to look for better paid work in mining and the developing railways. In Littleborough the strong family ties made some of the worst effects of poor working conditions tolerable, but on the other hand tended to support the use of child labour. Children were often recruited by the operatives to supplement their earnings which were based on piece rates. The cheapest solution, as in coal mining, was to use your own children.

In 1911 there were still 30,000 children working in the Lancashire Textile industry of which 56% were girls. Despite government legislation, many of the textile based Trades Unions and parents fought to keep this system well into the 20th century.

The 1850s

The growth and initial mechanisation of the textile industry with the recurring cycle of boom and depression was outlined in chapter 13. The 1850s were to be a new period of boom. The main reasons appeared to be the 'putting down' of the Indian Mutiny and the end of the war with China, allied to an enormous expansion of cotton growing in southern U.S.A. Raw materials were plentiful and cheap and the market appeared to grow effortlessly. For example, at this time many of the small sheds, including the cluster of Green Vale, Backing Hole and Sladen Wood expanded their cotton manufacturing capabilities. All three sheds were subsequently bought by Fothergill and Harvey in the 1870s and were used as a basis for expanding their manufacturing operations notably the making of khaki drill for service men's uniforms.

Cotton was already dominating the export markets which were evenly spread:
Balance of cotton exports (1854 - 56)

Europe	Asia/Africa	America/Australia
30%	40%	30%

154

Financing Textile Growth

To exploit this boom situation the textile industry needed large amounts of new capital and more suitable structures of ownership. This was the era of Co-operatives, Savings Banks and very significantly, in 1855 the Companies Act, which allowed individuals to invest in industry, with a liability for loss limited to the capital they had contributed. Thus if £15,000 was needed to open a new mill, shares could be made available at £15 a share. Anyone could buy a share by simply putting down an initial deposit on it and paying off the total value over a period. The individual liability would be the face value of the share.

The way was open to create large mills with integrated spinning and weaving, with a mass of workers' houses round them where employees lived. The employees could then have an investment in the business. The bad effect of this new legislation was that it drove the first significant wedge between ownership and operation of the mill. Professional managers saw the owners moving away from their factories. From Littleborough many went to live in Cheshire, Derbyshire, the Lake District and later to the south. By 1914 many of the old business elite, which in 1850 dominated the area, had deserted it. Exceptions included families such as the Harveys and the Laws.

An alternative business approach was for an entrepreneur to build a mill and then rent out parts or 'rooms', along with a share of the available mill power capacity. This was called 'room and power' development and enabled people with a small amount of capital to open up family-sized businesses, which had echoes of the old domestic hand-loom business. It also proved attractive to individuals who wanted to set up associated trades such as bobbin works or textile machinery repairs etc.

Every kind of individual was able to invest in textiles and many did, but the appetite of the textile industry for capital appeared insatiable. With poor investment structures and creative, but loosely regulated accountancy, the industry embarked on a massive expansion. No serious attention was paid to the inherent danger of over capacity and its implications in all but the most favourable trading conditions. The industry was clearly at risk.

The introduction of steam

As existing mill owners came to realize the gain in efficiency by using steam power rather than horses and water there was a steady conversion in the area. Examples start to appear in the local records from the 1850s:

1858   Higher Rakewood Mill: a water wheel and a new 14 h.p.engine installed. Hare Hill Mills: a 45 h.p. engine installed.
863   Uber Mill: a 30 h.p. engine installed.
1868   Lydgate Mill: Alfred Law and his brother stated 'the steam engine has become the sole source of power for the mill'.

In the Littleborough District in 1867 the machinery in cotton mills, that were powered by water wheels and steam engines, in total generated 429 h.p. Woollen mills and fulling mills contributed a further 229 h.p. The total of all woollen mills and cotton mills that only used water wheels was 131 h.p. making a total of 789 h.p. for the district. The pioneers in the industry could scarcely have imagined that 39 years later at the Sladen Wood Mill a 1000 h.p. engine would be installed to drive the machinery in a single mill.

Growth of the Mills

Between 1847 and 1867 the growth of mills continued:

1847	Lydgate
	Green Vale
1851	Brookfield
1856	Sladen Wood
1858	Rock Nook
1860	Frankfort and Broadfield
1863	Uber
1866	West View Mill and A. W. Laws
1867	Albion Mill

After this 20 years of expansion in the Littleborough district there were, for the first time, an equal number of cotton and woollen mills. Even in these heady days not every initiative succeeded. In 1875 a new company was launched called the 'Summit Spinning and Manufacturing Company Ltd.' It had a capital of £30,000 offered in £5 shares and it failed to get started.

By 1886 Fothergill and Harvey were extending Rock Nook Mill operations, spinning their own yarn and building local houses for their workers. Other operations were less secure, for example the Frankfort Mill was built and operated by a co-operative company who filled it with the last word in modern machinery. It proved, however, to be plagued by gross mis-management and the collapse of the company was attributed to the lack of directors with sufficient knowledge.

In Ealees large woollen mills were constructed by Messers William & Alfred Law, (Durn Mills) and Mr William Heap, (West View Mills), all of whom had small factories in the area previously. Also, in the 19th century there was another small expansion of the textile industry when the manufacture of hosiery was introduced:

1875	Lyons Mill: Joshua Street.
1887	Thomas Grimshaw's Sun Mill: Featherstall.

Slumps and Relief

The inherent instability in the whole textile industry was cruelly exposed when the American Civil War broke out in 1861. The southern ports of U.S.A. were blockaded and Lancashire lost the source of 80% of its cotton supply. Imports from India increased enormously between 1860 and 1866 and prices and quality fluctuated wildly. Buying became a gamble and soon mills were on 2 - 3½ day working. Relief committees were formed and by the end of 1862 their responsibilities had increased fourfold and they were distributing coal, money, clothing and paying to keep the children in school. By the middle of 1863 perhaps one quarter of the workforce, related to cotton, was out of work and another half were on short time. For some parts of the textile industry it was in 1864 that the severity of the depression lessened and relief was terminated. During this latest depression manufacturers combed the world for good quality supplies of raw material but the facts were that, without an increase in product price or increased output per mill, more mills had to close. It has been estimated that the profit margin on goods sold had fallen from 90% of the raw material cost to 20% or less.

Engineer James Stansfield of Todmordon and his helper Harry Calvert in the Frankfort Mill engine house 1926. A few days later the governor mechanism (centre) failed, the huge engine over-accelerated, the flywheel behind disintegrated and fragments were buried deep in the walls and ceiling. Frankfort Mill (1861) was demolished early 1960s. The large site is now operated by Green Bros, commercial vehicle dismantlers whose recovered engines find new uses all over the world.

This is a general summary of the impact of one more depression on the cotton industry but what was the reality for Littleborough? After Fort Sumter was surrendered (April 1861) and the American Civil War commenced, it was seven months before the cotton famine took a stranglehold on our local economy. In November 1861 Littleborough had 13 mills employing 1364 workers and of these only five mills were working full time employing 397 workers. Of the remaining eight, one mill with 81 workers worked a four day week, four mills with 814 workers were on a three day working week and three mills with 72 workers were closed. In summary, of the work force of 1364 people, 70% were on short time or unemployed.

To alleviate the worst of the hardship experienced by the families, a Littleborough Relief Fund was set up by various local business men. John Edward Consterdine, son of Betty Consterdine - partner with Joseph Kershaw in the firm Consterdine & Kershaw was the secretary. The fund was allocated to families 'so badly affected that they were in distressed circumstances'. In November the relief fund raised £427:1s. This sum was used to give 109 families (512 people) some form of relief. Fund raising took many forms, one was the production of a very high-brow concert given in December 1861 in the Littleborough Church School (later demolished to make way for the new Parish Church School). The programme included selections from Haydn's 'Creation' and Handel's 'Judas Maccabaeus' accompanied by an orchestra and chorus of 60 people. Tickets for the concert were 2/6 for a reserved seat, and 6d on the back row.

As recipients of relief had to be in need, those with any form of assets had to dispose of them, although consideration was given to those wishing to regain their assets later. As an example, a candidate for relief may have shares in the co-operative society. They were advanced money against the shares held, subject to a clause that allowed them to redeem their shares on easy terms within a named period of time.

157

Another way of helping the distressed families was the hiring out of unemployed factory hands. The Secretary of the fund advertised in March 1863 'to contract outdoor work to interested parties on reasonable terms'. The arrangement ran from November 1861 to March 1863 which marked the 'official' end to hardship in Littleborough.

It is interesting that Littleborough probably shared in relief that was obtained through the generosity of people living in the northern states of America. The Americans were touched by the acute distress of the textile workers throughout Lancashire and forwarded gifts of clothing, money and food for distribution to those who were suffering due to the blockade. That Littleborough people did benefit seems very likely, bearing in mind what happened some 8 years later. Chicago had expanded enormously in the 19th century and around 1830 they developed a 'balloon frame' house to accommodate the influx of people. In 1871 the balloon structure was proved to be a deadly fire hazard when the Great Fire of Chicago started in a barn and driven by a strong wind destroyed an enormous area of the centre and north side of the city of Chicago. This disaster gave the Littleborough people a chance to return the generosity the Americans had shown to them. Henry Newall, chairman of the Local Board, called a public meeting to consider the steps to be followed to help the victims of the Chicago conflagration. A resolution proposed by A. Clegg (Shore Mills), seconded by John Edward Consterdine (Consterdine Bros, Albion Mill, Featherstall) was put to the meeting as follows:

'That a committee be formed, for the purpose of raising subscriptions in aid of the suffering caused by the late destructive fire in Chicago, consisting of the following gentlemen: Henry Newall, treasurer, Rev. Thomas Carter, vicar, Messrs. A. Clegg, Alfred Law, Joseph Schofield and Frank Henry Shuttleworth, hon. secretary, with power to add to their number.'

By the end of November 1871 the Littleborough Chicago Relief Fund was closed and the donations raised came to £179.9s.9½ d. and so Littleborough did something to repay a debt and contributed relief to the people of the United States.

In general, with such a large number of mills existing in the Littleborough area there was never a period when they were all working at the same time. In an industry prone to boom and recession: Bank, Clough, Frankfort, Uber, Featherstall, Calliards, Hare Hill, Clegg Hall, Dry Dock and the Albion at one time or another were closed down due to bankruptcy. They sometimes remained closed for considerable periods and the partnership, which was still the common style of ownership, dissolved.

By 1873 yet another boom began, but this time the price of food soared and strikes broke out. The growth in competition squeezed the profit margins and unemployment increased and between 1877 and 1883 there was a string of bankruptcies.

Also, as the century moved on, it became more frequent for the premises to be converted to some other use, as the owners or partners stared at a very uncertain future in textiles. Following the virtual demise of the hand-loom weaver now it was the turn of the less resilient, less well-financed mills, or those wrongly placed in the market, to drop out of the textile industry.

In 1889 Featherstall Mill converted to the manufacture of travel luggage (Foxcrofts) as people in Britain gained mobility and could afford holidays. In 1893 the Uber Mill converted to making confectionery and when this failed the mill re-opened as the Victoria Bleaching & Dying Co. Ltd. It was destroyed by fire in 1916 and the company transferred to Clegg Hall Mills. In 1894 the Frankfort Mill converted to the production of soft drinks and this also failed. After a number of other 'attempts' in the commercial sector the mill became a storage depot for the Ministry of Food in the second world war. Later it was re-opened as a body building and paint shop for making wagons but this also closed.

In contrast to these moves out of the textile industry, in 1899 Fothergill and Harvey expanded the production capacity of cotton goods at Rock Nook mill, bringing their total capacity to some 1600 looms and 41,000 spindles. There was a great demand for cotton drill and other types of cloth and the merchanting operation run from Harvester House, Peter Street, Manchester was very successful. The projected future of the company looked very encouraging.

Manchester Royal Exchange

There was often an intimate connection between the early local mill owners and the Quakers, Unitarians, Congregationalists and non-conformity generally. However, the Manchester Royal Exchange became the centre for the business life of the textile industry and the absolute focus for cotton. It is the best example of the degree by which the economy of Littleborough was becoming a modest unit in a much larger picture. It was the focus of financial dealing and commercial operation for the successful mill owners. This was where the individual businesses were valued, bought and sold and financial deals arranged. In the huge building, manufacturers met merchants and discussed markets and the competition. It was also where finished and part-finished goods were bought and sold. In many ways it functioned like a large club with junior members (associate and support industries) all keeping an office or alcove in or close to the Exchange, to promote their business interests. Fothergill and Harvey set up their business in Peter Street, a few minutes walk away from the Royal Exchange. This remained their Head Office, commercial centre and administration centre. Initially manufacture was very secondary to trading but as it grew this was focussed in Littleborough for a long period, but in the most prosperous years they had units elsewhere and in the later fight for survival they bought and developed units abroad.

The Exchange was established in 1804, all sizeable firms involved in textile trading belonged and the membership figures are testimony to its pivotal importance.

	1809	1852	1860	1894
Membership	1543	3068	4209	7485

In the sumptuous reception rooms the cotton magnates received the greatest and most important people in the land and were pleased to be told that the Royal Exchange was called 'the Parliament of the Lords of Cotton'.

Technological change

As the century advanced, technology appeared to work against the interests of the working people in textiles. For example, in the 1880s ring spinning, which had been invented in America many years before, by a process of improvement gradually came to be a necessity for survival in the integrated spinning and weaving mills. Ring spinning was much quicker than the traditional mule spinning. Many thousands of the ring spinning units were installed but in the process this replaced skilled, well paid, male mule spinners by female machine minders of Ring Frames - on much lower pay.

Co-operation

Trades Unions

Over the years the fluctuations in trading conditions had deeply affected the lives of the workers. Prior to the formation of the unions one of the main results was a unilateral declaration of a reduction in wages by textile manufacturers, in February 1867. The Littleborough Flannel Manufacturers Association decided to cut the wages of their weavers by 1d in 1/-. This meant a reduction of 2/4d on the average wage of 28/-. The 50 weavers at Heap's West View Mills, Durn, went on strike for the restoration of the 1d. The strike lasted until the middle of April when they went back to work. The strikers sent out a hand bill thanking all members of the public who had supported them and also informed the public that the workers had been 'locked out' of the mill by their employers. 1869 - 1870 were another two bad years and in February 1869 short time working was in effect throughout most of the cotton mills in Littleborough. The cotton manufacturers agreed to a 30 hour working week 'for the time being' but trade showed no improvement and in October 1869 many of the mills were still working short time. The workers once again suffered a cut in wages. The remaining woollen mills were also affected by these trade cycles and two of the mills were on short time.

As the century came to its end it was clear that individuals had to 'come together' and that only co-operation and self help could protect them from the blizzard of change that had altered nearly every aspect of their life. One result of these conditions was the growth of Trades Unions for most aspects of the textile trades, such as weavers, beamers and spinners. The first union in Littleborough was the Friendly Operatives Self Actor Minders' Association which was formed in 1876, when it had nine members.

The state of the textile industry

If the workers were experiencing problems at the end of the 19th century so were owners, managers and merchants in both the home and export trade.

Communications were improving dramatically, old distinctions between the functions of each group were becoming blurred. Margins of profit shrank and competition was becoming intense. Aggressive American marketing was creating turmoil in the old buying patterns and elsewhere manufacturers were making alliances directly with retailers. Many of the bigger British firms were reluctant to face these challenges

The state of the Littleborough area

In 1890 Miss Jessie Fothergill, the novelist, was still living at Sladen Wood House, Summit, where she wrote a good many of her novels. In the prologue to 'Healey', the plot of which is generally believed to have been laid in Summit, she gives a description of the area as it appeared to her at that time. The whole district had been involved in the industrial revolution for some 120 years and notwithstanding the fact that it had been improved through the efforts of Mr. Gordon Harvey, especially in regard to the re-planting of trees and smoke emission, the description still makes a vivid summary of the near wasteland that resulted from the developments in the 19th century. She says:-

"A Town Village, the place is ugly, it is dirty, it has tall chimneys which vomit forth smoke, that clothe the land in a garment of smuts. It has Mills and Factories swarming with dingy looking hands, whose garments as they pass by, distribute odours of oil, fustian and cotton fluff. It has a long black canal, the banks of which are fringed with factories, stone quarries and foundries....Generally keen winds blow, and often smutty rain comes sweeping athwart the smoke from dawn till dark.....But the canal at last finds its sluggish way into green fields......and nearby are hedges, perhaps which late in summer, have been known guilty of - not bursting, for vegetation here never bursts, but of slowly, tardily and reluctantly unfolding into a semblance of hawthorn bloom. Such bleak moors, naked and gaunt for three quarters of the year, and for the other, dressed in a bright garment of purple heather, yellow bracken, and scarlet bilberry leaves....... This is not a lovable land, its very aspect suggests hardness, chills, bleak winds, howling and whistling over the desolate moors..."

The contrast with the picture of the environment in the first years of the 19th century is so stark that it is worth considering the degree of change the local people experienced in one lifetime. It could be argued the scale was unprecedented and may never happen again.

The local Textile Industry 1900 - 1950

This is the time when Littleborough finally became integrated into the UK economy and was influenced by the winds of change and the marketing and manufacturing struggles of major corporations at home and abroad. Our local economy had become a small sector of a much more widespread set of events.

The clothing industry

By 1900 the textile industry, but above all cotton, had transformed everyday clothing. Humble people could have changeable sets of washable clothing and had access to very good outer garments. Workers wages had doubled since 1845 and in the same period the amount spent on clothes, as a percentage of total personal expenditure, had risen from 6% to 12%.

Ready made clothes had grown to be an influential industry and a sewing machine was an everyday utility at home.

Textile Industry

The first decade of the century gave a deceptive picture of the prosperity of the textile industry. An examination of the Fothergill and Harvey Group would have shown a prosperous merchanting business in Manchester and in Littleborough a set of modern mills. These included Sladen Wood, Rock Nook and 'Schofield's' Green Vale mill with its own gas plant and variable speed motors driving the spinning frames. These mills were well maintained and a credit to their management as compared to industry norms. At the time a weaving shed manager could earn £1 10s to £2 per week and a clerk 12s 6d to 15s per week.

In the 20th century some segments of the textile industry, such as the hosiery industry, continued to expand with new mills opening locally:

Rock Nook Mill.

1910   Taylor and Stansfield: Newall Street
1938   H.D.Sturgess and Co: Box Street

Most impressive of all was that the early years of the 20th century represented the peak development of the Lancashire cotton mill as a symbol of the owner's pride in the achievement of the industry. At their finest the mills were perhaps six or eight storeys high, built and decorated in ornamental brick, with beautifully tiled engine rooms driving the great rope races carrying power to the multiple floors. There were acres of glass windows and above everything towered the great chimneys. They were an industrial statement of pride and confidence. Nothing so grand was built in Littleborough, our mills, in brick and stone were more basic in construction, although in nearby Todmorden the Mons Mill alongside the Centre Vale Park was a magnificent edifice.

The mainstream cotton industry appeared to be doing well and 1913 was the peak year for raw cotton consumption in Great Britain. This was turned into cloth by weavers and 80% of what they made was exported. The industry was so large that it is thought it represented some two thirds of all world trade. Cotton goods were a quarter of all British exports of which 40% went to India. Such a situation must have been recognised as unstable and likely to change gradually but we exacerbated the inevitable erosion of our market by enthusiastically exporting our latest machinery to our overseas markets or selling them our obsolete equipment at cheap prices.

Despite the evidence of over capacity and the vulnerable market situation there was one further ill-ventured expansion in Littleborough: the flotation of the Tyne Spinning Co. Ltd. in 1909. The firm went into liquidation in 1914 and its mill, which was built on the cleared site of the Littleborough New Mill, was never completed - stopping at

Mrs Martha Lord.

the second floor. It is not difficult to understand why another new mill would have appeared a sensible investment. In 1913 Lancashire still dominated world trade in cotton textiles. It must have been hard to forecast that by 1938 employment in the industry would be halved, cotton goods would be 12% of U.K. exports and our production would represent less than 25% of the world's cotton cloth.

Within the industry, on the eve of the war the Fothergill and Harvey mills had become a model for Lancashire, even though much of the welfare work was often unwelcome to their fellow manufacturers.

The life of a young mill worker

Today it is hard for us to conceive a full working life in the local cotton mills. Martha Lord was born in Shropshire in 1904, the fifth child of parents originally from Burnley. Her father was from a large family of six or seven and went to Shropshire to work on a farm, because it would be a better life in the country. Martha only had one clear memory of Shropshire; holding out her pinny to catch apples her older brother was shaking down.

When Martha was three, the family moved back to Burnley then went on to live in Cornholme near Todmorden where her father got work in a dyeworks. Her mother had an aunt Betsy, who lived in the Jockey Tavern on the main Todmorden road through Cornholme. In those days there had to be a woman living in a public house and the aunt had been taken ill, so Martha's mother went to live at the inn and took the children with her. It is probable that the aunt had what is now known to be Alzheimer's disease, at the time it was called 'the idiots disease' and sufferers were usually 'put away'. Martha's mother and family managed to look after the aunt for some years. Martha remembers how small the workers houses were, mostly two rooms up and down.

Often there was an attic, where the children of large families would sleep.

When the aunt died the family came to live in Littleborough. Martha was eleven years old. Her father found work at the dye works, off New Road, Dearnley behind the building which is currently Lazeez Restaurant.

At age twelve Martha set off with her older sister (age 13 years and 10months) to start work at Fothergill & Harvey's mill at Rock Nook. Soon after this time the law was changed so that her other sisters never had to start so young. Her younger sister stayed at school until age fourteen and then went to work at Whittle's Bakery on Whitelees Road.

Martha started work, as a'half-timer' at Fothergill's in the middle of the first world war. Each day was divided between work and school. She remembers clearly that there were no lights to be seen when the two sisters set out for the mill from their home in Inghams Lane (beside what is now the Waterside Inn, previously the Railway Inn). They had to get up in time to arrive at the mill at 6.0 am. on one week and 1.0 pm for the second shift on alternate weeks. On the early start they got a break for breakfast from 8.0 to 8.30 am.

The girls did not know the lie of the land in Littleborough and as incomers were very shy and frightened. The only way they knew to go to Fothergill's was the long trudge along Todmorden Road. Martha vividly recalls, 80 years later, passing Gale in the dark with the bitter wind whistling across the open area, as she remarked 'it is well called Gale' (some commentators believe the name refers to the Bog Myrtle, locally called 'gale' which grew on the marshy land there in abundance). The road used to flood very badly and this made the journey even more difficult. There was a tram going along the Todmorden road but the girls could not afford the fare. In the summer it was more pleasant to walk along the canal bank.

At the mill the girls were put into different rooms, one in the card room and Martha in the ring room. Martha remembers the misery of being separated from her sister and thrown into a strange world of bustle and the great noise of a mill shed. She was frightened of the machinery and already knew that the women might lose their long hair, their limbs and lives if they got caught in the great 'straps' that powered the machinery from the 'rope races' overhead. The noise in a mill was deafening to the degree that many of the operators suffered deafness at a very young age. The sisters missed each other enormously and missed the chance to help each other. They longed for the mid-day break when they could meet at a cottage where Fothergill's provided benches and tables for the workers to eat their lunch. Because they were so poor this was nearly always jam sandwiches along with a little tea in a screw of newspaper. The woman in charge would boil water for them, to make a hot drink and also provided some milk, for 2d each weekly. Sometimes if they had got through all the available work they would creep to a warm corner of the mill and fall asleep. Martha remembers being shaken awake and told to clear up the bobbins as Mr Ernst (Ernst Harvey, one of the owners) was coming round.

Martha remembers just how miserable the life was: she knew she would have much preferred to have been at school which she remembers with warmth and appreciation. Her mother had to earn more money and went off to do the laundry at the Wheatsheaf. This was the most prestigious hotel in Littleborough and at this time was a flourishing venue for 'travellers' (commercial) who came on business to the many mills. Someone had to look after the babies in the family so the mother chose one of Martha's sisters

Shore Mill, built by Mr Bamford in 1845, later run by Leech, Kershaw, Consterdine and Clegg for making fustian. Now demolished, the mill and reservoir are a site for new houses.

for the job. The school master used to comment wearily 'when I ask you why you were not at school yesterday do not tell me that you were looking after the babies again'

Both Martha's father and elder brother were in the army in the first world war. Her brother lied about his age and joined up when he was seventeen but said he was eighteen. He told his family he had volunteered because he wanted to see the world. He was killed on the Somme. Very poor, Martha's mother , in addition to working at the Wheatsheaf, took in washing from wealthy families which took all day to wash with a mangle tub and hand wringer. Even when he was back home Martha's mother said that her husband gave his family half his wage, but that it was the smaller half. Martha does not remember actually going hungry; one of the neighbours used to say that her mother could make a dinner out of a 'dishclowt'.

At work the employees were told little of what went on in the mill. Their world was limited to the machine they were working on. They had no idea of the wider picture of what was made or where it went. To quote Martha, 'nobody told us anything'. One thing she did discover from the other workers was that during the war they were making khaki and navy cotton cloth (mainly khaki) for the army and navy uniforms for troops serving in the tropical countries. She gathered that in previous wars all the uniforms were made in wool and this was a big change. She knew the material was very strong and she said occasionally damaged pieces would find their way home in the women's bags.

In the war, Mr Ernst Harvey's wife was moved to make a contribution to the war effort. She decided to come down to the dinner room in the cottage and give the women lectures on sound nutrition. She duly turned up in shiny leather boots (all the girls wore clogs) and a fur trimmed coat and large feather trimmed hat. The girls were admonished 'see you behave yourselves when Mrs Ernst comes'. She was in full flight about the virtues of making nourishing broth from vegetables and bones, 'as you can't get meat', when a bold woman from the back stood up and interrupted (Martha said the women who came from Rochdale were a rougher sort and more outspoken):

"Eh Missus, I want to know who's having all this meat off these bones we're stewing ..."

Martha said that they all had it on good authority from a servant, at Townhouse, the home of Gordon and Ernst Harvey, that they had chicken sandwiches for supper after their big dinner.

After she'd been at Fothergill's three years (during the first half of this time she was a 'half timer' at school) Martha's mother told her and her sister that they must go to work at Shore Mill because they paid better wages. They went but found it more daunting, more noisy, less friendly and there was not even a special place for them to have their dinner. They did earn more money, but sadly lost the Christmas party where, at Fothergill's, all the entertainment and food had been provided free.

It probably never occurred to them at the time, but later Martha was very conscious of the hard times they went through. Perhaps the deepest sadness was that they had lost most of what we regard today as the rights, pleasures and opportunities of being young.

The First World War 1914-18

When the First World War broke out many of the young men of Littleborough went to war, first as volunteers and from 1916 as conscripts. By 1915 most of the leading textile firms were dealing in government orders and the German submarine campaign led to rationing of raw cotton by the Cotton Control Board in 1917. All non-essential work was cut to 40 hours a week and to no more than half the available spindles. Despite all the mills working on reduced levels they were earning record profits. Restrictive labour practices had been relaxed and in many weaving sheds the workers were women.

A post-war world

Soon after the war, faced with striking workers, the industry conceded a 48 hour working week with no loss in pay. The industry was once more booming and wages continued to chase spiralling prices; some local workers experienced 25% to 29% increases in their wage packets. At just this time, both in Britain and elsewhere in the world, the growing clothing industry was starting to experiment with a new artificial silk called rayon which had been developed outside the mainstream of the traditional textile industry.

In the last months of 1920 the boom in the cotton trade once again collapsed. By the summer of 1921 there were large numbers unemployed or on short time. India had grown a home-based manufacturing industry and our market was disappearing. The Japanese cotton industry quadrupled its exports between 1913 and 1918, increasing its market share by 6% in the Far East markets.

Cotton-spinning wage rates were cut by 30% and the clothing trade rates fell by 12%. 1916 was the peak year in Lancashire for combined weaving and spinning firms, also for the firms specialising in weaving only. By 1928 the signs of contraction were everywhere; unemployment was high, under-employment was nearly universal with long unpaid holidays. Between the two world wars it was rare for a textile worker to look back on 12 months of continuous employment. Councils organised relief schemes, mainly involving road repairing or widening. Between 1911 and 1935 there was little growth in population: local birth rates fell to 10.4 per thousand compared with the national average of 14.7 and the death rate in our area was 16.3 compared with a national average of 11.7.

By 1928 the textile industry appeared to have a stable, if significantly reduced, situation. This plateau was illusory and in 1929 the textile trade plunged into depression once more and nationally unemployment in the cotton industry spiralled upwards from 9% to 40% in 1930. Already, back in 1926, the cotton employers had imposed an earnings reduction of 13% and the workers went on strike. The strike went to arbitration and the settlement agreed, led to a 6½ % reduction. There was another period with a damaging strike in 1928-32. The struggle between decent wages and declining profits and markets continued ending with a series of dramatic collapses of major textile concerns. In the Todmorden area for example, the largest spinning concern was sold for a token price while in 1926 the leading textile machine manufacturer collapsed and the work went to a unit in Manchester. By 1930 the biggest bobbin manufacturer was closed and the work moved to Liverpool. It became clear that the companies who were part of major conglomerates were most vulnerable. The Unions had a strong grip especially over the piece rates and the ratio of looms to workers and they fought modernisation. Employers responded with autocratic management and a decision to retain old machinery and to slash the workforce.

Throughout the 1920s there was a wish to ignore the most important results of the terrible war. The writing was on the wall that our export markets were shrinking rapidly and the national figure for cotton exports fell by 75% between 1929 and 1937. The Japanese had created an integrated industry, built up of a number of major units and had invested in the latest technology. They had also funded research to carry it forward in the future. At much the same time we still had masses of merchant convertors all pointed at specific markets. In 1920 the Manchester Royal Exchange had a membership of 11,539 which was to fall to 5000 by 1939. The period from 1920-31 was an economic catastrophe which destroyed a way of life that had grown and prospered for more than 150 years.

In 1926 Ernst Harvey died leaving three children, Alexander (Jnr), Charles and Barbara. The boys were too young to take over so a caretaker director, Alec Sandys, was appointed. He had the job of steering Fothergill and Harvey through ten very difficult years until in 1936 Alexander and Charles took over and ran the operation until 1946 when they were replaced by the creation of a public company with a board of directors.

From 1931 onwards the history in our area is one of a 'roller coaster', sometimes going up but inexorably falling to a lower level with businesses continuing to collapse. For example, in 1936 - 37 there was a minor boom and for the first time since 1920 a rise in cotton wages of some 6 - 7%. 1938 saw the loss of this gain and the numbers of spindles and looms fell below the 1916 level. Weaving sheds prospered or closed for complex reasons of market position, finance or management but times were unremittingly difficult.

Even the hosiery industry suffered in the general decline of textile manufacture and in Littleborough, Grimshaws, Cryers, and Taylor & Stansfield all closed down during the 1930's.

In summary, the U.K. industry had not adapted to the existing conditions so finally it was outside entities, first the banks and then the government (Cotton Spinning Industry Act 1936), which finally imposed amalgamation and the scrapping of surplus or obsolete operations. The following figures are eloquent:

Cotton Industry 1912-39

	Spindles (millions)		Looms (Thousands)
	Mule	Ring	
1912	45	10	786
1930	42	13	700
1939	24	10	495

In 1912 we had a huge market for low quality goods in poor countries. We did not accept until the 1920s that we would never return to pre-war levels. The Japanese embarked with a few high quality companies and started with cotton blends and 'high through-put' equipment. We lost our low quality markets as each country began to meet its own needs. Sadly, we were not ready for many years to compete in the new 'niche' markets of fashion driven textiles closely integrated to major retail corporations. We were not alone in Europe; only Italy, which had been at the poorest end of textile manufacture, was able to make a new start and subsequently prosper through companies such as Benetton.

UK firms finally began to group and consolidate their marketing operations, but they still resisted direct connection with the retailers and the consequent loss of control once they were dependent on direct trade organisations. Lancashire was locked into 19th century trading structures; there was both inertia to overcome and a major learning process to be absorbed to adapt to the new balance that was emerging between making textile goods and selling them.

By and large at this stage the mills in the Littleborough area were still in the hands of the families who originally owned them. For example, Sir Alfred Law still controlled the Durn and Lydgate mills. The workers were on declining wages and short time and their annual holidays often became a matter nearly of dread since they were not paid. The Unions campaigned for paid holidays from 1920 and achieved one week's paid holiday in 1939. However, war was to break out that year and there was once again the prospect of 'full employment'.

World War Two 1939-45

The mills were often re-opened not to work on government textile contracts but as military storage depots or in suppport of some part of the food industry. Early in the war the West View and Sun mills were both used to house soldiers in transit. Later the West View Mill housed R.A.S.C. soldiers who were subsequently shipped to the battlefields in the deserts of North Africa. It later reverted to a storage depot staffed by soldiers described as 'on war work'. Local rumour claimed that there were carefully guarded cells at the back of the mill. After Dunkirk the Sun Mill became an Royal Army Service Corps depot with a big staff of A.T.S. girls, many of whom were billeted locally. The subsequent history was less exciting as the Home Guard took over the basement for .22 rifle practice and then shared it with the Army Cadets and the Boy Scouts practicing for their marksmans badge. During the war the Breda Visada mill was partly

Sometime around 1930 this aerial view shows Fothergill & Harveys Sladen Wood Mill between Todmorden Road and the canal with the recently built houses at Timbercliffe on the hillside (Aerofilms library).

operated by prisoners of war. This caused much resentment as they were 'bussed' to and from Rochdale daily whilst the local workers got soaked, standing at the adjacent bus stops.

By 1941 the textile industry was short of labour and cotton and 40% of the cotton mills and the weaving sheds of Lancashire were closed. Prices were controlled and profits guaranteed on the Government projects, which were mainly military contracts and the utility clothing scheme (1941). The cotton workers were subject to 'essential work orders' which prevented them from changing jobs without permission.

The Textile Industry 1950 - 2000

The Aftermath of the Second World War

The European war ended in 1945 and the textile industry found itself in the forefront of a programme to revive industries fortunes with the slogan 'Britain's bread hangs by Lancashire's thread'. The textile industry responded in many ways: Fothergill and Harvey bought new companies and also created a number of overseas subsidiaries, including Australia (PTY) Ltd and Rhodesia (PTY) Ltd. The outline of this policy was decided towards the end of the war when they bought Ealees Mill from the Ealees Dying Company. This was followed by the purchase of Gale Mill in 1950 from Fredrick Scott, Printers. To support all these initiatives they also set up a new Research Unit in 1945 which was in place by the time they became a public company in 1946.

In the period immediately after 1945 both mainland Europe and Japan were dislocated and there were some five years when we were insulated against both, in terms of competition.

1950-65

The decline of traditional textiles and the rise of artificial fibre

Despite government help and strenuous efforts by the employers, by 1950 about one third of all spindles were idle, partly due to the shortage of labour. Our markets were slipping away and British West Africa, South Africa and Australia were our largest remaining outlets. The period was one when all possibilities were explored including: purchase of new machinery, establishing plants overseas, seeking niche markets, adopting new products, lobbying for input controls and subsidies and seeking to regulate or restrict competition.

Vertical integration, with all major functions of the textile industry under one roof or at least in one company was seen by some as the way forward. However this approach had already been tested and was judged to have failed in the USA so that by the 1960s the Americans were the prime protagonists of an 'old fashioned' protective regime to preserve their internal market. The large UK firms had money but lacked experience in overseas investment. The spokesmen of the textile industry declared the President of the Board of Trade had become 'Lancashire's 'Hangman' and the Japanese were demonised.

Many working people who were very conscious of the hard times experienced between the two wars, with poor wages and long bouts of unemployment, were not keen to go back into the mills. However, there was little else left to do locally, outside the service industries related mainly to transport and the retail industry. Slowly there was a radical overhaul of work practices and ways of payment. Modern machinery was introduced alongside evening shifts and mill nurseries. In the late 1940's we started to invite in migrants and displaced persons from central and eastern Europe, Malta, Germany, Poland, Ukraine, Czechoslovakia and Pakistan.

What work would the new industries give the returning men and the women? For many families and at many levels related to job opportunities, education and general conditions, it became an era of uncertainty.

Apart from the other issues there were disturbing signs that the rump of the local cotton industry was starting to contract again. Our scrapping and re-equipping programmes were not working quickly enough or widely enough. Japanese competition was reviving on a world wide scale with competition made more intense by the growth, in Western Europe, of a textile industry based on high technology, using modern techniques. At the same time low wage economies could, of all industries, expand most easily in textiles. By the late 1950's Britain's home market was flooded with imports mainly from India, Pakistan and Hong Kong, imported under Commonwealth Trading Arrangements.

The future seemed to lie in enforced spinning integration, professional management, revised labour practices and new technology. In addition it was planned to limit both internal competition and Japanese imports. In 1948 the Cotton Industry (re-equipment subsidy) Act authorised £12 million for spinners to re-equip with a 25%

subsidy. Only £2.6 milllion was taken up, since without world wide regulation of production it would not pay existing UK manufacturers to modernise.

The local response of Fothergill and Harvey was to consciously address the need to break with cotton and diversify. To survive in the 20th century diversity and specialisation both seemed important. The solution in the 1970s was to create separate divisions each with a clear focus:

Composite Division;

Carbon, Glass and organic fibre reinforced resins. The applications were aimed at the aircraft, medical and general engineering sector.

Industrial Textiles Design

This division was based on the skills of the traditional cotton industry which were turned to industrial uses for synthetic and glass fibres. Between 1971 - 1974 modern (foreign made) Ruti Looms were installed in Rock Nook and Sladen Mills with matching finishing plant. They chose to move into textile products including the weaving of glass fibre and other synthetic products for domestic and industrial use.

Tygaflor Division

This was given a separate company identity and specialised in the the use of PTFE (Polytetrafluoroethylene). One departure was the development, of a glass-based fabric coated with PTFE better known as Teflon. The trade name of the product was Tygadur and during the marketing great use was made of the old Fothergill and Harvey symbol of the Bengal Tiger. This logo, shades of the old cotton connection with India, can still be seen in Peter Street, Manchester carved in stone at the entrance to the old Head Office of Fothergill and Harvey. It also appeared in tiles on some of the mill walls. Today it is woven into the selvage of the fabric.

To support the diversification and speed up the entry into the appropriate markets Fothergills embarked on the purchase of a number of outside companies including: Martin Goacher Ltd., Ogden Smiths and Hussey Ltd., Technical Woodwork Ltd., Readimades Ltd., F & H (Crenette) Ltd. and Lantor Ltd. These purchases were to help the diversification away from traditional textiles; in addition companies such as Anodium Ltd. and Wills (Bridgewater) Ltd., were purchased for entry into new areas.

Looking outside Littleborough it is clear that all over Lancashire mill groups were belatedly rationalising their structures and turning to artificial fibres. In 1959, for the first time, cotton cloth imports exceeded exports in the U.K. Reeling under this and other blows the cotton industry was offered a government sponsored package for contraction and re-equipping. Many of the firms had only been able to survive because they had written off the cost of their buildings and machinery long before. The Act was a way out, and Littleborough was hit by a wave of closures (which also happened industry wide). The detail of the closures was complex but the result was that in the weaving sector only 30% of the looms remained in the early 1960s that had been in place in 1946.

Some firms did re-equip parts of their plant with impressive results. One firm with more than 500 old looms was able to replace them with 72 automatics. One weaver could handle 20 to 30 of these machines.

In the middle of this turmoil, Courtaulds and ICI, both giant artificial fibre manufacturers, revolutionised the structure of ownership in the textile industry during the 1960s. By 1970 there was virtually no cotton industry only a textile one based on artificial fibres. Courtaulds were deeply committed to rayon and lost their private war with ICI to the point where ICI made a bid to buy them in 1961. This bid was thwarted and Courtaulds decided to 'buy into cotton' to safeguard their rayon business. By 1968 Courtaulds controlled 10% of Lancashire's spinning capacity, 12% of the weaving along with extensive knitting finishing and merchanting capacity. ICI responded to this danger of the market being 'smothered', deciding to fund acquisitions through their allies, Viyella International and Carrington & Dewhurst. In 1970 these two merged to become Carrington Viyella with ICI holding a 35% share in the group.

1963 became known locally as 'the year of merger mania' with the Carrington and Viyella Groups, Courtaulds and Ward and Goldstone leading the way by buying up and consolidating numerous private firms into more 'viable' units. Mills were closed, new managers brought in, modern equipment installed, including break spinning and shuttleless weaving.

In all this activity very few of our local mills escaped direct or indirect impact from this commercial struggle. For example in 1970 Fothergill and Harvey bought part of the mill known as Breda Visada near the new police station. They set up a rayon mill and commenced to make 'art silk'. 'Fothergills' was finally bought by Courtaulds and it was reorganised into new commercial units, only to be disposed of piecemeal a few years later. A similar sequence of events happened to the Kershaw group of mills and these are summarised later in this chapter

Courtaulds alone spent £57 million on textile machinery and factories. British manufacturers were no longer competent to make such advanced new machinery so, between 1970-76, 89% of the firms who re-equipped went abroad to purchase.

The Carrington Viyella merger was not a success; in turn it was taken over by Vantona. The restrictions on imports were not effective and the new plants could not get consistent long runs to exploit the new equipment. Italy proved to be Europe's most consistently successful textile manufacturer in this era. They stayed with small runs, supplied textiles to the fashion conscious and eschewed the low quality products. Their forward integration was to the fashion markets. British manufacturing was seen as shoddy and lacking in style and chic.

By the early 1960s out of all the mergers and turmoil some modern units did emerge in our area, as elsewhere. These units were well equipped, highly organised, capable of efficient production, paying viable, if not high wage levels and fully exploiting multi-shift working sometimes based on immigrant labour. But it was no longer a cotton industry, rather an industry of artificial fibres and blends with cotton and wool.

The Kershaws: a local textile family

A specific example will illustrate much of what happened locally. The Kershaws were typical of the local families who entered the textile industry in the 19th century and made a considerable success of their business. They had a complex of mills and at the foot of Blackstone edge was Sladen Mill which was one of the earliest recorded water-power sites in Littleborough. The Woodcock Inn (now demolished) stood beside it and sitting on the hillside above the mill was a fine stone house, Hollow Field, where the Kershaws lived. The Sladen mill was the biggest of their mills and it was gutted by fire in 1901. The mill had been a 'statement of pride' about the confidence of the textile industry but it was replaced by more utilitarian space. The partially re-built structure was burnt down again in 1926. Meanwhile about a quarter of a mile away, up a side valley was another mill which they owned, the Wellfield Mill or to local people 'the Top Mill'. This was a fulling mill which beat, compressed and shrunk yarn. This mill was destroyed by fire in 1965 and its chimney became a local celebrity for a few days as it twice resisted the attempts to fell it with dynamite. Finally it emerged the chimney had two skins each more than 3' thick and a cavity between. It only fell after breaking into the cavity and manually weakening the structure. The work from the Wellfield mill was brought down to the once more restored Sladen mill. By 1967 the Wellfield work was housed in brand new premises beside the Sladen mill. The Charles Kershaw (1927) company was now part of the Ashton Group for whom it bleached, dyed, and finished cotton piece goods. The new mill claimed total integration of the latest ideas in chemical processing, machinery, building construction and design, services and effluent disposal. The opportunity was taken to introduce a simpler and more effective bleaching process using hydrogen peroxide. The initial outcome of all the changes was that productivity doubled and it was claimed the high quality of the product was maintained.

The Chief Engineer of the Ashton group said:

'The plant is laid out in accordance with the best American and Continental practice maximum attention has been paid to illumination and to walls and floors. The latest equipment for air conditioning and steam extraction has been installed. Along with the bright airy office working conditions are ideal'.

The Senior Management said:

'We are now equipped with both a mill and technique which are unsurpassed in the bleaching field'.

Probably none of these people or the workers could have guessed that within a few years they would have been taken over by Courtaulds and not much later a large 'for sale' notice' would be displayed in 1980. It was bought by an entrepreneur and split into units. The units have housed plastic extrusion, engineering, a firm dealing in brick and stone, and a unit that dyed and finished textiles. This unit at least, still needed the soft, pure water from the moors which played such a part in the history of the textile industry generally.

The world's verdict seemed to be that the U.K. textile industry had re-organised too late to suppport a major general product market. The future for our firms seemed to demand a blend of innovation in the product and strong marketing. In the spring of 1959 unemployment in Littleborough was 9% which was 3 times the national average. Increasingly people lived in the district and worked elsewhere with Manchester as the obvious magnet.

The end of the Fothergill and Harvey Group

In 1970s Fothergill and Harvey continued a determined drive to transform their business and were amongst the first to move into the 'Aramid' fibres and carbon fibre products. This move was made in co-operation with the Royal Aircraft Establishment, who provided technological backing, which enabled Fothergills to maintain their leading role. Despite diversification and modernisation, an apparently unstoppable trend led to Courtaulds P.L.C purchasing the Fothergill and Harvey Group to provide itself with a base to enter the world of advanced fibre technology.

Within a few years Courtaulds had to withdraw and in 1995 Fothergill Engineered Fabrics emerged from the break up, as an independent, private, limited company. In 1997 it had 130 employees and was confident of a modest expansion. Its basic objective was to be amongst Europe's leading suppliers of woven and high performance textiles - in a very capital intensive industry. The products find outlets in ships, computers, space and defence applications, special coatings and glass and aramid woven protection.

Some of the technology is fascinating. For example: in terms of bullet penetration a glass woven fibre is said to be three times as strong as steel. Kevlar, a new woven product, is said to be three times as strong as glass-based fabrics and a recently specified product aims to be three times stronger than Kevlar. However bullet penetration is being improved in a matching way! Finally, it appears there is much less resistance from current materials to a strong stab from a fine pointed weapon - so another technical challenge exists in this area.

It is very encouraging that, depite all the contraction in business and loss of employment, a local initiative has managed to retain a position in one really innovative sector of the new fabric industry. Another part of the dismembered Fothergill and Harvey Group was incorporated into a different area of high technology, modern cable manufacture, when it was purchased by Raydex (CDT).

The Woollen Industry

The woollen industry started centuries before cotton but it also had its severe problems and set backs as the 20th century progressed. In the 1970s the once flourishing woollen industry had been reduced to the following mills:

> C.W.S Hare Hill Mills: closed in the late 70s
> Sykes and Olivers Dry Dock Mill: closed in 1979
> A. & W. Laws Mills: closed in 1973

Laws Mills were bought by a Rochdale group who were working with man made fibres. This work continued until a serious fire in the 1980s lead to the demolition of the mill. The fire was so serious that local properties had to be evacuated for some days including the nearby old people's residence. Emergency accommodation was found mainly with other local families.

With the loss of the cotton and woollen mills it is clear that Littleborough had totally lost the textile industry that had suppported its growth in size and its prosperity for more than 150 years.

Some units still remain in specialist areas. For example Walsden Printing Co. does bleaching at Gale Mill in preparation for printing the cloth at the Walsden unit.

Earlier, the tenacity and continued prosperity of units at Rakewood was noted. John Clegg opened a mill there to spin cotton waste, which he converted in 1863 to the more profitable business of taking prepared wool and making it into 'Welsh flannel'. The mill was driven by water power and a beam engine. The area being remote, orders came from manufacturers by homing pigeons housed at the top of the mill. When John died in 1873 his widow carried on the business which at this stage used the most primitive tools and techniques. In 1890 they got the first 'tenter' machine and when the widow Ann died in 1892 the business went to the sons Edwin and John. Edwin

Shore House, home of the mill owning Clegg family; now demolished.

carried the business forward and in his time the firm made a major contribution to the manufacture of 'Lancashire flannel' which became second only to the Welsh original. In 1912 it became a limited comapany J Clegg & Brothers (Rakewood) Ltd. and in 1916 John and Henry Clegg took it over introduced modern procedures and enjoyed a period of great success. The mill ceased weaving in the late 70s but continued as bleachers and dyers. At the year 2000, though much contracted, the mill still finishes some woollen goods on a site which can be proud of 137 years of wool finishing managed by one family, including (a wry comment) more than 70 years of flannel.

Apart from these survivors the industry today only lives in the street names, old buildings, accessible knowledge and examples of the main elements of the processes, which can be seen in a spread of industrial museums in north east Lancashire.

The death of the textile industry

The problems which led to the virtual demise of the textile industry in Littleborough district were the same problems that affected all Lancashire and indeed other parts of Britain. The consensus appears to be that there was a lack of investment in modern textile machinery until it was too late, which left us using the spinning mule long after the foreign competitors had installed faster ring spinning frame and automatic looms. As we slowly modernised we sold our older equipment on the 'far side' of the world only to find that they had assembled it, improved it and with cheap labour were taking our markets. The trade recessions became more prolonged leading to a world wide slump in the 1920's and 1930's and after the second world war the overseas competition became fierce.

Britain was weakened by the loss of an Empire and through fighting another lengthy war. Despite late attempts at modernisation and amalgamation to create viable competitive units, it was too late. In the late 1940s Cleggs Shore Mills installed the latest textile machinery under the guidance of the Shirley Institute, in a completely modernised environment. They were determined to keep at least a diminished market. In 1948 they amalgamated with another firm to become Clegg Orr. In 1964 this unit was absorbed into Viyella International who closed the mill down in 1967 with the loss of 500 jobs. This was the last surviving cotton mill in the Littleborough district. In the 70's and 80's the Clegg Mills were used by a pharmaceutical manufacturer prior to closure and subsequent demolition. The site is being developed with over 100 houses (Edmunds Close etc). One reminder of the Cleggs are the workers houses that they built in the nearby Hodder and Ribble Avenues.

In 1965 Fothergill and Harvey abandoned the spinning and weaving of cotton and devoted their efforts towards the manufacture of goods from artificial fibres. The local opinion was dismissive of this move; the local newspaper headline read 'The Python drooped his head and became an artificial silk worm.' The underlying fact was that demand and consumer taste were driving the industry and the remaining British firms could not react to it.

From the base of 1939 figures, by 1980 consumption of raw cotton, the output of cotton yarn and cloth had all fallen by more than 80% or more. At the same time between 1950-80 employment in the cotton sector fell by 70%.

In the last 20 years of the century computer design and machine control have afforded another opportunity and in the remaining rump of the industry there are healthy signs that the conscious economy in all areas and the identification of specialised markets are transforming the units into world competitors.

Epitaph: the Albion Mill

In searching for a suitable epitaph for the period a brief history of the Albion mill will serve.

In the 1840s a Consterdine (Betty) and a Kershaw (John) rented part of Shore mill to weave fustians and corduroys. In 1851-2 they moved the work to a new mill on Canal Street built on the 'brook field'. (This mill was finally demolished in the 1930's and its chimney felled in 1952).

Consterdine's wife left the original partnership for cotton spinning and built a mill at Featherstall in 1867. This was the Albion mill and she traded under the name Consterdine Brothers & Co. Cotton Spinners and Manufacturers. The brothers were her two sons. The business closed in 1878-9 and one brother became a small shop keeper selling jams and preserves. The other brother was found dead in 1885. To quote the Rochdale Observer 'shocking suicide of Littleborough Gentleman'. He was found by his wife 'with his throat cut and covered in blood: a large carving knife was found by the body.' His wife lived to be 91 and is in the family grave at Holy Trinity church.

The Albion Mill was built from brick manufactured at the Chelburn Brickworks. The only stone used was for the cills and an ornamental frame round the main entrance dated 1867. The site was a triangular piece of land at the Featherstall end of Willliam street.

The land was let on a 999 year lease at an annual rent of £55 - 2s. In 1876 the Consterdines got into a dispute with the workers who were locked out. There was physical violence and one of the pickets was fined 40/- or a month in jail for an assault on a 'scab or blackleg'; an ex-employee who was strike breaking.

After the Consterdines' business failed (circa 1878) a cotton waste spinner took on the mill and produced warps and wefts until 1891. Next came J T Jackson of Hurstead who produced more specialist yarns and wefts until 1917 with a labour force of some 24 men as mule spinners (they spun the cotton to yarn and wound the yarn onto spindles). Following the First World war a company founded in 1917, The Albion Mill (Littleborough) Ltd, retained the Albion mill until 1962 and produced yarns and wefts by mule and ring spinning. After the Second World war commercial production was resumed, but the number of spindles (19,000 in 1870's; 10,800 in 1938) was reduced below 10,000 in 1958 and in 1962 the mill closed.

During its lifetime workers who mainly lived near the mill, would often take their breaks at home and use them for cleaning, shopping and caring for their children. The mill had no canteen and no modern toilets, using the infamous 'tub closets'. These were carted right through the sheds to be emptied, a practice which ended in 1947.

The mill opened again in 1965 as Boro. Candlewick Textiles manufacturing bedspreads from artificial fibres, so ending 95 years as a cotton mill. The company operated until 1998 when the mill closed for the last time.

The land was sold for residential development. In March 1998 the Albion Mill, perhaps the last purpose- built mule spinning mill in Littleborough was demolished. In its lifetime, except for an extension, few changes had been made to the main body of the mill. The interior had massive timber binders, floor joists and staunch iron supports. There was extensive woodwork in the offices and the exterior was Flemish Bond brick. It was a splendid example of a spinning mill of the mid-1800's. The demolition can be seen as a serious loss of a building of special architectural and historical interest which we may come to regret.

The main textile story was over by the 1980's and in Littleborough (as throughout the whole of Lancashire) everyone recognised that employment within the textile industry, on a big scale with jobs for life, was a thing of the past.

CHAPTER FIFTEEN

THE NINETEENTH CENTURY

PART FIVE : THE GROWTH OF LITTLEBOROUGH
1800 - 1850

With a picture of the rise and decline of the textile industry in Littleborough (chapters 13 & 14) it is possible to step back in time to 1800 and look at the impact on all aspects of our society of these sweeping events.

In chapters 11 & 12 there is a description of our area and its communications along with an outline of the impact of the introduction of the canal and the railway. These developments provided the basis for the growth of a range of new industries alongside the massive growth of the textile industry.

All these events gave rise to dramatic changes in how local people were employed and where they lived. It was the time when the focus of living moved away from the hill settlements, like Smithy Nook and Whittaker, down to the valley bottom centring on Littleborough.

Littleborough village in 1800

By the end of the 18th century there was widespread insecurity, as traditional work no longer provided an adequate income and many of the alternative occupations were hazardous, unregulated and did not provide enough work for the people. One result was that in our area many families were crowded together in inadequate premises. New industries were welcomed, mining and lime burning for example offered some spasmodic work. The fact was that the traditional ways of living were declining and Littleborough was on the threshold of becoming a 'textile town'. Soon the main river valley and the tributaries were harnessed to provide water-power for mills that were carding, spinning and weaving.

So, in 1800 all over our district there were small weaving sheds and in addition, within each small commnity and the surrounding farms, people were spinning yarn and weaving cloth. Much of the quality of their life was still rural.

The population explosion which was happening at a national level was also reflected locally.

	Year	Population
Blatchinworth and Calderbrook	1800	2000
	1821	3143
	1841	4466
	1851	4600

Littleborough at the beginning of the 19th century, at a casual glance, was a small hamlet with three coaching houses, whose prosperity was based on the increased traffic with the coming of the turnpike roads. A closer look would have revealed the growth of new facilities and services such as the provision of a regular mail delivery.

Sometime around 1900 the corner of Littleborough Square was home to at least four small businesses including Wild the Shoemender.

A map of the Littleborough area in the early 19th Century shows that small communities have grown up at the significant road junctions with modest 'ribbon development' on the older roads. Even in 1850 the centre of Littleborough is not notably bigger than Featherstall; Calder Moor is a sizable independent community as is Durn. The most prominent map features are the tenter grounds which had rows of frames on which manufactured cloth could retain its shape whilst being stretched and dried.

In Littleborough there were a number of houses with large gardens and the river, running through the town, was mainly in its natural watercourse with a number of bridges over it. The area that is now the centre of Littleborough, was called Marsden Holme. The Saxons settled here early in the 11th century and it still retained the place name which they gave to it. The literal meaning is 'the meadow land in the marshy valley.' (Holme - meadow; den - valley; and mars - marsh).

This low lying part of the district had not been greatly developed over the centuries, most of the land was still being used for grazing. The village of Littleborough was built on seven modest hills. The actual hills have almost disappeared, but we still retain their names: Chapel Hill, Seed Hill, Will Hill, James Hill, Bare Hill, Hare Hill, and Shore Hill. Until the late 1800s Hare Hill and Shore Hill play a small part in Littleborough's growth as the former was owned by the Newall family and the latter was too remote to play a significant part in the first developments.

Of the remaining five hills, James Hill was fairly large at this time and covered with market gardens, but when the valley road through to Todmorden was made in 1824, James Hill and Will Hill and probably the others as well, were brought down to their present level, the top soil taken to form the road over Marsden Holme (Gale Flat). Bare Hill, as the name implies, was bare at this time, without a single house or farm. Before

SOME FEATURES OF LITTLEBOROUGH IN THE EARLY 19th CENTURY

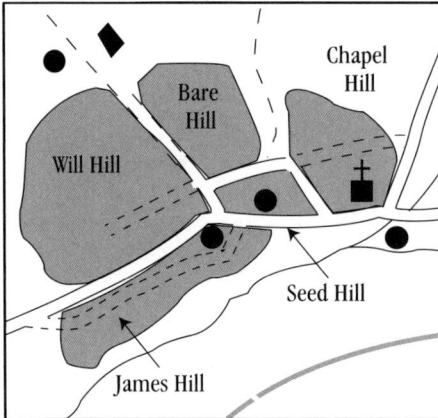

The Hills of Littleborough

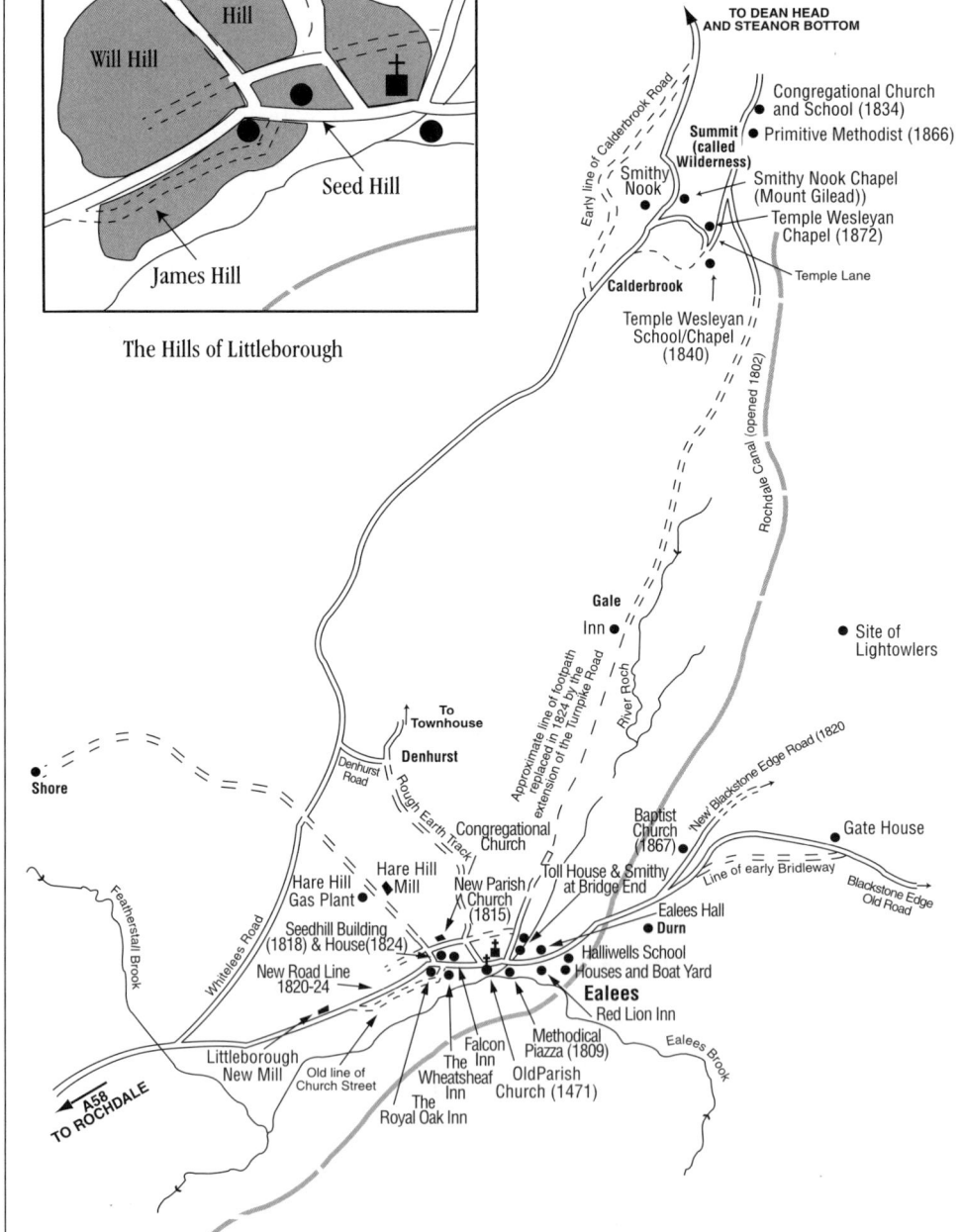

Will Hill

Bare Hill

Chapel Hill

Seed Hill

James Hill

TO DEAN HEAD AND STEANOR BOTTOM

Early line of Calderbrook Road

Congregational Church and School (1834)

Primitive Methodist (1866)

Summit (called Wilderness)

Smithy Nook

Smithy Nook Chapel (Mount Gilead))

Temple Wesleyan Chapel (1872)

Temple Lane

Calderbrook

Temple Wesleyan School/Chapel (1840)

Rochdale Canal (opened 1802)

Gale

Inn

Site of Lightowlers

Approximate line of footpath replaced in 1824 by the Turnpike Road extension

River Roch

To Townhouse

Denhurst

Denhurst Road

Rough Earth Track

Shore

New Blackstone Edge Road (1820

Gate House

Congregational Church

Baptist Church (1867)

Line of early Bridleway

Blackstone Edge Old Road

Hare Hill Gas Plant

Hare Hill Mill

New Parish Church (1815)

Toll House & Smithy at Bridge End

Ealees Hall

Durn

Seedhill Building (1818) & House(1824)

Halliwells School Houses and Boat Yard

Whiteleas Road

Featherstall Brook

New Road Line 1820-24

Ealees

Red Lion Inn

A58 TO ROCHDALE

Littleborough New Mill

Old line of Church Street

Falcon The Inn

Wheatsheaf Inn

Methodical Piazza (1809)

OldParish Church (1471)

Ealees Brook

The Royal Oak Inn

180

the construction of the canal and railway, Chapel Hill was a natural extension of the Cleggswood Estate of Thomas Thornhill, covering the land represented by the Parish Church and school between Lodge Street and Todmorden Road and stopping short of Newall Street. It formed the end of Ealees. James Hill ran from the centre of Littleborough between the A58 and the river to Box Street. Though covered with market gardens at the start of the century the area around the present day James Hill Street became known locally as Bogey or Boggie Hill and it became a notorious part of Littleborough - said to be full of drunkards and disreputable lodging houses. Certainly conditions were very poor with excreta observed in open drains at the end of the century, it was 1950 before some of the very old property was finally demolished.

The village started to grow in the 18th century. For example between 1786-99 houses were built fronting Church Street, from a point opposite the United Free Methodist Church as far as Hare Hill road. In addition Littleborough New Mill was built at the Featherstall end of the run of houses on the site opposite Charles Street.

An increase in tempo began when the canal was opened in 1802. At the time the whole district had a population of about 2000 people and Littleborough village had a passable road to the larger community of Featherstall on one side and the 'new' upland road to Summit. From the centre of the community there was a 'cut' through the fields to Laneside then on to Calderbrook, which was a thriving hamlet. At this time people thought of themselves as living in a location such as Shore or Gatehouse and Littleborough was reserved for those in the lower lying central area. The present Littleborough square was a sunken green hollow with a stream through it which ran behind a hillock on which 'The Royal Oak' inn and farm stood. There was a whitewashed 'Wheat Sheaf' building on the slope and some three cottages facing the 'Falcon'.

At the beginning of the 19th century there was only one church in Littleborough. The Holy Trinity church (1471) stood between the present Parish church and the river and it was the last building of the village, on the line of the present road (along the valley bottom). There was a long gap before arriving at a farmhouse called 'the Brow', where Gale public-house now stands.

The next religious building to be built in Littleborough was a chapel, the 'Methodical Piazza', in 1809. It was sited where the railway arches cross the river Roch in the middle of Littleborough. It takes an act of imagination to see it surrounded, as it was, by green fields, with the river behind it and the lovely valley of Marsden Holme studded with tree life for its whole length, but especially in its higher reaches, as at Shop Wood, Sladen Wood, Grim Wood, Light Hazzels Wood, Chelburn Wood and Steanor Bottom Wood. Today these woods have almost entirely disappeared, or are represented by a few stunted trees

In Littleborough the Royal Oak, the Red Lion and the Falcon had large posting stables and grazing land to provide accommodation for the stage coaches between Manchester and Yorkshire, passing through the village. The Falcon was the pre-eminent coaching hostelry and John Travis claims it was the official 'change house' for horses. The Royal Oak was the richest in farmland. The 'Royal Oak' farmlands at that time went by the banks of the River Roch to Featherstall water and round by Whitelees to Hare Hill, and included James Hill, Will Hill and Bare Hill. On a map (1879), of the Peel family estate, an 'ancient highway' is marked from behind the Royal Oak going down James Hill at an angle towards Will Hill to meet the main highway, Church Street, between the present Morgan and Winton Streets.

Bridge Terrace and 'The Methodical Piazza' seen from Todmorden Road, probably in the 1940's.

Early in the century, by the Royal Oak there were a number of houses and houses-cum-shops and opposite, adjoining the Falcon, was a cart track that ran behind the Hare Hill Mill to Denehurst. Another cluster of buildings centered on the church and the old church school, extending to properties around Church Street which were built early in the century. Of course there was no Gale or Gale Road but behind the Red Lion were a cluster of buildings and cottages associated with the boat yard on the canal. These buildings were mainly swept away with the coming of the railway.

By 1818 the old Seed Hill building was erected with Seed Hill House being built in 1824. Nos. 96-102 Church Street carry date stones indicating that they were built in 1829. The most substantial buildings, between Hare Hill Road and Steanor Bottom, were probably the 'Old Sheaf', the Royal Oak and the Old Falcon Hotel. Round each of these buildings were a number of smaller ones. What is currently the most thickly populated part of the village was then and for a good many years after this time, practically non-existent. Much of Church street was not built, there was no Victoria Street, Hare Hill Road was a modest earth track, there was no Gale Road and no Summit.

A 'new' highway was constructed in 1820/24 which ran between James Hill and Will Hill, replacing the ancient one. It left the Royal Oak and passed through an area of market gardens. The lowland farming was mainly dairy cattle and in 1824-5 the owners of the Royal Oak placed a barn and shippon on James Hill, once the new highway was completed. It was only in the early 1900s that these buildings were pulled down to make room for 'The Queens' cinema.

The meadow land farmed by the owners of 'the Falcon' extended from where the church is today along one side of the river to what is now Gale; the 'Red Lion' farming the land on the opposite side of the river. At Gale there was a farm which went by the name of 'the Brow' but soon after the present road was made, in 1824, this farm was

Greenwood's Sadlers on Church Street at the back of the 'Royal Oak'. The barn became the site of 'The Queen's Cinema'.

pulled down and the public house named 'Gale' was built. A cotton spinning mill was built behind it by the Mr. Newall of that time. Of all the buildings 'the Sheaf ' which started modestly, was to become the most ornate.

An enthusiastic traveller's account in 1840 describes the flower gardens around the properties sloping down to a still unpolluted river Roch and the attractiveness of the James Hill area where the local gentry were starting to build fine houses. This must be qualified by the 1851 O/S map (surveyed 1847/8) which only shows two cultivated plots, one behind the site of the Trades Hall club and the other the vegetable gardens of the Falcon covering the ground west of the current post office round to the Cenotaph.

The 1851 O/S map shows the toll house and other buildings on what is now the square including the Wheatsheaf Inn, the Royal Oak and its outbuildings. The houses built by Sladen, the clerk to the church, on James Hill St, the first United Methodist Free Church chapel and the stone houses built in 1799 near Winton Street are all recorded. The Holy Trinity Church sits on Chapel Hill and the new houses can be seen on Ebor Street. Across the road is the Methodical Piazza and houses front the road.

The early 19th century Littleborough was a great contrast to the crowded state of the village centre today but by 1850 many recognisable landmarks were in place.

Commerce and Industry

Even at this early stage of Littleborough's development there were already identifiable areas focussing on commerce and industry.

Ealees and Durn

With the exception of Town House (Ton House) this is the oldest part of our village and the name Ealees is of Saxon origin. When the Saxons settled here in the 5th century A.D, following their usual custom, they gave it a name which described the

183

The view towards Littleborough from Halifax Road, Durn, about 1900. The buildings (near right) have long gone - the stone walls, other cottages and Durn Co-op remain today. The Uber Mill (left) burnt down in 1916.

area: 'Ea', meaning water (or a river) and 'lees' cultivated land. To the Saxons Ealees meant the 'cultivated land near the river.'

One of the very early stone buildings in Littleborough was called Ealees Hall. This was a fairly large two-gabled house which stood just beyond the present railway arches. The hall was pulled down in 1837, when the site was required for building this part of the railway. Probably, with the exception of Lightowlers (Lightolres), Ealees Hall was the oldest house in the Littleborough area. The original Lightolres was not the present house of that name; it stood where the farm does today. Every vestige of this old house has also disappeared.

Starting with early examples of substantial houses, from the introduction of the local spinning and weaving of woollen and cotton goods Ealees has been a centre of industry. An inventory in 1910 showed that Ealees and Durn district included: Uber mill, Frankfort mill, Durn foundry, the mortuary, pipeworks, Durn mill, West View mill and a number of smaller collieries and mills further up the Ealees valley.

The Old Smithy

Until the introduction of railways around 1840, using a horse was the quickest way of moving from place to place and around it grew up a set of related industries in wheels, carts, carriages and gear. It is not surprising that, after the new Blackstone Edge road had been completed in 1820 and the present main road to Todmorden in 1824, the large number of stage coaches and other traffic passing along these roads necessitated some larger and more convenient place for shoeing the horses and other necessary repairs than the Smithy at Calderbrook. So in 1825 the 'Smithy' was built on land at Marsden Holme (Maden Square) adjacent to both toll roads and close to the toll house.

In the Littleborough area Galloways were still a very common working horse being ideally suited to the many poor moorland paths. Families travelling with packhorses or

sometimes using them to pull a cart, would call on the upland and urban communities to sell lime, coal, 'lading cans' and a load of 'sandstone' to scour the stone flags of domestic kitchens. This trade is still remembered by the name of an inn, on the road from Littleborough to Rochdale, called 'The Sand Knockers'

When the Beautiful Littleborough Society was formed by Gordon Harvey they planted trees at Maden Square in the 1920s. They discovered a stone behind the smithy which originally formed part of the old doorway. It had the inscription '1825' and the sign of a horseshoe carved on it.

Littleborough in 1850.

The Ordnance Survey map of 1851 shows some of the impact of the previous 50 years of development (see p.186).

The life of the people

At the beginning of the 19th century, in a society still rooted in agriculture and with few other opportunities for earning money, the food of the people was rough and coarse. It consisted chiefly of porridge and milk, or oatmeal and water, transformed into parkin, cake-bread, or stirabout. The stirabout was often the basis of dinner, with a bacon collop (slice) served with the fat yielded by roasting or frying. This formed one of the better sort of meals.

Wheat flour was very expensive and could not be afforded by the poor, except for sizing warps with and occasionally to make a loaf or a few muffins, or at other times for a flour suet parkin baked on th'back-stone. The parkin, when ready, was cut into shares by the mother and dealt out, a share to everyone. With a pot of mint or penny royal tea, 'sweetened' with treacle, it was a most substantial meal. Such an occurrence happened perhaps once a week and was counted as a red letter day. But

185

BLATCHINWOR

47

B

Whitfield

Gale

Calder Moor

Littleborough

Featherstal Mill

Featherstal

Rake
Wood

L

1676

Hollingworth Hill

Hollingworth Reservoir

Little Clegg

oftener than not it was a 'mess of chell porridge' sweetened wi' treacle, three times a day. Chell porridge was made by taking a few spoonfuls of oatmeal and mixing it with cold water and then boiling well and afterwards adding treacle as a sweetener. There was only a scattering of wooden shops selling necessities and a market which was originally on the forecourt of the Royal Oak but was moved, by the owner's request, to the site where the Coach House is now. There are some indications that local commerce in food was becoming a more profitable activity, such as the growth of market gardens alongside the large kitchen gardens attached to the major houses and inns.

Fred Jackson contributed an interesting slant on the local social conditions in the early part of the 19th century. To the problems that might arise from a generally low standard of diet and poor physical living conditions, he added another factor:

"The making of the canal, reservoirs and railway had led to a large influx of strangers into our district. A good many of these on the completion of the above undertakings settled amongst us and some of them were of great help in the development of both Summit and Littleborough. Others were of a more undesirable character and helped considerably in lowering the tone of morality in the village. At this time there were at least seven public houses in the village of Summit and Smithy Nook alone and it should be remembered that at this time there were practically no restrictions on their opening and closing, some of them were open day and night and drinking and immorality was rife among a certain section of the community. Instead of 'Wakes Week' being a thing to look forward to, it became a nightmare to the more law abiding people, in striking contrast to what it is today. Even in the late 19th century, when I first knew the area, it was a common occurence for men to go on "Th' Rant" (drinking) for a week or a fortnight at a stretch.

Apart from the heavy drinking other conditions of life in a large number of villages and towns early in the 19th century were in a deplorable state and our district was no exception. No provision whatever was made for either the spiritual or mental welfare of the inhabitants."

Religion

Anglican Church

We have seen how the Abbot of Whalley reluctantly allowed the building of a church in Littleborough and much later the break away of the Protestant Movement from the Catholic Church. This split coincided with the end of the 'Middle Ages' and from AD 1500 to 1800 there was a struggle between two sets of believers.

Fred Jackson gives a summary of the local situation at the beginning of the 19th century.

"The religious life of the district was at a very low ebb at this time. Although the local population in 1817 was nearly 3000 people the only place of worship between Rochdale and Todmorden was Littleborough Church, and at this time it was very small, only capable of holding 200 people at the outside. According to Fishwick it was in a very deplorable and dilapidated condition."

The new Parish Church

The present church was built in 1815 and stands about 15 yards to the north of the old one (1471). There is the suggestion that the timing was in response to the recent building of the Methodical Piazza on the far side of the river. Alarm grew with this very visible spread of non-conformity. However, from 1824 there were Government grants to allow new Anglican churches to be built and with hindsight Littleborough may have acted too quickly by building the new parish church between 1815 and 1820 and paying for it by public subscription. Elsewhere, parish churches were rebuilt or extended with money demanded in reparation, after the defeat of Napoleon (1815) and the ending of the Napoleonic wars.

The new church was 'Gothic' in style with a small steeple, a bell and a clock. A contemporary view of it was:

'a painfully plain oblong building with galleries on three sides and seating for 401 people'.

In 1890 John Travis wrote:

'the venerable edifice of the old church was taken down and replaced by a neat erection of debased architecture.'

He also quotes Baines's History of Lancashire where it is indicated that the Parish Church was 'rebuilt' at least twice between 1471 and 1815.

For more than twenty years after this time it stood on an eminence, with the ground sloping gently down to cross where the present main road is to reach the site of the old chapel.

The graveyard was extended for a second time in 1820 but it was not until the early forties that the graveyard took its present form. After the opening of the railway for passenger traffic in 1839, the stage coaches were soon driven off the road and the large posting stables of the Falcon became obsolete and were turned to different uses. The large coaching house next to the Falcon was taken over and used by Englands, joiners and builders, for the best part of a century. This building was subsequently transformed by a community effort in the 1980s to become the Littleborough Coach House. Close by, soil was taken from the local 'hills' where other coaching stables had been sited, and it was used to raise the church grounds to their present level. At the same time the graveyard was walled and railed round. The iron railings surmounting the walls were removed for melting down in the second world war and today only the sockets remain visible on the cap stones of the wall.

Fred Jackson felt that the established church even in the early 19th century had made very little effort to improve local matters.

"St Chad's, Rochdale was very opposed to any fees, oblations or dues being diverted to the Parish Churches of either Littleborough or Todmorden. The result was that both found it difficult to carry out their work. All marriages from either village had to take place in St Chad's, Rochdale, or an extra fee had to be paid. It used to be a common practice for wedding couples and their friends to walk three or four miles over the hills to St Chad's to get wed before the morning service, then after a short rest at some public-house in town to walk back again."

As we follow the overall development of religious practice in our district in the first half of the 19th century the keynote is diversity.

Non-Conformist Religion
Methodism

After the methodist 'Plan of Pacification' in 1795 many Methodists split away from the Church of England, though others kept their links. By the 19th century there was enthusiastic local acceptance of Methodism, led by Charles Wesley.

In and around Littleborough, for some 150 years Methodism deeply affected how people lived and what they thought. Fred Jackson experienced in his life time the power of Methodism, perhaps in its most prosperous era and observed many signs of the decline of its influence by the 1920s. He records a loving picture of the methodist way of life as he experienced it in our 'upland community'.

"Smithy Nook Chapel (Mount Gilead)

In an old number of the 'Methodist Magazine' I find the following particulars in regard to the commencement of Smithy Nook Chapel. The writer says:

'Our connection was introduced there about the year 1817 by our friends in Todmorden, who were part of the Halifax circuit. The late James Butterworth, once a local preacher among the Wesleyans, invited our friends at Todmorden to open a cause at Smithy Nook. They commenced preaching in a small room and formed a class. The cause prospered in such a manner that a chapel was soon after erected, which was numerously attended and the sittings well let'.

The writer goes on to say that he had pleasing recollections of former days when he again visited the place in 1826-7, when he was stationed in the Todmorden Circuit. He was delighted to find there was still the same lively kind of singing and the same love for the plain, pointed methodist Gospel, so that he felt it quite a treat to visit the friends at Mount Gilead.

'A tale is told of this early preacher running a 'mission' at Smithy Nook and the difficulty he had in getting the people to attend. Times were bad for the hand-loom weaver at this period, and the loom had to be kept going to provide food for the children, so he decided that if the hand-loom weavers could not go to the mission he would go and see them. He made his first visit to 'Old Kitty' and began 'holding forth', but Kitty went on with his 'weyvin', but bye and bye the minister got so excited that he upset the candle. It fell on the warp which Kitty was weaving and "brunt it out." It stopped Old Kitty's weaving but whether it led to his conversion or not, history is silent. Another weaver visited was John-o'-Mary's, but more often he was known as 'Butter Teeth'. John did not like his loom work (weaving plain calico cloth):-

"There be no more cally looms there,
There be no more cally looms there.
In Heaven above, where all is love,
There be no more cally looms there."

For many years after Mount Gilead was opened for public worship, the people connected with the place held anniversary services called 'Th' Singing' and a band of musicians regularly attended on these occasions. They came from the Ripponden valley by way of Blackstone Edge, arriving on the Saturday evening. After being refreshed with a good 'Baggin' and plenty of 'penkie' (home brewed beer) they had a rehearsal in the Chapel, in order to be in touch and tune for the morrow's performance. The inhabitants took a lively interest in the success of their 'Little Gilead' and although only poor, usually made preparations to feed and lodge the visitors in a right welcome manner, having them billeted out at different houses, where one or two could be accommodated. For weeks before the event came off, there was a great deal of making ready, not the least important being the brewing of home-made beer, a palatable and harmless drink, with which the players and singers might "wet ther' whistle". The band played at each service on the Sunday and did not return home again till the following day, when they wended their way leisurely back over the 'edge' towards Yorkshire. They were a fine body of men were these old musicians. I used to know a few of them in my young days. How they loved their fiddles! How tenderly they would care for them and how jealous they were of anyone laying unholy hands upon them!

In addition to these 'borrowed' fiddlers, Smithy Nook had a few of their own. There was Jim-o'-Jamie's and Charlie-o'-Jamie's, Jim-o'-Butts, and Old Jonas. At one of the rehearsals the three younger fiddlers decided to play a trick on Old Jonas. They got him to sit 'on th'end o'th form', and at a given signal they all got up and poor Jonas was dropped on th' floor, but this did not stop him fro' fiddling; he fiddled th' tune out on th' floor.

Once the choir was singing the anthem 'Who is the King of Glory' in which first the altos, then the sopranos and then the bass sing out, asking the question. One of fiddlers turned to his mate and said: 'Here, reight that rosin here Bod; we'll show 'em who the King of Glory is.'

Edwin Waugh had such fiddlers in mind when he wrote the poem entitled 'Eawr Folks':

> Old Jonas were a fiddler, and'
> >   Aw fain could yer him play,
> Fro' set o' sun, till winter's neet,
> >   Had melted into day.
> For eh' - sich glee - sich tenderness,
> >   Through every changing part,
> It's th' heart 'at stirs his fiddle,
> >   An' his fiddle stirs his heart.
>
> When th' owd brid touches trembling strings,
> >   At knows his thowt so weal,
> It seawnds as if an angel tried
> >   To tell what angels feel.
> An' sometimes wayter in his e'een
> >   At fun has teyched to flow,
> Can hardly roll away afore
> >   It's washed wi' drops o' woe.
>
> Then here's to th' owd musicianer,
> >   Aw wish long life to thee.
> A mon that plays a fiddle weel
> >   Should niver "awse" to dee.

Ah, well! - other times, other manners. On Sunday, September 2, 1923, I had the pleasure of being present at the installation of their new organ. Although Smithy Nook was by far the oldest Chapel in the district, going back for at least 110 years in continuous occupation, yet up to the above date they had never had an organ installed. The Minister spoke of it as progress. I could not help asking myself the question 'Progress in what? In a deeper religious life?' We have gained immeasurably in some things, yet I wonder sometimes whether we have gained anything in real happiness for the mass of the people. We may sneer at the old hand-loom weavers and say that theirs was a religion of the heart, of the emotions; ours is a religion of reason. In those days, we are told, that if the minister touched the springs of their emotion , shouts of 'Glory, Hallelujah, Amen' would fill the place. Some little time ago I was reading a description of one of the early "Sings" at Smithy Nook and it shows that in their singing they rang the heart. What did it matter if their pronunciation was all wrong, they felt and believed what they were singing.

One old lady, in 1850, left on record her experience of a visit she paid to 'Th' Sing' at Smithy Nook in her young days. In describing the singing of the anthem, or chorus, she was most critical of their pronunciation of the words used, the beating of the time with the foot, the swaying of the body, so as to indicate a lively appreciation of the movements in the singing and playing. She often went through the parts in imitation of the style of singing: "Glowrifi yer Feyther, Glowrifi yer Feyther, yer Feyther who is in Heaven, and praysethe His hoally naome'.

The place was lighted with candles and it was quite an event to the younger people to see the caretaker going round during the service with his 'snuffers' to snuff the candles. In 1868 gas was introduced for the first time at Smithy Nook. Of course, when the new lighting arrangements were completed they must have special services to inaugurate it and Old Adam Mills of Wardle was selected to preach the sermon. He was noted for preaching what were called black sermons and on this special occasion he exceeded himself. There was quite a crowd to see the new lights at the evening service and Adam was in his element. He was describing the torments of hell in picturesque language and said he fancied he could hear the old clock pendulum in these lower regions saying as it swung to and fro , 'Lost, lost, lost, lost.' Just as he was repeating the word 'lost' all the lights went out. My friend said there was a general rush for the door and it was some time before the service could continue.

Another popular local preacher was Mr Abram Pilling. He was full of fire and action. On one occasion he got wound up to such a high pitch that he lifted the Bible up in his hands and then banged it down on the book-board of the pulpit with such force that both Bible and book-board crashed down into the singer's pew below. Fortunately none of the singers was hurt.

It was surprising how some of these old preachers got carried away with their preaching. One of Gilead's own locals was trying to describe the unlimited power of the great Divine, and said 'he has power to do aught. He could bore a hole through a tunnel. I suppose he meant he could bore a hole through a rock.'

Temple Wesleyan Methodists; Temple Lane.

The Wesleyans at Summit claimed that they have had an unbroken continuity since the time of John Wesley, who visited the Rochdale District in 1749. Or what is more likely still is that the Society was formed as the result of the visit of the Reverend W. Grimshaw, Vicar of Haworth in 1747. In the 'Life of William Grimshaw' there is a reference to Deanhead:

191

'Mr. Grimshaw has introduced the preaching into a dark and ignorant part of Lancashire called Deanhead' (now Summit).

The Society first met in the home of Mr. and Mrs. Clegg at Deanhead, who opened their house to the methodist preachers including William Grimshaw and John Wesley himself. Jonathan Maskew was their first resident preacher in 1753. For the next 86 years until 1839 they met in each other's houses. Maskew was a very serious man and his friends said that they had never known him to laugh. Fred Jackson speculated that this may account for the slow progress they made at this time.

"I may be wrong, but it seems to me that there must be something radically wrong, either with the parson or his religion, if he cannot unbend occasionally and indulge in a hearty laugh, even if the laugh is against himself. Anyway such was the character of the man who became the founder of the Temple Methodist Society".

Later Mr Clegg died during Maskew's ministry and Jonathan Maskew married the widow, left the ministry and settled down on the farm at Deanhead. It was in the home of John Maskew, son of Jonathan Maskew, that the Society met in 1839. This was in a group of houses called 'Temple' which are still standing on the Calderbrook Road, close to Stoney-Head. When the Society removed from the home of John Maskew they found premises on Temple Lane. This building served as a school-chapel for over 30 years, until a separate chapel was built and opened in 1872. This chapel was demolished in the 1980s; on the same site some of the stone was used in the construction of a house in an unusual decorative style. The old school-chapel was used as a day school for a good many years and did a great amount of good in giving a grounding in the three 'R's' at a time when such places were practically non-existent in the district.

Littleborough Wesleyan Methodists: The Methodical Piazza, MDCCCIX.

This Chapel was built in Littleborough by the Wesleyan Methodists in 1809 and was the oldest chapel in the district. The building that it adjoined was dated 1805. John Travis (1890) speaks of it as 'the old place near the Roch bridge which for some time had the only Sunday School in Littleborough.'

Previously the Wesleyans had a small chapel, which was a converted house, at the top end of the village. It consisted of two rooms, a bottom room and a gallery which was made by cutting away part of the chamber floor to provide more seating accommodation. To make it better for the congregation to hear and join in the services, the pulpit was fixed in one corner of the bottom room, so that the preacher could be seen from all points.

The Methodical Piazza was built below the Parish Church on the far side of the river Roch. Locally it was described as being at 'bridge end' along with the houses on Ebor Street and those in front of the chapel and the 'toll house' ie. houses at the end of Littleborough Bridge (see 1851 census). When the railway line was built, the viaduct in the centre of Littleborough was almost on top of the chapel. The noise of the railway made the chapel virtually unuseable and it was closed in 1861. For some time it was used as a private house. The building survived until 1950 when it was finally demolished by the municipal authorities after an ownership dispute.

Rakewood Methodists 1821

This group opened a chapel in 1821 which was closed in 1870. The building was on the old road up to Schofield Hall and was later converted into a house called 'Rydal Mount'. In 1876 a new Rakewood Weslyan chapel was opened.

'The Methodical Piazza' at Bridge End, erected in 1808 with the canal built 10 years earlier in the foreground and the railway viaduct, thirty years later, behind; a time of great change in Littleborough.

Primitive Methodists: Ebenezer Chapel, Summit.

About the year 1865/6 the Primitives of the Knowlwood Circuit (Todmorden) began to extend their activities in the direction of Summit and Littleborough. Their first meetings were held in a top room of one of the houses near to the Summit Inn and were so successful that they decided to build a small chapel and school. Trustees were appointed and according to the trust deeds, land was bought on the Sladen Wood Estate from John and William Crabtree in 1866 for a term of 994 years. By another deed dated March, 1867, the trustees mortgaged the land and chapel to secure the sum of £300 and interest to J. Newall.

The Primitive Methodists became as staid and respectable as any other of the religious bodies of the community, but in 1866 and for a good number of years afterwards, they worked more on the lines followed by the Salvation Army.

Camp meetings, outdoor meetings, singing in procession through the streets and preaching at prominent street corners on the way, were the common methods of procedure, with those early 'Ranters' as they were called. Love feasts, experience meetings, prayer meetings and class meetings all added fervour and zest to their indoor meetings.

The Doctrine of everlasting damnation was thundered into the ears of all, but especially it was made vivid and terrible to the young, whose lives in many instances were made miserable by it. Even grown ups were mentally and spiritually ruined, by the ever present nightmare of hell. Some of the itinerant preachers raged and fulminated about fire and brimstone, outer darkness and the eternal torment which awaited the sinner. Although common at this time such preaching died out at the end of the 19th century.

Much later Fred Jackson mused about it in relation to Methodism:

"As the people got more liberty, more knowledge and more sympathy the preaching of 'hell-fire' became unnecessary. Perhaps at this earlier period this style of preaching was necessary to rouse the people to a knowledge of their shortcomings. I wonder what kind of preaching would be required to rouse the people out of the indifference and apathy to which they have fallen today, both in regard to religion and politics?"

Feeling between Anglicans and Non-conformists ran very high in the 19th century. For example, Miss Jessie Fothergill, novelist and local churchwoman, appeared to resent the introduction of severely doctrinal religion into our locality. In her book, 'Healey' she was very sarcastic; one of the principal characters is a local preacher in the Primitive church named Abraham Cryer, cheat, fraud and hypocrite are epithets she applied to him.

"He had put on his Sunday clothes and with them his Sunday manners. The manner in which he went to kneel down and utter a carefully prepared extempore prayer... He is a very religious character, quite the brand snatched from the burning. I was passing the tabernacle of the Primitives the other night and I heard the voice, as it were, of a mighty preacher, with groans and sounds of awakenedness from the congregation. No doubt it was Mr Cryer expounding the word; he is not the first person whose preaching and practice have failed to be in unison".

Fred Jackson concludes that whatever may have been its deficiencies at the outset, in its later days the primitive methodists were a powerful aid for the uplifting of the religious and social life of the area and became 'one of the most forward' in this respect. It was, in his opinion, very fortunate in its choice of ministers, who were broadminded, sympathetic and tolerant. At a personal level he said it had been a pleasure to listen to their preaching and to have their friendship. He argued that it spoke well for them that, for a good many years, Gordon Harvey gave them a donation of £30 per year on condition that they had a resident minister in the district.

Fred ended his consideration of these matters with a sentence that will raise sympathy from anyone who has experienced a desire to learn about his 'roots' or how his area came to develop.

"It has been rather difficult getting some of the foregoing facts together. It is a pity that all the old records and minutes belonging to the place have either been lost or destroyed, and in a very few years' time all the old people connected with the place will have passed away. It has been a pleasure to me to have been able to preserve at least a little of the old history."

In summary, under the Methodist umbrella many forms of worship developed including Methodist New Connection, Methodist Unitarian and Primitive Methodist all alongside the mainstream Wesleyan Methodists.

Baptist's Church

In the area of the non-conformist Churches, Baptists are a much older grouping than the Methodists. The Baptists had internal distinctions between Particular Baptists,

General Baptists and Independent Baptists. In the first half of the century Baptists in Littleborough walked to Ogden for services and it was 1861 before they opened a meeting house in Durn and 1867 before they replaced it by their 'Iron Chapel' (see chapter 16).

Congregationalist Church

In 1824 a small group of men and women at Summit wished to worship God in accordance with the dictates of their conscience. They met in an upper room over two cottages situated at the top end of Summit Village. They were visited periodically by the minister of Providence Chapel in Rochdale, the Rev. John Ely and a group of his workers. This minister was mainly responsible for the forming of this little local group into a recognised church of the 'independent' order. In 1825 such a church was formally constituted. Eight years later in 1833, Mr Henry Cheetham, a member of Providence Congregational Church, was ordained and became its first pastor. Shortly before this ordination a scheme had been launched for the building of a chapel. The 'Ebenezer Congregational Chapel' was built at the top end or 'old part' of Summit and was completed in 1834. It was to stay open for 141 years and finally closed in 1975.

Up until 1865 if you were a congregationalist and lived in Littleborough, your nearest place of worship was Ebenezer Congregational Church, Summit. Even for keen walkers this was daunting in bad weather.

Summary of the Religious situation in 1850

By 1850 there were ample seats in churches for everyone who wanted to go and a breadth of belief to cater for most needs. The Roman Catholics were the exception with no local church. More concerning was the social gulf that existed between the 'respectable working class' and the 'undeserving poor' who had no decent clothes to wear. Attendance at church could be three times on Sunday.

Looking back from 1940 and contrasting religious conditions then with the early 19th century, Fred Jackson remarked:

"we have gained immeasurably in some things, but I wonder sometimes whether we have gained anything in real happiness for the mass of the people. The handloom weavers may have been poor in the material things of this world, which we think so vitally necessary to us, but they possessed something which we, in the hurry and bustle and stress of the present age, seem in a great measure to have lost; that is deep religious convictions."

Education and the local schools 1800 - 50

At the beginning of the century education provision was mainly associated either with the religious groups, or the private enterprise of some teacher. Reading and writing were the main subjects and pupils paid one penny weekly. Most children were busy with industrial tasks either in their home or in the mill so they were lucky to get any 'schooling' and if they got 2 or 3 years it would be between the age of 5 and 9. By age 9 they were full time in the mill or a domestic workshop. Of children at school only a very small number were 'free pupils' and boys outnumbered girls 2 to 1.

By the middle of the 19th Century there were many more individuals and institutions addressing the education of our local people. The longest established school was Halliwell's Endowed School founded in 1688. In 1827 it was being conducted by Mr. Thomas Sladen, the clerk's son. The scholars were taught reading and writing, and paid 1d each for the Sunday morning's tuition. This is the first mention of Church Sunday School in Littleborough. They had to attend very early in the morning, read their lessons and then write out a copy. Afterwards, they were marched off, two by two, in procession to the church where they were again taught the Church Catechism and remained to the morning service.

There were also some Dame's schools in Littleborough at this time which took pupils at rather high charges. The main problems with these schools were lack of continuity of teachers and the pupil's spasmodic attendance or total absence when work was busy. Such a Dame's School existed at Hollingworth. Austin Colligan, in his history of the Lake (The Weighver's Seaport), describes pupils learning the alphabet from letters carved on a large stone over the fire place.

Around 1836-7 a school was opened at Smithy Nook. In that year a man named John Thomas, who formerly kept a beerhouse at Deanroyd, Gate End, removed to the neighbourhood of Handle Hall and kept a day school for children. This remained until Thomas was a very old man.

In 1839 the Temple Methodist school and chapel opened in Summit and this was to be an early example of the development of chapel-cum-school which was to spring up in all parts of our community in the following years.

In 1844 a small parish school was built in the N.W. corner of the church yard. For years it only took a few boys and it reached no academic standard until 1865 when a new headmaster set targets. It was however renowned for the church teas.

The pattern of education was changing. Formal state intervention occured in the Factory Act of 1833, which insisted on half time education for employees under 13 years old (morning or afternoon, often rotated). The legal age for starting work was eight. The education would be carried out in one of a number of kinds of school, which was sometimes maintained by the millowner. Frequently however, the employers evaded the regulations by employing the children in a so called 'relay system' embedded in the Ten Hours Act of 1847. This Act was designed to extend the protection of legal working hours for children to include women. Due to poor drafting unscrupulous employers could sidestep the 1833 Factory Act and this was only remedied in 1874,

It was a privilege to become a 'half timer' and you had to achieve a Learning Certificate to qualify. Another group of schools was called the Ragged School Union. These included the 'Dame' schools which usually only taught reading and knitting and sewing but not writing or arithmetic, indeed many teachers could not write. Private elementary schools taught reading, writing, and arithmetic, with optional extras like geography and grammar for an extra fee. Non-conformist 'Church' and C. of E. 'National' schools taught the bulk of the children and someone had to pay, usually family or employer. On average they admitted two boys for every girl and of the children, up to a third were half-timers. By the middle of the 19th century charges had risen to 2d for a dame school and up to 6d for a parish school. Private schools charged on sliding scales based on the subjects taught. The Church and National schools aimed at orderliness, efficiency and achievement of the three 'Rs', their syllabus became known as the 'monitorial system'. The nature of most of the teaching was to rely on the virtue of repetitive learning and drill using lists to be committed to memory. It was said that the lists were never forgotten but rarely used!

Nearly all children went to Sunday school. These schools taught religious knowledge and reading and some taught writing.

By the 1850s schools following the Monitorial System were steadily growing in size and they were the major benefactors of industrial growth and National Education Grants, which grew from £30,000 in 1839 to £837,000 in 1859.

The first reliable picture of the general pattern of education came from the Educational Census of 1851 and the overall picture in the Littleborough district was:

80% of our children went to a local chapel school (non-conformist) whereas the national average was 50%.

60% of the non-conformists were methodists.

20% were baptists.

Newspapers

Cheap printing and the rapid growth of news sheets, papers and books, made an enormous impact on education and society generally. Amongst the working class there was a thirst to learn to read and write and their leaders recognised the prime importance of these skills in improving worker's lives. There are many stories about the men getting together after the second Sunday service to read and discuss the content of the weekly newspaper they had bought jointly. Fred Jackson gave a very good picture of how such material was obtained locally:

"Newspapers were 10d (tenpence) each at this time. This price was quite prohibitive for any single individual, so they clubbed together and met at each other's houses, generally on Sunday afternoons to read and discuss the week's news. There were John Cryer (Jons-o'-Jacks), William Kershaw (Will-o'th Butes), Edmund Crossley (Ned-o'-Nicks), William Chadwick (Will-o'-Cuts), William Dawson (Billy Dussel), Sam Woodhead (Bowing Sam), Jim-o'-Butts, Bob-o'-Jamies, and a good many others who formed these clubs for getting the week's news and discussing it.

For a great number of years the paper was distributed by a Todmorden man named John Schofield (Jack-o'-Steens). He was a short squat, rough-looking figure who went bare-headed summer and winter. He lived midway between Todmorden and Walsden. During the greater part of the week he was brewer, gardener, and general manservant, but at the weekend he would fetch the papers from Manchester, selling them on his way back through Littleborough, Smithy Nook, Walsden, and Todmorden, when the papers were tenpence, ninepence, sevenpence, and down to the time when they got to fourpence halfpenny (4½d) each. He usually started from the Golden Lion Inn, Todmorden, about noon on Fridays, when the coach arrived from Wakefield Market bringing the state of the same. John waited for the letter containing the market reports, and then immediately setting out to trudge the whole distance to Manchester (20 miles) delivered the letter at the office of his paper, to be printed the same night, then retiring to rest and calling for his papers the following morning, would start off on his 20 mile walk back, selling his papers by the way, arriving at Smithy Nook in winter generally about nightfall, on the Saturday, where there was always one appointed to meet him."

Co-operation

From the the start of the 19th century the working people began to realise the impact of the industrialisation of their working lives and also their family life. By the

1820's there was a widespread belief, led by Robert Owen, that there was a need for a wider socialist vision of life. It was no accident that it was in Lancashire and Yorkshire that the thinking was centred. In 1831 there was the first ever Co-operative Conference with some 56 societies attending and representing a membership of 3000 people. Literacy was spreading and there were papers like the Lancashire Co-operator and in 1831 the first workers' wholesale company was announced. These developments were a false dawn and the depression between 1831 and 1834 both checked the growth of co-operative ideas and indeed reduced the existing co-operative base. It was in the 1840's that a revived textile economy became the basis for the co-operative movement. In the interim the dream of truly co-operative 'people's communities' driven by utopian ideals had been exchanged for more focussed objectives with the quality of food and availability of goods high on the agenda. This time it was the Rochdale Pioneers (1844) who first implemented the key essentials of a members owned enterprise, a share in the management and the profits and a democratically elected management with half yearly elections. This pattern was to play an enormous part in working people's lives.

It is fascinating to consider how all the same ideas were tried in the worlds of retail and wholesale selling and manufacturing of consumer goods, education and leisure pursuits and in the world of textile manufacture. For example in the 'ten co-operative principles' which were published, was the principle of 'one man (sic) one vote'. This came to be accepted as basic in politics after a long struggle to include women. The attempt to apply the same idea in conducting industrial affairs was subsequently blamed for the failure of many enterprises. Finally, it was seen that different sub-sets of the co-operative ideal failed or were successful in each of the sectors.

The application of these ideals in the retail and wholesale sectors was to be dominated by the Co-operative Societies who for many years could claim one paid up member in every household within communities such as Littleborough. The Co-operatives from the beginning were an attempt to improve the living standards and widen the intellectual horizons of the working people, who grasped it avidly. Between 1844 and 1853 thirty nine new societies were formed and a great new movement was under way.

Town and Community Development.

In the 50 years from 1800 Littleborough changed from a 'village' to a small town, dominated by mills.

In 1836, George Swindles (grocer, hatter and draper) introduced gas on a small scale to a few shops and the Falcon Inn. He also built nos. 28 (1836 date stone), 30 & 32 Church Street.

No. 30 became the first post office in Littleborough (address for letters: Littleborough via Manchester). It remained the post office for some 44 years until Winton Street P.O. opened. In 1859 Mr William Rigg, letter carrier, was to be given a cash prize for good performance but, on his father's advice, he was given a coat instead. In 1862 a letter posted in Rochdale up till 3.45 pm. would be delivered in Littleborough the following day. With an extra stamp if posted before 5pm. the letter would be delivered in Littleborough that evening.

Later, Nos. 28 & 30 were occupied by the Co-operative for the sale of wet fish, fruit and flowers.

Before the age of the motorcar, the narrow entrance to Hare Hill Road about 1890, bounded by Robert Hall - Grocer and Corndealer and the old houses, later replaced by Seed-Hill Buildings 1902.

At the beginning of the century, Hare Hill Road was entered by a constricted junction off Church Street which could be described as an alley. It was in 1794 that the houses at the Church Street end of Hare Hill Road were erected and 1818 when the old Seed Hill building was put up. The space left between the houses was seven to ten feet, as being quite sufficient for a horse and cart to pass through. Further up Hare Hill Road on the right was the site of Hare Hill Mill, a four storeyed building which for many years would further restrict the width of the road. This mill had been built by the Newall family and opposite it they built a gas plant in the 1840s. Only a little higher up at Lane End Cottage (later called Calder Cottage) the road became an unsurfaced earth track. In 1824 surveyors of the township called a public meeting to decide on the need of a good road from Shore to Caldermoor, known at that time as Turf House Lane, and Caldermoor to Littleborough. A follow up meeting took place in 1832 convened by John and Thomas Kershaw, surveyors:

'to take into consideration what means must be taken to raise money to complete the road leading from Shore to Littleborough'

A start had been made in the previous eight years. In December of the same year the gentlemen of Blatchinworth and Calderbrook were requested to meet the surveyors:

'for the purpose of laying a rate upon the inhabitants of the said division towards completing the new line of road leading from Hare Hill Mill to Littleborough'

In 1847 the road known today as Hare Hill Road was called Hare Hill Mill Road and later Hare Hill Lane. By 1875 the section between Church Street and Sale Street was called Hare Hill Road and beyond that as far as Whitelees Road it was called Hare Hill Lane. In 1876 the local board requested tenders to widen and level 'Hare Hill Road'.

In the 18th century Hare Hill had been a pleasant area with few houses. The gas plant was constructed to supply gas to the growing number of mills in the area and was destined to become the Littleborough Gas Works. It was a squat building with a tall central chimney, which dominated the left hand side of Hare Hill Road just beyond the 'cupola' capped building belonging to the Co-operative Society which was on the right. Hare Hill mill was demolished in the 1930's and the only remains are a truncated chimney, a section of the engine house, and part of the office block. The rest of the building visible today was built by the Co-operative Society for factory space. The Gas Works continued to expand and during this development the site was very badly contaminated and acres of land in the immediate area were denuded of vegetation. By 1900 there was an apparently never-ending stream of horses and metal shod carts carrying coal from the railway yards to the gas plant, over stone setts, so that there was filth and pollution everywhere and the noise level was intolerable.

The gas works finally closed in the 1960s and the gas-holders were demolished in the 1970s. Examination showed that the whole site was severely polluted and could not be restored for housing or a nursery or school because of the cost. Finally the whole area was skilfully planted and landscaped to make an open wooded area which has created a pleasant open space in urban Littleborough: things had come in a full circle in a period of 200 years.

An old local almanack published in the early 1860s by B. Rigg and Sons, Littleborough concluded a survey of Littleborough at that time:

"There is little difficulty in predicting a brilliant future for Littleborough. There is an abundant supply of coal, stone and good water. It is still the great highway between Lancashire and Yorkshire. New mills, new mansions and new houses are rapidly springing up and with a few more years of progress Littleborough will cease to merit the first half of its name."

From this point on Littleborough had become part of the great changes which were happening everywhere in Britain, although for the next 100 years the local people clung doggedly to old traditions and loyalties.

Inside the gas-works at Harehill Road, this view shows part of the gas and coke making plant in 1953 when the works was under the control of the North Western Gas Board, Oldham-Rochdale Group. The site is now landscaped.

CHAPTER SIXTEEN

THE NINETEENTH CENTURY

PART SIX : THE GROWTH OF LITTLEBOROUGH

1850 - 1900

Shop-Keeping

As Littleborough began to grow from a village into a town, one major source of employment was to be shop-keeping for the provision of retail goods and services. Fred Jackson gives a delightful description of the antecedents of today's businesses as they had been in the older communities along the trade routes on higher ground.

"The Village Shop

In the 1850s there was only one shop in Smithy Nook and Summit and it always went by the name of "Sam'l Cryer's Shop at Lighthouse". Sam'l was getting on in years, so his son, Abram-o'-Samels, generally looked after it for him. From all accounts, it was one of those village shops so general at that time, where you could buy almost any of the things required in everyday life. My friend, who gave me some of these particulars, says he well remembered his mother telling him one day to go to Abram-o'-Samel's

For a pound o' meyl (meal)
An a red brush steyl.

Preserves and syrup were kept in huge jars at the grocer's shops at this time and people had to take their own pots or jars to put it in. It was ladled out according to the customers' requirements. Pots and jars were scarce and sometimes Samel had to lend them one, but it was a strict rule that it must be returned as soon as possible. One of these pots had been kept too long by my friend's mother at one time and some excuse had to be made for it. He had to keep repeating to himself all the way from Newgate:-

This is Samel Cryer's pot,
It's been put in th' cupboard and quite forgot.

As our local poet says in one of his poems, probably describing Abram-o'-Samel's shop:-

He'd simples, cordials, balsams, gums
For every ailment sent
And fooak forgeet ther brittle thrums,
Wherever Samel went.

He made fooak's wills an' gave advice
To keep 'em eawt o'law.
He'd draw a tooth, an' just as nice
He'd draw a plan an' o.

He'd toffee nicknamed Swaggering Dick,
    For th' lads to race up th' hill,
He'd cheesecakes (kussins) rare and thick, ·
    For t' wenches' sweet goodwill.

He'd maxims good for t' gradely poor,
    Directions wod to do,
But he never sent 'em fro' his door
    Beawt fillin' t' meyl bags, too.

And Will-o'-Samels, or Willie Cryer as I knew him when I first came to Summit, was a chip off the old block, one of nature's gentlemen, modest, retiring , kind-hearted and always ready to do a good turn to anybody. Willie was the youngest son of Old Samel and as soon as he was old enough he went to work for John and William Crabtree, of Steanor Bottom Chemical Works, where he later became a partner in the firm. Young Samel, another brother, became steward for Dearden, Lord of the Manor of Rochdale. Old Samel had also three daughters. Thos. Ed. Lord (organist) married one; a Mr Thompson, who was the pointsman at the house near Summit Tunnel married another; the other daughter, Betsy, was never married."

(There was a shop, possibly this one, trading at Lighthouse, Calderbrook until the 1960s, it is now a private house)

Littleborough: a growing town

Looking at Littleborough after 1850, things were changing dramatically. Following the major growth in population in the first half of the century the growth can nearly be characterised as an explosion in the second half.

Population	1851	4600
	1861	4860
	1881	7891
	1891	8384
As above plus Butterworth and Weurdle (+2962)	1901	11166

Between 1850 and 1900 the population doubled and due to boundary changes nearly 3000 more people were added. Compared to other Pennine towns which increased by some 40% in the same period, Littleborough's increase was truly dramatic. This increase focussed on the town centre whilst the outlying districts declined. Moor edge farms, small mills and all the associated activities withered and people moved downhill. It is estimated that the stock of housing on the edge of the moor fell by 20% and the population living outside of the Littleborough urban area on upland sites fell by 70%.

The population growth initially came from short distance migration into Littleborough and from neighbouring counties. As transport links improved migrants came in from southern counties, Ireland, Wales and Scotland.

In 1850 81% of the population of Littleborough were migrants (born elsewhere) and almost all of them had come from the counties of Yorkshire and Lancashire. They averaged a 20 mile move from Yorkshire and 4.5 miles (ie from Rochdale) within

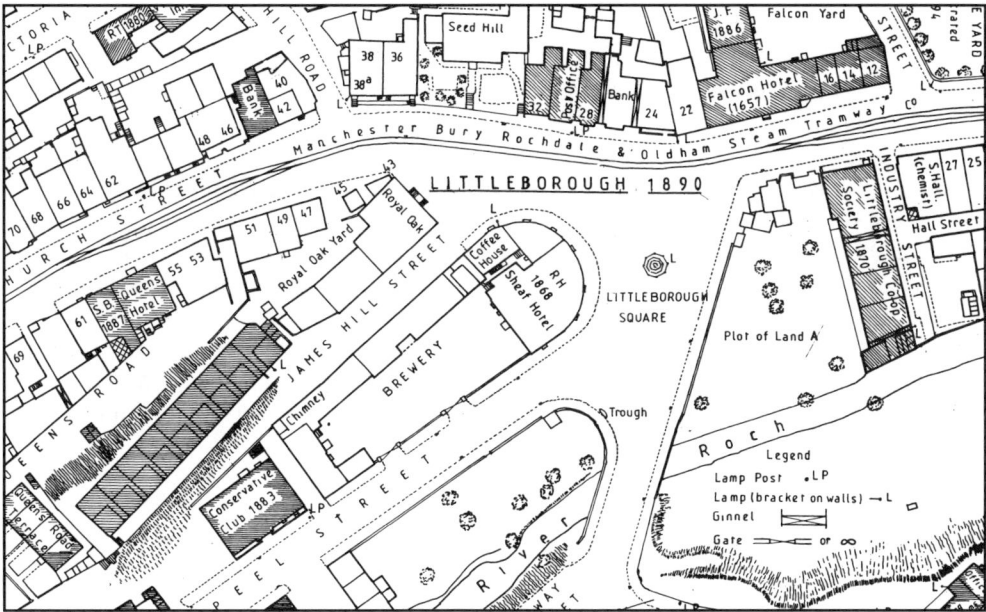

Littleborough Square in 1890. The square was lit at night by a large central gas-lamp. The open plot to the right later became The Memorial Gardens.

Lancashire. In 1891 46% were migrants and 36% came from Yorkshire or Lancashire. The distances moved were still low but in both samples nearly all migrants were adults but very rarely a full family. The family moves which did happen were mostly within the county of birth. Nevertheless, by the end of the century there were some nine families from Suffolk, Norfolk, Shropshire, Scotland and Wales living in Littleborough.

In the second half of the century Littleborough experienced explosive growth, with mills, coal mines, foundries, roads, a developing canal and a railway, new trade and industry. The migrants seized the opportunity offered, by moving to the area. In 1851 manufacture employed 47% of the migrants and all other categories (mining, trade, building, transport, professional and clerical and public service) had less than 5% each. 25% of the migrants did not declare their employment and less than 5% were employed in agriculture. In 1891 the main changes were that manufacture only employed 44% of the migrants, trade had risen to 15% and agriculture had collapsed to 1½%.

In both 1851 and 1891 the majority of 'heads of migrant families' took work in the woollen or cotton industries as fullers, weavers and printers and the indications are that the major way of recruitment was by word of mouth between friends and families, supplemented by newspapers and news sheets. Out of the industrial growth came opportunities in transport, shops, building and other trades. These jobs were well paid as compared with agricultural labour rates.

Work and more money meant a rapid growth of new activities. Every hamlet had a non-conformist chapel for worship, education and social meetings, Hollingworth Lake became a centre, initially for day trippers. It rapidly developed into a location for two or three day holidays and luxury goods began to appear for sale beside the necessities.

Agriculture

In earlier chapters the total dominance of activities based on the textile industry has been outlined and in looking at the statistics on occupations it is clear that by the 1890s agriculture no longer made any significant contribution to the wealth of our area.

The Littleborough area, although covered with a healthy blanket of trees and plants in the past, has never had extensive areas of high quality agricultural land and at the beginning of the century oats were the dominant crop with extensive meadows to accommodate the coach trade. By 1866 arable farming had almost ceased, only compensated for by a modest increase in pastoral farming. The industrialisation of the community created a demand for dairy products. Farms moved to grass and meadow with milk cows. Farming was further depressed by a series of bad years in terms of the weather and cheap imports of wool and meat from Australia and Argentina. The small upland farms and small-holdings could no longer support a family and many were vacated and vanished back into rough moorland.

Pig keeping increased from the middle of the century to provide the new factory workers with bacon and pork. Much of the land round Littleborough was lost to agriculture; it was polluted and rendered sterile or greatly reduced in value as the

Haymakers and helpers of all ages pause for a rest at Lower Townhouse Farm in the summer of 1890.

result of industrial development. The land that was still cultivated tended to be rented, with the remaining small-holdings and farms having between five and fifty acres of land each.

It is interesting that both the Falcon and the Royal Oak were still actively farming in the centre of Littleborough village in the 1880's. These are late examples of a very ancient dual function of being both a farm and an inn which was once common around Littleborough.

Religion

In the first half of the century there was an enormous increase in population and for many of the working people their day off may well have been entirely spent in attending church or chapel services or in activities related to and organised by the same institution. Well might an old lady, aged 87, say; 'you know the Greenhill chapel was all our life'. This from someone who was a young girl in 1910.

Churches and chapels continued to extend their work of Sunday Schools, libraries, book clubs and burial clubs. Combined with social activities, it meant the facilities were open and active most or all evenings of the week. Although population growth slowed during the 1850s-60s it started to grow again and the 'Sunday Schools' in many cases became day-long teaching institutions. 1870 -1890 saw a burst in chapel building and in the late Victorian period non-conformity was widely embraced locally and predictably; it was synonymous with the Temperance movement.

The Anglican Church
The Parish Church
Fred Jackson gives a lively sketch of some of the events related to the Parish Church.

"The church formerly had a tower, but in 1860 this was partly pulled down and the present steeple created in its place. The tower benefactor was Mr Lawrence Newall, landowner and gentleman, who wished to make a gift to the church which would be visible from his home at Townhouse across the fields. At the same time he built the Gale inn and a cotton-spinning mill alongside it.

In December of the same year the church clock was purchased by public subscription and erected and lighted before the end of the year. Some alteration was also made in the interior of the church by the purchase and erection of a brass lectern (1866) in the form of a spread eagle, which somehow began to be spoken of as an innovation and one that could be dispensed with. Afterwards (in the quaint language of an old writer) 'the eagle took flight', but how was not publicly known. At any rate it flew over the high hill called Lobden to the Whitworth side, being lost for some weeks, but at last discovered in a morass almost buried. After a very wet time it was unearthed and restored to its old place. I think that we are a little more tolerant today than they were at that time."

(Substantially the same story is found in Travis. Though perhaps less amusing, a detailed account of a second theft of the brass lectern can be found in the book 'The Village Church' by Austin Colligan. Once again the eagle and its stand disappeared and many years later first the stand and then in 1942 the eagle was recovered. This was widely reported in the Rochdale Observer and elsewhere. The irony was that in the interim the church had bought a new eagle, so today there is a shiny eagle and lurking in the shadows a rather discoloured but very well travelled bird with a proven survival capability.)

Thought to have been taken about 1860 this early photograph of Holy Trinity Parish Church shows the old vicarage to the left and open ground, which later became the school site. The long flagstone wall appears to be on Lodge Street.

If the Anglican Church was seen to have lost ground to the various non-conformist groupings, a major change in the conduct of local church affairs came about when Dr Salts was apppointed vicar and dominated the religious life for the next 38 years (1872 - 1911). He ardently supported the church schools at the Parish church and the one which had been opened at Calderbrook St James. This initiative was rewarded as in the late 19th century the parish church school grew to be very important in the local educational picture along with the Methodist day schools on Church and Victoria street. Each held more than 300 pupils at one time or another.

Dr Salts also set about refurbishing the many beautiful stained glass windows in the church. Supplementing refurbishment he also added extra windows, mainly through patronage from the congregation, as he formed new and positive relationships with the community.

In 1876 Mr W Law, who owned mills at Durn and Lydgate and built Honresfeld as a home for his family, offered £4000 for the building of a new chapel. Dr Salts accepted this offer gladly but was dismayed when the Parish Council voted it down. Law withdrew his offer expressing both annoyance and disappointment. The matter became the subject of a protracted dispute and it was the 3rd August 1889 when the foundation stone of the new chancel was laid, 318 years (to the date) after the first dedication of the church. The new chancel added 57 new seats in the Parish church. The handsome east window (created in 1842) was refurbished and reinstalled on the side of the church that it occupies today. The window is full of crests and coats of arms. There was a great celebration when the building was complete. Mr Law was a forgiving soul as well as a generous one and regardless of past history, in 1892 he installed a new organ in the church.

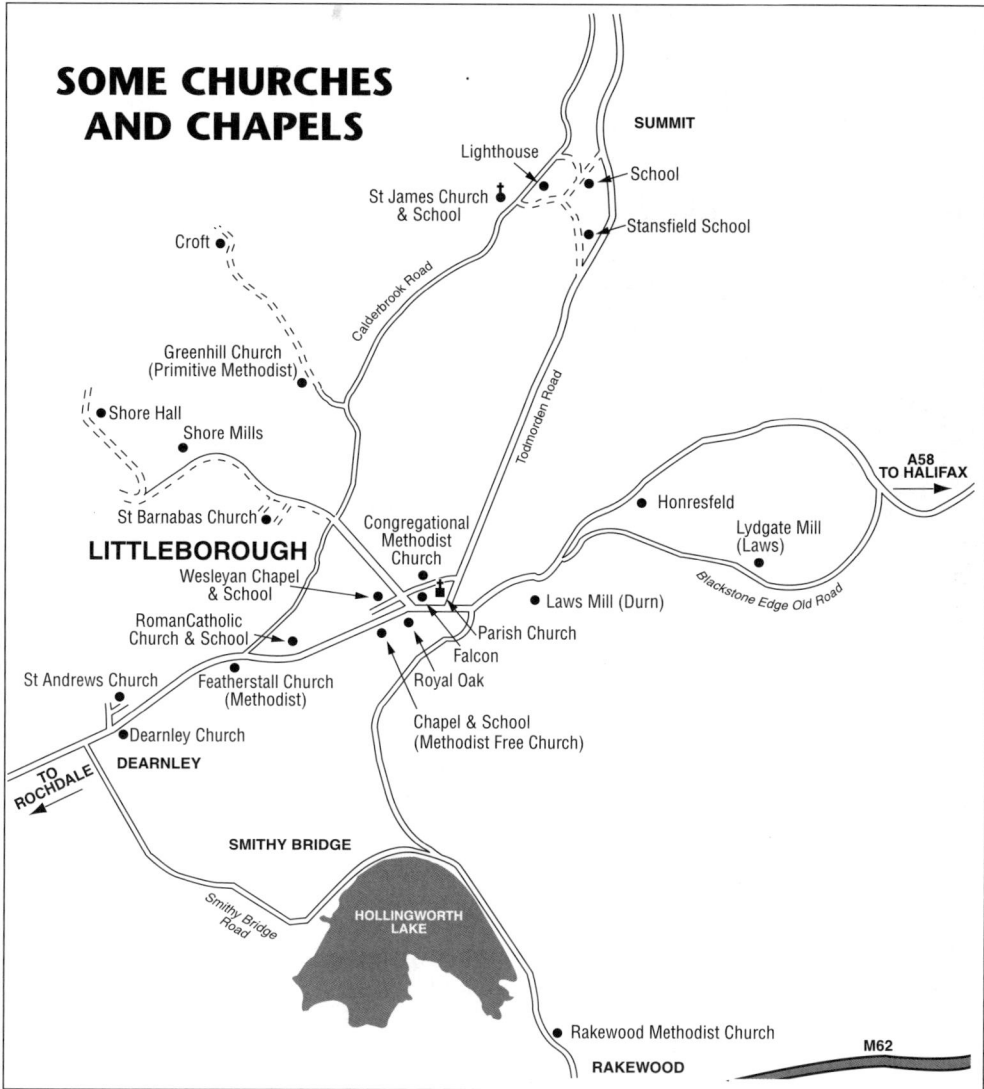

SOME CHURCHES AND CHAPELS

SUMMIT

Lighthouse

School

St James Church & School

Stansfield School

Croft

Calderbrook Road

Greenhill Church (Primitive Methodist)

Shore Hall

Shore Mills

Todmorden Road

A58 TO HALIFAX

Honresfeld

Lydgate Mill (Laws)

St Barnabas Church

Congregational Methodist Church

LITTLEBOROUGH

Laws Mill (Durn)

Blackstone Edge Old Road

Wesleyan Chapel & School

RomanCatholic Church & School

Parish Church

Falcon

St Andrews Church

Featherstall Church (Methodist)

Royal Oak

Dearnley Church

Chapel & School (Methodist Free Church)

TO ROCHDALE

DEARNLEY

SMITHY BRIDGE

Smithy Bridge Road

HOLLINGWORTH LAKE

Rakewood Methodist Church

M62

RAKEWOOD

It is appropriate to dwell on the Law family as typical of a new kind of rich local benefactor. The Laws were 'incomers' by local standards, a family who emerged in the 1820s. Wm Law and J Fletcher started a small textile mill and subsequently built the Lydgate Mills. The sons of Wm Law, John, William and Alfred went on to build the Durn mills. John had a son Alfred who later became Sir Alfred Law M.P. but John himself died young. Alfred and William went on to develop the mills and William became the church benefactor, with great loyalty to the Parish Church. This tradition was followed by Sir Alfred. Honresfeld was built by W & A Law after they out-grew Bent House. Today all members of the family have died or moved away from the area and Honresfield has been adapted to become a 'Leonard Cheshire Home' caring for the severely ill.

Mr Alfred Law who with his brother William built Durn Mill in 1864. Local materials were used; bricks from Rake Pottery and iron pillars from Schofields Foundary.

St James' Church, Calderbrook

The foundation stone of Calderbrook Church was laid on August 23rd, 1860, by James G. Dearden Esq., son of the Lord of the Manor of Rochdale, to mark his 21st birthday. The cost of purchasing the site and all costs of erection were paid for by his father. The laying of the foundation stone was a great event, a district holiday was declared with banners, dinners and widespread events including processions, cavalry, salvoes of gun fire and much eating and drinking. Although the church was completed in 1863 it was not opened until 1865 when it was licensed for worship. A Sunday school was started in the same year. In 1896 a new Parish was declared at Calderbrook, but on the day it had not got a vicar, a curate, or a churchwarden. All these omissions were corrected within a few months but it was 1910 before the vicarage was built. Prior to this date the vicar(s) had lived in various houses locally.

In 1873 a new national school, St James' Church Day School, was built by the Church and opened at Calderbrook. There were some 40 pupils initially and it had little furniture, except 'a few books and an easel' and one teacher. By 1891 there were some 55 children and in 1894, when the Mount Gilead School closed, the figures in that year rose to 138 children. As with so many of the church schools the history was one of frequent shortages of money for materials, for heating and to pay the teachers. The school over its lifetime experienced a number of total closures for repair or because of fever or other illness. For example, an extension was completed in 1896 but only after a long period of disruption. The strength of the school (and the other similar schools in the locality) was their close links with the community and, at best, care for the scholars made up for many of the other deficiencies so that old scholars will argue they were very happy at such schools.

In time it became obvious that a new school was necessary to meet the development needs of the area. The Church and the Education Authority agreed that St James' School and the Summit Board School should be amalgamated to form one school to be known as Stansfield Hall Primary Interdenominational Controlled School. This joint school opened in January 1917 although the St James' building continued to be used for teaching the younger children of the new school until the early 1980s, when the main building was extended. The old St. James' School was converted into a home for the elderly.

Honresfeld, the grandest Victorian house in the district, built for mill owner William Law and later to become one of the first Cheshire Homes.

James G. Dearden lays the foundation stone at st James Church, Calderbrook, 23rd August 1860.
INSET. Calderbrook Road, early 20th century.

St Barnabas, Shore

In 1870 rooms were taken at 'Sunny Bank', Shore for 'Services and School'. In 1874 Dr Salts had the Shore school built (£1500) and in 1891 the Rev. M.E. Pett accepted responsibility for the Shore area, in addition to acting as curate at Holy Trinity. He lived in Shore Hall. Following an old tradition he 'discerned' the need for an evangelical mission to the people of Shore (see the history of the Dearnley Church) and organised a series of prayer meetings. The meetings were held on the lawns of the 'Shore Mills House' (the Cleggs home). Even at this late date the chemistry of a sympathetic mill owner, an active clergyman and a major local work force was a success and the meetings were very well attended. Based on this success the Revd. Pett organised an appeal for public subscriptions and subsequently a very successful Bazaar which raised £544. The decision was made to build a church on land below Turf Terrace. The Revd. Pett appeared to have a real talent in encouraging local giving from mill owners, the growing middle class and the local workers. In 1901 the church was consecrated with the completion of the nave portion of the building and the existence of the parish was declared, the chancel and tower were completed in 1907. The parish was put under the control of the Rev. Pett who continued to develop it until 1928 and it is still the centre of worship in Shore at the end of the 20th century.

St Andrews, Dearnley

If St James's Church can be seen as the gift of a rich man to the Anglican Church the story of St Andrews' is in striking contrast. The area was part of the St John's, Smallbridge Parish in the late 1880s and money was being saved, in modest increments, for a 'New Church' fund, with Dr George MacGill as the treasurer. The area had been classified as a missionary one and had a modest iron church and a day school. The whole issue of to build or not wavered back and forth, with rather lukewarm support from the church authorities. Nonetheless, in December 1892, the local building committee authorised the preparation of plans for a church costing no more than £2800. In February 1893 an architect Frank Oakley was instructed to proceed with detailed work. The site proposed was thought to be over a coal seam so initially this had to be inspected and the 'forty yard' seam was found to be 40 feet below the surface. Since 30' was the critical minimum depth the scheme went forward and a small stream crossing the site was diverted

Plans to incorporate the old iron church as extra temporary space were rejected. The idea of using the diverted stream to generate electic light for the church was also rejected in favour of lighting to be achieved by driving a dynamo by a gas engine. Finally, only the organ came from the old iron church.

In September 1895 the church was consecrated in a modest ceremony. During the celebrations the major contribution to the building project, made by Dr George MacGill, was recognised. The church was at the north, Dearnley, end of the long narrow parish which extended to Smithy Bridge and the Hollingworth Lake area.

A further point of interest is that the first vicar appointed, Father George Oakley (brother of the architect who built the church) stayed with the church for 28 years (1895 - 1923) and had already been the assistant vicar responsible for Dearnley since 1892. He was a caring and co-operative man with a strong Anglo-Catholic faith and a doughty supporter of the day school. He was also a poet, a local historian and story writer who achieved some popularity with books including his 'In Olden Days'. The 1914 - 18 war took a heavy toll both of the man and his church congregation and this was compounded by the death of his wife in 1920. He finally resigned in 1923 and moved to a Parish in Yorkshire where he had close friends but no longer carried responsibility for the Workhouse at Birch Hill and its associated units, which had been a growing and unpaid burden.

At the end of the century between 1895 and 1900, as well as St James' Calderbrook, St Andrews, Dearnley and St Barnabas were all made parishes.

From this time onwards the history of St. Andrews parallels others outlined in this story. Its members fought the battle to keep their children in touch with the church, since they were its future. They struggled with falling congregations and the ever present need of money. They bought a house to be used as a vicarage, later replacing it by a more suitable building. In the period between the wars they struggled with further decline in attendance and the loss of many men from their congregation. In 1939 there was good news with the gift of a new Hammond Electric Organ.

Today St Andrews Church is well attended by an enthusiastic congregation whose members in recent years have carried out improvements to the interior of the church, enabling the various groups to enjoy and make full use of the building. Church activities range from toddlers to mothers'union meetings, performances from the St Andrews' Singers to the event of the year the Annual Autumn Bazaar. The church has also welcomed other local groups such as the Littleborough Chernobyl Childrens Project which provides assistance and holidays in our town for the unfortunate young victims of the nuclear disaster in the Ukraine in 1986.

Non Conformist Churches

It is a comment on the powerful appeal of the non-conformist faith in the Littleborough area during the 19th century, that by 1860 no less than 16 non-conformist chapels had been built, (and only one closed). By comparison, the construction of St James' Church (1865) came 400 years after the building of the Parish Church. There is evidence that the latter was rebuilt at least twice during this period.

Littleborough Wesleyan Methodists

In 1865 the Victoria Street Wesleyans opened a chapel at Will Hill after the closure of the Methodical Piazza subsequently adding a school in 1873. Along with the Church Street (Free Church) Methodists, they became the leaders in non-conformist affairs as both had regular ministers and large congregations, so in some aspects there was rivalry between the two chapels. Both chapels are now demolished, the Victoria Street site was redeveloped as the 'Littleborough Home' for the elderly.

In 1868 a group of members from the Stubley Primitive Methodists disagreed with some of the teaching, declared themselves 'modern' Methodists and opened a meeting house in Dearnley. After a period of independence they joined the Wesleyan Circuit (Rochdale) and have survived ever since.

In 1876 the Rakewood Wesleyan Chapel was created and finally in 1888 the Featherstall Methodist Chapel was opened. Built on the site of an older 'preaching house' it became a Labour Club in 1968, a Hosiery Works in 1975 and for a time it housed a gardening business prior to its current use as a hair and beauty salon.

Primitive Methodist Church Croft/Greenhill Church (1850)

Outside Littleborough, where Calderbrook Road starts to rise, a valley runs up to the left. A narrow road up the valley deteriorates to become an earth track as it starts to climb the moor.

About a mile beyond the present buildings was the hamlet of Croft which had fourteen cottages in 1850. A small building in the Croft community became the home of the Croft Primitive Methodist Church which was given the official title of Croft Greenhill Church. In the early days it was referred to as the Croft meeting house. Only the foundations of the houses and the original Preaching room can be found today. The first members of the church were from the cottages and the many small farms surrounding Croft at that time. On Sunday, in the early days, members were seen coming into the hamlet carrying their food for the day in a handkerchief.

In 1852, when established, the Croft Society joined the Knowlwood Circuit of the Primitive Methodists (centred on Summit/Todmorden) and regular services were instituted twice a day each Sunday. Preachers came regularly from Summit and by 1857 the trustees were considering a room in Littleborough to give a base to extend their 'cause'. Nothing came of this immediately and when, in 1864, sanction was given for the construction of a new chapel; no less than four of the trustees could not write so put their X on the document. In 1866 the new chapel was opened (in its present position) lower down the valley. By this time Greenhill was providing its own share of 'local preachers' who had qualified by examination and by 1868 the Society boasted three Superintendents, 14 male teachers and 13 female teachers. The following year they formed a Band of Hope which remained very active for the next 25 years. In 1882, 25 years after Greenhill first raised the matter, the Littleborough Circuit was formed and 'Croft' was transferred from Knowlwood to Littleborough. By 1890 Croft had 32 trained teachers and an attendance exceeding 100 both morning and afternoon. The music tradition stayed strong and a pipe organ replaced the harmonium in 1889. In 1893 Samuel Cryer, who had been a Superintendent for a long period, died and was greatly mourned. This appears to be the same man who Fred Jackson celebrated at the beginning of this chapter. In 1894 the Church was invited to put forward a member for the new School Board, which was a considerable compliment and in 1898 they purchased Rose Cottage as a residence for their minister. By 1900 the church was healthy, well equipped, mature and an accepted part of the local community. Despite a loss in numbers Greenhill is still active today, supporting and teaching religion, providing companionship and contributing to social life.

Stubley Primitive Mehodist

This chapel was opened in 1855 on Featherstall Rd (High Street) and it continued to serve the local community until 1979. When it closed planning permission to convert it to a house was granted, on condition that the facade was retained substantially unaltered. It can be seen today.

Other Methodist Chapels

In 1839 the Temple Methodist School and Chapel at Summit opened and in 1851 the Methodists at Shore followed suit.

The Smithy Bridge Methodists opened a meeting house in 1856 (circa) followed by a chapel in 1863; by which time they were part of the United Methodist Free Church. Around 1868 they built a larger chapel across the road and used the old one as a school which was greatly extended in 1903. In 1975 the new chapel was closed and demolished and the old chapel resumed its religious function.

In 1866 the Summit Primitive Methodists opened their chapel. Despite belonging to different Methodist strands the two Summit chapels always maintained cordial relations. At the centenary celebrations of the Summit Primitive Methodists in 1966 it was said there had been no substantial alteration to their chapel since it had opened! To mark the event they redecorated and 'modernised'.

There were other chapels often united under the banner of the the United Methodists Free Churches. Many of these chapels were small and were were driven by the personal leadership of an individual or family and failed once the leadership disappeared.

Examples in Littleborough include: 1870 Church Street opened (closed 1938), 1874 Queen Street opened, 1881 the Zion Chapel opened, at the junction of Shore Road and Calderbrook Road, but was converted to a workshop in 1940.

The Baptist Church

In October 1861 the Littleborough Baptists opened a meeting house in a three storey 'loomhouse' (weaver's cottage) at Shore Hill, Durn. In 1863 there were 339 members at Ogden (the mother church) and Littleborough had 67. It was decided to build a chapel at Durn, in Littleborough and it was completed in October 1868. Its foundations were

The Iron Chapel at Durn Baptist's built together with the brick school room below in 1868. The later stone chapel (1886) was demolished in the 1980's and a few houses built.

stone but above ground it was built in iron and wood. It could seat 500 people, had a Sunday school of more than 100 attenders and was built for a cost of £800. By 1874 the Littleborough Baptists were independent of the Ogden community. Sadly, by the early 1880's it is recorded that 'members of the Congregation sat with their umbrellas up during services' owing to the iron corroding and the rain coming in. The iron church was closed in 1885 and a new stone church was built; at the opening ceremony in 1886 scaffolding collapsed with many injuries. The architect was Henry Shuttleworth who (in 1872) became the first Clerk and Surveyor to the Littleborough Local Board. The new church could also hold 500 people but the cost of the replacement was £2250. The chapel flourished for many years though, after 1939, the congregation declined and in 1960 it closed, was converted to industrial use and subsequently demolished. The site was redeveloped for residential use.

Congregational Church

The minister at Summit decided that the number of worshipers who were travelling to Summit from Littleborough justified a local place to worship. A room was hired on Church Street which soon proved too small, the present premises in Victoria Street were opened in 1869 and by 1874 the building of the chapel and school was complete. The church was small catering for working people 'who laboured under very unfavourable circumstances'. It has withstood many trials including the anniversary service in 1907. There is a terse remark that 'the weather was tempestuous and the offerings were small'. The church survives and actively serves the Littleborough community today. In 1972 the Congregational Church in England and Wales, amalgamated with the Presbyterian Church to form the United Reform Church.

Roman Catholic Church

It was 1820 when the first R. C. priest was appointed in Rochdale, his church being a room over a public house. Soon after that in 1829 the Act of Catholic Emancipation removed many of the limitations and restrictions on Roman Catholics holding office, being M.P's etc. and finally in 1851 the Catholics completed the Formation of Hierarchy which gave them a administrative structure of diocesan administration. The Catholics call the subsequent period the 'Second Spring'.

A mid-century stock-taking of the condition of Catholicism in England suggested there was an intelligentsia (the Oxford Movement), some old established families (none in Littleborough) and that the most numerous group locally were Irish immigrants. Following the Great Famine (1840-60) significant numbers of these immigrants had filtered into our area, frequently as itinerant labour to help with harvesting and they continued to do so up till 1900. They were predominantly manual workers, often had their family with them and had tended to settle in small groups near the communities where they found work. These were the groups who were to re-establish the Roman Catholic Church in our community.

In the 1870's the nearest Catholic church was at St Patrick's in Rochdale and the small group of Catholics walking to Rochdale from Littleborough on Sunday were frequently taunted by some locals in Smallbridge, with remarks about T'Irish, Cathlicks, Red Necks and personal remarks about their women. One Sunday morning this came to a pitched battle and the Catholics were clear winners with two of the more vocal and aggressive taunters thrown into a small river with broken bones. The return from church was met by policemen who challenged the Catholics over the morning's violence. Having heard their case apparently the policeman in charge accused them of being fools to have done it in daylight with so many witnesses and let them pass. These men and women were to become the nucleus of the congregation that formed St Mary's Parish, Littleborough.

By 1880 there was a small group of regular Catholic worshippers in Littleborough but as they had no church they were considering supporting the construction of one in Todmorden. They then switched to the possibility of buying the Methodical Piazza but it was too expensive. The construction of a new workhouse in 1874-6 brought more families into Littleborough and under the guidance of the manager of the Stansfield Print Works they rented a piece of land on Featherstall Road along with an empty cottage on James Hill. The latter was soon replaced by a larger building on Brown Street - 'The Public Hall'. By 1878 there were 225 declared Catholics in the Littleborough District. After inspection in 1879 Mass was permitted on their premises within the Parish of St Mary with a resident priest. Many of the first priests came from abroad, for example from Germany. By 1881 plans were formulated to use the Featherstall site to build a school. When the contract was awarded the parishoners volunteered to do all the basic digging and sewering for the building. They started in March and finished in May. The building was to be 2 storeys high with a capacity for 120 children on the ground floor and 4 rooms above as the priest's residence and to hold 350 worshippers. The final building cost was £2 per seat. In January 1882 the first Mass was said in the new building and a month later they had the first Irish Evening. In Littleborough, factories, the railway and the canal were all expanding, quarrying was very active, and brick and tile works were springing up. More working families flooded in and up to 1900 there was little continuity of staff either in parish matters or staffing for the school. Poverty meant that it was difficult ever to initiate a solution to obvious needs. From the 1890s the parish was classed as a 'poor mission' and the sixth priest to be appointed (in 1902) spent his first night sleeping on the floor in bitterly cold weather with no bed linen. He left in 1904 and the need for a change in fortunes for the church was clear.

Summary of the religious situation in 1900

For the Anglican church it had been, compared to the previous period, a half century with many innovations and some solid progress.

For the Non-conformist group it will perhaps be seen as the apex of their existence. Methodism was spear-headed by two Anglican priests and it incorporates some of the ceremony. However, the pragmatism of many of the 'well-to-do' sponsors of the new chapels and the simple but deeply held beliefs of many of the communities, who wanted a church that understood their hard life, led to many of them breaking away to become 'Primitive or 'Independent Methodists'. The ceremony was minimised and the main focus became a sermon. In the 19th Century this was sometimes delivered by a 'ranter' who, as Fred Jackson described earlier, could create a highly emotional atmosphere.

For the Catholics locally it was a new beginning with both hope and success. At the end of the century all denominations encountered problems with loss of influence, declining attendance, declining income, deep concern about the place of church schools and a growing debate on the place of religion in the 20th century.

CHAPTER SEVENTEEN

THE NINETEETH CENTURY

PART SEVEN : THE GROWTH OF LITTLEBOROUGH

1850 - 1900
(Continued)

Education

Education has always been an important part of the fabric of any society and we have traced its development in the Littleborough area from the first established school, Helliwells Endowed School which opened around 1688 (see chapter 9). Most development of education facilities after this time was prompted or supported by churches and combined rudimentary learning and religious education. This position started to change in the first half of the 19th century (see chapter 15). As in trade, politics and agriculture the second half of the 19th century sees events and legislation from outside playing an ever increasing part in local education.

The Education Act (1870) established a framework so that the Board structure had the the authority to implement greater State intervention in Education. Boards were authorised to set up schools, levy a local rate to pay for them and the act gave the Board discretionary powers to enforce attendance at school up to the age of 13. By 1874 some 5000 new schools had been founded under this act. There was great resistance to the concept in Littleborough, which had Church of England, Non-conformist and Catholic schools. All of these groups were deeply opposed to any split between Church and State education. The opposition was led by the Rev. Doctor Salts, Vicar of Littleborough. Gordon Harvey was the local champion of State education with a renowned rallying call: 'Because our parents used rowing boats, must we never have steamers?' Harvey won the argument and in 1894 the local Board created their first Board school. In the following years Board Schools were to replace a wide range of the local schools that previously existed. Some of the 1870 legislation affected local education much sooner, for example, by 1872 there were public examinations under government inspection covering reading, spelling, dictation, slate and mental arithmetic, English grammar and geography. To meet the costs new education rates were levied. In 1880 another Education Act made 'schooling' compulsory.

A new Education Act (1902) abolished the 'School Board' structure and passed the responsibility for education to 140 newly created Local Education Authorities and through them, for elementary education, to the recently formed Urban District Council; which was authorised to levy rates to finance this level of school, including church schools. Government grants and general provision for the Church and other 'voluntary schools' was not as generous as it was for L.E.A schools; so the battle still raged over the separation of Church and State in the field of education. In 1906 Mrs Beswick Royds, of Pike House, offered to pay for anyone who would go to London to demonstrate against the latest proposals which, in her view clearly tipped the balance

Alexander Gordon Cummins Harvey, 1858-1922.

further in the favour of state education. The story is that every member of Littleborough Brass band volunteered to assist in this onerous task!

An interesting 'snapshot' of our local educational development can be presented by following the growth and decline of the many initiatives that were mounted to extend the education of our people.

1688   **Helliwell's Endowed School** Privately funded teaching under the wing of the Church. Initially the teaching was done in the chapel (see chapter 9).

1844   A three-roomed **Holy Trinity Parish School** was opened, which subsequently became the National School in 1865 (at which time they also started night classes). It was sited on Lodge Street and in the early days the school was both cold and damp. This school was demolished in 1877 to become part of the playground for the New Holy Trinity C. of E. Day School

1856   The origins of the **Smithy Bridge United Methodist Free Church School** were in the top storey of a three-storey loomhouse on Smithy Bridge Road which had 46 attenders when it opened.

1857   The headmaster of the Helliwell's Endowed School, in Littleborough, was Mr Wainwright. In 1858 the unfortunate Wainwright was 'murderously attacked and robbed in a railway carriage travelling between Littleborough and Manchester. The assailant was given penal servitude for life.' A new **Ladies School**, run by Mrs Lee of Blackstone Edge Road advertised for pupils.

1863   **Smithy Bridge United Methodist Free Church School** (old school see 1856)) opened. The building cost was £500 and it could accommodate 400 pupils. It started with 124.

1867   **Mount Gilead School** (Smithy Nook) was a small school, built by the Chapel, costing £500. This remained open until 1894 when the 50 children attending at that time were moved to St James' School.

1869   **St Andrew's (National School)** started as a day school in 'the old garret'. In 1871 (at Dearnley) a large rectangular room was built with 3 folding partitions to make four classrooms with another classroom attached to the side of the main building. This school was closed when the new St Andrew's school was opened near Birch Hill.

1870   **Many Chapels** announced that they were holding **evening lessons** or running 'Young men's mutual improvement societies' and a small **C. of E. School** was opened in Shore.

1872   A lady in Rochdale advertised she would give **weekly piano-forte lessons** in Littleborough; another lady announced the creation of a **'select school'** for young ladies, in Victoria Terrace, Gale. Miss Schofield set up a **Day School** in Featherstall. **The Featherstall Independent School** was opened in a large house on Chapel Hill, Victoria Street.

   Government Science classes are advertised in Littleborough. These include: Building Construction, Applied Mechanics, Machine Construction, Practical Plane and Solid Geometry. These classes were being conducted in the Parish Church School in 1885 when it was stated they had, during the first 50 years no less than 80 different teachers.

1873   The 'select school', which was in Victoria Terrace, Gale was taken over by a Mistress who claimed references from nobility and clergy.

A. Holt advertised a **'Middle Class School for pupils of both sexes** - preparing them for public examinations, night school in French, Drawing and English. He quotes references from a London College in Isleworth and a Professor at Owens University, Manchester.

An **'Academy for Gentlemen'** is advertised on Hare Hill Lane by a Mr Dalby. Since he had five wives perhaps it should have been an academy for ladies? **U.M.F.C.** School (United Methodist Free Church) was built on Peel Street. The cost was £2000 and it was to provide accommodation for 700 pupils with a hall, 5 classrooms on the ground floor and 11 classrooms on the first floor.

St James' Church, Sunday and Day School, Calderbrook was opened at a cost of £1000. It could accommodate 40 pupils on a 3 year course. It started with a few books, a black board and easel. It was extended in 1896 at a cost of £1200. The school closed in 1969 and some 78 pupils transferred to Stansfield Hall Primary Interdenominational Controlled school in 1970 (the buildings of the old Summit Board School). The old church building was used as an annexe to the main school accommodating the younger children.

1877   **Holy Trinity, C. of E School** opened on Victoria/Lodge Street replacing the 1844 Parish School. It took 4 years to finance and build, the cost was £3000 - £4000 and the ground floor accommodated 199 boys and 64 infants, the upper floor accommodated 216 girls. The building was extended again in 1909.

1879   **Wesley Methodist Free Church** opened a school on Victoria Street with space for 250 pupils.

1882   **St. Mary's Roman Catholic School** opened with a school room to accommodate 120 children, replacing the earlier meeting rooms.

1884   **Extension** of the U.M.F.C. School in Peel Street (see 1873). A new classroom on the ground floor would accommodate 100 infants. Two classrooms on the first floor would handle 80 children. The headmaster, Mr Nuttall became Clerk to the Littleborough School Board in 1903. His school was put under Board Control in 1894. By 1898 H.M. Inspectors reported the buildings were unsuitable and that grants would be terminated in 1902. When the Central School opened in 1902 534 pupils transferred from Peel Street to the new school in 1903. They marched in their Sunday suits to the new school and each pupil was given chocolate and an orange. This march ended the identity of a school whose children were known as the 'committed Free Church pups'.

1894   Helliwells School is closed. Only a small square structure remains as evidence of the old school - next to an enlarged dwelling house (often referred to incorrectly as the old school). The **Victoria Street Board School** was opened by the the Blatchinworth and Calderbrook School Board taking over the premises of the Wesley Methodist Free Church School (see 1879). The pupils remained the Wesleyan 'bulldogs' to their friends.

1895   Evening classes started in the Victoria Street Board School on Mondays and Fridays with an initial enrolment of 75 males and 186 females. There were soon many complaints about interference from political meetings, Bazaars and rehearsals of the 'Messiah'.

1897   **The Summit Board School** was built. This was the first school built by the Littleborough School Board (formed 1894). G Harvey was chairman of the Board and it was opened by Mrs George MacGill. There was an infants room for 60 children and 3 classrooms for 186 pupils. The Victoria Street Board School (1894) was recognised as a Higher Standard School but by 1900 there was strong external pressure on the School Board to provide better accommodation.

In this abstract you get a very fair picture of who was involved in education and the demand, need and respect for education at this time. The students conditions were often cold and bleak and the staff to pupil ratio was often awesome. Pupil absenteeism was rife especially when the textile industry was in the boom periods. Turnover of teaching staff was very high; one sad letter of resignation complains 'I do not like Littleborough at all, I do not like its fogs'. Throughout the century there is the tension between the Church Schools and the Board Schools. By 1870 it was accepted nationally that education was a duty of the State and this view challenged the church's traditional place in teaching and the right to combine it with religious instruction. In 1894 the Board schools became dominant and the church schools survived under the 'dual

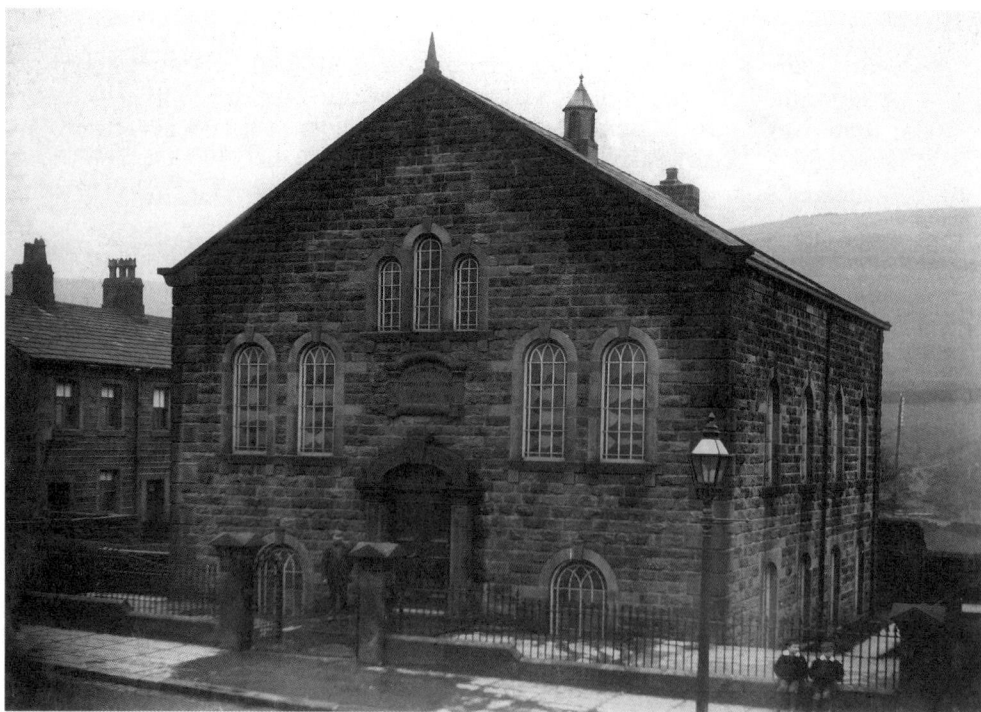

Littleborough Primitive Methodist Chapel 1866.

control' arrangements. These allowed the churches to continue to be a powerful influence in running their own schools and gave them a level of funding - but this fell short of the funding to the Board schools and to compete the churches had to undertake all kinds of fund raising activities.

Perhaps the most common was the bazaar; for example those held at the Parish School. This was a serious undertaking with an executive of pehaps 12 prominent local men, numerous committees and elaborate stalls. The refreshment stall would be 'manned' by up to 25 women and there would be light music all day and bands and dramatic entertainments each day and evening. The General Regulations and Rules of Etiquette were prominently displayed and prove the existence of a wry sense of humour.

1. No one may come into the Bazaar without paying but anyone may pay without coming in.
4. Examine your change before leaving or leave it with us.
8. Visitors should try to be present at the Opening Ceremony each day.
9. All should purchase from each stall, and should let their generosity exceed all their other virtues.
10. No less than £1500 should be aimed at by all Workers and Visitors.

It was not uncommon for a bazaar to continue over three or four days.

The contribution of the Co-operative movement to education in this half century should not be under-estimated. The guiding body of this organisation, the Co-op Union, recommended that 2.5% of all profit should be used to help those who 'would otherwise be deprived'. The main activies were to create libraries, newsrooms, publications and formal classes at every level of achievement. As an example, by 1877 Rochdale Pioneers ran 14 libraries and had 14,000 books.

The libraries were often sited on the upper floor of selected retail shops.

Co-operation
The Co-operative Societies

Co-operative ventures were to become a national institution but in 1850 they were modest little enterprises which opened after the mills shut (6pm) and were serviced by members who sold one or two commodities such as flour or oatmeal. In our area the link with the textile industry was always very important. In a world where much of the food was contaminated there was as much emphasis on purity of food as there was on cheapness. Of various experiments, the movement came to be modelled on the Rochdale Society (Toad Lane 1844), which established two principles - paying interest on share capital and distributing part of the profits in the form of a dividend to all who had made a purchase. The movement expanded by increasing the number of shops, staying open all day and diversifying the number of goods sold (millinery, dress making, clogging, shoes, and an ever widening range of food and drink). By 1863 Co-op's were so widespread that the North of England Co-operative Wholesale Society was created. The path was wide open to commence manufacturing many of the goods the societies sold and to create an effective wholesale to retail operation.

As the outlets grew so did other arms of the co-operative idea and based on the structure of the textile industry, the natural centre for the new units was Manchester.

They included the Wholesale Agency Ltd. (later the C.W.S.) 1863, Co-op. Insurance 1867, Co-op Union 1871 and later the Co-op Bank and Press. Each unit built major premises and spawned subsidiaries, including the Rochdale Paint, Varnish and Colour Works. All manufactured goods were produced under trades union pay and conditions and the organisational structure was designed to enable worker involvement, loyalty and solidarity.

The last quarter of the century saw a dramatic rise in working class living standards and the co-operative movement shared in this. In 1899 there were 1500 retail co-operatives and sales were 6% of national retail sales.

Membership and size of dividend grew so that, by 1900, members were able to enjoy 3s for every £1 spent in many of the individual societies. Co-op 'divi' was still a major element of the domestic budget in the 1940s. The Co-operative Movement became part of the social fabric, organising events, funerals, concerts, sports days and holidays. From the earliest times they supported educational initiatives and pioneered the ideas which developed into the Workers' Educational Association and Co-operative colleges.

Littleborough Co-operative Society of Industry Ltd.

In much of this development Littleborough was not exceptional. It started in 1850 with a 'small shop' at 84 Church Street with 31 members and a share capital of £96. The reality was that it was the front room of a cottage belonging to James Hall one of the founder members. The original members were mainly fullers working at Sladen Mill on an average wage of 10s per week so the money laid out represented a big sacrifice and an act of faith. The Rochdale Pioneers had been formed in 1844 with their new initiative of linking the dividend to the amount of purchase rather than a pay back on money that had been loaned. Littleborough was one of the first six to follow suit. The shop had a flagged floor, rough fixtures and was lighted by paraffin lamps. It opened when the mills closed and all the goods were bought in bulk and measured out. The main commodities were flour, oatmeal, lard, bacon, sugar, butter, cheese and eggs.

It was 1852 before any Acts existed to control the activities of co-operative societies and demand records be kept. Average sales for the first 6 years were £2,580 (100 years later the figures were 3000 members, £87,000 share capital and £200,000 average sales). The original single outlet became many.

True to its full name the Co-op built Industry Street in 1861. This covered the strip of land west of the present post office running round to the Cenotaph in the Square. The street included a butchers shop, a grocery warehouse and an abattoir. The warehouse later transferred to Peel Street in 1923 and was subsequently destroyed by fire. The abattoir lasted until the second world war when it closed under a government scheme to abolish small abattoirs. It was re-let to a private slaughterer in 1953 until it closed in 1963. The buildings were sold off and later it was partly destroyed by fire in 1978. The damaged buildings were converted to self contained flats in the 1980s.

The local co-op rapidly became a major part of the growing urban community. In 1868 the Littleborough Co-op commissioned 48 stone houses for their workers to be built on Bare Hill Estate. The streets were named Pioneer, Leah, Jerrold, Smith and Nelson. Pioneer is self-explanatory, Leah was a founder member of the society and manager for 34 years, Jerrold, Smith and Nelson were named after members of the

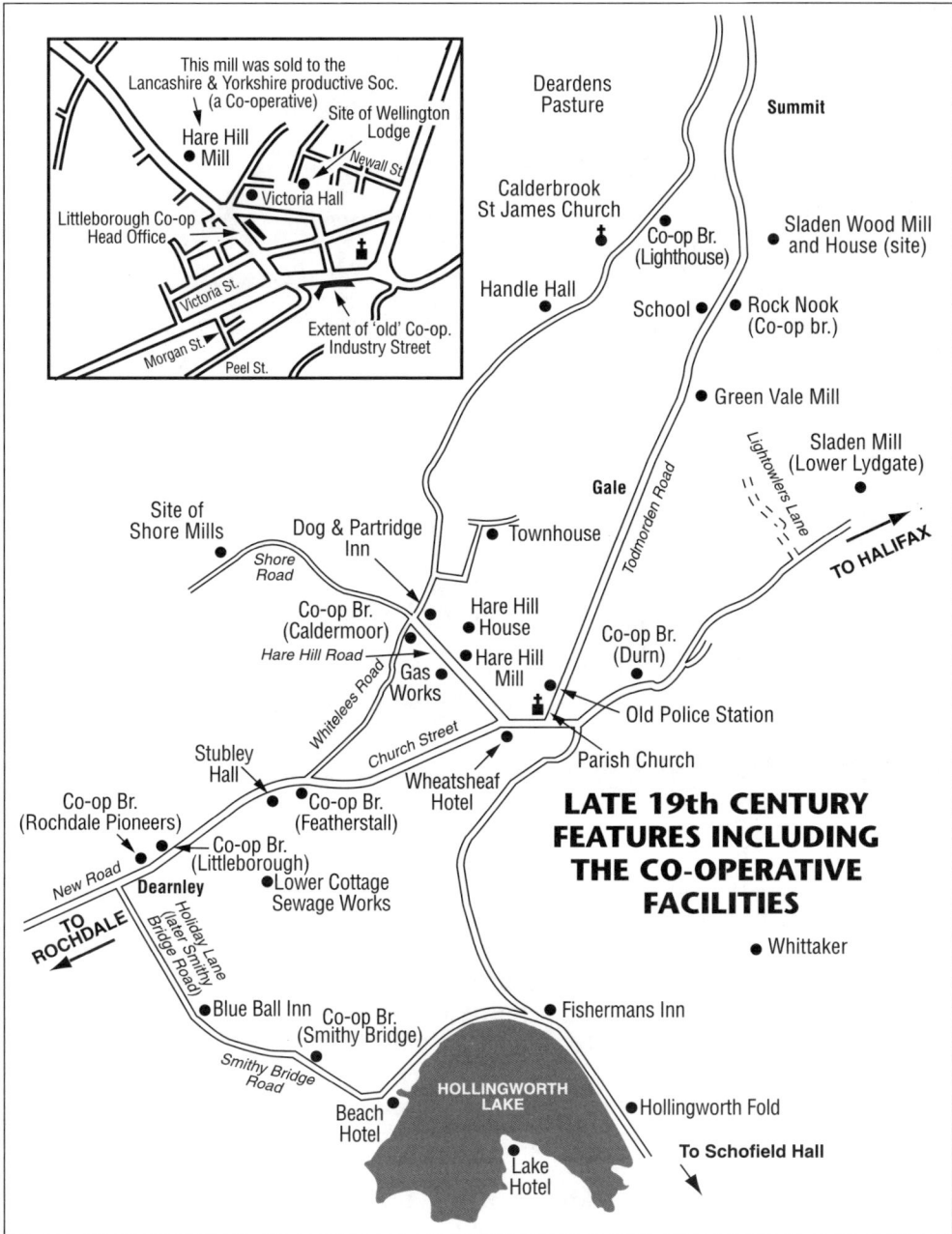

This mill was sold to the Lancashire & Yorkshire productive Soc. (a Co-operative)

Site of Wellington Lodge

Hare Hill Mill

Newall St.

Victoria Hall

Littleborough Co-op Head Office

Victoria St.

Morgan St.

Peel St.

Extent of 'old' Co-op. Industry Street

Deardens Pasture

Summit

Calderbrook St James Church

Co-op Br. (Lighthouse)

Sladen Wood Mill and House (site)

Handle Hall

School

Rock Nook (Co-op br.)

Green Vale Mill

Sladen Mill (Lower Lydgate)

Gale

Townhouse

Todmorden Road

Lightowlers Lane

TO HALIFAX

Site of Shore Mills

Dog & Partridge Inn

Shore Road

Co-op Br. (Caldermoor)

Hare Hill Road

Whitelees Road

Hare Hill House

Gas Works

Hare Hill Mill

Co-op Br. (Durn)

Old Police Station

Church Street

Stubley Hall

Wheatsheaf Hotel

Parish Church

Co-op Br. (Rochdale Pioneers)

Co-op Br. (Featherstall)

Co-op Br. (Littleborough)

New Road

Dearnley

TO ROCHDALE

Holiday Lane (later Smithy Bridge Road)

Lower Cottage Sewage Works

LATE 19th CENTURY FEATURES INCLUDING THE CO-OPERATIVE FACILITIES

Whittaker

Blue Ball Inn

Co-op Br. (Smithy Bridge)

Smithy Bridge Road

Fishermans Inn

HOLLINGWORTH LAKE

Beach Hotel

Hollingworth Fold

To Schofield Hall

Lake Hotel

Newall family who owned the land. In a similar manner Wellington Terrace was built in 1874, but is was subsequently sold.

In the October of 1868 the Caldermoor branch of the Littleborough Society was opened (cost £1500) and in 1869 the total sales figure of the Littleborough Co-op for

Jerrold Street, off Bare Hill, 1998.

a year was £4641 with Caldermoor contributing £1030 and Rock Nook £925. Caldermoor in the early days did a significant sale of provender and offals to farmers but later lost the business to a farmers' co-operative.

From the outset the co-operative ideal embraced much more than retail shops. In June 1860 the Littleborough Manufacturing Company Limited was founded with a capital of £20,000 which was to be raised by selling 2000 units of £10. The aims and objectives of the company were:

'The company is originated based on the success of the principle of co-operation whereby the savings of the working classes may be employed generally to their greatest advantage'

The minimum deposit on a share was 5/- and then 5/- per month until it was fully paid. At the end of the first year the capital required was increased to £100,000.

In 1870 at the 75th quarterly meeting of the Littleborough Society, which was held in the large room over the new branch store at Caldermoor, a dividend was declared of 2/- in the £ for members. The following year the dividend was 2/- in the £ for members and 1/6d for non-members.

In the following years there grew up a central nucleus of Provisions, Ladies and Gents Outfitting, Footwear, Furnishings, Greengrocery, Fishmonger, Clogger, Abattoir -

all housed in separate shops including a splendid domed building on Hare Hill Road for administration and other facilities. Scattered around the edges of the village were the all important Branch general purpose shops. The following is a small sample of the mass of activity in this period which was based on the fact that costs were stable and from 1850 to 1877 sales increased annually, they decreased in real terms in the following years up to 1884:

1868   Tenders invited for the erection of a co-op store at Caldermoor, at the junction of Hare Hill and Whitelees Roads.

1869   The opening ceremony of the Rock Nook branch. 150 people sat down to tea, to celebrate the opening and the 20th birthday of their co-op society.

1872   Formation of Featherstone and Dearnley Co-op.

1874   John Molesworth (solicitor) informed the Littleborough local board that Hare Hill Mills was to be re-let to the Lancashire & Yorkshire Productive Society. The new tenant was happy to allow the board to retain the fire engine house and oil room for the time being. The new company was a co-operative and shares could only be purchased by other co-operatives.

1875   Smithy Bridge Co-operative (1873) had 118 members and declared a dividend of 2/10d in the £. In the December tenders were issued for a co-op store at Smithy Bridge and a new branch at Featherstall during 1877.

1877   A newsroom was opened at the Caldermoor branch of the Littleborough Co-op Society of Industry Ltd.

1878   A meeting was held by the Littleborough Co-op Society 'for the purpose of taking into consideration the propriety of increasing the share capital invested in the Lancs. & Yorks. Productive Society Ltd'. It was agreed subject to the other societies increasing their share also. In the August of the same year the directors of the Littleborough Manufacturing Company Ltd. arranged a £12,000 mortgage with the Littleborough society. In the November the shareholders voted to liquidate the Lancs. & Yorks. Productive Society Ltd. In December a news room was opened at Featherstall co-op which was 'well appointed with 3 daily papers, several weeklies and periodicals.'

1883   Central Offices and shops built on Hare Hill Road (£4300). The shops included ladies and gents outfitters, grocers (the 6th branch) and confectioners. There was also a newsroom and a lending library.

1887   A serious crisis due to the failure of the Frankfort Cotton Mill, on Halifax Road. This mill was known as the 'Co-op Mill'. Many of the employees were co-op members and had induced the society to invest £28,000 in the mill which gave the society two members on the board. When the mill failed the society lost £22,000, and the share value fell seriously. One good outcome of this disaster was that for the first time the society appointed a professional auditor.

1897   The secretary was found to have embezzled a large amount of money which led to another serious drop in share prices.

1900   Jubilee Celebration. This was euphoric: as the society had made a excellent recovery during the last three years, after a period in the doldrums. In fact they promised their members that they were 'well on the way to make the working class into a new Capitalist Class.'

The Co-operative Wholesale Society Flannel Factory, Hare Hill Road Littleborough, portrayed about 1910. The artist has drawn the buildings accurately but the foreground especially is a little idyllic.

From the Trade Directories of 1888 and 1890 it is possible to build a picture of the size of the co-operative movement in the Littleborough area.

Littleborough Cooperative Society of Industry Limited

Richard Law, manager (1888) Thomas Leah (1890). Leah lived in a co-op house, 3 Wellington Terrace.

Central Stores: Church St.
Offices and stores: 40, 42, & 44 Hare Hill Road.
Branches at: 33 Church Street, Caldermoor, Featherstall, Rock Nook, Durn and Lighthouse.
Butchers: Church St. and branches.
Linen and Woollen Drapers: Church St.
Grocers and Tea dealers: Church St and branches
Dearnley and Featherstall Co-operative Society Ltd.
Location; 84 New Road Dearnley
Grocers and tea dealers
Linen and Woollen Drapers
Smithy Bridge Co-operative Society Ltd.
James Royds manager
Linen and Woollen Drapers

Friendly Societies

The nature of these societies was that a group of people would get together and agree conditions under which they would all pay subscriptions regularly. The money saved would be used to alleviate distress, most commonly bereavement or illness. They gloried in rich names including, Oddfellows, Ancient Order of Foresters, Royal and Ancient Order of Buffalos and a Women's Friendly Society. Many of these societies

226

Central Premises · · · · HARE HILL ROAD.
Now comprise Registered Offices, Board Room, &c.; Grocery and Provision, Drapery, Millinery, Dressmaking, Boot, Tailoring, and Bakery Departments; Co-operative Hall, Stables, &c., &c.

The Co-operative central premises, Hare Hill Road about 1900. Today only the corner stonework remains, when the dome was taken down in 1987 it was rebuilt as a feature in a garden at Clough Bank.

were associated with a public house where they met and subscriptions might be 5p or 10p per calendar month.

Town and community development

Littleborough was growing very fast and the old framework of supervision was creaking. From 1858 local Boards could be set up to provide appropriate sewage disposal, street lighting and public health services as well as to raise a levy to build pavements and tackle river pollution. Rivers were a serious issue locally, having become the dumping ground for all kinds of waste and sewage. In our valley such activities had exacerbated the already serious problems from flooding.

During the 19th century houses were built in large numbers. For example nos. 23-33 Whitelees Road were built and are very typical of the period and on Church Street nos. 15 onwards were being constructed. In 1861 a survey claimed that Butterworth and Calderbrook alone had 1,017 houses. A good stone house built between the Parish Church and Victoria Street was let at 5s 6d per week which represented nearly a third of a skilled working man's wage at the time. Smaller houses were available for 2s.0 or 3s.0. Workers' houses were usually 'back to back' terraced houses with only 'party walls' at the sides and rear of the building. There was no back door and the dwellings were either 'one room up and down' or two. Later, these houses were often 'knocked through' to make larger ones with a bathroom and kitchen.

Prior to 1870/71 there was no legislation on sanitation as regards household materials, rubbish or excreta. Owners and occupiers make their own arrangements for disposal. Rural dwellings and farmhouses had 'middens' and spread the soil on the fields, others arranged collection for subsequent use as manure. Others proceeded more informally with the 'bucket and chuck it' system.

Early local bye-laws called for one 'petty' for every four dwellings. Collection was arranged with local farmers. If collection was done by the board they would advertise for tenders for the annual collection of the ashes and excreta. Thus lavatory facilities were at the end of each street and on wash days the streets would be blocked with clothes hung across them between the houses. There was no running water in the houses so toilet sets were essential and a bucket parade was usual each morning, often accompanied by a macabre sense of humour. The pail system lingered for many years in Littleborough and even up to the 1970s there were still over 100 pail closets in use.

There was an alternative to a pail for disposal of night soil as the water closet developed. These took the form of a tippler or tumbler - which used waste water from the kitchen sinks. The water ran into a pivoted earthenware reservoir. At a critical point it passed the balance point and tipped over allowing a concentrated rush of water down a drain to a separate building in the yard. Here it washed away any accumulated solid matter from the pan moving the night soil to a lower level for clearance by the soil cart. In the late 1960s there were still more than 100 tipplers in use locally and only in the 1970s were they replaced by fresh water flushing cisterns.

The manager of a section of a mill tended to live in the same street, as the workers, but in a better house. A replacement for the manager often moved into his predecessor's house. Resentment only grew up when they moved away. Some of the houses were built on low-lying land and were soon unfit for habitation. Evidence of this is still visible at the Church Street end of Hare Hill Road, where stone houses were built on damp and unstable foundations. They soon began to tilt and though most have since been demolished one or two remain today. Many of the gaps on Victoria Street are the sites of houses that tilted so badly that the top stories had to be removed and finally the houses were demolished. Flooded cellars remain a serious problem in the town centre at the end of the 20th century. Drainage and clean water were basic for health and the river beds had to be cleaned out.

A great contrast to the workers' housing was seen in the house building for the successful millowners. They often lived close to their mills in spacious well built stone mansions. The Cleggs lived in Shore House, the Newalls in Town House the Fothergills in Sladen Wood House. All these were houses of substance and there were many more such, as Wellington Lodge and Hare Hill House. The owners were men of considerable wealth but it is clear they were totally involved in the direct control of their mills during the 19th century and in most cases could walk to their work. Houses, of course, demand roads and in 1861 Hare Hill Road and Victoria Street were constructed. The entrance to Hare Hill Street at the beginning of the 1850's was very narrow and much later was still described as 'an alley'. Width restrictions were not finally removed until 1915. On the new streets purpose built shops were constructed, unlike the converted cottages on Church Street. Status building continued on Victoria Street despite the insecure foundations and many buildings started to shift, tip or sink. It was said that it was cheaper to get drunk in the Victoria Hotel (corner of Hare Hill Road and Victoria Street) than anywhere else in Littleborough, as the floors already sloped so severely. Bare Hill Street, Peel Street and Morgan Street were all under construction. Cottages, mansions, places of worship, shops and a Public Hall were all soon built. The face of Littleborough was changing, as were people's lives. Probably anticipating her husband's initiative to change the church tower to a spire (1860) so that he could see it from his

The Wheatsheaf Buildings on Littleborough Square, 1999.

drawing room, across his meadow, Mrs Newall in 1858 arranged a three day event to raise money for a new public clock, or more politely a 'Horological Desideratum'. In one day she raised an astonishing sum for the time of £127.

The working day became 6am to 6pm and 2pm on Saturday. Before it had been 'all God's hours' or eleven to eleven on the day or night shift working for a master. Regular wages were paid, whereas previously it had been once a month or six weeks or when the stage coach passed. Children started work at age 10 rather than 7 - and only if they passed their 2nd Standard.

Progress was possible, John Hurst, a cow lad on a farm behind Wellington Lodge, played cricket with the Newall lads and taught them skittles. In due course he got the job as landlord of the Dog and Partridge. He brewed his own beer, had his own gas generating plant, raised a large family and amassed a lot of money. His son pulled down the old Wheat Sheaf and erected the building we know today, it was a pioneer hotel in the area. Called 'Hurst's Folly' by the local wits it was foredoomed, but despite all this cynicism it thrived.

Gas was first introduced into the Littleborough district in 1843 by Messrs. H. and Lawrence Newall, chiefly to supply their Hare Hill Mills. They were able to supply only a few houses in addition to the mills with the new illuminant. It was sold to these at the rate of 7s (seven shillings) per 1,000 ft. Many other local people had also made their own gas for private use including the owners of Green Vale Mill and John Hurst of the 'Dog and Partridge'.

It was not until 1866 that the Littleborough Gas company was formed (under the recent Gas Acts) to supply the whole district. This came about through the initiative of

A postcard scene from the Victorian heyday, The Beach Hotel is on the left, its outdoor dance platform in the centre, with the old Lancashire and Yorkshire Hotel behind that.

John Hartley, of the Falcon and one George Swindells, grocer. Gas of course was to be widely used for street and domestic lighting and for cooking. Both gas and water were very quickly made available through pipes and taps to most parts of Littleborough.

Throughout the century there were bad periods like the Hungry Forties before the repeal of the Corn Laws, when Ernest Jones and Fergus Connor incited 10,000 people at an outdoor meeting on Blackstone Edge. Then in 1862 there was the Cotton Famine when wages fell below 1/6p per week. But throughout it all there were the three days of Rushbearing when the village centre was filled with hurdy gurdys, brandy snap stalls and booths all the way from Hare Hill Road to the Falcon. And the 'Wrigley Thrutch' was run at Lydgate for a prize of half a sovereign and well wishers would throw buckets of water over their runner. Saturday excursions to the Hollingworth Lake were a great day out and 80,000 bream and perch were put into it for the delight of the anglers.

In 1868 a drought stopped many of the mills working in August though Dearnley Colliery was able to provide a water supply to local households which was distributed by carts. The amenities were in the hands of the Guardians of the Poor (Wm Heap & John Tetlow in 1867) and the suspect sanitation was in the hands of Surveyors.

The size of the surveyor's problems are illustrated by the comments of the members of the local board about Hare Hill road.

July 1872	Drainage in the road is simply abominable.
	Cellars in many cases are nothing better than cesspools.
	Low lying property has become the receptacle for the sewage of higher property
August 1872	The highway is a pestilential place

It was in August 1872 that tenders were invited for the first public sewer. This was to run from Hare Hill Road down Victoria Street along Todmorden Road and Church Street through the Square to discharge into the river near the railway bridge. Subsequent extensions went down Todmorden Road and from Durn under the canal to join to the main sewer in Church Street. Slowly the network of sewers was extended throughout the district. It was the late 1800s before a sewage farm was constructed near Lower Cottage below Stubley Hall.

One Surveyor was immortalised for a more attractive job. He became the man who introduced a steam roller to Littleborough which immediately got called 'Big Ike'. The roller weighed 15 tons and was delivered by rail in 1878. Its trial run was to the top of Blackstone Edge and it was followed by members of the highway committee and many thrilled spectators.

In 1870 Local Boards were formed with Henry Newall as Chairman in Littleborough. Rates were set at 1s in the £ and the Board met in a room above the Gas House (built by the Newall family). Sub-committees met in the upper rooms of a house along Church Street. Nearby was a night school for spinning and weaving.

The cricket club was founded with 30 members and in its second year, membership had risen to 78. A playing pitch was made available at the foot of Newall meadow from which the club moved , after some years, to the present ground on Hare Hill. The club engaged its first professional player in 1875.

For many years the Royal Oak barn acted as a local prison but Littleborough got a new police station in 1871, sited between Newall Street and Victoria Street on the Todmorden Road. This was vacated in favour of the current site on the A58, in the 1960s. The old site could be located by the date stone that remained over the door for many years but which was removed when the front of the building was refurbished.

In 1872 Littleborough was still surrounded by considerable meadow and pasture land and the gardens and mansions of the more opulent classes. There was plenty of coal, stone and good water to be found outside the centre. Handle Hall and Dearden's Pasture formed a much advertised picnic spot near the recently built Calderbrook, St James' Parish Church.

Visitors coming from the station were likely to see a pack of galloways or 'gals' waiting for their loads of lime in the station yard. These pack horses were still the main carriers of goods to the upland communities but they were universally gaunt, lean, ungroomed and unkempt. They were always muzzled not because of their savagery but to stop them wasting time browsing as they travelled.

When the Turnpike Trusts closed (1875) the maintenance of roads fell to the local Board. From that time the records are full of initiatives to widen, surface or strengthen local roads and bridges. Road surfacing was simple if time consuming.

The first roadwork undertaken by our local Board was to repair a footpath alongside the turnpike from Littleborough to Summit. Using ashes they repaired the left hand side as far as Gale then the right side to Summit. The board's responsibility initially covered the old turnpike roads, Halliday Lane (previously Holiday Lane), subsequently Smithy Bridge Road), Shore Road and Hare Hill Road.

Welsh stone was delivered to Smithy Bridge wharf, Schofields Foundry wharf, Smithy Bridge and Littleborough railway stations. Tenders were invited for spreading, watering and rolling of the roads under Board control and the inspection committee gave rewards

Alongside the Parish Church opposite the Trades Hall, the last steam tram to leave Littleborough.

to contractors for the best maintained sections. In 1888 the Littleborough Square was laid out using Whitworth setts. Road setts were used throughout the district and after the second world war hot or cold asphalt was laid over them. Surface dressing by tar spraying and chippings were frequently done later. Tar was laid over an area, chippings were spread and the surfaced rolled with a steam roller (Big Ike).

At the same time the rapid expansion in travel turned people's thoughts to solutions other than riding a horse. In 1879 a fund was launched to provide a railway station at Summit. The initiative failed and the money had to be returned to the subscribers. At the end of the 20th century a station at Summit is once again being discussed! The underlying need for better communications remained and was only solved with the coming of tramcars in 1907. Horse buses started to run between the town and Rochdale with a 5d charge inside and 4d outside. There were two horses with the facility of an extra chain horse at the front. The vehicles often paid a boy to ride the bus and blow a horn at every public house on the route. Wooden shops were springing up all along the more used roads in the area and a few in this style, if not the original wood, have lasted until the year 2000.

The steam tram arrived in 1882, half joke, half nuisance and rarely clean. The car was hauled by a squat steam locomotive which at the Littleborough terminus (by the Parish Church) ran round a loop to be ready to take the car back to Rochdale. It was frequently demonstrated that it could be quicker to walk to Rochdale. The service was run by the Manchester, Bury, Rochdale and Oldham Tramways Company which, despite the name, never did connect to Manchester.

This is a good point to summarise how the local people saw themselves, through the 1879 Trade Directory. Littleborough was part of the township of Blatchinworth and Calderbrook. They were proud of the scenery, the hills and the attractions of Hollingworth Lake. Spinning and manufacturing cotton was the staple industry followed by flannels,

Littleborough Square about 1900. Tramlines are laid but there seems no evidence of the motorcar. The Wheatsheaf, the Royal Oak and The Falcon Hotels are much as today. The 'shop' in the centre was Martins Bank, later Barclays; in the 1970s it served as a youth employment office and since 1979 has been a bookshop.

baizes and fulling operations. Alongside these were the sanitary tube works, stone quarries and oil refineries. Since its purchase from a private company in 1866, the Gas Works was an important new utility which had already cost an extra £27,000. The Local Board was formed in 1870 and their main offices were at the Gas Works. Commercially there was great interest in the new powerful communication links by the canal and the railway. Beyond business the biggest element emphasised in the local life is the position of the church. The rebuilt Holy Trinity had two satellite units dedicated to St James's and St Barnabas. There were numerous dissenting places of worship 15 of which were itemised in 1879, covering Wesleyans, United Methodists Free Churches, Primitive Methodists, Independants, Methodist New Connection, Baptists and Congregationalists. Some 180 people are indexed for their perceived importance or their place in public service, followed by an itemisation of the main occupations and the number of companies involved. A few of these are listed:

Architects (2), Banks (2, both Branches of London banks), Beer Retailers (19), Blacksmiths (6), Boot and Shoe Makers (9), Brewers (1, Littleborough Brewing Co.), Cloggers (8), Colliery Proprieters (11), Calico Printers (3), Cotton Spinners and Manufacturers (15), Dyers and Finishers (5), Farmers (61), Fire Brick and Sanitary Tube Manufacturers (9), Fulling Mills (13), Inns, Hotels & Public Houses (28), Manufacturers of Flannels etc. (8), Solicitors (1, Molesworth John and Son), General Shopkeepers (54), Quarry Owners (5), Carriers (4), road, rail, general carrier and omnibus. The omnibus ran from the Falcon hotel to Rochdale via Dearnley and Smallbridge several times a day.

In addition to these occupations there is a mass of other trades covering every aspect of retail needs. It is clear that the community is just emerging from an agricultural way of life, is essentially still self supporting, and has no need to look beyond the village to buy the necessities of life.

By 1883 there was a Littleborough newspaper and in October 1883 it was delighted to report that 'The Great America Aetherscope, Pepper's Ghost and Spectre Company' would come to Littleborough for six days. It all demonstrated the astounding effects of the new electric light. In this era Ceylon tea became available and Mr Consterdine introduced a display of 'The New Gas Cookers'. It was the heyday of characters and nick-names. Jammy Flup the bookmaker, Owd Calib the hen doctor who made 'owd brids int'young uns' and many more.

In September 1883 the New Temperance Hall, later the Victoria Hall, was opened in Littleborough. There was a crowded 'blue ribbon' meeting where hundreds of people were not able to get in. The Chairman's report was robust:

' the Oldham people thought themselves very clever building cotton mills, if they built one at a cost of £1 per spindle - the Trustees have built a nice building here at a cost of £1 per head. He had been told that within a mile of the centre of Littleborough there were at least 20 places of worship and their schools, which says much for the enterprise, morality and religious well being of the community. Then he thundered: 'Unfortunately these are not the only buildings to which the public resorted. They had the Wheat Sheaf, the Royal Oak, Red Lion and many more besides. He should like to see these places appropriated to another use, which would not be harmful but beneficial.'

This is the Victorian era and soon after the opening, the following series of reports about a dance in the Temperance Hall are found in the Littleborough 'News'.

'First week: a dance will take place in the above hall - STRICT PROPRIETY
Second week: the dance announced in the above hall is suspended.
Third week: the Temperance Hall is pleased to announce a new
                   (and we hope more careful) secretary has been appointed.'

There were in Littleborough at this time 'gangs' of Liberals, Conservatives, Blue Ribbon Temperance Hot Gospellers and the New Salvation Army. There is a record that the Salvation Army fought a battle to oust the Blue 'Ribbers' from the Methodical Piazza. They hired youths who sent a hail of stones and other missiles through the windows. The mayhem only melted away with the arrival of the law in strength. There was also the Littleborough Public Brass Band which between 1882 and 1886 had outstanding sucess in National contests. At York they apparently not only beat the Black Dyke Mills band at performance but on the York station afterwards recreated and won the 'wars of the roses'. Those not detained returned to claim a total victory! To end a rumbustious period Littleborough suddenly became famous as the home of 'a great pig' owned by John Alletson. The animal was of a volume and proportion that can only be reported as world beating. It was sold to Blackpool but it had to arrive alive. Littleborough did it proud and the beast was played down to the platform by the Brass Band and accompanied by a great and appreciative crowd. It was accompanied by four 'minders' to Blackpool and its final fate was glorious but too sad to report.

The Local Government Act of 1888 created new County Councils elected by ratepayers replacing the old system of County Magistrates elected by Lords Lieutenant. Thus, in 1889 the next step in restructuring our administration framework came, with the creation of the Lancashire County Council with a range of responsibilities. Prominent among the people elected to this new body was Gordon Harvey, who led the long battle for 'Board Schools' in Littleborough. His next step in politics was to become

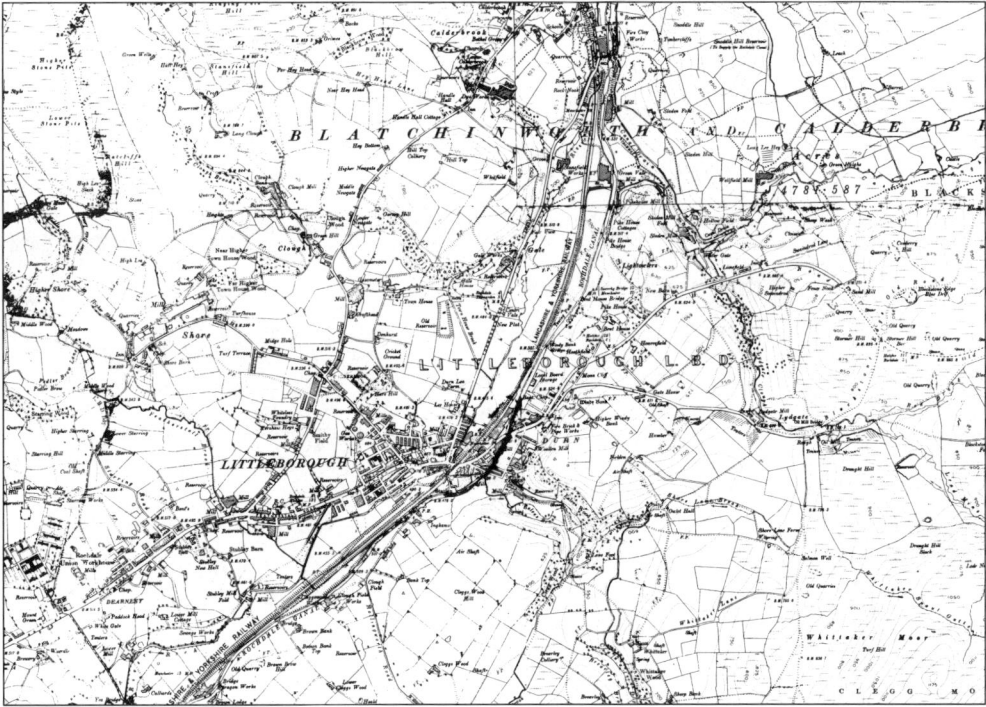

The Littleborough District 1891 from the ordnance survey, kindly loaned by Rochdale Libraries.

Rochdale's member of Parliament at the Liberal Landslide election in 1906. The creation of the County Council was followed in 1894 by the District and Parish Councils Act establishing Rural and Urban District Councils, replacing Parish Vestries and also establishing female representation. Littleborough was declared an Urban District Council (U.D.C. or abbreviated locally to 'the District'). The excitement was great and celebrations were widespread - if slightly naive. One banner said it all:

> 'May our rates be small, prosperity great and happiness for all'.

The local U.D.C. structure was made up of 3 electoral wards (later four: Blatchinworth, Butterworth and Weurdle, Calderbrook N and S), 3 councillors per ward, a Clerk and a Chairman and Vice Chairman. The U.D.C. broadly took control of all utilities, and transport including public provision. District road building and maintenance were a U.D.C. responsibility and when School Boards were abolished (1902) the new Education Act passed their powers to the local Councils. All kinds of schools, including Church Schools, were to be supported by the rates system, up to varying levels. Other responsibilities were for local housing, public cleansing, sewage, lighting, parks and refuse. From the beginning there were many responsibilities that were divided between the U.D.C. and other committees or the County. These included child care, education, fire services, health, classified roads and bridges, shop acts, planning, police, public health, libraries, food and drugs, diseases, representation of the people and quarter sessions. To handle the range of work the U.D.C. had some 8 officers who between them worked with the local committees and also county and other agency officers and committees.

An occasion for a large congregation to hear 'outdoor preaching' sometime before 1900, on the area which is now the recreation ground at Hare Hill. On the right is Frankfort Mill.

In 1892 Littleborough claimed a first in England by appointing Mr James Cryer of Lyons Mill as a magistrate, said to be the first working man in that position.

During the 1890's there was still an old apple tree growing near the Square. The road running from the square towards Gale was known locally as 'Tall Hat Row' as an ironic comment on the up-market stone houses being built there.

'Who dosta think's baan to live in them grand 'ouses'? asked the natives. 'Naught but tall 'ats, I'll gammon!'

For the first time red brick appeared in a number of housing developments between Bare Hill and Newall Street.

In 1893 Littleborough enjoyed what was billed as a world swimming championship at Hollingworth Lake. The estimates of the crowd in the newspapers varied from 40,000 to 110,000. An Englishman, Joey Nuttall, swam against an American called McCusker. The Englishman won and the newspapers revelled in headlines claiming the Lake had been drunk dry in the subsequent celebrations.

June 1897 was Queen Victoria's diamond jubilee which Littleborough celebrated royally, with the centre piece being an enormous bonfire on Blackstone Edge at the top of the Roman Road close to the site of the Aiggin Stone. It is estimated that some 75 tons of material was carried up to form the beacon.

When the Boer War broke out in 1899, Sergeant Christie from Littleborough was called as part of the Burnley Militia. The people of Littleborough gave him a rousing send off with the Summit Band carrying him shoulder high in a torchlight procession. After the celebration he rode a funeral horse to the station. He got as far as Bury barracks only to be rejected on medical grounds. By the end of the day he was back home and from then on he was known as South African Jack by succeeding generations

This magnificent bonfire was built on the top of Blackstone Edge to celebrate Queen Victoria's Diamond Jubilee in 1897.

of children. In all about 15 local people died in that war - a pale shadow of the horror to come in the 20th century.

Women in Littleborough

With Queen Victoria on the throne and the century closing it is interesting to review the place of women in our long local history.

In the early chapters of our story there are few references to any named character, only say a head on a Roman coin or a reference in the Domesday book to the Saxon owner of the lands. Significant references to women do not exist. In later years, although women had no place in the official hierarchy of the church or local government, they are occasionally mentioned. In the Middle Ages, in our area, such mention was usually to record marriages, with the important emphasis being on land and property. In the last four centuries women do start to emerge because of their own abilities. For example, Mrs Taylor, a widow who inherited property on Whitelees Road and built on that inheritance to leave a substantial amount of money at her death. We also hear of women outstanding professionally like Ailse o' Fussers (see chapter 11) who organised a string of packhorse ponies carrying cloth, lime and fuel across the uplands. She overcame difficult terrain and obvious danger with courage, skill and determination.

In the 19th century, women begin to be mentioned more frequently, particularly those who had inherited wealth or married a newly rich mill owner. One example of such a woman was Mrs Beswicke-Royds, of Pike House, who seems to have had a social conscience and involved herself with many beneficial causes in the village. Just like her men folk, she had her name engraved for 'posterity' on the side of a chapel school.

Jessie Fothergill

Another talented woman who is remembered in Littleborough, is Jessie Fothergill. She was the daughter of the T. Fothergill half of the firm ' Fothergill and Harvey' who set up as textile merchants in Manchester. Thomas Fothergill was a member of an old Quaker family with strong Rochdale connections whose initiative led to the buying of the Sladen Wood Mill before he entered into partnership with Alexander Harvey. It was also the first mill where the firm got experience of manufacture and where Gordon Harvey, Alexander's oldest son, learnt his trade. Born in Cheetham Hill, Manchester, Jessie moved to to Sladen Wood House at Summit on the death of her father. This was of course originally the mill manager's house and became so again when Gordon Harvey moved into it. Like the Brontes before her, Jessie loved the hills and the people who lived in 'the thickly populated districts of the valleys below'. She would visit people in their homes, loved to talk and the working people of Summit accepted her. It was these meetings that gave her the material for the novels she started to write. For example *Probation* gives a vivid picture of the hardships of the workers in the late 19th century. *Healey* is a thinly disguised picture of Summit with a closely observed description of the atmosphere in workers' homes and the power exercised by the ranting preachers over the simple people at that time. She also achieves a very good representation of the dialect which was still the natural form of speaking for most of the local people (see extracts from her work in chapters 14 and 15). Using pseudonyms, Rochdale and Littleborough were her settings, for example Rochdale became Thanshope.

Jessie Fothergill stands in the fine tradition of women writers in the 19th century who found an outlet for their talents in writing about the industrial society around them. Sadly, she died at the age of 40 in 1891 whilst visiting Berne in Switzerland.

Enid Stacy

During the 19th century, there was growing across Britain a new women's movement, to struggle for equal rights for women and especially equal voting rights. A young woman, involved with those women's struggles, brought Littleborough closely in touch with those wider movements.

Our story starts modestly enough when Percy Widdrington, a divinity student and ardent Anglo-Catholic came with his wife, to the Parish of Calderbrook in 1901. In 1903 she was pregnant with her second child and while making tea for a friend her husband heard her cry out once and she died at his feet. She had suffered a massive heart attack aged 35. A sad story but not an unfamiliar one at first sight, until you dig deeper.

Percy Widdrington was a promotor of the early Christian Socialist Movement and he met his wife to be when they were electioneering for the International Labour Party on behalf of Ramsay McDonald. Her maiden name was Enid Stacy.

Enid Stacy had a degree, was a member of the Fabian Society, was awarded a lectureship and held a high administrative post in the International Labour Party. But it was not academic honours or renown that drove her, but a deep conviction to help create a society where everyone had equal opportunities. Age 24 she led a long strike in Bristol of women confectionary workers, 'the Sweet Girls'. As a result she was victimised and unable to get work, so she came north, where she helped workers in Nelson, Burnley, Rochdale and the Colne Valley.

By 1893 she was living near Kendal in a colony, set up by a clergyman, as a cheap alternative to a rate supported workhouse. The clergyman decided to evict Enid and her friends, whom he saw as agitators. He hired 'twenty assorted roughs, from the beershops at 5s each'. Enid described the violence that followed:

'Ted Childs was lying senseless on the ground. Jack Moore was struggling with three or four .... meanwhile they had quite succeeded in ousting our small band of five .... all had been severely handled. The police utterly refused to take any steps to put a stop to what they knew was an utterly illegal procedure. Such is the power of the money bags, outward respectability and the parson's coat!'

There was an outcry and Enid became even better known, In that year she gave 50 lectures and subsequently averaged over 300 per year. A typical note from her pocket book read 'August 8th, Rochdale. Went to Littleborough to finish meetings of yesterday and answer questions. Open air. Good meeting. Topic *'What socialism is'*.

Enid Stacy

In 1896 at an International Conference in London, of some 450 delegates she topped the ballots to act as their representative, in two key areas. They had a Peace March on the Embankment and Enid's signature is prominent on an often quoted resolution which began 'that peace between the nations of the world is an essential foundation of International brotherhood and human progress ... that wars are not desired by the peoples of the earth ... and are against all the real interests of the workers ....'

In 1898-99 she toured the country with the Clarion Van taking the socialist message into the small country towns. Everywhere they struggled against paid ruffians and un-sympathetic police. In one such struggle the police refused to believe a mere woman could be in charge and so served a summons on a Liverpool clerk who was helping. When Enid was called to give evidence the papers reported 'I fancy she was rather a surprise packet for their Worships. They didn't expect anything like that and were evidently much impressed ... clear and logical manner, never hesitating and never contradicting herself in any particular ... the Magistrates dismissed the case.' As the 'Vanners' moved on her fame had gone before and thousands turned out to hear her speak on such topics as; *'Industrial Crises: their cause and cure'*.

As Enid's fame as a platform speaker spread wider, she was invited to the United States, where she did two tours. Most of her abundant energy was given in the States to supporting the cause of women's suffrage, in Philadelphia, Buffalo, Cleveland and onwards; speaking to ever larger audiences. Percy her husband wrote from Calderbrook ...'indeed good news. Two hundred and sixty dollars: why it is as much as a member of the leading professions receives. ...We shall be glad of some extra money this year. Things are beginning to look very shabby, curtains especially. The cold in my study is *arctic*, so much so that I find that I positively must have a pair of thick window curtains.' Enid had ended the century in a very different world.

This was the woman who died in the Calderbrook Vicarage. There were many moving tributes, but one from a close woman friend will suffice. She recalled their early campaigns,

'more often than not it was her hard-won earnings and often hours of hot baking that paid for the cakes we ate so thoughtlessly. Her shoes were literally worn out, tramping for sale of tickets and organisation work of every kind. Later as a platform speaker, it was her brilliance, incision and logic which won the day with her audience from Littleborough in Lancashire all across the United States.'

Her gravestone is found in the Calderbrook Church graveyard. For many years commemorative sevices were held in her memory drawing large crowds to Calderbrook church. A role model for succeeding generations, her niece and biographer wrote:

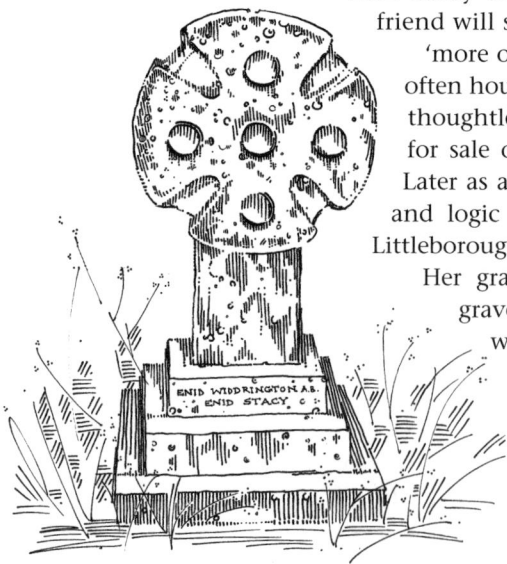

Enid Stacy's grave at St. James Church Calderbrook.

'She hardly ever spoke in London: she never stood for any public office. She asked for nothing except to be free to use her talents to further the liberation of men and women and deepen their awareness of how to grow unhindered into fuller humanity. That is why ordinary folk did not just admire her as a clever outsider, but loved her as one of their own, helping them to enrich their own lives.'

Reading of these women, so talented and committed, it would be easy to assume that women's place in society had changed considerably. But this was not so. Examine a brochure for the Littleborough Grand Floral Bazaar in 1910. The executive committee, whose picture opens the book, consists of twelve men and is headed "Are you good men and true" and to help says this is a quotation from Shakespeare. Under 'AND ALSO' are listed no fewer than 17 women. It was to be many years before women progressed from being 'and also'.

Leisure, culture and entertainment

With the growth of Littleborough there was an audience for music, brass bands, scientific societies, chess clubs, drama societies, sporting and leisure activities of all kinds, including the following:

Littleborough Cricket Club.

The club was founded in 1859 by five local gentlemen at a meeting in the Falcon Hotel. A subsequent public meeting enrolled 30 members. The evidence suggests that the club had started some time prior to this date as a level of organisation is already in place. The first ground was on Wellington Street but it was moved when Mr Henry Newall (first President of the club), offered a field opposite his residence on Will Hill. Matches continued there until 1872 when the club moved to its present ground. Within a few years of the formation of the club teams were visiting neighbouring areas such as Healey, Fieldhouse, Newbold, Todmorden and Walsden. Later they went to Elland and Bacup.

If the mill owner's family were involved there was a good chance of visiting 'on full pay' given the appropriate sporting prowess!

The first record of scores in a cricket match is for a game between Rochdale and Littleborough in 1863. In 1864 when Hollingworth Lake froze over Littleborough played Rochdale at cricket on the ice. Skates provided a substitute for the spiked boots but it was disputed who won. The club moved from Wellington Street to the present ground in 1872. In 1892 the South East Lancashire League was formed (later the Central Lancashire League), Littleborough joined in and won the cup (subsequently winning on a further six occasions 1911-12-17-19-21 and 31). Team travel became more regular and more regulated. The metal pavilion dating from the 1870s was replaced by a brick pavilion which was itself destroyed by fire in 1967. By the 1880s the cost of membership was around 5s per year and the cricket club was running other events such as annual sports days, concerts and light hearted games of Clown Cricket played to to raise money for charity. It was 1874 when the first 'professional' (John Huffin, Notts.) was engaged on a regular basis. By 1880 the club's splendid record of professionals was well established when Walter Robinson, Lancs. led the team to a stream of successes. This was a period of considerable popularity for the game of cricket.

Hollingworth Lake - the 'People's Park'

By 1850 the old lodge had become a lake which was the focus for leisure and pleasure for an ever increasing hinterland of Yorkshire and Lancashire people. Visitors were exhorted to choose between the pleasures of the lake and the drama of Blackstone Edge. The hotels all promoted the idea of a two day stay as the minimum necessary to explore the area.

At the beginning of the century there was accommodation at the Fisherman's Inn and the Blue Ball at Smithy Bridge supplemented by rooms in surrounding cottages. By the 1860s two more big hotels, the Beach and the Lake Hotel, each with extensive gardens had been added. Other, more modest accommodation was growing up as fast as people could build. The railway companies seeing the attraction of the area started to bring large numbers of people from Lancashire and the West Riding. To understand the appeal perhaps the following quotation from a railway poster will help

'You are out of your everyday world, transported suddenly from the regions of smoke and dirt and the sound of busy life to where nature herself appears to be making a holiday. The Lake is teeming with life -'.

There was a good basis for these claims as a visit to the Lake Hotel illustrated. To get there you could walk round to 'the back of the Lake', or take a 'car', or buy a ticket and cross by the ferry at a penny a trip. The booking office on the west bank was available for booking of accommodation, dinner, entertainment etc at the hotel and was connected with it by 'subaqueous telegraph'. The Lake Hotel had extensive facilities for pleasure activities and a very large garden surrounded by ornamental iron palisades. The existence of the garden explains the dense areas of rhododendron that are found on that side of the Lake today. There were bowling greens, croquet courts, and a dancing floor capable of accommodating 2000 persons under a covered area. There was also a gas-lit viewing stage to watch events or spectacular fireworks etc on and around the water. Next to the hotel was a life-sized model of a ship-wrecked sailor created by 'clay moulding'. Large clocks announced the times for the ferries. There was rising competition between the ever increasing number of hotels springing up in response to the increasing prosperity in urban areas. In 1872 the following hotels advertised in a trade journal as being immediately accessible to the lake: Hollingworth Lake Hotel, Yorkshire House, Fisherman's Hotel, Star Hotel, Beach Hotel, Queen's Hotel, Lancashire and Yorkshire Hotel, Royal Oak Inn and the Lodge Inn. The need seemed unlimited, for example the area claimed to have housed the 6000 miners who came to a conference at the lake in August 1866.

The Rowing Club was formed in 1860 and in 1862, it held its first Regatta. The peak of the exploitation of what we would call the leisure and tourist industry came between 1850 and 1900. There were ups and downs: for instance the Rowing Club faltered but was restarted in 1872 and never looked back.

In 1860 J. Sladen of the Beach Hotel had sole rights of letting out boats on Hollingworth Lake. His fleet included two steamers and 30 boats. Two years later there is a description of the crowds at the lake and of the many waggons with gaily covered awnings and three steamers on the lake, one with a band on board. Writing in 1872 it was said that on a fine day 'an apparently countless number of boats are plying' and another says 'there were ambitions to be the Henley of the north.' Fishing was further promoted and the lake filled with dace, perch, bream, gudgeon and trout for lovers of 'piscatorial pursuits'.

The lakeside was filled with stalls, lock-up shops, snack bars, entertainers, gypsies, professional photographic rooms, bazaars, fairground rides and fortune tellers. In short it was homely, pleasant, very varied and an ideal foil to the grimness of much of the everyday life of ordinary people. There were interesting communities nearby to visit and explore such as Hollingworth Fold, Schofield Hall and Whittaker.

The climate was perhaps more severe than in recent years and the lake got a reputation for its ice skating with excellent conditions in 1860 and in 1864 (2000 people on the ice) and more recently in 1912 and 1947. There were other sports around the lake more common to the whole of the area such as cock fighting and foot races. In 1883 Sunday boating was legally allowed and in the 1890s the lake was attracting huge crowds. Swimming competitions were very popular and numerous professional swimmers including Captain Webb used it for cold water training. By the end of the century it unfortunately had lost its 'tone' and a mix of drinking, fighting, vulgarity and poor service heralded a precipitous decline in its fortunes in the next 50 years.

A Victorian Pastime

Although neither well known or popular it is not entirely surprising, given the skill of the local people in building in and carving on stone, that a very early leisure activity were the stone carvings on the rocks known as Robin Hoods Bed on Blackstone Edge. Amongst many inferior and undesirable attempts of recent years there are some fine examples of carving designed to record the existence of 'old' Littleborough family members such as 1827: S Butterworth and 1832: H Newall of Town House (1815-1886).

Before cameras were commonplace local photographers satisfied the demand for family portraits.

CHAPTER EIGHTEEN

THE TWENTIETH CENTURY

PART ONE : AN ERA OF SOCIAL CHANGE

1900 - 1950

Late in the 19th century we achieved reform of the army, the civil service, the police and there was cautious encouragement for both education and the trades unions. Public health was vastly improved through enhanced sanitation and the provision of clean, edible food. Councils were actively encouraged to build and rent houses. The combination of better organisation and better wages brought holidays for example, the official bank holidays, rail and steamer trips and a vast variety of weekend special offers. The urban population had access to the hills and moors and rambling became a major leisure pastime. Bicycles became very popular everywhere while cheap travel was becoming possible. Suitable newspapers were published for the 'ordinary people'. Regular church going declined in the towns, with the exception of the Methodist Church which served the new working class.

As the 20th century began a Liberal Government, with Labour support, promised more reforms in areas of trades unions, school meals and medical services. The latent tension between the House of Commons and the House of Lords flared up in terms of paying for such reforms - however the 1882 Reform Bill had already reduced the House of Lords to a very low level of influence in key legislation. By 1903 'votes for women' was on the political agenda but up to the 1914 - 18 War they still did not get a vote. In 1918 some women were allowed to vote but it was 1928 before all women achieved the right - and Britain became a democracy.

The first World War was a disaster for Britain with one million dead and 2 million wounded. We entered because we feared German domination and the trigger was the German invasion of Belgium in 1914. We sent a large expeditionary force which, together with the French, stopped the German advance outside Paris. For the next three and a half years, during which millions died, the Western Front did not move more than a few kilometres in either direction. Germany was aligned with Turkey, Russia (to a degree) with France and Britain. One side or the other gained advantage, never supremacy, but in 1918 the last German mass attack drew the U.S.A. into the war committing 250,000 more soldiers to the struggle. In 1918 the Germans accepted failure and surrendered. Eight million young men were dead and twenty million seriously injured.

The war had united Britain under David Lloyd George but after the war the divisions became apparent. Some women got the vote, but most lost their jobs and lost their equality of pay because of the intense pressure to find work for the returning soldiers. Managers who had worked and consulted with trades union leaders suddenly turned away and bitter strikes broke out especially in the traditional industrial areas. New competition from America, Japan, East Europe and elsewhere meant there was an enormous downward pressure on wages.

By the late 19th century 1½ million people had left Ireland and by 1926 its population was halved. The divisions became more violent. After a series of terrible atrocities on both sides, and civil war, Ireland was split - first by the formation of an Irish Free State which later, in

Town and Country still meet close to the heart of Littleborough.

245

The Rochdale Canal at Ealees, seen from Taylor Terrace.

Steanor Bottom Toll House.

246

The recreation grounds.

Hare Hill Road, 1985.

A professional cycle race speeds through the square, 1993.

248

Hollingworth Lake, looking towards Rakewood.

The Lady Alice with The Fisherman's Inn beyond.

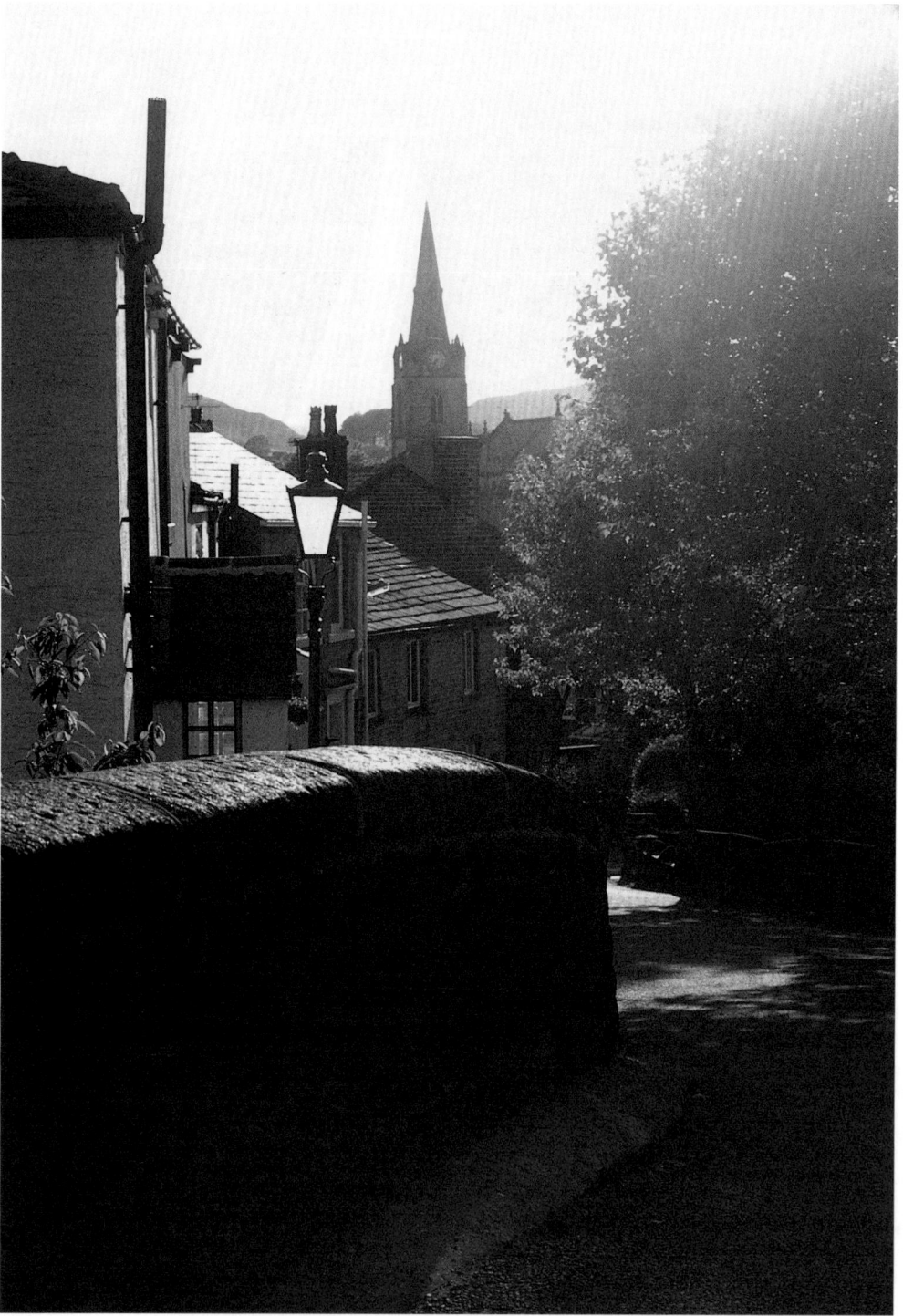

The cottages on Ealees Road.

The rush-bearing festival has been successfully revived in recent times.

A veteran from the 1950s this Rochdale Corporation double Decker bus has been lovingly preserved, in its original livery. Littleborough had a regular 10 minute service to Rochdale 3, 3a, 6 and 6a which travelled a route from Summit to Newhey. For journeys to Halifax the Hebble bus passed through the Square and over Blackstone Edge.

1937, became the independent Republic of Eire, with Northern Ireland remaining in the United Kingdom.

In 1922 the British Coalition Government collapsed and the new three party system of Liberal, Conservative and Labour Parties began to take shape. In 1923 Britain's first Labour government was elected. In May 1926 the miner's dispute triggered the General Strike, which escalated to most of the unions and nearly led to a national shut-down. After nine days the T.U.C. called off the 'General Strike'; in December the miners returned to work, on lower wages and working longer hours. From 1929 to 1933 there was a depression, especially in the old-established industrial areas, where unemployment figures were highest and poverty deepened. It was the coming of the next war that finally restored full employment.

Textiles for uniforms, ships for war, coal for the arms factories, slum clearance, more leisure and holiday industries all brought work. Abroad Hitler and Mussolini had earned some admiration for their achievements in economic areas. They were also becoming increasingly aggressive and were threatening war. Our politicians appeased them - against the background of an electorate still carrying the raw scars of the world's most bestial war. In September 1939 Germany attacked Poland and in the same month Britain and France declared war on Germany.

For six months we had a 'phoney peace' which was used to evacuate many of our children from the big cities. When they arrived at their billets, their appearance was often a shabby testimony to the poverty in which they lived. A blackout (no lights outside from dusk to dawn) was imposed and gas masks were issued to everyone. In 1940 France surrendered and the British troops, along with many French, were driven into the sea and only saved from final disaster by the evacuation at Dunkirk. The land battle on the continent was lost and the next step was a battle for control of the air. With France defeated Britain was alone, but Hitler decided, in 1941, on a policy of bombing and starving Britain into submission while simultaneously to attack Russia. This led to Russia entering the war; in December of the same year (1941) Japan attacked the U.S.A. It was now a World War with Italy, Germany and Japan fighting Russia, Britain and America. Though on rations, most of the British population were actually eating a better diet than pre-war; everyone was absorbed into the war effort. The Allies gained air supremacy commencing massive bombing attacks on Germany. The German submarines were eventually sunk or driven into hiding and in 1943 the allies invaded Italy. However the single most important factor was that the Germans were utterly defeated in Russia. In 1944 the Allied Expeditionary Forces landed in Europe. In 1945 the Germans surrendered.

In the Far East the Japanese had expanded their conquests during 1942 with fearful consequences. In response the U.S.A. marshalled huge armies and navies first containing Japan then, with their allies, commenced to attack. With increasing dominance in the air and naval supremacy, the attack was focussed on the Japanese mainland culminating in the dropping of the world's first atomic bombs on Hiroshima and Nagasaki. The slaughter was immense and within five days the Japanese surrendered. Since then, the military necessity for this action has been bitterly contested and despite the devastation and suffering brought to the civilian population this marked the beginning of the nuclear arms race between U.S.A and Russia. Continued development means that we now possess weapons that can destroy the earth.

The second World War over, everyone expected a job, a house, good medical care and decent schools. In 1945 a general election was held and to the surprise of many, there was a massive vote for the Labour Party, to implement a promise of 'fair shares for all'. The new government delivered jobs for all, and universal health insurance. There was also protection for mothers, the ill and the elderly. The National Health Service was free for everyone; the money being raised by taxation. House building was a key issue and local Councils were seen to be at the heart of the solution.

After the latest war it was clear our iron and steel, coal, shipbuilding, wool and cotton industries were ill-equipped and had lost their markets. A great swathe of industry including railways, steel, airlines and gas was nationalised, but by 1946 shortages were widespread. During the 1950s and 1960s Conservatives came to power and they set about adapting the major Labour reforms to make them work within their vision of the world.

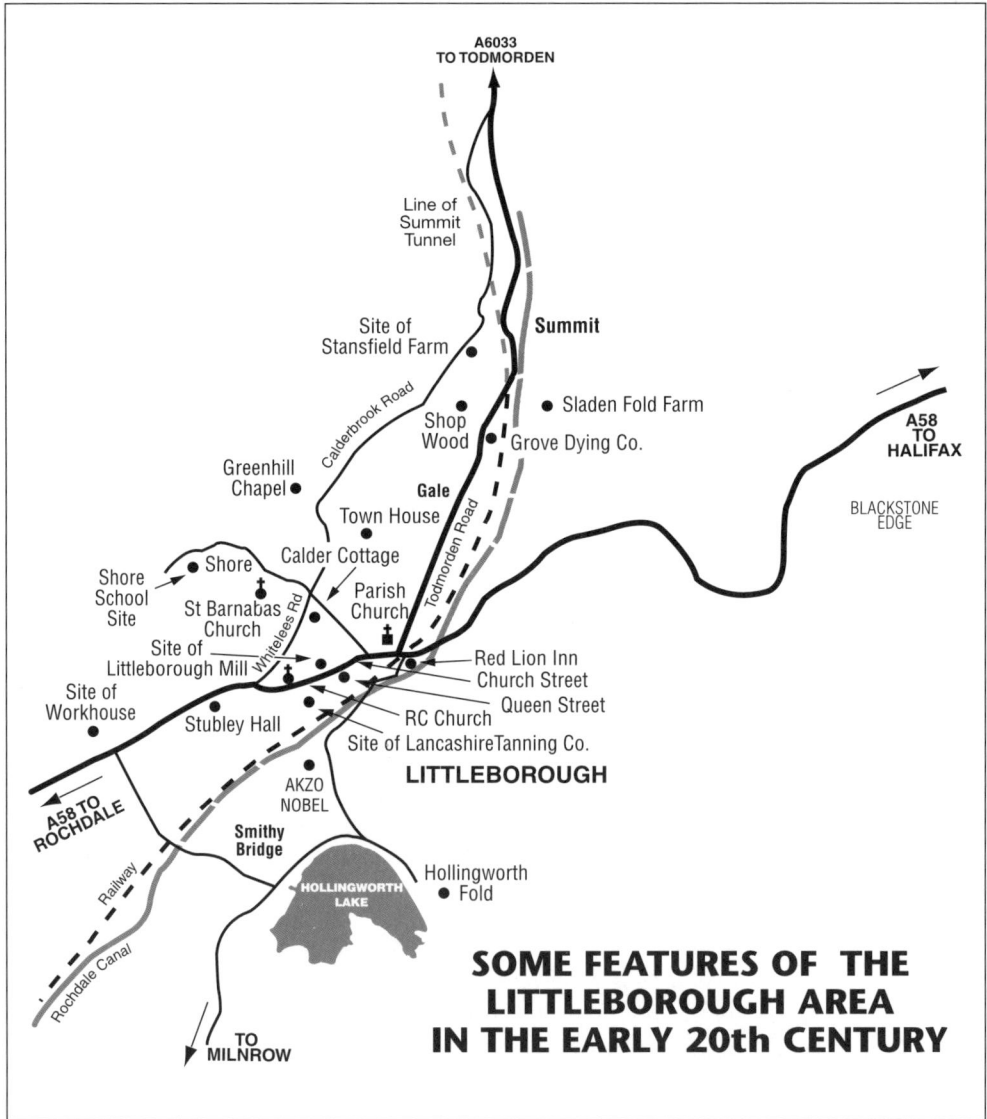

SOME FEATURES OF THE
LITTLEBOROUGH AREA
IN THE EARLY 20th CENTURY

General Conditions

The industrial picture of Littleborough was of a small town dedicated to textile manufacture and the industries associated with it (see chapter 14).

In terms of the environmental picture we entered the 20th century with a landscape that had deteriorated drastically over a hundred years, was extensively polluted, littered with derelict sites of defunct industrial initiatives and nearly denuded of trees. Literally our area was a dirty place to live. The problem was recognised and during the first half of the century a number of initiatives were mounted to start a change for the better. Gordon Harvey, although one of those who profited most from the local textile trade, recognised the many ills that came with it and encouraged the creation of 'the Beautiful Littleborough Society'.

This Society is the direct predecessor of the Littleborough Civic Trust and the letter confirming its formation remains a statement of many of the objectives of our National Civic Trust today:

BEAUTIFUL LITTLEBOROUGH SOCIETY

Dear Sir or Madam   Nov 6th 1919

A Society bearing the above title was formally given birth at a small meeting held on Oct. 16th 1919 & received the enthusiastic support of A G C Harvey Esq. James Edwards Joseph Nuttall Counc W Law Counc S Nuttall Joseph Dearden & Mr Fred Jackson, & others

1st	The objects shall be to create amoungst all residents an appreciation of the beauties of the district and an interest in its History its Geological formation its Scenery its vegetation & its Architecture.
2nd	With these ends in view, the aims of the society will be to preserve all that is interesting or beautiful, to keep records of objects of interest which are disappearing, to watch for and try to prevent the disfigurement of the locality, to sysematically plant trees & shrubs, to encourage the local Authority in all endeavours at neatness and general improvements, to insist that all powers for the prevention of nuisances including the pollution of the Atmosphere shall be used, to encourage the training of children in the care of flowers and growths, & to promote a knowledge of good taste in local & domestic architecture.
3rd	The Officers shall consist of a President (who shall be the Chairman of the District Council when he is willing) Vice Presidents a Committee of 12 who shall appoint a Sec & Treasurer.
	Any resident may be a member who is willing to subscribe 1/- per Annum or who will plant or give a tree, or perform some similar act in futherance of the Societys objects. An Annual meeting of the Society shall be held at which the accounts shall be presented & the Officers Elected.
P.S.	Will you please attend a Meeting in support of the above objects on Friday Evening Nov 14th 1919 in the Textile School Hare Hill LBoro at 7.30 PM.

Mr FRED JACKSON
SEC. PRO TEM. Calderbrook Terrace
L.BORO

Early tree planting group at Summit with young helpers in attendance.
The man in the bowler hat at the back is almost certainly Fred Jackson.

Fulfilling their objectives, in due course they planted trees on all the approach roads to Littleborough, notably those on the line of the main road between Gale and Summit. Here, owing mainly to the efforts of the society, hundreds of trees were planted. Shop Wood, which was formerly an ash and rubbish heap, a nuisance and an eyesore to everybody, was reclaimed to almost become the wooded vale it had been centuries before.

The Grove Dyeing Company, on the road to Summit, set a good example to other firms by planting trees and shrubs around their reservoir and works, helping to restore it to a pleasant area.

These pioneering efforts were of course supplemented by numbers of private gardens and other guarded spaces where plants still grew: typical examples of these were Stubley Hall, or the gardens and woods that Gordon Harvey planted around Town House to make it 'look like' the Lake District and the flower displays grown by Daisy McGill under glass (said to include Orchids) at Calder Cottage.

Finally the purchase by the U.D.C of the Hare Hill Estate gave public ownership of extensive parkland and large greenhouses which were a source of pride for everyone. The grounds of the house needed little alteration to make a typical Victorian park with rockeries, weeping trees, rhododendron shrubberies and, of course a bandstand. It is little changed nearly a hundred years later.

Population

At the beginning of the 20th century the boundaries of Littleborough were redefined to include Butterworth, Weurdle, Blatchinworth, and Calderbrook North

256

Hare Hill Park,
the Council offices and surroundings, 1951.

and South. Throughout the first half of the century, of the total population, women represented 52-53%.

Year	Total Population
1901	11,166
1921	11,488
1931	12,028
1951	10,932

The population had risen rapidly during the last hundred years and at the turn of the century was stable; the main source of employment was in all aspects of the textile industry.

Industry and Commerce.

Littleborough entered the 20th century with its economy totally dominated by manufacturing industry either directly involved in textiles or supporting the sector.

The Textile Industry

Generally, if rather bitterly, it was said that one of the most popular local events in the first half of the century was the occasion of the felling of the many factory chimneys.

Typical of a situation that was repeated many times was the closing of the old 'Littleborough Mill', its demolition and the raising of the Python Mill on the site. This was a rather handsome mill which was taken over by a Dutch company, the Breda Visada Co. Ltd, who made viscose rayon fibre. Throughout the second world war it was

257

Crowds gather, some on the rooftops, to watch the razing of the mill chimney at New Mill (near the present Health Centre) 24th August 1907.

One of the few remaining mill chimneys in the district, at Rakewood, looking towards Wardle.

occupied making axles for Churchill tanks, but post-war it passed into the hands of British Anka only to be closed. Most of the plant was removed and the bulk of the building was demolished.

Chemical and associated Industries

Through the textile industry Littleborough developed a degree of expertise and a number of modest firms specialising in some chemical based supporting industry such as bleaching and dyeing. From the 1930s, for many years Littleborough was the site of a major subsidiary of one of the world's biggest tanning companies:

Lancashire Tanning Co. Ltd.

It would seem unlikely that a major European company, Adler and Oppenheimer (A&O), with a number of large tanneries in Central Europe would become deeply involved with Littleborough. However, in the early 1930s one of their directors, a Mr Power, went to Berlin and when he saw what was happening to the Jews he urged the senior management to consider moving to England. Commercially he emphasised that there was not enough leather processing capability in Britain in the event of another war.

Messrs. Bevington and Sons were their U.K. agents and one of their directors went to search for suitable premises. They found an empty mill in Littleborough which was sited between the railway and the river Roch. The factory had been a mill processing artificial silk but had closed down 10 years before and in general terms was in a dreadful state with all the drains blocked. Upon closure the owners had removed all machinery, fixtures and fittings, including simple things like door handles. Undaunted, the firm retained an architect and an engineer converting the buildings into a tannery which was to employ 400 workers. Such a plant needs a great deal of water so part of the work was to dig a well and it is believed that it was the first mill in the district to build its own sewage plant. All this negotiation and conversion took time and production only commenced in 1937. The situation in Europe for the Jews had become increasingly perilous; already some senior staff were living in Manchester and elsewhere.

A&O had chosen a young member of the family, Werner Treuherz, to run the factory in Littleborough mainly because he could speak English and had spent six months in England, including a term at the London School of Economics. He was brought up in Alsace where his playground was one of the company's tanneries and in early manhood he was given the opportunity to work in all the various parts of the A&O company. He was due to start in Littleborough in July 1936 but was tipped off about the intention to put him in a concentration camp and fled to Britain in April of the same year. The tanner, Mr Huber and several managers were brought to Britain from Europe. The property, owned by the Littleborough Unit of A&O, known as the Lancashire Tanning Co. included one of the oldest buildings in Littleborough, Stubley Old Hall. Werner Treuherz converted this into a house to receive guests, also making a home for his family. Many years later he remembered with great affection the pleasure he found in living there and the help that gave to an exile, under considerable stress, to settle down in Lancashire. He regretted the subsequent loss of atmosphere within the house as it was adapted to commercial catering but acknowledged that conversion had preserved the external facade and shown respect for (in his words) 'its dignity'.

Factory production started in 1937 and the product was usually called 'Upper Leather'. This was suitable to make heavy boots such as those needed by the Army, Navy, Air Force and Land Army to name some of the more obvious customers. After the war it was estimated that the Lancashire Tanning Company had produced some 66% of such leather needed in the war effort.

With the war over, the factory switched to working with fashionable leather with gold and silver lame (interwoven metal thread), for ladies' shoes and handbags. Although a major departure from the earlier business the new product sold well with Werner Teuherz visiting Italy, America and South Africa, to support the sales effort

The generally accepted cycle for a business enterprise is that the first generation creates the business, the second generation enlarges and consolidates and the third generation loses interest and moves on. In the case of A&O it was Hitler who drove them out of Germany and caused them to place their main assets in the Americas. With hindsight Werner Treuherz admits to making a wrong decision some time after the war, when a Yorkshire tanner made an offer for the products, plant and customers of Lancashire Tanning Co. and he opposed it.

<table>
<tr><td>

LANCTAN

MADE IN ENGLAND

CALF

THE LANCASHIRE TANNING Co. Ltd.

CHARLES STREET

LITTLEBOROUGH

Manufacturers of high class Chrome, Calf and Side Upper Leather, used by the Leading Shoe Manufacturers in this Country and exported to all parts of the World

</td><td>

E. Clegg & Son Ltd.

SHORE MILLS
LITTLEBOROUGH
LANCASHIRE

Over 100 years ago was founded at Shore the firm of E. Clegg and Son Limited, Cotton Spinners and Manufacturers. Throughout the years expansion and modernisation have combined to place the firm amongst the most efficient and progressive concerns in the country. Large sums of money have been spent in the institution of up-to-date machinery and amenities, and the 750 employees of the firm, engaged in producing high quality yarns and fabrics, spend their working day in clean, warm, well illuminated, air-conditioned rooms. They also maintain their own Cricket, Football, Chess, and Table Tennis sections, and organise regular dances and outings.

Amongst the principal products are Drill cloths for overalls, Spun Rayon and Fine Cotton Cloths for dress goods, and Cotton Sheetings. The sheeting is made up into Sheets and Pillow Cases and marketed by a Subsidiary Company, Shore Sheets Limited, and are sold in white and many attractive shades.

In this firm are open many opportunities for boys and girls on leaving School, and the Personnel Officer would be glad to interview anyone who is considering taking up employment in cotton.

We invite you to inspect our works and see for yourself all that happens between Raw Cotton and Finished Cloth.

</td></tr>
</table>

Advertisements for two of Littleborough's biggest employers, from the Councils Coronation Souvenir Handbook, 2nd June 1953 (price 9d).

From a series of photographs taken at Fothergill and Harveys in the 1950s this group is noted as 'Tacklers, Weavers and Smash hands at Rock Nook Weaving shed.

Sadly the ultimate decision lay with the units in the Americas, who preferred to use their money on the New York Stock Exchange, and having no interest in a tannery in Lancashire sold it, having dismissed Werner Treuherz.

The tannery at Littleborough was closed down by the new Yorkshire owner, the jobs disappeared, all valuable equipment was removed and it became a depot for lorries. The tannery had become the victim of the 1960s phenomena 'asset stripping'; subsequently the mill was burnt down. In 1998 the site was cleared redeveloped for residential use.

After the tannery closed people living near the site expressed concern that the ground was infected with anthrax. The potential danger came from the hides imported mainly from South America which were said to be infected. The Lanctan management claimed that during the period when they ran the tannery there were no cases of human infection due to the expertise that always existed together with a range of precautions that were in place. Such as the appointment of a factory doctor (Dr Vining), who attended the mill regularly.

261

Two of the Hess fleet of chemical tankers, based at the works off Hollingworth Road about the mid 1950s.

AKZO NOBEL

On the Hollingworth road there is a site that for many years has supported a variety of chemical based industries:

In the 1930s an 'artificial silk' (viscose rayon) plant was opened on the site which was previously occupied by the Cloughfield Oil works. An older resident recalls that it was possible to go there and buy candles. The site was taken over by Hess Products (later Armour Hess) and more recently by AKZO Chemie Company now called AKZO NOBEL (see chapter 20).

Retail Sector

Shops and shopping

Local shopkeepers formed the Littleborough Traders' Association to protect customer loyalty; it offered credit through members' shops. Collectors were paid to bring in the periodic payments. The struggle to hold their local business, as the market got more mobile and discerning, was underway. This struggle was to intensify throughout the 20th century and it has been fought with vigour in Littleborough. For example, in the 1930s a schoolboy called William Meredith was out delivering The Littleborough District News from 5 am onwards on his bicycle before going to school. The area he and his family covered was from Blackstone Edge to Smithy Bridge collecting the free paper from the Trades Hall. The paper was produced by Vic Crossley who was editor, advertising manager, local news hound and recorder of social events. Heavily advertising what was available in our town, but happily mixing in locally written poetry and serious material, this paper survived into the 1950s.

By the 1930s there were many shops open that older Littleborough residents will still remember at the year 2000. Apart from the numerous Co-op outlets there was John Walsh - men's outfitters, Eddison's - ironmongers, with beautifully made wooden trays containing a world of screws and nuts and bolts, Craven's & England's - chemists,

This busy shop on Church Street sold health products; later 'Halls chemist' until well after the Second World War. It is still busy today - as the betting shop next to Littleborough Post Office.

Manager and young assistant, Durn Branch Co-op.

Whittles bread van fleet; no 50 was acquired new about 1933 and was used on the Huddersfield run, usually with local driver Jack Harwood. Basically an Albion, the body was built by George Henderson, established at Frankfort Mill yard.

Whittle's Bakery Christmas party, about 1950.

Parry's - shoe shop, Greenwoods - gramophone shop and Arthur Smith's fish shop. In the square was Lawson's coffee shop and Leach's 'tin Lizzie' shop. On Church Street was Cleggs, the publisher of the Littleborough District News.

The contribution made to our town by the shop keepers goes far beyond the supply of goods. For example in 1848 Mr Arthur Holden opened a shop at 83/85 Church Street selling household goods and furniture. The whole family lived above the shop. As both family and business increased he moved 'home' to Todmorden Road and later Featherstall Road. With, by then, a much larger family there were still family members living on these roads in 1984. Mr Arthur's first deliveries were by horse and cart followed by vans and eventually by a grandly named pantechnicon for the furniture removals. He started making furniture with a workshop in Queen Street employing nine men, joiners, cabinet makers and upholsterers, to supplement the shop which employed five. He expanded into the funeral and undertaking business which his son joined at 95 Church Street. Their business and name is still there, at the end of the 20th century. Mr Holden served as a district councillor, was Chairman twice and in later years his daughter Alice Holden followed in her father's footsteps as a councillor and also became Headmistress of Shore School. In 1936 Mr Holden was presented with his Chain of Office by Sir Alfred Law, a fitting recognition for a family which has given so much to our town for more than 100 years.

A rapidly increasing population, modest prosperity and the growing specialisation in factory work not only meant success for retailers but was an opportunity for those who supplied the goods to them. James Henry Rhodes Whittle, the son of a farmer, was born at Cleggswood in 1856. A few years later the family moved to Rakewood and Henry (his preferred name) began working for Clegg and Brothers at Rakewood Mill. By 1881 Henry had married and set up house with his wife Jane at Benny Hill. In 1893 the couple moved to Featherstall where Henry Whittle began in business as a baker and confectioner. According to legend Whittle, with the help of his two sons-in-law began selling bread door-to-door from a wheelbarrow. Within a few years they were doing a roaring trade and were able to establish an ambitious bakery at Featherstall Mill. Soon Whittle's horse-drawn vans were a familiar sight and in 1911 the concern became a limited company with Henry Whittle as managing director. In 1912 purpose built premises were acquired and modern machinery installed. The company always prided itself on its innovations and in the 1930s developed a number of techniques which they subsequently marketed under brand names. By the early 1930s the workforce was more than 200 yet it remained a 'family firm'; when Henry Whittle died in 1934 all sections of the firm joined in a remarkable tribute to their senior employer. James Butterworth, one of the sons-in-law, took over and was followed by his own son Albert who was the senior executive when the company was finally acquired by Sunblest Bakeries in the 1950's.

Transport
Horses
Although there was a near total demise of the horse as a beast of burden in the first half of the 20th century, it will be clear from the accounts of the growth of businesses in our area they were still playing a vital part in local 'carrying' for much of that time. As a by-product they still gave great pleasure at the fiercely competitive local shows and fairs where scores of horses, which had been cleaned, prepared with gleaming brass and polished

The FINEST LOAF THAT'S MADE

WHITTLE'S **PURITY EIGHT**

made by
Hy. WHITTLE LTD.
LITTLEBOROUGH

PURITY

THIS ISN'T A BOAST—IT'S A FACT

From St. Barnabas Jubilee handbook 1951.

leather, were submitted for judgement. Although they were declining fast, the underdogs of the horse world, the pack horses, were still actively carrying to the less accessible areas.

Tramways

The original horse-drawn public transport was first replaced by vehicles driven by steam. Then in 1903 the first electric trams ran to Littleborough and from this time trams played a major role in transport in the early 20th century. The Manchester, Bury, Rochdale and Oldham Tramways Company, which was the local owner, was municipalised in 1904 and the electric trams were extended beyond Littleborough to Summit in 1905. About 1½ miles beyond Littleborough this became a link point between the trams and the growing Yorkshire bus system.

Much of the tramways were single track with loops at intervals, to pass each other. From Littleborough going to Rochdale the first passing place was at the meeting of Featherstall and Whitelees Road. Timing at these points was very important but 'waiting' for the 'other' tram was very common. The electrification and extension of the track to Summit led to the need to create a triangular network of tram tracks in the square at Littleborough. This could accommodate through traffic and trams from either end which wished to turn round. Trams continued to serve the area up till the 19th October 1930. This was a Sunday; on the following Monday, omnibus services took over from the trams in the Littleborough area.

Afterwards gangs of men, up to 15 or 20 strong, were out in the district removing the tram lines. They took out the 'setts' removed the lines and then restored the road; the whole job being done with traditional tools and hand carts. The job was finally completed in 1933.

Buses

Most tramways were abandoned in the 1930s in the face of increasing competition from the municipal bus operators. The change came about by a long series of amalgamations and integrations of the web of existing track (varying types, gauges etc.) and a gradual rationalisation of the patchwork of different methods of transport.

Dressed for a parade, Crossleys of Morgan Street.

Electric trams passing at The Royal Exchange, Featherstall Road, before 1914.

Pulling up the tramlines at Summit, early 1930's.

The York to Liverpool Express passing Fothergill and Harvey's.

Railways

The railways continued to develop their services but as the 20th century advanced they started to lose their passenger traffic to the bus companies and other motorised transport.

The Canal

Regular traffic on the Rochdale Canal ceased after the 1st World War although some sections were used up till 1945. In 1923 the Canal Company sold its supply reservoirs to Rochdale and Oldham Corporations including the right to supply water to industry.

Haulage

The significance of many of the transport developments and the importance of the textile history is perhaps best illustrated by the impact they had on local people and the kind of life they were able to create.

Around 1880 William Burrill, who was a farm foreman in east Yorkshire, got a job with Joshua Hoyle, a cotton manufacturer in Lancashire. The job was to be the farm bailiff for a number of small farms that the manufacturer owned. The move improved William's pay to £1 per week and provided a small farm to live in.

Later he moved to Stansfield Farm, Littleborough, where he continued with a herd of dairy cows as the basis for a milk delivery round in the Summit area. With modest success he moved to Sladen Fold Farm, expanding the milk business, but he also commenced casual carrying for the expanding Fothergill and Harvey mills. Initally it was by horse and cart but as the business grew he started to look at the opportunities offered by motor transport and decided that this was the future and finally ceased the milk business. Eventually he had some 40 horses carrying coal from Littleborough station sidings to the local mills. He had also become the transport contractor to the Rochdale Canal Company, moving goods from the canal wharf to the local mills and cotton pieces back to the wharf for barge transport to Manchester.

During the First World War the use of barges was considered too slow by the government contractors consequently khaki cloth, a Fothergill speciality used for soldier's uniforms, had to be taken by horse-drawn vehicles direct to Manchester. The horses were changed at Middleton to maintain the pace so the carters worked a very long day.

After the war when Rochdale Canal Co. ceased to operate as an independent contracting carrier Burrills lost an important sector of their business. In answer to this latest business challenge William Burrill bought two lorries (Maudsleys) to carry cloth into Manchester. Soon after, there was yet another slump in the cotton industry with mills on short time and many closures. There was no work locally so William's son Henry had to resort to 'tramping'; that is taking a load to a destination and when it was delivered taking another load to a second destination and so on. In later life one of Henry's most amusing stories related to collecting a fairground carousel at Southampton Docks and bringing it to Bolton. He helped the showman erect it on the fairground and collected the takings until he had covered the cost of carriage!

During his journeys he had noticed the West Riding was more prosperous than Lancashire, so the family bought a small transport business in Bradford which had contacts in the import and export trade. The result was that they started regular runs

A major change in public transport.

This fine example of motorised transport was a 3 way tipper wagon owned by William Burrill of Springfield Avenue.

between Bradford, Liverpool and Birkenhead, carrying manufactured goods on the outward journey and wool from various parts of the world on the return. William Burrill died in 1925.

Henry took over the fleet which by then had grown to five vehicles (all four wheel Maudsleys). He was like his father both in enterprise and in his far-sighted view of the business. As soon as six-wheeled vehicles came onto the market in 1929, Henry bought two at £1000 each. The business continued to prosper and expand and in 1931 they started to buy AEC vehicles with pneumatic tyres and diesel engines. Diesel was 4p per gallon; petrol was 10p.

At the outbreak of the Second World War they had 25 vehicles and employed more than 50 men. The firm was based at the canal wharf, Littleborough; a convenient half way point between Merseyside and the West Riding. After Dunkirk, when the allied forces were driven out of Europe, the transport industry was divided into sections and required to move armaments and materials concerned with the war effort. One local task was moving Hurricane fighters to the north of Scotland for shipment to Russia.

Shortly after the war the Labour Government was elected and the business was nationalised. Henry retired and died in 1978.

William (Bill), Henry's son, worked for some years with the nationalised British Road Services but in 1957 took over a transport business in Rochdale which he resold in 1988 as a going concern (now part of Meek Distribution, Rochdale). He retired in the same year; the family is no longer connected with the transport business.

There must also have been something about the area around Dearden Street as, not far from the Burrill's site the Leach family ran Leach's Transport successfully for many years, before relocating to Rochdale.

William Leach was born in 1870 and owned a cycle shop at 32 Church Street where he was helped by his daughter Doris and his sons, Harold and John Alfred (Jack). In 1908 he became the local Raleigh Agent in addition to marketing his own cycles, including the 'Wardleworth'. He also sold petrol from a pump outside the Royal Oak. The petrol was delivered to him in drums by horse and cart.

Jack Leach with his Albion short wheelbase, 5 ton tipper lorry; the Albion Mill is in the background. The DK registration was common in the district as all new vehicles were licensed locally at Rochdale.

271

Leach's Taxi.

Todmorden Road, winter 1947.

Soon after the first world war he started a taxi business, seeing the opportunity to chauffeur local mill owners like Sir Alfred Law and Gordon Harvey. The sons, Harold and Jack, became well known in our area for their achievements in motor cycle racing, hill climbing, speedway and associated competitive sports. They continued the taxi business but diversified into coaches and coal tipper wagons. Jack bought his first tipper wagon in 1931 when he was 24 years old to start carrying coal for the local mills. The company continued to develop and was soon supplying the needs of Adolph Hess (now AKZO), The Tannery, Fothergill & Harvey, Cleggs (Shore Mill), Taylor (Builders) and many more. The former stables at the rear of the Red Lion were used as workshops.

In 1950 Jack bought the petrol station known as Central Garage on Todmorden Road and a plot of land on the opposite side of the road which became one of the first developed areas on what is now the Industrial Estate.

From 1960s to the 1980s the company expanded, primarily using flat wagons, employing between 10 and 20 local drivers and mechanics at various times. The company remained in Littleborough until 1994 when, due to further expansion, they relocated to Rochdale where they employ some 100 people at the end of the century. They became a limited company and the current managing director is John Leach, son of Jack.

Religion
The Anglican Church
The Holy Trinity Parish Church

After the new chancel was built in 1889 and the east window was resited there has been only modest change to the physical state of the church. The original clock face became illegible and had to be replaced by a secondhand one of smaller dimensions, the surrounding space being cemented up. A single bell remains in the tower, however, bell ringing has been replaced by mechanical chimes. These broadcast a recording of bell ringing at Westminster Abbey. The machinery was installed with money allocated from the funds available to provide a memorial to those who died in the 1939 - 45 War. A memorial cross was also erected in the church-yard. The original graveyard became full and was closed for use in the 1940s. Internally there were small changes relating to decoration, convenience and to accommodate gifts from parishioners.

The more significant changes came from the arrival of Dr. Salts who dominated his parish from 1872-1911. He was deeply involved in the late 19th century disputes about the chancel, parish boundaries and the fate of old graves but was also responsible for

Holy Trininy Church, INSET Rev. Dr A Salts.

protecting and expanding the beautiful glass in the church, the new organ and much else, notably in the area of education. In 1900 he appointed Joe Preston, a certificated teacher of first grade (Cheltenham College for Teachers) as head of the parish school. This appointment greatly improved the standard of conduct and teaching. Dr. Salts retired in 1911 and found a worthy successor in the Rev. A. F. Gaskell, a brilliant scholar who stayed for 40 years. This man served both the parish and the diocese, outside his main work key interests were books and cricket (President of Littleborough in 1936 and later). When he died in 1957 the Bishop of Manchester said, 'today we have interred the most intelligent minister in my diocese'.

St Barnabas Church, Shore

The church was consecrated and the Parish established in 1901 and it was to have an unusual record of being served by seven incumbents only, in the next hundred years. Up till the 1960s there was little physical alteration to the fabric after the church was completed during the first decade of the century.

Non Conformist Churches

Primitive Methodist Church, Greenhill

Looking at the church records you see a steady growth and the recording of the deaths of members who have given 50 years, or more, service to the cause. The 1914 - 1918 War was responsible for the death of 43 of the scholars and teachers of this little church. By 1921 normality was restored and the Sunday School membership was growing steadily in numbers so the issue arose of a new school. A bazaar was proposed to raise the money needed and this took place in March 1923 in Littleborough. It raised £600 and on this basis it was decided to go forward. It was 1925 before appropriate land was secured but

St. Barnabas Church, Shore.

when building tenders came in they were too high so more delay ensued. In 1927 young church members took the matter into their hands commencing to level the site, remove dirt and waste and start work on the boundary walls. Their work reduced the overall bill by £800 and a new tender to complete the building of £2495 was obtained. In 1928 the new school opened. The last Quarterly Circuit Meeting was held in 1932 before the amalgamation of the three main branches of the Methodist Church. In 1940 the organ at Mount Giliad's Church (the original purchase was recorded by Fred Jackson, see chapter 15) was bought and the school and organ debts were all cleared by 1941. The Second World War totally disrupted local life again but mercifully only two scholars died in this war. With the war over, young people returned to church but had to struggle to find work. The church, which had been in existence for 100 years in 1950, is typical of the local devotion, service and continuity of worship by men and women of which they were rightly proud. When they did their roll call at the centenary they again found many members who could claim at least 50 years of continous service.

Looking back, nationally non-conformist activity peaked in the early 1900s; from 1922 to 1929 Sunday School enrolments fell by 20%. With a fall in congregations smaller groups were left with large chapel buildings and mergers and demolitions became inevitable. As early as 1891 'Particular' and 'General' united, in 1907 the 'New Connection' merged with United and in 1932 the Methodist circuits were 'rationalised' to attain a more fitting coverage of falling congregations.

The decline of religious attendance was blamed on picture palaces, wireless and other distractions. Certainly the wireless (or radio) had been rapidly absorbed as an integral part of everyday life. Church leaders had then to re-think their position and even use the new developments to allow them to reach the people once again and so reverse the decline in the size of their congregations.

Roman Catholic Church

The Catholic mission moved into the early 1900s as a healthy but poor organisation. There followed a period of increasing prosperity which was reflected in an increase in membership and income which allowed improvements in general conditions. As with most other aspects of life, the 1914-18 war halted progress deeply harming the life of the church. The aftermath was the need to revive all aspects of the church life. By 1927 the school was greatly enhanced. There was also recognition that a new church was long overdue, as the current structure had shown serious signs of faults from the early 1920s. This objective was achieved in June 1930 when the new church was completed. At the time it cost some £6000 and when rates and other costs were added this was to prove a heavy burden on the parish.

(The old 'Iron Church' of St Mary's was purchased by the Mission of St. Hilda (C. of E.) and re-erected at Hollingworth Fold. The main family there was headed by John Hall and the revenue from his estate had been used to provide schools at Ogden and Hollingworth. This revenue was now used to buy the old Catholic Church.

The men of the Parish, as at the start of St Mary's, did the digging, sewer work and plumbing, dismantled the building and re-erected it in 1931. In 1975 it was divided into two sections, a church and a meeting place, the church being cared for by the minister from Milnrow Parish Church.)

The Catholic community continued to expand so that the men's club had to move

St. Hilda's Church, Hollingworth Fold.

Birch Hill Hospital (formerly The Workhouse).

out of the site to a building in William Street purchased in 1931 (Jubilee Hall). The William Street site was later absorbed by the school and the men's club had to find a new site again. On the eve of the second world war there were 650 committed Roman Catholics in Littleborough.

It is worth noting that from 1874 until 1948 (Health Acts) the priests of all denominations had onerous duties in relation to the work house (then part of Birch Hill Hospital). This was compounded by lesser responsibilities at the Cottage Homes for Foundling Children on a nearby site. These both fell within St Mary's Parish and the priest did the duties without reward or any compensation. In a year the priest might do 250 - 300 visits, on any day, at any time, in relation to these duties. For 40 years Rochdale had resisted the concept of a huge centralised Work House (called 'Bastilles') that the Poor Law Amendment Act of 1834 demanded. One was finally imposed at Dearnley in 1877 when the headlong rise in the cost of poor relief under the 'old poor law' made change inescapable. The architect of the Bastilles was Edwin Chadwick who designed them to be, in his own words, 'uninviting places of wholesome restraint'. Just as Littleborough Central School was was one of the last of its kind to be built so was the new work house. Some of the early bleak austerity of construction and the severity of living conditions was relaxed. The result was a fine structure with a distinctive, even magnificent, mock gothic tower. The buildings soon held hundreds of people putting an enormous burden on St Mary's Church and school. The expanding hospital compounded the problem. Finally, Rochdale Board was one of the only three Unions that did not pay allowances to visiting priests. This was a long and bitter dispute never fairly concluded. It was 1930 before Rochdale took over the whole area, the hospital, the workhouse and related institutions. In 1948 under the control of the Ministry of Health, officially-appointed ministers were given an annual stipend for their work but by then the workhouse cottage homes were closed.

At the end of the 20th century the Health Authority are likely to shut down most of the medical facilities at Birch Hill and move them to an expanded Rochdale Infirmary.

Part of the site is already planned to be used for private house building and this site includes the 'gothic tower'. The Rochdale Observer are running a campaign to retain the tower as an prominent landmark visible for miles around and also because it is of historical importance.

The Second World War revived all the strains and misery already familiar to the middle-aged in Britain. At the end of the war St Mary's faced real problems with financing the school which was a 'dual control' unit. This meant there was dual management with representatives nominated from the 'Authority' and the 'Church' but it also meant the school did not get as much funding as state schools.

In 1946 a member of the church became the first Catholic councillor but, shades of the old prejudices, another councillor was overheard saying:

'if we are not careful these Catholics will soon be running the place!'

After the war there was the need to restore many years of deterioration of fabric and furnishings. The Pennine climate is unforgiving about neglect.

CHAPTER NINETEEN

THE TWENTIETH CENTURY

PART TWO : AN ERA OF WAR

1900 - 1950
(Continued)

Education
The Central School

1900 was a critical date in the development of education in Littleborough because the District Council secured the Hare Hill Estate from Major Newall. This estate came to house the Central School, Textile School, Library, Council Offices, School Board offices, Fire Station, Park, Recreation Grounds and other facilities.

For education it was invaluable as it made available the opportunity to build a new school on a near perfect site. It must be remembered that the Central School was built at a time when the School Boards were rapidly being phased out and it was 'illegal' for them to make provisions for anything but basic education. However some of our local schools were about to have their grants withdrawn because of inadequate facilities and the local School Board had, for its nine year life (1894 - 1903), Gordon Harvey as its Chairman. Thus there was an immediate need for a new school at a time when the Board had a Chairman who was both politically powerful and who had considerable social influence. Under his direction the Board researched and submitted a most ambitious plan for a new school. The controlling Board of Education promptly refused to sanction all the proposed rooms designed for advanced instruction. There was a compromise and in 1901 all the substantial aspects of the original plan were approved and a grant made of £13,648 for building costs.

If the controlling board thought they had, in some way, limited the development by financial constraint they had seriously underestimated the local competence to put up fine quality buildings at a very low cost. For nearly a hundred years this had been the hallmark of our local mills and chapels. Contracts were let within days and building started immediately. It was a truly handsome site of some 8300 square yards and the buildings and grounds were laid out to 'be in keeping with the park and surrounding areas'. The result was a dignified stone structure, two storeys high, with the ground floor designed for infants and the mixed school and the upper floor full of special art and science rooms. Special attention was paid to the furnishing and equipping of all parts of the building, a lesson learnt from the experiences in the 19th century.

The formal definition of the function of the school called for it to:

> Replace the Victoria and Peel Street Board Schools (current student numbers 1035)
> Accommodate the evening classes in Science and Art housed in
>   the Technical Institute (150 - 170).
> Accommodate the commercial and domestic evening classes conducted
>   in the two Board Schools (200+)
> To provide more, and more advanced, day classes.

Littleborough Central Board School.

It is little wonder that the chairman of a progressive South Wales Board saw the finished school and wanted to know 'what magic had let the Littleborough School Board get such a school scheme past a conservative Board of Education'. It was generally admitted to be the finest facility to be found in any similar district in the country. Gordon Harvey wrote that the pleasure it gave him to help establish the school exceeded any achievement in his notable political and commercial careers. The school was opened in 1903, the existence of a School Board was ended and control moved to the Local Education Authority.

The school became an integral part of our community and for example made great efforts to keep in touch with its ex- pupils during the First World War.

When more normal life was resumed after the war the school enjoyed great staff stability with, on average, 15 teachers. In a period of 16 years there was one retirement, one marriage and three promotions to headships. It was said that to work in the school with its range of facilities was to have one of the better teaching jobs in the county. In due course the school was recognised as a centre for School Certificate training and the first group sat the exam in 1924. Gordon Harvey founded the Alexander and Amelia Harvey Scholarships 'to help and reward advanced scholars'. Perhaps one disappointment was that one pupil sat the Higher School Certificate exams in 1926 succesfully and two were successful in 1927 - after which submissions ceased. The Second World war interrupted the normal routines and again the school played its part, but at the end of the war all was to alter greatly.

A teaching job in the school was always one of the 'plums' of Lancashire Education but the 1944 Education Act planned great changes. Distinctions were established between Primary and Secondary Education, the compulsory curriculum was widened and outside and extra activities were included. The keystone to a successful education became to show that pupils were 'prepared for life' and the 'Central' was created on the principle of an 'All-through school'. Not many of these survived as long as ours in Littleborough.

Littleborough Central School, 1925.

It is appropriate to leave this phase of the school history at 1953 when the school celebrated its 50th birthday in the same year as the coronation. Ex-teachers and headmasters and their current counterparts all defined the important and basic objective of the school since its founding as:

'Training in character and to create good citizens, who can fill both their civic and communal duties'.

Again with apparent unanimity:

'Academic success and intellectual brilliancy are not enough in themselves'

Sobering statements for a late 20th century society dedicated to performance tables.

It would be wrong not to allow the school children a joke in all this serious material just as their teachers did at the Jubilee.

Teacher: 'In the Middle Ages a sheep cost 6d.'

Pupil: 'Please sir, how much did they charge then for a quarter of liver ?'

Adult Education

Adult evening classes started in September 1895 under the management of the Littleborough School Board. According to the log book, on the first evening 41 males enrolled for writing and composition and 90 females for one or more of 'writing, composition, arithmetic, domestic economy, needlework and cookery'

In the early years there was much emphasis in the writing classes on 'transcription of a letter on note paper and addressing the envelope'. The domestic economy class went into the practicalities of 'starching and ironing' but the direction of the study of 'skin and its uses' is less clear. Could this anticipate sausages for supper?. Beginners in writing at an early stage had to battle with the challenge of 'long looped letters' above and below the line such as *'h'* and *'y'*

Lessons in history were introduced 'in anticipation of the lesson on the Progress of India' and they began with a brief sketch of the foundation of our Indian Empire.

Littleborough Central ; the staff 1947.

At the turn of the century a complaint emerged that 'the roll has decreased by 30 during the month, many students not putting in an appearance after the first two nights. By 1902 there is a 'decided falling off of Students'. About this time drawing and home nursing were introduced as subjects.

Among the dryness of the meticulous recording of 'numbers present' there are glimpses of the close knit nature of our community. For example 'Ethel Leach, one of the most regular and industrious of the evening scholars, sustained a serious accident at Shore Mill. It has been found necessary to amputate her right hand. Much sympathy for her and her widowed mother is felt in the evening school.'

The Parish School

1900 saw a new era with a new Headmaster, Joe Preston. Generally the school was rated as being better controlled and the quality of work much improved. Under the then existing system of grants to schools there was a direct correlation between performance and the size of the next tranche of money and 'the high Principal Grant' was recommended. The school was competitive academically but was also very active both in sports and in the life of the town. Staff numbers rose to 10 with a new infants class in 1909 after extensive modifications and additions to the existing building. The 'Bazaar' now came into prominence as the struggle to pay for the facilities was heightened by the cost of the improvements. With education re-organisation the pressure for further building improvements continued and the Holy Trinity was declared a primary school with pupils up to age eleven.

Ministers were never paid very high salaries but at this period they had to act as entertainers, youth organisers, business men, social secretaries: all in the context of a job based on Christian leadership. From the beginning of the story of Littleborough and especially from the 18th to the 20th century much of the help for the church and the school came from the traditional local families or the new traders. An honourable

The Parish Church School and extensions 1909, an extra storey was added to the nearer building in 1999.

The Parish School Cricket Team 1928, Headmaster Mr Joseph Preston (left) and teacher Mr John Crowther. Even in summer everyday clothing was heavy; some of the boys are wearing clogs.

family list; Holt, Newall, Law, Helliwell, Lightowler, Kershaw, Clegg, Stott, Beswicke-Royds, Molesworth and Harvey.

Summary of the position of local religion and education in 1950.

After the new Central School was built it was 50 years before the Lancashire Education Authority built another school in the area, the High School on Calderbrook Road.

In many areas, teaching became equated to the new state schools while the connection with chapel and sunday school withered. The compulsory school syllabus became much wider and the range of knowledge tested by exams became the same throught the whole country. Teaching was no longer locally based.

The 1914-1918 war had an enormous effect on people but perhaps the cruel contrast between fighting for 'a land fit for heroes' and the subsequent unemployment and strikes of the 1930s was to be most influential factor. People no longer looked for leadership from the chapel or local prominent people. There was more awareness of the need and opportunity for change and a readiness to criticise traditional values.

In the religious sphere locally it was 'The baggin preachers', that is the travelling lay preachers, who were seen as the strongest survivors. They knew their Bible and their fervour was genuine. They also had close links to the community life. The whole position of the established church became open to discussion and attendance continued to decline. The elderly lamented the 'loss of the children from their churches' which they saw as the result of the closure of church schools. Their own fathers had forecast the likely outcome of the closures and all the evidence proved they were correct to foresee a great loss to religion.

Summary of Education changes (1900 - 1950)

1900   **Smithy Bridge School** This was the second school to be built by the School Board. It had accommodation for 19 infants and 154 children of either sex.

1902   **Littleborough Central Board School** was the last Board School to be built in our area. It was designed to accommodate 262 infants of both sexes and the facilities included a hall and four classrooms. For 504 older pupils there was a Hall, eight classrooms, a laboratory and balance room, physics laboratory, dark room, lecture room, prep. room for advanced students, art room and a cookery and laundry room. This school was designed to replace the Victoria Street and Peel Street Board Schools which had, in aggregate, 1035 pupils and also provide accomodation for the evening classes in Science and the Arts which were currently held in the Technical Institute and were attended by 100 - 150 students. Finally it absorbed the Commercial and Domestic evening classes which were conducted in the Victoria Street and Peel Street Board Schools. The Central School was demolished in 1996.

Fred Jackson had the deepest appreciation and respect for the value of education. As an elderly man in 1930 he looked back and had his last word on the changes going on around him.

"What a contrast between the well-equipped schools which we possess today (1930s) and the schools of the time of which I write (1820s). Even at a much more recent date than this they were very little better. I wonder sometimes when I see so large a number of our lads and lasses hanging about the street corners or going to the pictures or more questionable amusements several times a week and seeming to have no other interest in life, whether they value the educational facilities which are offered to them so freely today. Have we made them too cheap? In the old days we thought nothing of walking miles to hear a lecture or attend classes on subjects we were interested in, although it meant denying ourselves things which are thought to be absolute necessaries today."

Social and cultural development of Littleborough

General Conditions

Ordinary people found that they were part of a better organised, better paid workforce with more spare time, embedded in a more orderly society. In Littleborough, the main facilities were controlled by the Urban District Council. Social and other facilities revolved round churches and chapels, and a growing number of societies and independent sports clubs.

Nevertheless, it is worth mentioning that at the beginning of the 20th century there were still undertones of violence and illegality never far from the surface. As an example, a Sheffield firm could advertise in Littleborough the availability of a 'Saloon Pistol Knife'. This was a pen knife, a protector blade (could be used as a bayonet) also a pistol of advanced design. It makes our Swiss Army Knife look innocuous. The knife was advertised for 'self defence'.

There was also widespread suspicion about the number of largely unexplained fires early in the early 20th century. In 1901 there were: Lydgate Mill, Beach Hotel, Sladen Mill, Trafalgar Mill, 1903 Eafield Mill, 1906 Gale Mill, Clough Mill etc. The message of the legend of the Phoenix arising from its own funeral pyre seems not to have been entirely lost among Pennine business communities.

Many new technical facilities were developing; for example electricity was known in the 19th century and was available in Littleborough from 1900, although public supply only commenced in 1911 and it was 12 years later before most people had access to it.

One of the most lasting changes for the benefit of Littleborough people was the purchase of an estate in 1901.

U.D.C purchase of the Hare Hill Estate

Hare Hill Estate was a major facility bought by the council in 1901 which ensured that Littleborough, unlike many small Lancashire towns, still has a 'green heart' today.

For many years the estate was in the hands of the Newall family who were very large land owners around Littleborough. In 1876 H.G.F. Newall married Barbara S. Gibb from Bute, Scotland. At marriage a settlement was made from the estate: all lands and mills in the townships of Blatchinworth,Calderbrook, Wuerdale and Wardle, all rentals, tenancies, rents and buildings, including mines and minerals, were put into a trust to provide Barbara with £700 per annum during her lifetime. The trustees were also authorised to grant short term leases and offer land for public uses such as roads and reservoirs. Included in these arrangements was a mansion house called Hare Hill with its stables, offices and lands including meadow lands already on a lease. A second house

Hare Hill Park; the monkey Mephisto's grave...   *and The Water Wheel.*

involved was Wellington Lodge, outbuildings, stables and garden which was occupied by J. Taylor Rogers. Rogers was a prosperous brick and sanitary tube manufacturer whose eldest daughter married George MacGill who was part of the family which dominated the medical profession in our area for 120 years.

In February 1901 the same H.G.F Newall, then resident at St Andrews, Fife, sold the main part of the Hare Hill estate, including Hare Hill house, stables, outbuildings, gardens and plantations, to the Littleborough Urban District Council, for £323-19s-8d annually, as a 'perpetual yearly payment'.

This magnificent estate provided facilities and space for Council Offices, Fire Station, Carnegie Free library, bowling greens (1903), tennis courts, paddling pool, bandstand and other facilities. The volunteer Fire Brigade involved some 13 men and had a horse-drawn fire engine. Unfortunately the horses used were those owned by the Council for general work so they had to be 'rounded up' before being hitched to the engine. The Carnegie Free library did not allow you free access to the books. You addressed an indicator or index and then approached the librarian who would get the book for you. The library also housed a collection of books from the Beswicke-Royds collection at Pike House. These were only available to students who made an extra payment.

Many of the park facilities were given by caring individuals or organisations: it was Mr J Cryer who presented the bandstand in 1902 and the Co-op who presented the drinking fountain in 1903. In the same year the Central School was opened, increasing the focus of activity in the centre of Littleborough. The fire station remained behind the current bowling greens until the Fire Services Act of 1947 opened the way for a new and modern fire station to be built in 1951, on part of the old tenter field belonging to Calder Cottage, between Whitelees and Hare Hill Road. It is ironic that at the end of the 20th century the facilities of the park look rather neglected and two of the most

Hare Hill Park in 1910; the bandstand, the drinking fountain presented by the Co-operative Society with Hare Hill House and conservatory, in the background.

enduring features appear to be the folly erected to drive a small water wheel and a small grave of a monkey, the pet of the Newall children, which at the end of the century usually has fresh flowers brought by the children of local people. There must surely be a close connection with the 'monkey steps' behind Town House which was also lived in by a branch of the Newall family.

Private and Local Authority Housing

The problem in housing, in the first half of the 20th century, arose in relation to both the quality and the quantity available. Most families lived in rented houses and in common with other Lancashire towns, much of the housing was terraced or back to back of poor quality, damp and poorly maintained. By today's standards the living conditions of many of our citizens were very bad. Quite commonly the houses were only heated by one coal fire which often served as the only cooking facility. Gas was the usual source of light until the end of the first decade and despite the availability of electricity, gas for lighting was not unusual even up to 1950. Perhaps the main urgency for better housing and more of it came from overcrowding; families of five or more had to manage in small two bedroomed houses with no bathroom or inside toilet. This was a national problem, which could only be met by programmes of council house building (see p.288).

In 1922 there was a new initiative with the first housing estate, at Calderbrook, to be built by the local authority. From that time a whole series of authority-built houses were added at Calderbrook, Smithy Bridge and Shore. This building phase finished around 1930. A Government Act of 1929 abolished the Boards of Guardians and in April 1930 Poor Relief became the responsibility of the County Council.

Littleborough Fire Brigade, about 1900.

From 1933, nationally, there was a start on new housing programmes, along with related social legislation such as the creation of new welfare and maternity clinics and one was established on chapel hill. Littleborough only had one other small residential development in this phase.

The second world war intervened so that the next major increase in Local Authority housing stock took place in the late 1940s, primarily at Shore and Hollingworth Lake. In the 1950s there were further developments, of which the largest was at Barnes Meadows. The 1960s was a time when additions were made to existing sites across our area until political decisions terminated any further building. Subsequently four complexes of sheltered housing have been built by our Local Authority. Towards the end of the century there has been a number of initiatives to allow occupants of Local Authority housing to purchase their own homes. Though this has been a benefit to former tenants, who have been able to purchase good quality houses at a modest cost, it has also been controversial. The main issue is that the Local Authorities were not allowed to spend any of the income on renewing their housing stock.

Road construction

From the beginning of the 20th century, the Urban District sustained a continuous programme of widening roads, opening up turning areas and both widening and strengthening bridges. The entrance to Hare Hill Road from Church Street was widened where Robert Hall occupied one of the 'custom-built' shops at this junction, directly opposite the Seed Building. At the beginning of the century the walls of the shop were covered with trade names, many of which we still recognise today such as Fry's Chocolate, Colman's Starch and Mustard and Hudson's Soap. Hare Hill Road was

1920s	**Caldermoor**	Brooklyn Avenue
		Calder Avenue
		Clough Road
		Mount Avenue
		Springfield Avenue
		Moorfield Avenue
	Dearnley	Lightburn Avenue
		Smithybridge Road (A58 end)
		Stopford Avenue
		The Elms
		Whitegate
	Shore	Furness Avenue
		Welbeck Avenue
1940s	**Shore**	Sawley Avenue
		Tintern Avenue
	Smithybridge	Beechwood Avenue
		Cleggswood Avenue
		Little Clegg Road
1950s	**Shore**	Melrose Avenue
	Smithybridge	Walmsley Avenue
	Caldermoor	Calderbrook Road (Low Nos)
		Laneside Close
		Whalley Avenue
	Stansfield	Drake Road
	(Barnes Mdws)	Grenville Walk
		Hawkins Way
		Howard Way
		Norfolk Close
		Raleigh Gardens
		Sydney Gardens
		Barnes Meadows
		Calderbrook Road (High Nos)

1960s	**Caldermoor**	Ashworth Close
	Smithybridge	Queens View
	Durn	Saxon House
		West View (Odd Nos)
		West View (Even Nos)
	Calderbrook	Shakespeare Close
	(Stansfield)	Temple Lane
	(Barnes Mdws)	Barnes Meadows (Bungalows)
	Shore	Ribble Avenue (from Shore Mill)
		Hodder Avenue -ditto-
Others	**Durn**	Rake Terrace (1930)
	Shore	Kirkstall Avenue (1938)
	Dearnley	Halliday Court (1975 Sheltered)
		Crowther Court (1975 Sheltered)
	Littleborough	Hare Hill Court (1971 Sheltered)
		Olive Standring House (1988 Sheltered)

TO TODMORDEN

Barnes Meadows
(Stansfield)

Calderbrook Road

Calderbrook

Todmorden Road

Halifax Road

Shore

Shore
Road

Hare Hill Road

Whitelees Road

LITTLEBOROUGH

Durn

A58
TO ROCHDALE

Dearnley

Hollingworth Lake Road

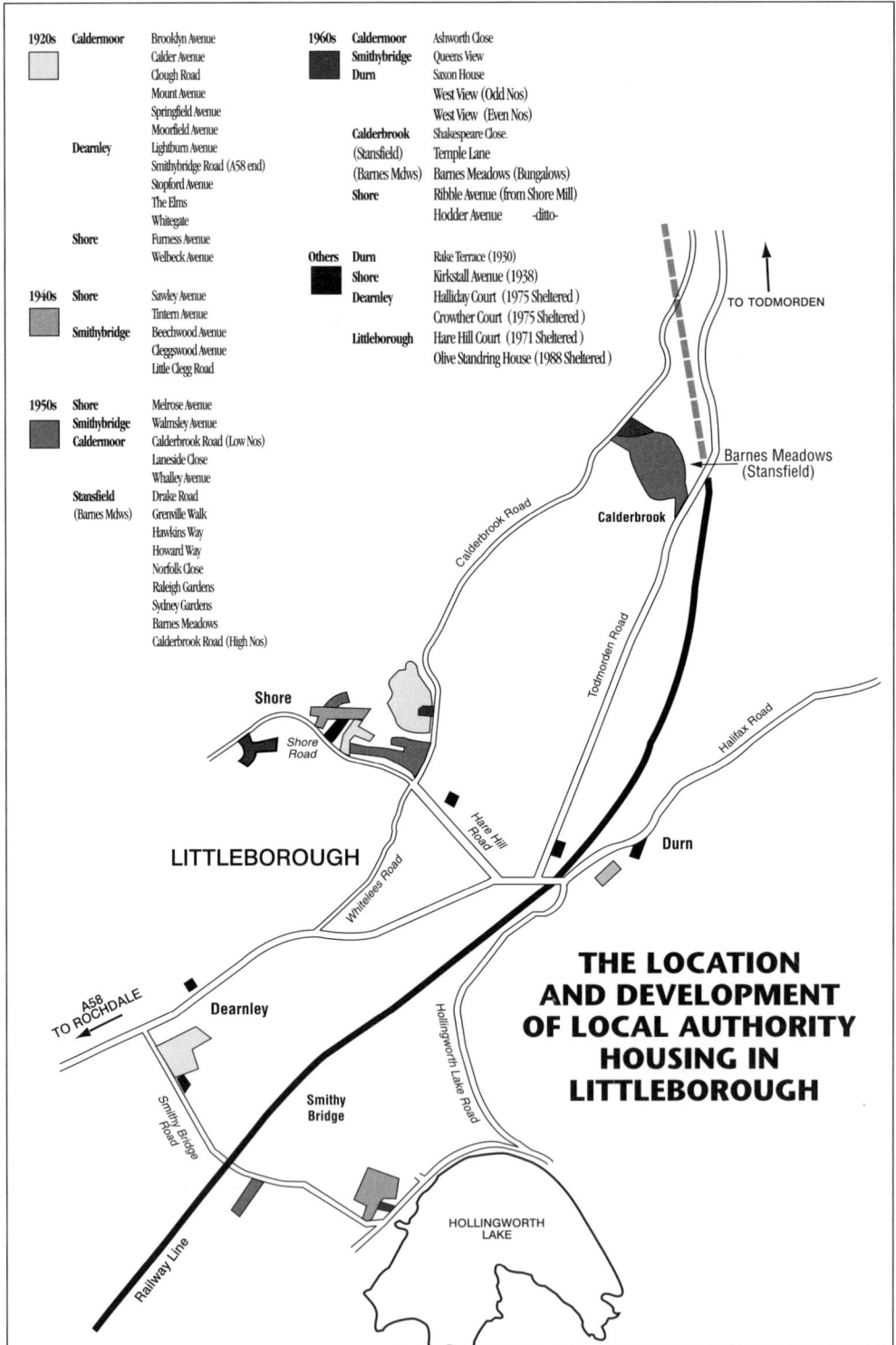

**THE LOCATION
AND DEVELOPMENT
OF LOCAL AUTHORITY
HOUSING IN
LITTLEBOROUGH**

Smithy Bridge Road

**Smithy
Bridge**

Railway Line

HOLLINGWORTH
LAKE

further widened in 1930 followed by a similar improvement in 1931 on Todmorden road. In the 1950s the U.D.C. listed these activities at length when called on to justify its stewardship.

Leisure Facilities

From the late 19th Century we have tracked a rise of leisure and cultural activities which become even more marked in the first decade of the 20th century. It is surprising how many societies, organisations and facilities grew up around Littleborough at this time. To itemise them all is not possible, but the following is a sample of the variety and popularity of some of the main ones.

Traditional Events

Firstly there are the survivors from earlier times, traditional events that had demonstrated great capacity to entertain over the centuries. These include Mummers, Pace Egg Plays, May Day Celebrations and Maypole Dancing, Whitsuntide Walks (on Friday) and Clog Dancing, Rush Bearing and Chapel Sings.

Rushbearing was the time when fresh rushes were carried into the church and spread on the floor. Only the wealthy had seats or private stalls, ordinary people stood, or sat on the floor. The rushes provided warmth and comfort for bare feet and to sit on. When the poorer parishioners were too old to sit in this way, in many churches they were given a ledge to lean against along one wall. This is said to be the origin of our phrase 'gone to the wall', to describe an irreversible event, usually unpleasant! The Rushbearing Festival was revived in 1991 when the Rochdale Morris Dancers and the Littleborough Action Group joined forces to stage a two-day event, which included a Shopping Festival.

The Littleborough Carnival is another more recent event that has also been revived periodically. Its origins appear to have been in very popular cycle parades that started in the 1880s and which grew to become the current carnival. By 1911 the Cycle Parade included quite elaborate trade displays, one of which was a bicycle dressed up to evoke the mining community, accompanied by two boys carrying miner's lamps. This won a second prize. There were notable carnivals in 1937 and 1962. In the 20th century they have been associated with the Littleborough Trades Association and the event has been linked with a Littleborough Shopping Week.

These carnivals were typified by fancy dress, trades floats, jazz bands, decorated cars and bicycles, best-dressed horses and ponies. The day culminated with a bonfire on Blackstone Edge. Money collected along the Carnival route was supplemented by donations from a large number of other events or entertainments. The collection was given to one or two charities which were active locally.

In the early years of the century many of the events included a section for the best presented horse etc. Such events brought out large numbers of horses and a demonstration of the real meaning of horse power. In daily life teams of horses were taking raw cotton to the mills, finished goods to the railway waggons and coal from the railway sidings to the gas works.

Holidays and Wakes Weeks

In Lancashire each town had it's own traditional week (between June and August) each year, increased to a fortnight in the 1950s. Latterly in Littleborough, Wakes Weeks

The corner of Hare Hill Road (now Rif Raf), about 1910.

This visiting fairground ride appears to be set up on open land near the gasworks.

The cycle parade on Halifax Road, near the Red Lion, about 1910.

Whit Walk passes over Littleborough Bridge, photographed by Harold England, Photographic Chemist of Hare Hill Road, in the late 1940's.

The rush cart at Caldermoor, 1997.

The Whitsuntide procession 1910 on Church Street in front of what is now the Post Office.
The church railings were later removed for the war effort in the 1940s.

were two weeks in June and one in September. These weeks were chosen by the workers as the sunniest weeks of the year. The start of the Wakes week was the time when the mills went quiet and the railway stations were heaving with people, all determined to get to the sea side. Littleborough was 'closed down' and the streets for a period did not ring with the noise of an army of working people in clogs walking to the mills. Even in the 1960s the air was notably cleaner during the holidays.

Cinemas

The Queen's Cinema was given planning permission by the Littleborough U.D.C. in 1912 on a site on Church Street almost oppposite the entrance to Hare Hill Road. It was already in existence housed in an outbuilding which had been the barn of the old Royal Oak coaching house and farm. The new 'Picture House' belonged to the Picture Theatre Co. Ltd. Up to the 1950s it was still flourishing and was substantially improved during its life time, only to be closed later and replaced by a car showroom in the mid 1960s. Finally office accommodation was built on the site.

The King's Hall (Reform club, Chapel Hill) is a good example of the varied use of one Littleborough building. In March 1909 there was an advertisement announcing the opening of a 'New Skating Rink' at the King's Hall. This was roller skating which has

Maypole Dance, July 18th 1908, opposite the Summit pub.

Thousands gather for a major occasion in the square about 1900.

The Parish Church Football Team 1914-15.

been popular from time to time with another skating rink at Butterworth, Featherstall. In 1917 the Rochdale Observer covered the opening of the 'King's Hall Cinema' but its life, as a cinema, was short. The Victoria Cinema on Sale street had a longer and more varied life. It started as a Temperance Hall in 1883 built for the society known as the Blue Ribbon Army. It was closed in 1894 and offered for auction. In 1910 an advertisement announced the Victoria Billiard Hall was open with ten tables and by 1913 it had become a cinema. It had a film each day of the week and a matinee and two evening performances on Saturday. It was 2d in the pit, 3d in the stalls and 6d in the circle. The cinema closed in the 1960s to re-open as a Bingo Hall. The game of Bingo was so popular that special busses regularly brought players from Rochdale. In its turn Bingo declined and the 'Vic' again became a snooker and billiard hall; an activity which has been re-invigorated by television coverage of the major competitions.

Finally there was a cinema on Brown Street, Will Hill, the shell of which was still recognisable in the late 1990s.

Singing

The Littleborough Choral Society was formed in 1857 and was still a healthy organisation in the first decade of the 20th century. At the end of the century there is still support for a wide variety of entertainment involving live music and singing in the churches, chapels, clubs and public rooms such as the Coach House.

Cricket

1911 and 1912 were great years, if not the greatest years, for cricket in Littleborough. The club had two professionals, Bowden and Buxton, known affectionately as 'the busy B's' who made a devastating combination which bowled Littleborough into winning

The Queen's Cinema 1961.

the Lancashire League two years in succession. It was a tradition followed by such stars as Leslie Warburton and the West Indians, Garner and Sobers in later years.

Cycling and walking

In 1909 the Littleborough Cycling club had 90 members. The President of the Club was James Taylor Rogers who lived in Calder Cottage (formerly Lane End) at the top of Hare Hill Road. His name is remembered today in 'Roger's Path' between the house and the Fire Station. The Pennines were the playground for local hikers and cyclists. Fred Jackson used to take out the apprentices from the mills for walks and was an early camera enthusiast.

The Rochdale Co-op. Holiday Association rambling club was also very active, often coming to Littleborough for their weekend walks.

Running

There was a thriving Harriers Club and also activities such as the 'Wrigley Thrutch' which was an annual foot racing event held at the Lydgate Inn 'for a purse of gold'.

Today there is still a great appetite for running as a leisure activity, whether as training for other sports, competition running or simply for exercise.

Hollingworth Lake

The first signs of the decline of the leisure and entertainment industy around the lake were seen at the end of the last century. In the first quarter of the 20th century the decline became a collapse when most of the hotels and boarding houses were

296

Littleborough Tuesday Cricket Club, about 1907.

either demolished or turned to other uses, domestic or commercial. For example the Lodge Inn at Rakewood, first licensed in 1826 was closed in 1916 and the license lapsed in 1917. It became a private house called 'Lodgeville'.

Town and Community Development

In retrospect it is hard to visualise the first half of the 20th century locally, except in terms of what happened before or after the two world wars. These became a constant reference point for two generations; the material on the town development is presented to reflect this.

Co-operation
The Co-operative Society

In the first half of the 20th century once again the co-operative movement showed many similar developments to the textile trade. After 1900 amalgamation of the many societies began and diversification became commonplace.

1901   A bulk coal business had grown up in the Grocery operation and it was decided that it should diversify into 'bagging' coal. This grew rapidly into a new department.

1902   At this time the issue of tin 'checks' was used to record the amount of any co-op purchase. In 1902 the co-op changed to a 'metallic check system'. Of various denominations these checks came to be accepted as money by the local publicans, but at a much lower exchange rate than their real value.

	This value was set annually after the accounts were closed and the 'divi' was declared. Theft of checks became a common petty crime.
1904	In April the Caldermoor Branch had a bad fire caused by a cigarette. There was a cloggers shop, which was entered by outside stone steps, over the main store. When the branch was repaired the cloggers shop was re-sited in an adjacent cottage.
1905	Durn Branch, number seven, was opened.
1906	The Littleborough Co-op erected further buildings on Bare Hill Street, including a bakery (finally closed in 1947 when the machinery was declared obsolete) and a hall. The cost of the various buildings was nearly £800 and the hall had a seating capacity for 400 people. Apart from being an assembly hall it was also a centre providing 'high and funeral teas'. The hall continued as a function room for many years, with dancing on Saturday nights, until it closed and converted to commercial uses (including furniture making).
1910	Diamond Jubilee. This was a good time for the co-op, which had experienced thirteen years of continuous growth in membership and sales. The auditors report said that in comparison to societies country-wide the growth showed 'outstandingly excellent progress'.
1913	The new central premises were developed with boots and shoes, tailoring (a new departure) and a Colonial meat shop. The Summit Branch was opened at 78 Todmorden Road.
1916	The tea room moved from the hall to a new, 60 seat, cafe on Hare Hill Road, over the new confectionery department.

The Co-op Hare Hill Road,1910.

The former Durn Branch 1999.

In 1916 the Trade Directory records the following units for the Littleborough Co-operative Society for Industry:

Offices and Central Premises	44 Hare Hill Road
Fruit and Flower branch	31-33 Church Street
Centre Vale branch	
Featherstall branch	
Durn branch	
Caldermoor branch	Hare Hill Rd.
Dearnley branch	84 New Rd.
Lighthouse	Calderbrook
Rock Nook branch (Leased premises)	78 Todmorden Rd.
Summit branch	

In addition there were branches of two other co-operatives in what is considered as the Littleborough area:

New Rd Dearnley	Owned by Rochdale Equitable Pioneers Soc
Smithy Bridge branch	All owned by the Smithy Bridge
Antioch branch	Co-op Society
Rakewood branch	

The period before the first world war was one of pride and self-confidence which was amply justified by the results. In 1914, in Lancashire, half a million people were members of the co-op, the equivalent in many communities to a member per family. In the same year the national membership was over 4 million.

Throughout Britain other forms of union, such as Trades Unions had achieved a position which commanded attention and respect from the employers; in Lancashire this came about primarily from the struggles in the textile industry.

The local position, is possibly best represented by the experience of people such as James Shackleton Shepherd. He was born in 1870 and lived much of his life in Oak Street, Ealees. He was employed for 25 years as a compositor by Jackson's Printers, Eclipse Works, Peel Street. One day he was dismissed to make way 'for cheaper labour'. His union, the Typographical Association, black-listed the firm and achieved a payment of 4 gns. hardship money for him.

'Getting coke, Littleborough Gas House, Coal Strike 1912'. In the background is one of the two gasometers.

Mr Shackleton Shepherd was a resilient man who continued to live in Oak Street until he died in 1911. He was not always unlucky as, in 1911, he won a competition organised by Tit Bits and got a £200 prize. For some, this was a year's wage at that time. His name commemorates (through marriage) a connection with Shackleton the famous antarctic explorer.

First World War 1914-18

The First World War brought tragedy into our community and a lull in the development of many of the social and cultural aspects of life, cutting through Littleborough lives, purposes and ambitions.

The first real impact came in 1914 when thousands of young territorial soldiers of the Manchester Regiment camped in the Ealees valley. They were befriended by the local people until it was their turn to sail to war in the Dardanelles, dying as they left their ships with no hope of fighting their way off the beaches. For many years afterwards Manchester people visited Littleborough to see where their children had been for their last days and say thanks to the people who had been kind to them.

Another clear memory is of the time in 1916 when a Zeppelin flew over Littleborough. It was night and pitch black but the noise was very loud causing a number of residents who lived near the railway to flee with their children to take shelter under the arches. The Zeppelin was apparently shot down over Manchester.

It is hard to express the sheer size and bestiality of this war. With the territorial basis of army units it meant that our small town, like many others, suffered devastating numbers of casualties in very short periods.

Manchester 5th Battalion-transport at Hollingworth Lake.

Manchester Regiment Camp. Ealees Valley 1914.

What follows is a summary of a large collection of newspaper cuttings made by a Littleborough family during the war years. Through it you may get a glimpse of what the local people saw of war through their newspaper. Week by week they read of deaths, of men 'missing, believed killed' or captured, men who had been their friends and neighbours. Each announcement had a photograph and what you come to recognise as a nearly standard text. During the period that the family cut out these pieces they recorded the following deaths: 1 major, 1 lieutenant, 6 sergeants, 3 corporals, 6 lance corporals, and 88 other ranks including, privates, drivers, gunners, riflemen, signals and machine gun corps. The age range of the other ranks was 19 - 26; few of any rank were over 30. The method of notification of death is often by an account from a fellow soldier, followed up by an official confirmation. Some notifications are chilling: killed instantly, killed under trying conditions, killed by gas, killed by multiple wounds. It is hard to comprehend the anxiety of the families faced with 'the twins died on the same day', or 'brothers died within one hour' and often 'died from the wounds in hospital'. What the enemy started, infection appeared to finish in many cases.

In addition to the newspaper records there are the personal memories, letters and the oral tradition passed down by families. One of our earliest deaths was Tom Wild killed on November 1st, 1914. Another volunteer, Thomas Lewis, enlisted aged 48, in a battalion known as the 'Old tough un's' and he died in France two years later. By early in 1915 some 300 men from Littleborough had enlisted. In 1916 the generals decided on a 'great push' to finish the war. The push failed and many of our local men died at this time. At home, the Littleborough Company of the 9th Battalion, Lancashire Volunteers were addressed in the Co-operative hall by Sir Richard Adkins M.P. with A.J. Law presiding.

Birch Hill Hospital was used as a military hospital (see notes on Dr George MacGill), and those new patients classified as 'walking wounded' were expected to walk to the hospital from Rochdale station. Many were not really fit to walk and bystanders rushed back to their houses to give the wounded men everything they could to help. When the wounded soldiers arrived at the hospital, it was like a base hospital behind the lines.

Two or three beds were pushed together to accommodate the maximum number of patients and above the beds further stretchers were balanced on the bed rails. Billiard tables and other bits of furniture provided a base for more beds. The military funerals for those who died were carried out at St Andrews church.

The total death toll in this war was terrible. For example 52 workers from Shore Mills gave their lives (not all Littleborough people) and in all our local churches and chapels there are tablets with the names of the dead. During the war the services of remembrance were carried out nearly every week.

When conscription was introduced in 1916, tribunals were set up to arbitrate on who should be exempt from call up or whose conscription should be deferred. Deferred is a poignant description for families such as that of R Chadwick, who was deferred for personal reasons until the 30th June 1917 and died in action in December 1917.

On the 17th June 1922 the Littleborough War Memorial was unveiled by Major Sydney Gowland in the Square. On the wall behind the memorial 269 names are listed of men killed in the war. The names listed are those which relatives submitted, in response to a request for notification by the authority. There is considerable evidence that a number of families either chose or omitted to submit names so there is little doubt that the total number killed was significantly higher. Every year on the nearest Sunday to the 11th November (Armistice Day) a remembrance service is held at the memorial. Until well into the 1960s local workplaces and schools held a two minutes silence in remembrance of those who died in both world wars. Over the decades the potency of war imagery can appear reduced, but as we approach the end of the century there is evidence that our young people are keen to preserve the respect for Armistice Day.

In the local newspapers it was normal to publish the workplace of a deceased soldier and their trade; this gives a snapshot of the businesses offering employment in the area in 1914. The employers who lost employees included: Ealees Dying Company, Alfred England Joiners, Croft Head Mill, Shore Mills, Rochdale Observer, Shuttleworths architects, Littleborough Dyeing Company, Grove Dye works, J Bright & Bros Ltd, W.H. Heap Ltd, West View Mills, Wellfield Mill, Albion Mill, Fothergill & Harvey, Uber Mill, Spotland Council School, Cryers (chemical and rubber) Smithy Bridge, E Taylor & Co. pipe and brickwork, Fredrick Scott and Co., Argenta Meat Co. Summit,Woodhalls Billiard Hall, Hurstead Mills, Turner Bros Asbestos, Ealees Mill, Gale Print Works, Littleborough Cooperative Soc Ltd, Post Office, W.H. Heap Ltd.

The young men from Littleborough, who died, were largely employed in the textile industry and its associated trades. A number still lived on farms but were classed as weavers; in addition there were bricklayers, jiggers, musicians, labourers, clerks, finishers, fire beaters, sizers, and other trades.

The ramifications of the first world war were endless for our country and our community. It was said that Gordon Harvey, our enlightened mill owner, lost both heart and spirit when we plunged into the war. He was not only a business man but a politician, environmentalist and a confirmed European. He was strongly opposed to conflict as a solution to our problems but failed to attract enough support to 'head off' an Empire which was sliding into war. He is attributed as being the first man to use the words 'League of Nations' (in 1916) as a possible way to end wars. Such a league was formed later and is the direct predecessor of the current United Nations which to no small degree holds most people's hopes today for a path towards peace in the third Millennium.

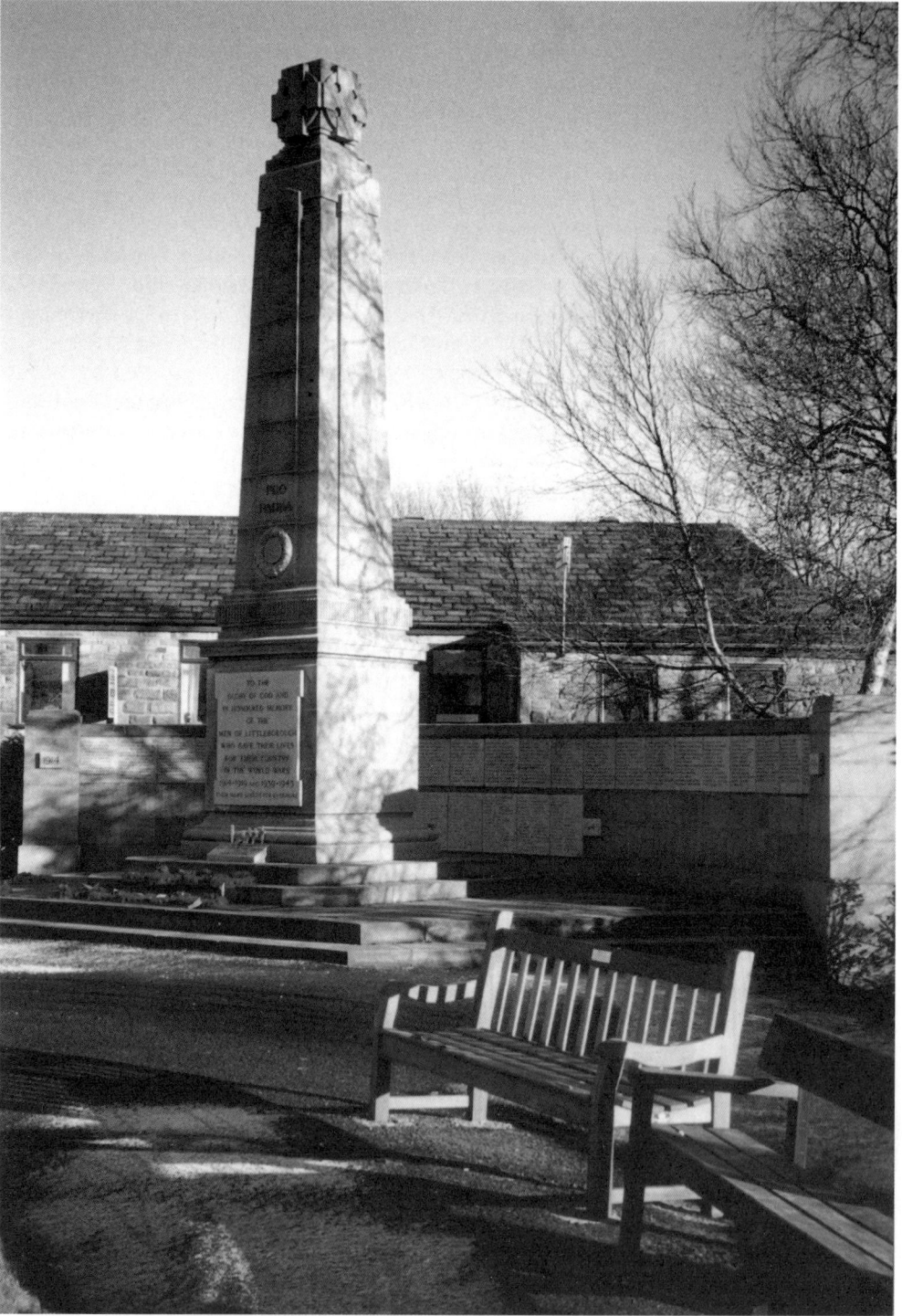

Littleborough War Memorial.

Between the Wars

Gradually people were experiencing more leisure and had more money in their pockets. One result was that many of the pre-war cultural organisations were either re-formed or expanded. Light music, choral Societies, orchestras, brass bands (which first emerged in the late 19th century) all thrived again and ballroom dancing became fashionable. For older people there was a sense of loss and inevitable change. A late middle aged man wrote:

'We, like Littleborough, must go forward, we cannot go back. Where once was peace, today is bustle. We appear to be working at tremendous high pressure. American idioms are displacing the dialect. There is a price to be paid for progress.'

However, Littleborough appeared in some ways to ride the post-war depression (1930s) without the dire effects experienced elsewhere. Some claimed, including our own U.D.C in a promotional leaflet, that this was because we still had such a variety of industry and trade in one small town. Public life in Littleborough was said to have been managed at this time by co-operative non-conformists (Liberals) and mill-owning non-conformists (Liberals). Although this was probably said with tongue in cheek, an examination of the mayors appointed in Littleborough tends to support the general idea.

Co-operation

With so many changes happening, one stable element was the Co-operative Society movement. Dividends fell but stabilised around 2/6 in the £ and they continued to pay interest on the share capital.

1914-1918	The society bought its first motor car and built a garage
1915	Further extensions on Church Street and a dairy opened on Victoria Street. Major improvements to the cafe and the millinery department.
1918	Opening of the fish and game department.
1919	Sales continued to rise but inflation is eroding the profits and the dividend fell from 3/0s (for the last 13 years)to 2/0s in the pound.
1921	A world wide slump and the dividend fell to 6d and wage levels in the textile industry collapsed. From 1921 onwards there were few new developments, cotton no longer flourished and economically Littleborough ceased to expand. The population was to decline by some 2000 people.
1924	Sales hit a low of £110,000 and gradually rose to £148,000 by 1930.
1931	The year when the world experienced the greatest economic slump so far.
1932-1939	Sales increased annually but it represented mainly inflationary value and profits stayed stubbornly low.

In 1919 the Co-operative College was founded nationally along with a variety of youth organisations designed to promote co-operation. However, in 1921 the movement decided to abandon their Reading Rooms, with the adoption of a Free Library Service - which they had been instrumental in promoting. There were real concerns about the fact that the social class at the heart of the co-operative movement were employed in textiles, mining, ship building and other heavy industries and in areas like Lancashire and industrial Scotland they appeared to have achieved saturation membership. Thus the 1920s and 1930s saw much encouragement for the first major amalgamations on commercial grounds; which clashed with the fierce local pride of societies and raised the

The Juvenile Rechabites boat trip, 28th August 1909.

prospect of a serious clash with the root principles of the business. New departments, shops and services became the focus, with both travelling shops and delivery services of bread, milk and other goods. In all this period the co-op based education committees still flourished and remained an innovative force.

Sport and Leisure

Immediately after the 1914 - 18 war some events which had been popular rapidly revived. Typical of these was the holiday trip in a barge. A religious or other group would hire a barge which could hold some hundred or more people (rather appropriately) packed like sardines. They would often go the length of the 'long pound', the three mile lock-free level to Rochdale and then on to Hartley Farm in the Ashfield valley. This rural spot was widely advertised as a place where 'refreshments may be taken'.

Most sports teams were still based on places of worship, but 'leagues' were growing up which were totally independent.

Cricket

Casualties had sadly depleted the fine pre-war cricket team and a Memorial tea room was erected in 1921 in memory of the lost members. As years passed cricket once again became popular attracting thousands of spectators for a match of quality in the 1920s. By 1932 the club was once again amongst the finest in the north of England. Five teams played league cricket weekly and the first women's team was playing matches. This was a pioneer movement formed in 1931. No matches could be played in Lancashire so they applied to and were accepted by the Yorkshire Women's Cricket Federation. In their first year they were runners up to the Holme Valley Ladies.

Littleborough Women's hockey team, 1928.

Unstoppable, they formed a Lancashire side (mainly from Littleborough) and played the Yorkshire Ladies at Bradford, 9000 people watched a match which Lancashire lost by a narrow margin and regrettably it was the same story when the return match was played at Hare Hill. Throughout the 1930s Ladies Cricket attracted large numbers to evening games. The Littleborough Cricket Club also had a growing tennis section with new courts and its own small pavilion. In October 1932 the club ran a two day Fair to eliminate debt burden that existed and also to celebrate the fact that they were Central Lancashire League Champions again. The champion club successfully dismissed its debt. Between 1932 and 1937 was another golden era for cricket in Littleborough. The teams won many, indeed nearly all, of the competitions they could enter and it was said the players and the townspeople alike lived 'from match to match'. In 1936 they ran a second Village Fair to make the major sum of money needed to 'Buy the Cricket Ground' on which they played. With some 800 members and a committee filled with the 'great and the good' from the area, the cricket club was the most important social organisation in our town.

From 1939 onwards cricket faded into the background in the face of the second World War.

Hollingworth Lake

At Hollingworth Lake there was a gradual increase in sailing and a real upsurge in rowing all of which was stimulated by the launch of the 'T.S. Palatine', a shore based establishment, at the back of the Lake run by the Navy League. This offered cadet training in seamanship. Once again the Lake began to act as a focus for growth of leisure and sports activities, notwithstanding the large growth of residential premises on the north side of the lake.

Second World War   1939-45

There were many-fund raising schemes with names like 'Wings for Victory', 'National Savings', 'War Weapons', 'Dig for Victory'. Locally the war meant billetted soldiers and evacuees. The Council Offices in Hare Hill Park were sandbagged, a searchlight battery was sited at Hollingworth Lake and redundant canal boats were moored as booms over the reservoirs to stop seaplanes landing. Littleborough people were called on to take evacuees wherever they had room, as the area was relatively safe from bombing.

A story is told about the arrival of the first train load of evacuees in Littleborough and how all the Littleborough ladies turned out to receive them. When the train arrived they apparently ignored the organisers and swept up the nearest child and most likely took them off to be given a 'hot brew'. The harassed officials only learned later where the children had gone! They came from Manchester, Liverpool, London and the south coast. The receiving families were paid 10/6 weekly for a mother and small child or a child alone and 15/- for a young person over 16 years old. A school dinner was provided for 6d per day.

Chapels took on a new function as 'British Restaurants'; Wakes Week became 'holidays at home'; mills became service barracks or depots. Even the weather contributed to wartime austerity giving us a very severe winter in 1939/40. Ice on Hollingworth Lake was more than 1'6" deep, houses were buried in snow and a R.A.F convoy was snowed up in Littleborough. The weather was bad in 1942 but in 1947 we once more experienced the paralysis of the trans-pennine routes for a period of weeks due to the worst weather on record at the time.

Fortunately the worst of the war locally was bombers jettisoning surplus bombs on the moors and a strong rumour that the best 'off-ration' bacon was available for purchase in the Police Station! (See chapter 14 for further details of the war as it related to the textile industry).

Plaques behind the war memorial sadly record 84 more of our young people killed serving their country.

Post War Period

Co-operation: the Co-op. Movement.

During the Second World War despite loss of staff, shortage of raw materials, price controls and rationing, the trading operation and the dividends held up very well. This was because the basis of the co-operative trading was non-luxury goods. 'Divi' had become a household word among working families. From this time onwards business conditions are routinely described as 'difficult and uncertain' and the appetite for change and innovation appeared to decline. In the ten years after the war the local co-op made few innovations beyond a re-model of the bakery and the introduction of a travelling shop doing home deliveries.

From 1946 onwards the changes of habits and fierce pricing from competitors put enormous pressure on the movement. Dividends shrank, profits disappeared and discount savings stamps no longer attracted the customers.

In 1950 the Littleborough Co-op had 60 male employees and 41 female. More than 80% of the households belonged to the society but lamentably, although well over 50% of the members were women, there had never been one woman on the committee of the society.

An independent Commission of Inquiry was created in 1955 to analyse the existing situation and the future direction of the Co-operative movement. The senior managers were aware that the new predators in the retail market could see an enormous soft target.

The 1960s were the peak years of trading for the movement with 12% of the national market. This figure was to fall to 4% by 1994. In the movement the changes were being faced. Some aspects of the total business held up much better than others; for example in 1968 the Funeral Business took 25% of the national market. At that time, although membership was still 13 million the management saw that overall decline was evident and likely to increase. It was clear that centralisation, amalgamation and specialisation were key elements in any plan to ensure survival. The problem was that the 'business' was so huge and its principles so deeply rooted, that change would be slow and painful. It was a long time before Late-night shopping and Sunday shopping were acceptable to the membership.

Sport and Leisure
Cricket
After the second world war cricket slowly recovered and this was the era when overseas professionals were introduced. The club developed new facilities, finance was sound and youth coaching schemes were introduced. In July 1998 the Rochdale Observer published a photo of the 1948 Littleborough Ladies Cricket Team which, from the account, was flourishing. It is a strong recommendation for cricket that at the time of publication eight of the team were still alive and well and five of them still met regularly.

Towards the end of the century the club is secure, with a strong social life contributing to the well-being of the community. The cricket is still greatly enjoyed but they have not yet broken the highest recorded match score which was 350 against Royton in 1911 nor beaten their lowest score which was 12 against Moorside in 1917.

Unfortunately the tennis section of the cricket club declined and the courts were finally closed.

Littleborough Cricket Club, Central Lancashire League Champions, 1932.

Landscape and Environment

Looking back as an old man in the 1930s Fred Jackson has the last word on the environmental impact of the many changes that had happened during his lifetime. It must be borne in mind that Fred, who spent a life working in the textile industry, had always been interested in geology and geography. From a physical viewpoint Fred echoes the conclusions of Jessie Fothergill some 30 years previously:

"I know of scarcely any area of the same size which has suffered more from the effects of 'industrialism' on its natural scenery than the Roch valley above Littleborough. Perhaps some part of this is due to its geological formation, one half of the area from the Summit Inn to Rock Nook being very rocky owing to the Millstone Grit out-cropping to the surface, while below this point the strata at the sides of the valley belong to the softer Lower Coal Measures. Added to this the valley is so narrow in some places, as at Rock Nook, that the road, railway and canal take up nearly all its available width".

The next two generations were (nearly) able to forget such issues, as we appeared to expand our control over and use of the environment. Only today are we starting to face the size of some of our underlying problems and understand the meaning of phrases such as a 'sustainable life' or the word 'development'.

CHAPTER TWENTY

THE TWENTIETH CENTURY

PART THREE

1950 - 2000

Introduction

During the 1950s and 1960s the Conservatives came to power and set about adapting the major Labour reforms passed by their predecessors. They emphasised the importance of market forces, entrepreneurial activity and business success. They encouraged the ownership of houses, the attraction of having a motor car, a television, a holiday and luxury domestic goods. Young people got much attention and were demanding changes in how we organised education and leisure. Wages were rising but so was inflation and once again we had national strikes and national discomfort. Machines were replacing people and Germany, Japan and the U.S.A. could, in many cases, make things cheaper and better than we did. Notably Germany and Japan, who had been prevented from making armaments during the 'Cold War' era, focussed on commercial technological innovation. By 1964 the Empire had gone; Britain was no longer a great industrial power and fifteen years later had 3 million people unemployed while only the south-east of England remained relatively prosperous. To combat this situation policies were introduced to promote business, to de-nationalise and to cut public expenditure.

Street party for the Coronation, Walmsley Avenue, 1953.

Since 1945 mainland Britain has enjoyed years of peace, yet in that time we had experienced a bitter struggle in Northern Ireland with many soldiers, policemen and citizens killed. From the 1960s women had progressed towards gaining equal rights, notably in education. However, women still did not have easy access to child care, still earned less than men and still had not gained equal representation in government or the professions. The concept of family had been under strong scrutiny, one in three marriages ending in divorce. Fewer and fewer people attended church. In the 1950s and 1960s our policy of encouraging immigrants to satisfy the need for cheap labour in the brief textile boom resulted in compact pockets of ethnic minorities in many Lancashire and Yorkshire towns. Not withstanding the Race Relations Acts there were many problems of race and culture that remained to be resolved. Young people were again the focus of unemployment in a divided society with growing concerns around the developing drug culture. The Welsh and the Scots were looking for more independence and potential separation from England. The gap between rich and poor had grown and confirmed the split between north and south. As a world trader, our position continued to deteriorate and there were global problems shared with Europe and the rest of the world, in areas like genetics, health and the environment.

In 1997 the Conservative Government was defeated after 18 years of continuous power. It was replaced by a 'new' Labour Government which won a huge majority. The vote was generally seen both as a vote for 'change' and an expression by the electorate of deep unease. It is right to touch on these serious matters as we end our local story at the year 2000. Reading the story highlights the fact that each generation has faced challenges and often the people were unaware of the the factors that were about to transform their lives. At the Millennium we can argue that we are in a better position to respond to new challenges than any of our ancestors.

A statistical profile of Littleborough.

Starting in the 1980s there has been a growth in available statistics about Littleborough so that the general picture of what life is like can be more adequately quantified.

Population of the Littleborough District

Date	Total population
1951	10,932
1991	11,692

In the 1950s and 60s there is some evidence of a drift of people away from Littleborough, which ceased between 1960 and 1970. The population appears to be stable or gently increasing at the Millennium. Following a centuries old pattern there are fewer males (5,657) than females (6,035). Of the total population 1% is of a non-white ethnic origin.

Living conditions

84% of the total population live in owner-occupied properties and 11% in Local Authority-rented accommodation. Looking at the type of dwelling: 2,367 were terraced houses, 1,492 were semi-detached and 588 were detached. By households, 28% had no car, 48% had one car and 24% had two or more.

Employment pattern of Littleborough Residents

On the last count there were 5488 working people living in Littleborough (employees and self-employed), some working outside the area

312

For Littleborough residents the major sources of employment in descending order are: Manufacturing, Public Administration, Education , Health Distribution, Hotels and restaurants, Banking, Finance, Insurance, Agriculture, Service industries, Transport and Communications and Construction

The profile of the categories of work, in percentage terms, is not notably different from the national profile except for a higher percentage of workers in manufacturing.

Jobs available within Littleborough

In 1991 there were 2990 jobs available in Littleborough of which some 290 were self-employed. These figures do not appear to have changed substantially during the last 15 years of the century. The employment pattern of the 2700 jobs was:

Manufacturing	1400
Public Administration/Education/Health	500
Distribution/Hotels/Restaurants	500
All other categories	300
	2700

Manufacturing, at 52%, is the *dominant source of employment* within the Littleborough boundary and presumably has been so since the industrial revolution.

The initial comparison is with the figure for *all working people* living in Littleborough where manufacturing falls to 29% of the sample. By comparison the figure for Rochdale Borough is 30% and the national figure is 18½%.

From the material presented so far it is possible to believe we have 2700 jobs in Littleborough and some 5500 employed people living in Littleborough so the rest must go further to find work. Further examination shows this to be wrong.

The facts are that:

1340 people both live and work in Littleborough

1650 people **come from outside the town** to work in Littleborough

Summary

Of the 5488 working people living in Littleborough 75% commute to work outside the town.

1650 of the people who work in Littleborough commute into the town ie. 55%.

600 of the people who commute into Littleborough have what could be described as a 'long drive' from the 'far side' of the Rochdale Township, Greater Manchester, Calderdale and Rossendale.

Despite its heavy focus on manufacturing, Littleborough has consistently had one of the lowest un-employment rates of the 20 wards in the Rochdale Borough (second to Norden and Bamford). In April 1988 it was at 2.5% (135 people) with a Borough average of 6.0%.

On these criteria during the next century Littleborough must examine the implications of the current pattern in the kind of work we have, the movement of people in and out of the community and the impact of their legitimate needs.

The characteristic feeling of 'living in a corridor', being 'different' and being somehow more secure 'up the hill' will not go away. It has been a theme throughout this story. One of the first records mentioning our area was a medieval complaint by a Yorkshire man, about the difficulty of travelling through the outskirts of Littleborough!

At the Millennium Littleborough is a relatively prosperous suburb on the edge of an enormous urban area. It may be a very legitimate objective to ensure that we stay that way, but we must digest the idea that residents will routinely travel some way for work and will have to share their facilities with many visitors.

Industry & Commerce

Within the framework of the picture of what Littleborough is and what work exists at the end of the century a sample is given of three companies that between them provide some 20% of the available jobs.

Fothergill Engineered Fabrics/Fothergill Tygaflor: Todmorden Road.

These units are the direct survivors of our biggest local company which was built up during the growth and decline of the textile industry. There is considerable detail given in chapters 13 and 14 and it is sufficient to say that today their survival and prosperity rest on the manufacture of industrial textiles and PTFE coated products. To maintain their position and prosperity demands not only advanced manufacturing skills and marketing techniques, but also a high level of research and development. Much of the finished product is exported.

Raydex (CDT) Ltd: Church Street.

Raydex (CDT) manufactures high performance cables and bought this subsidiary from Courtaulds when Fothergill and Harvey was broken up. It employs some 100 people locally with a Head Office at Skelmersdale.

CDT (Cable Design Technologies) provides enhanced performance wires and cables. Customers for these products are organisations such as the Ministry of Defence, the Civil Aviation Authority, British Rail or those who supply to them. The products must conform to stringent standards in the definition of materials. The PTFE material, introduced to Littleborough by Fothergill and Harvey, is at the heart of the solution to these problems.

The importance is obvious in, for example, the aviation industry. Key circuits must continue to work for a defined period of time and are vital to everyone's safety in the event of a localised fire on a plane. Elsewhere, for a diving bell a cable may have to be able to resist severe abrasion, or perform consistently in conditions that exist in very deep sea water.

In the plant, there are systems installed to ensure that such quality is achieved. It is pleasing that the enormous efforts made by Fothergills, which we have recorded in this story, are being carried forward and developed to give us a local share in the newest technologies.

AKZO NOBEL: Hollingworth Road

AKZO Nobel merged with Nobel Industries in 1944 to create one of the world's major chemical companies. The company is organised into business units with 34 sites in the U.K most central functions are sited at Hersham, Surrey. AKZO NOBEL Chemicals Ltd. business unit has two major sites in Britain, at Littleborough and Gillingham (Kent).

314

'The Sinking Buildings' on Victoria street, about 1940, caused by a geological fault.

Littleborough specialises in products to provide surface coatings, resins, detergents, disinfectants, cleaning formulations and associated products. Of the 130 people employed on the site almost 80% live in Littleborough (1998).

Major companies such as AKZO NOBEL are constantly looking for joint ventures, alliances and partnerships to get the economy of scale and better marketing positions. In this search they have added a footnote to our story of the growth and decline of the local textile industry.

In the account (chapter 14) there is a summary of the enormous impact, on our textile companies, of the development of artificial fibres and the long struggle between I.C.I and Courtaulds to obtain the dominant position in the new markets. It was Courtaulds who bought the Fothergill and Harvey group, to gain position and expertise in some advanced technological areas. Now years later, Courtaulds the predator, has become the victim of just such a takeover by AKZO NOBEL who wanted their coating technology and market outlets. Other saleable elements, such as the Courtaulds fibre interests are being sold as independent companies.

Retail industry

The shops and related services have continued the fight to survive against the growth of superstores, the much greater mobility of the local population, and new opportunities to buy goods from catalogues and other outlets. The Carnival, the direct successor to a similar event in the first half of the century was revived in the 1960s. Supplementing these activities the Action group have initiated a 'village fete' and the

'Christmas Festivities, aimed at helping local shopkeepers. A recent count of the number of privately-owned shops produced a list of some 50 businesses in the central area of Littleborough. These shops provide a personal service that cannot be matched by supermarkets and department stores.

Agriculture

At the end of the century we still have extensive areas of high moorland bordered by fields. It is a fragile habitat, but important for animals, birds and humans. Pennine farms vary from 5 to 50 hectares and the overall quality of the land is poor. It gives rough grazing for sheep, beef cattle and some dairy cattle. Some of the farms are not self supporting and the owners need to supplement their income with other work. Agriculture makes a very modest contribution to the wealth and employment in Littleborough. In terms of the overall development, with an accent on the leisure industry, it is very important that we develop a strategy to preserve the many important and interesting aspects of our stretch of countryside. This is a general problem, which is being tackled throughout the country, as the century comes to an end. The forecast might be for a very modest level of traditional jobs in farming, more new jobs in areas of development and conservation, but in total agriculture will not be of great significance in our employment statistics.

Transport

The M62: Lancashire / Yorkshire Motorway

As we moved to the 1970s following government re-organisation a very ambitious engineering project was agreed right on our doorstep. It was proposed to build a new Lancashire / Yorkshire Motorway, the M62, passing within two miles of Littleborough.

The project involved the construction of the highest bridge in Greater Manchester (the Rakewood Viaduct with four spans, each 150' high) and the excavation of the largest 'cutting' that exists on a road scheme in Europe. The scheme was proposed in 1961, agreed in 1964 and begun in 1968. The M62 is a six lane highway through the Pennines, the highest point crossing Rockingstone Moss at 1200'.

With time the Rakewood Viaduct, behind Hollingworth Lake, has come to be seen by many as a workmanlike piece of road engineering which is not too obtrusive in the surrounding hills. The cutting through the Windy Hill section is 120' deep and was designed to keep the road surface below the prevailing cloud level. The conditions for carrying out these enormous engineering projects were demanding: the peat is 20' deep in places and the average rainfall is 60" per annum but falls of 12" in a month are not exceptional.

The initial impact of the opening of the motorway was a miraculous lessening of traffic on the utterly congested roads of east Lancashire and west Yorkshire. It immediately made the location of Littleborough attractive, as a potential home base for people who might work 20 miles away. It also gave an economic impetus by encouraging new industrial estates and distribution centres in the area. With house prices reaching very high levels in Cheshire and south Manchester the motorway helped to create the right conditions to attract people back to our area, leading to new housing and improvement of much of the old.

The Railway

The sale of the railways to private interests in the 1990s has led to change and in the first years of operation a great deal of dissatisfaction. However in one area, dear to the heart of many Littleborough residents, there has been progress; this is the height of the railway platform. For many years the platform has been too low and there were small steps which were rushed out when the elderly or infirm could not get in or out of the carriages. More recently the platform was raised, but not enough, until finally the platform has been raised yet again to allow satisfactory entry and exit to modern carriages.

Many travellers will observe that the opportunity is now open to restore a regular and reliable operation. It is also sad to observe the currently inadequate shelters provided for passengers on our exposed platforms and the lack of enough seats and the un-heated state of the main waiting room. It appears to be a situation that will not bear comparison with even the late 19th and early 20th century.

Religion

In general, at a national level the number of people attending church has continued to decline but there are signs of an encouraging stability, even modest growth in our local area. The churches still provide a real focus for social as well as religious activity in the second half of the 20th century.

The Anglican Church

The Holy Trinity Parish Church

There have been no significant architectural changes to the Parish Church in recent years. One change has been the laying of the gravestones on the ground producing a more open aspect to the area round the church and allowing for easier maintenance. It also emphasises the importance of the existing mature trees in the town centre.

St Barnabas Church, Shore

In the 1960s, St Barnabas Church purchased the 'old Shore School' from the Local Authority to be used as a parish hall. It is sited on the left of Shore Road a short way beyond Ribble Avenue. Subsequently, the church decided to adapt the rear part of the St Barnabas Church to serve as a new parish hall. The old school was sold to a private developer who converted it into several private homes in the early 1990s. The new parish hall was part of a bigger plan to join St Barnabas with St James, Calderbrook in a Joint Parish with one priest. The vicarage at St Barnabas was also sold and is now a private house.

The grave of the man who was the original inspiration for this story of Littleborough, Fred Jackson, can be found in the graveyard of St Barnabas Church.

Non-conformist Churches

Of the non-conformist churches many were demolished or turned to a new use including:

Demolished: Shore, Temple, Rakewood, Church Street, Victoria Street,
  Smithy Bridge (Chapel).

Converted: Featherstall, Zion, Ebenezer, Smithy Bridge (school).

These lists are a reflection of a country-wide contraction of church owned property. The leaders of the non-conformist churches are looking to centralise and focus their activities, build up youth opportunities, encourage women to participate and lead, spread their social net in different ways, encompass modern developments, start to rebuild socialisation etc. Serious thought is being given on how to re-engage with schools. Some such mix of ideas must be necessary to revitalise the institutions.

The closures of churches are bound to be sad, especially for those who have attended for a life-time and can remember how much labour and loving care was invested in the buildings. Typical of the closures that have happened was the service in 1990 at the Summit Methodist Church. They celebrated 125 years of Christian worship in the chapel, with a moving final service of great simplicity, after which the church was closed.

St Mary's Roman Catholic Church

In recent years, compared with the turbulent past, the church has experienced financial stability, horizons have widened, social gatherings changed but the basic objectives spelt out in the 1870s remain. An important part of the work of the church is to ensure the prosperit;y of the school. It may be a struggle in terms of providing all the desirable facilities but is seen as vital by the adults in the church 'in order to have their children educated according as conscience desired and in the Faith they themselves worship'.

---------------- CHAPTER TWENTY-ONE ----------------

THE TWENTIETH CENTURY

PART FOUR: GOODBYE TO THE SECOND MILLENNIUM

1950 - 2000
(Continued)

Millennium
Latin for 1000 (mille): Millenarianism, the belief, inspired by biblical references, that in the near future we will experience a thousand years of Christ's reign - over a chosen people.
Naturally attractive for the disoriented and those without much other wordly hope, millenarian movements have recurred throughout Jewish, Christian and Islamic history - they were widespread in mainstream British Protestantism of the Reformation in the 16th and 17th centuries and during the French Revolution.

'Companion to British History 1955'

Education

After the 1944 Education Act the following significant changes and developments relating to education have been implemented:

1964   New High School built on Calderbrook Road at a cost of £242,000.
1968   St James's, Calderbrook closed as a school. All pupils transferred to the new Stansfield Hall Primary Interdenominational Controlled School. St. James ' School ceased to exist but the building was used as an annexe to the new school until 1980. Immediately after this time the building was converted to a home for the elderly.
1990   Littleborough High School was closed, mainly due to falling rolls.

At the end of the century many Littleborough people believe there are serious problems in the area of education. Notably, there is no authority-controlled secondary school in the Littleborough area which has a population of some 13,000 people. They are asked to look for places in relatively inconvenient (in transport terms) areas like Milnrow, Wardle and Rochdale. This presents travel, social and financial implications, which many local people see as unsolved. Gordon Harvey would surely wonder at the change, from a position of providing our children with the very best within the town, to the current situation.

The education supported by the co-operative movement has changed but is still active. They have moved the focus onto links with schools and colleges and supporting local vocational training; Co-op Retail Services have sponsored a computer package in this area. The co-op movement still helps young people, through the 'Woodcraft Folk' organisation, with 26 branches in the United North West Trading Area and 251 nationally (1992).

Co-operation

Of the three great C's the Chapels have dwindled, the Cotton has gone, so what of the great Co-operative idea?

The Co-op's Independent Commission of Inquiry started its work in 1955 and the outcome was a dramatic reduction in the number of societies nationally from 467 in 1967 to 55 in 1994. There were many parallels between the contraction of the co-op movement and that of the textile industry; with rationalisation, reduction and finally the closing of many of the manufacturing plants. For the Co-op, the outcome was that most of N.E Britain is serviced by the Co-op Retail Services Ltd and most of Lancashire by the United North West Ltd. Along the way the mergers have spawned units such as Price Fighters, Late Shops, Convenience Stores, Supermarkets, Normid Super-stores and Hypermarkets.

The United North West still represents one of the biggest co-operatives in Europe and the Cooperative Retail Services, which started as the amalgamation of the dozens of societies which were non-viable, has developed increasing specialisation and recognisable marketing labels.

It was the development, by new commercial companies, of multiple stores and discount supermarkets, all focussed on the traditional markets of the co-operative movement, which forced the co-op to retrench and reorganise. In the first half of the century the large retail margins in the co-op movement had supported 'divi' at 2/6 or 3/0 in the pound. Margins shrank and 'divi' became stamps and then disappeared. With it went services like the 'annual children's treat'. Between 1958 and 1994 the co-operative's share of the retail market fell from 11% to 4%. In the same period the number of co-op shops fell from 30,000 to 4,500. Today the co-operative no longer plays such an active part in the social development of communities, by providing facilities to help all aspects of working class life. Nevertheless, the co-op remains a very big business with its principles still intact and with evidence of a revival in its commercial success in a very competitive arena.

In 1950 the Littleborough Co-operative Society celebrated its hundredth anniversary. The 31 members who joined in 1850 had become 3000 and the original share capital of £96 exceeded £87,000. The average sales in the first six years were £2580 per annum whilst the sales in 1949 topped £200,000. In 1950, Littleborough Co-operative was the premier trading concern in the district. It is little wonder that they celebrated that anniversary with pride, which was shared by the community. The Celebrations lasted from November 4th to the 18th and included a Grand Concert, Pageant of Fashion, Centenary Ball, Children's Night, Grand Whist Drive, Aged Folks Nights, Childrens Play, Employees Party, Grand Closing Concert and much more. There were competitions for babies, window dressing, sales and numerous other 'flutters'.

The following is a list of the Littleborough Co-operative units that existed in Littleborough 50 years ago (circa 1954/55 Trade Directory).

31 Church Street	Grocers
33 Church Street	Butchers
105 Featherstall Rd	Grocers
59 Halifax Rd (Durn)	General
32 & 34 Hare Hill Rd	Footwear
35 Hare Hill Rd	Milliners

38 Hare Hill Rd	Confectioners
40 Hare Hill Rd	Butchers
42 Hare Hill Rd	Grocers
44 Hare Hill Rd	Drapers
103 Hare Hill Rd	Grocers (Caldermoor Br.)
Lighthouse Calderbrook Rd	General
84 New Rd Dearnley	Grocers
76/78 Summit	Grocers (Holme St, nr. Temple Lane?)
193 Todmorden Rd	Grocers (Centre Vale?)
Smithy Bridge Co-op	General (Owned by Rochdale Equitable Pioneer Soc. Ltd. Previously the Smithy Bridge Co-op Soc.)
120 New Rd Dearnley	Vacant (owned by the Rochdale E. Pioneer Soc.)

From this time the contraction of the co-operative retail outlets gained momentum. Events were overtaking the smaller co-op units and in 1968 Littleborough Co-op was absorbed into the Rochdale Pioneer Society which after a series of mergers became part of United North West. In 1986 the buildings that had been the main office and the associated shops of the Littleborough Co-operative, on Hare Hill Road, were partially demolished with the rest converted into a mini-market as part of a larger co-operative group. This was later supplemented by the purchase of the 'Low Cost' super-market that had been built recently, on the old goods and coal yard, adjacent to the railway station.

Despite the severe contraction in the number of co-op outlets throughout the country the co-operative movement still provides active support for a range of charitable and social services including women's rights, domestic issues, help to working women and Women's Guild. There are still many co-op recreational halls supporting community activities. The widespread involvement in locally organising events such as day trips, or running penny bank schemes to help people save, have died out or become part of specialist organisations such as 'co-op travel' who serve much wider areas. One growth area has been in a startling amalgam of new and worthy causes mixed up with a determination to have fun. These now include poetry festivals, young people's poetry and film and video festivals. An event at Burnley which combined politics, marquee displays and amusements attracted an attendance of 18,000 people in 1993.

A reasonable conclusion might be that the co-operative institution is still very much alive, very deeply rooted in the community and still part of the social fabric in Littleborough and Rochdale. You may also conclude that for a community to have an identity it still needs a co-operative vision.

Growth of Littleborough
General Conditions

In the 1950s population in the area was declining; there were many acres of derelict land and the rivers were polluted. Unemployment figures were relatively high mainly because of the collapse of the textile industry. Bronchitis and asbestosis were common following years of inadequate safeguards for the health of industrial workers. Such problems were not solved easily. The local economy was often described as 'exhausted' and the 'swinging sixties' were clearly happening somewhere else.

Local Authority and Private Housing

Littleborough entered the 1950s with a large housing stock of 'back to back' houses of an unacceptably low standard. A programme was started for the conversion and improvement of some, with the demolition of the rest including many derelict properties. Prefabricated houses were placed to meet some of the most urgent needs and a programme of development of housing estates initiated.

The major step was a programme of new housing to be built by the local authority in a number of council estates. The first were built in 1922, more houses went up both at Shore and Hollingworth Lake in 1952, followed by further development at Calderbrook with the subsequent major expansion in the Stansfield estate in 1955. There was a pause until 1962 when Calderbrook and two years later, Hollingworth Lake, were further developed. The Saxon House sheltered accommodation block was a new departure in 1965, followed, in 1967, by a new estate placed on land that had belonged to Shore Mill. In 1968 Stansfield was extended yet again. Between 1971 and 1975 more sheltered accommodation was built at Hare Hill Court and further housing provided at Smithy Bridge and Dearnley. In 1988, with the opening of the Olive Standring House to provide further sheltered accommodation, the programme of Council house building ended.

In the same period there was also the building of private estates, notably Bents Farm and around Hollingworth Lake; both were constructed on 'green-field' sites. In addition there were two other significant developments of more than 100 new houses, on the old industrial sites of the Shore Mills and the Lancashire Tanning Company. Finally there has been much private building of houses 'filling in' smaller mill sites such as the developments at Grove and Albion and one of some significance on the old site of the Central School, close to the centre of Littleborough.

In summary, only a few late 20th century housing developments have been carried out with a concern for the environment, traditional building materials and building design. Other estates show less regard for such issues. On the uplands another form of housing regeneration was in full swing: the conversion of old houses, farms and barns into homes. There has been a complete re-occupation of communities such as Bent House on the Halifax road and the hamlet of Whittaker, which is designated as a conservation area. Considerable care has been taken to maintain much of the earlier architecture during the conversion of ancient buildings to provide modern living accommodation.

The housing developments have tended to bring in younger families who, associated with the upland developments, have made their contribution to a wider range of activities in the area. There is now a healthy growth in community and leisure activities such as sports, walking, running, gala events, cycling, horse riding, sailing and sailboarding.

Medical Facilities
The MacGill Family

When looking at the medical facilities in Littleborough it is worth stepping back some 120 years to a time when a young doctor arrived from Scotland in 1873. Born in Kirkcudbrightshire in 1840, educated at Glasgow University and Queen's College, Belfast, he came to assist Dr Lister in Littleborough. This was a time when young professional Scotsmen were emigrating to all parts of the globe. The local growth of

1076
8·233

Town House

Reservoir
1086
2·066

1078ª
660

ROAD

S

FP

Near Higher
Town House Wood
1077
3·158

547

CALDERBROOK

1087ª
·123

SPRINGFIELD AVENUE

Resr.

1028
2·870

BROOKLYN AVENUE

594

MOUNT AVENUE

BM 529·15

1027
7·981

MOORFIELD AVE

1018
·627

CALDER

Cro

ROAD

AVENUE

584

1025
4·455

AVENUE

WELBECK AVENUE

Denhurst R

9

FURNESS AVENUE

ALL AVENUE

WHALLEY AVENUE

518

986
2·362

572

BM 515·85

Midge
Hole

Moorfield House

550

BM 535·93

Allotment
Gardens
988
3·614

984
1·059

581

CALDERMOOR

TCB BM 510·52

515

517

Dog & Partridge
(P.H.)

Meth.
Ch.

983ª
1·727

Grave Yard

Rese
6
7

ALFRED STREET

Vicarage

983ᵇ
·490

SALTS STREET

HENDERVILLE ST.

983
2·084

K STREET

INGLIS ST.

FP

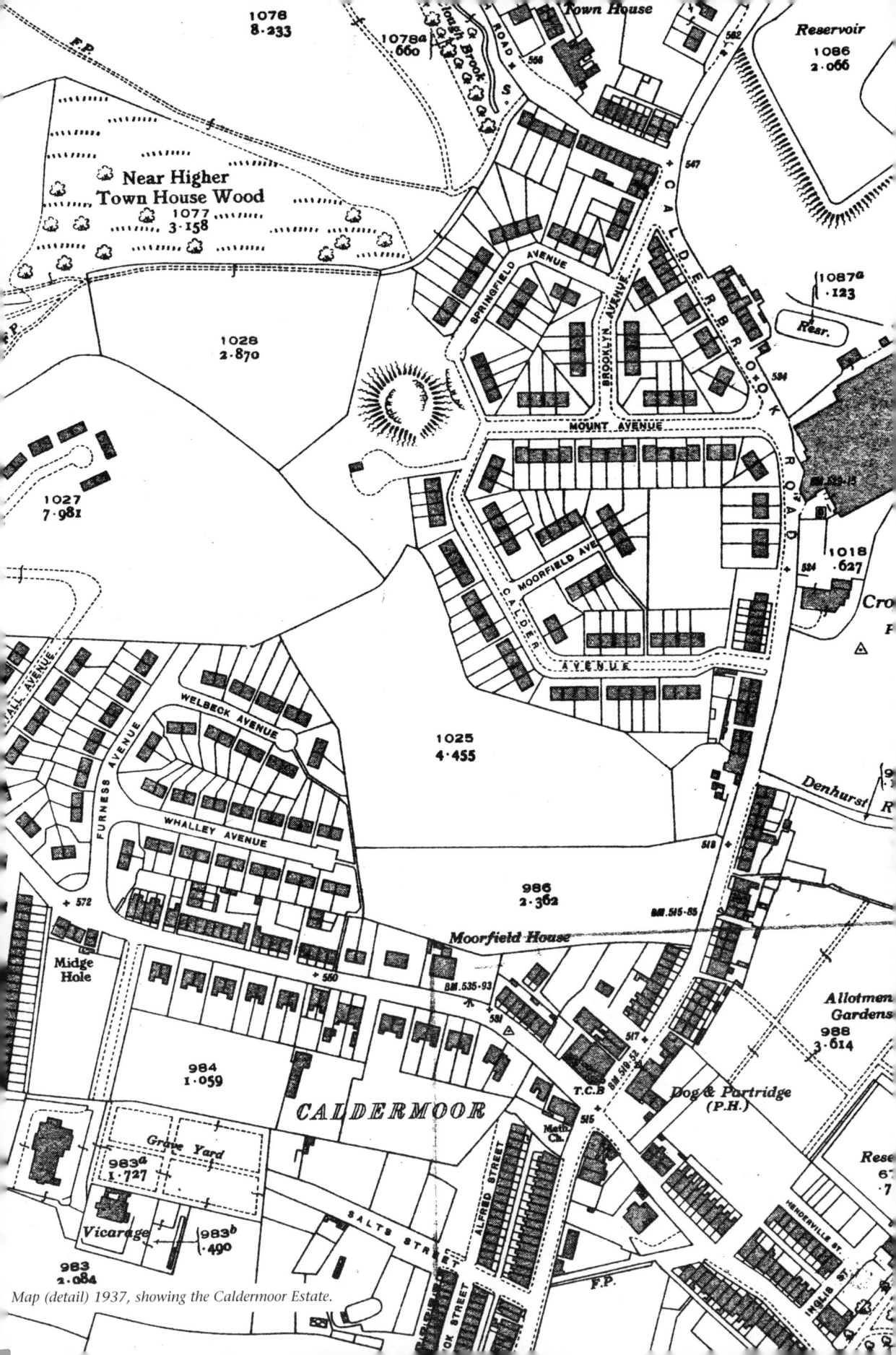

Map (detail) 1937, showing the Caldermoor Estate.

population in Littleborough, the increase in prosperity generally, must have attracted an ambitious general practitioner. Dr George MacGill was to become the longest resident medical practitioner in our area. He lived in Hollinbrook House on Church Street and died in 1921, aged 81. In later life it is said that he resisted having a motor car and chauffeur still preferring to travel round the district on horse-back.

In 1876 he married Fanny, the daughter of Mr & Mrs Rogers, who lived in Calder Cottage at the Calderbrook end of Hare Hill Road. They had four sons and two daughters. Of the sons, James, Donald and Roderick all became doctors and practised in or around Littleborough. The fourth son, Cameron, managed his father's farm in Scotland.

In 1923, after Dr George died, Dr James (Jim) moved into Hollinbrook House and when Dr Roderick married (a girl from Kirkcudbright) he went into Hollinbrook house in 1931. Mrs MacGill (Fanny) died at Calder Cottage in 1934 aged 78 and Miss Daisy, one of her daughters, died there in 1959

The service to the community of this family, was widely recognised and it stretched into the third generation when the son of Dr Jim, Peter, also qualified as a doctor and practised in Littleborough from the 1950s until he finally emigrated to New Zealand in 1976.

Dr George was perhaps one of Littleborough's best known and respected residents. He was familiar to everyone for more than 50 years. In 1874 he was appointed the first official Medical Officer for the Littleborough district, which appointment he held until he resigned in 1877. He was the police surgeon for many years, the public vaccination officer and for many years the parish medical officer. In the early 1900s a branch surgery was opened in Smallbridge which Dr Donald looked after as the principal G.P. In the 1914-18 war, Dr George was the medical officer in charge of the Birch Hill Auxilliary Hospital and was awarded the MBE for his services. An Anglican, his efforts elsewhere played a major part in the creation of St Andrew's Church, Dearnley. He was the 'people's warden' there for 25 years and his name and contribution are recorded in a stained glass window within the church. On his farm in Scotland, managed by his son Cameron, they bred Hackney & Clydesdale horses, Ayrshire cattle and collie dogs.

Like Gordon Harvey, in his own profession, George MacGill seemed to find the right time and possess the right qualities to leave behind him a benign history of help in Littleborough, which still lives in the memory of many people today. For example older people speak of the 'MacGill Houses' which dated from the time when various members of the family lived in them. By the 1960s when the government began introducing a new set of medical standards it was decided that the best solution was to focus local medical care at Hollinbrook House. By 1960, of the MacGill family, only Dr Peter MacGill was still in practice.

There had been other doctors in Littleborough prior to George MacGill and there were indeed two other practices of long standing in the mid and late 20th century. They were run by Dr Vining, who practiced from his home/surgery on Hare Hill Road, and was mentioned earlier as the doctor attending at the Lancashire Tanning Company, and Dr Michael-Phillips who practiced on Church Street. Both of these men were well regarded and long remembered by their loyal families of Littleborough patients.

Perhaps the single most helpful characteristic needed during a visit to a doctor, prior

Calder Cottage: a 'MacGill House' for many years.

to the opening of the new health centres, was patience. There were no effective appointments systems then. A visit to the doctors surgery could be over in 15 minutes or could take two hours. It all depended on how long the queue was.

Recent medical developments

As the scope and responsibilities of the practices continued to grow, in 1976 the doctors in the 'MacGill' practice moved from Hollinbrook House to the present premises, the Littleborough Health Centre, on Featherstall Road. Within a few months Peter MacGill left for New Zealand and the connection with his family ceased. Soon after the move to Featherstall Road the doctors adopted the name Littleborough Group Practice. In the later part of the 20th century the growth of medical facilities has been determined by the growth of the National Health Service and the need to develop many new services and centres for treatment.

In Littleborough, as elsewhere, people look first to their local General Practitioners for medical help and advice and through them to the Birch Hill Hospital or the Rochdale Infirmary for hospitalisation depending on the illness or speciality involved. At the end of the century (1998) we have the following practices and related treatment centres in Littleborough :

> Littleborough Health Centre, Featherstall Road, five doctors.
> Village Medical Centre, Peel Street, two doctors.
> Church Street Surgery, one doctor.

Within these centres there are highly trained practice nurses, district nurses, health visitors and community midwives. They are assembled to provide a wide range of family care services and have a responsibility for pro-active health promotion.

The Dog and Partridge football team 1963. The pub later changed its name to the Caldermoor in 1968.

Wrapped around this core are further layers of social service, some voluntary, some run by the authority and some privately initiated. Typical of the private sphere are the seven private nursing homes in the Littleborough area. Other essential services contributing to our general health are of course the dentists (2), chemists (2) and opticians (1) together with many units giving help and advice on disability, care in the community and providing facilities such as sheltered housing.

Even such a brief review of the range of services leaves no reason to doubt that the National Health service will always be amongst the biggest elements of our national budget and deserves to be treasured in terms of the quality of life we enjoy.

Social, Leisure and Sport activities

In this section there are many voluntary sector initiatives that frequently start with one objective and end up meeting different needs in our community. The initiatives vary in age and there are too many to mention them all, but a review of some gives a deeper feel of where our society has grown from and how it changes. You may ask where are the Guides and Scouts and many other organisations that some time in life give us so much help and pleasure? The current selection leans towards those with a unique Littleborough orientation; the revision of this area can be a pleasant challenge to the next edition of Littleborough's story.

Littleborough Prosecution Society

This society has been very much a part of the fabric of Littleborough and the picture outlined is the society, as seen through their minute books.

Formed in 1875 it appears to have been a co-operative project to protect the interests of local farmers. From the beginning, the pattern of book-keeping was settled and has lasted until the end of the 20th century. The main elements are 'cash in' from new members and 'cash in hand', on one side and the expenses of an annual general meeting and dinner on the other. The major actions recorded in the early years are a series of meetings. It appears that any member could call a committee meeting at any time, at his own cost, to vent a concern and to seek help to get justice. To clarify this; here is a summary of some of the issues that arose in the 1870s and 1880s which led to a meeting.

> The removal of broken bricks.
> Wooden fencing broken down wilfully.
> Claim by John Mathews for damage, from the acts of Mrs Yarwood.
> From Timothy Laycock, farmer, against Hy. Magson for wilfully breaking
>   windows and other damage.
> For 32 yards of wall top stones knocked off between Steanor Bottom and Summit.
> Lane Colliery vs Schofield and Molesworth for trespass. (Trespass appears to be
>   the biggest single issue with members).
> Severe attack by a dog on a member out riding his horse near 'Rushtons' house.
> By Hollingworth Lake Company (1878) for 2 steamers released from their moorings
>   and found at the Fisherman's Inn the following morning.
> For dangerous loosening of some coal wagons from their chains.

The Prosecution Society appears to have acted like an early insurance company. Payments have been recorded from members, to help defray the cost of cases that are disputed. For example such costs arose for 'large bills' at the time when a member offered a substantial reward to catch a vandal. The bills appear to be posters put up throughout the district.

Printing costs have always been a serious item in the books, for example a significant charge for 200 copies of a large circular with all members' names on it. In 1891 this could well be an invitation to the annual dinner. Certainly by this time the dinner was a major affair: the entry for 1894 records gallons of beer, 'one bottle' of special beer and other drinks all at a cost of 7/3d. The society which was still recording the payment of court fees at this time imposed a fine on 'non-attenders' at the committee meeting of one shilling. There were also payments for recruiting new members. The recurring costs of letters sent out to trespassers are prominent at this time.

In the early 1900s the cost of the annual dinner includes a pianist and by the 1920s one or more singers. The original function of the society seems to dwindle and the last business payment was recorded in 1924:

> 'Paid to William Marshall's account for Poultry Trespass; 6.0d.'

Through the 1930s the Society prospers and we find two well known Littleborough caterers, Whittles and Lords providing the dinner, often called the 'feed'. In the late 1920s and 1930s the practice of members calling meetings appears to be replaced by quarterly meetings which themselves appear to die in 1949, except for the December 7th meeting to finalise dinner events and later to plan the 'annual trip'. The society at this time had the whole range of officers, presided over by a Chairman, a very healthy membership and sound finances. The following years see a regular increase in new membership of some 12 annually and in 1954 Mr Higginbotham retired after 41 years service as Secretary. He was presented with a Westminster Chimes Clock with a suitable inscription (£11.15d). It was also in this year that the Society decided to make the Conservative Club its 'headquarters' for the all important A.G.M. and dinner. Around this time the 'day out' starts to figure, the first event being to go to Morecambe in a coach provided by Leach's (see chapter 18). The annual dinner date by now is 'traditionally' on the first Thursday of each year and there is no further mention in the books of what could be described as business or commercial or legal matters. There is however regular and serious consideration about the dinner, hot or cold, two singers or one, a ventriloquist and a comedian. In 1956 the 'day out' went to Skegness. It started with breakfast on the way followed by a full day which ended with an evening event on the way home. The dinner in 1957 had the full complement of entertainers with singers, comedians and pianists. The prior committee meeting decided on 4 turkeys, 3 chickens and plenty of roast ham as back up, in case everyone turned up. The birds were gifts from the members and after due consideration the pudding became apple pie and custard. The late 50s may have been one of the high points of what appears to be a very happy society. Two years in succession the membership increased by 17 people and at the 1960 dinner 128 members sat down to eat and 32 new members were recorded in the previous year.

Inevitably, at this time there start to be regular records of the death of older members and also a pointed note 'that if members are not attending the 'feed' they are expected to pay their subscriptions just the same'. Modern costs and technology also obtrude with subscriptions being raised to 10/-, raffles being introduced and a microphone being hired from 'Parry' (the electrical shop in Littleborough) for the artistes. Much of the earlier printing costs have moved to become payments for material placed in the Rochdale Times.

In 1971 Thomas Lord retired having been Chairman for 30 years. He recalled that during his service he had been called to pay for rose trees that his sheep had eaten; more seriously he observed that the society in its entire existence had only had 5 secretaries. The meeting closed, as it always had, with 'the Queen'. 1975 saw the 75th Anniversary when 94 members attended the dinner, anyone not attending had to pay 25p to remain a member. The dinners in the late 70s were well attended but through the 80s the society declined; in 1989 only 26 members attended the dinner. In 1990 there is a minuted apology for a poor meal, a unique comment on what had been otherwise an endless record of digestive satisfaction. In the 1990s there have been ups and downs, the worst being a poor attendance of 33 members and a cryptic remark that 'the entertainer turned up but disappeared'. By 1997 attendances were back to the level of the 70s and the society seems to be set to continue to provide a focus and much pleasure for its members.

Trades Hall Club

This club, sited on Church Street, is over 75 years old. The origin of the club was an organisation called the Trades Hall Littleborough Co. Ltd. which later became Littleborough Trades and Labour Council. In 1917 the Trades Council moved into new offices in a building which had been the Horseshoe Inn and still has the name carved into the stonework above the door.

Initially, the forerunner of the Trades Hall Club rented the basement of the old inn where they installed a billiard table. Later, when the Trades Council disbanded,(1922-23) the club moved to the upper floor, a concert room and a games room were developed with a shared bar and the constitution was revised to the form it has today. Finally the ground floor came vacant which had been the offices of the Littleborough News (see chapter 18) and later, lock-up shops. The club purchased them and today they are the bar area.

The club has always been close to the heart of Littleborough and claims 600 members including some 50 honorary life members (who are over 65). The horse shoe symbol is used by members of the club as an emblem on their pullover.

The Trades Hall.

Apart from supplying a congenial central place for people of like mind to sit and talk, drink and play games it also runs events such as bingo nights and provides live entertainment. A resilient organisation it is remembered how, in the Second World War, a kitty was kept at the bar and any local soldier home on leave was sure of a drink. Resilient also in the fact that by word of mouth it not only survives but its membership grows and with gradual improvement to the facilities it continues to contribute to the life of the community.

Littleborough Peace Group

The two preceeding accounts are of organisations that have lasted and served the community for many many years. In the same period dozens of other initiatives have come and gone and it is interesting to look at the growth and activities of a much more recent local group. During the 'cold war' with Russia, after the second world war, groups belonging to an organisation called Campaign for Nuclear Disarmament grew up all over Britain. Their distinctive symbol was to become known as the peace symbol world wide. Rochdale CND was formed in the late fifties and a group in Littleborough decided there was enough interest to form an independent group in 1981. Their brief was that of the parent organisation, to oppose militarism, the use of weapons of mass destruction and to promote peace and social justice. From the start women's voices were strong and when the Greenham Women started their non-violent actions against the U.S. Cruise missile base in 1981 the Littleborough women were there. The group works by publishing pamphlets and newsletters, giving out leaflets and using the media to forge links with activists locally and throughout the world.

Their mandate has always embraced humanitarian activities and in the late 90's repeatedly Littleborough women have driven ancient trucks carrying aid directly into the conflict areas of the former Yugoslavia. They were also founder members of the Chernobyl Children's Project in Britain, sending aid to Belarus and bringing children back to Britain to help their recuperation. The children have suffered from the appalling aftermath of a nuclear reactor explosion in 1986. Many of the children suffer severely from radiation linked illness, but such visits give them a chance of extending their life and our community has given them the help both generously and willingly. We did, after all, do a similar thing for our evacuees in the Second World War.

Littleborough Action Group

Started in 1985 this group has promoted the well being of local commercial and business interests, to retain healthy locally based activity in the town centre. It has created events and printed material that have provided our independent shop keepers with outlets to promote their goods and also actively supported retailers over issues such as their rates and parking problems. At the other end of the scale they have worked to form alliances with significant outside groups. The objective is to bring money and commercial activity into Littleborough, which in turn would exploit the many skills that exist locally by widening the scope for self-help.

Littleborough Civic Trust

A unit of a country wide organisation, it has a local membership of some 80 people, whose mandate is to preserve and improve the general conditions, both for leisure and work, in the Littleborough Area. The Trust has existed in Littleborough for 30 years, having grown out of the Rochdale Civic Trust. It focuses on environmental issues primarily in urban areas and plays an active part in planning, conservation and associated matters. It has a proud record of achievement in a number of local projects including the preservation of the Steanor Bottom Toll Bar, the formation of the Country Park at Hollingworth Lake and the conversion of the Falcon's stables into the Coach House information and community centre. Smaller projects have included restoring an area of land by clearing up litter and replanting it and planting a new wood. The Trust also works with our authority to achieve protection for valuable local buildings by listing them, as subject to special building regulations or, in the case of the Littleborough town centre and Whittaker, by creating conservation areas. A branch of the Trust has always been interested in walking the footpaths of our area and actively reporting blockages and obstructions to the local authority where these occur. The Trust has also produced a book of walks, to guide the growing volume of people in Littleborough, or visitors to it, who wish to walk on our moors, tracks and footpaths.

We are very proud to add this present book, The Story of Littleborough, to the list of achievements, as the result of three years of hard work with the co-operation of literally hundreds of local people.

Littleborough Coach House Trust

The Coach House started and has continued to be, a voluntary sector project. The idea grew from the need for a facility for meetings and activities, for the people and organisations of Littleborough, in the centre of the town.

Earlier in the story we recorded the rise of stables beside the major coaching houses in Littleborough and the decline of that trade as the railways were established and motorised transport introduced.

Around 1870 a journeyman carpenter, James England, came from Addingham in Yorkshire to carry out some work on Stubley Hall in Littleborough. When this work was completed he decided to stay and set up a business in Smithy Bridge. About 1880 the stables of the Falcon were available and he brought his business to Littleborough. In the heyday of the business the part of the present Coach House occupied by James England had been a farm with cow stalls, the other part of the Coach House was

The Coach House and Heritage Centre.

originally the horse stalls for the stage coach. In 1886 when Falcon Cottage was built next to the Coach House James got the contract for the joinery work. At the time there was an open market in the Falcon Yard every Friday and another part of the stables was used to store the market stalls. James England died around 1900 and his three sons, Alfred, John Edward and Walter became equal partners in the running of the business.

The sons flourished and soon there were 20 joiners employed. The firm undertook major projects as sub-contractors to Dryland and Preston, Builders. The projects included the joinery work for the new Central School in Littleborough and also for E Clegg & Sons, Shore Mills. The same combination did major contracts on Gas Works, Hospitals and other business sites.

The carpentry business followed the classical pattern; the first generation established it, the second enlarged it and the third saw its decline. After the carpentry business and wood yard finally closed the property reverted to the brewery and the opportunity emerged to get a long lease.

Littleborough Civic Trust negotiated this agreement and a saga of conversion began. Initially it was carried out by the Trust but, because of the seriousness and the detailed demands of such a large project, it rapidly drew in a number of other voluntary organisations and finally created its own organisational set up. With the financial help of Fothergill and Harvey, the Greater Manchester Authority and innumerable other smaller contributions from the community; phase one of the present fine facilities were opened in 1983. Today they include an Information and Heritage Centre, rooms available for large and small meetings, facilities for arts and crafts exhibitions, a cafe, a bar and a major function room with a handsome wooden floor for bigger meetings, dancing and all kinds of social functions.

A survey revealed that, in 1987, it was used by some 35,000 people who came from all parts of our community and beyond. Income has in recent years hovered around £20,000 per annum and expenditure has been held to a comparable figure. Although this development can rightly be seen as a excellent achievement the demand to raise some 40% of the income annually by fund-raising events continues to put pressure on those directly involved. The Coach House Committee is seriously considering further developments and sources of help, to lessen the burden on their active members.

Public Houses

These institutions have played an honourable part in much of the Littleborough story over the centuries. Their popularity and service continues unabated into the 21st century. They are not only a congenial place for a drink but frequently act as a social centre for large groups of people providing rooms, service, good food and entertainment. Regrettably there is a tendency for the breweries to rename pubs for reasons of fashion but we are fortunate in having a history of Littleborough Pubs written by the late Alan Luke which records much of what happened in the past and up to 1983. Alan, a local teacher, was a founder member and activist in the Littleborough Historical and Archaeological Society.

Cinemas

Today Littelborough people have to travel to the Multiplex Cinema development in Sandbrook Park, Rochdale or alternatively, to the more warming experience of the Cinema at Hebden Bridge.

Cricket

By 1959 the Lancashire Cricket League was facing contraction and had recognised an overall decline in playing standards. Attendances were being measured in hundreds rather than thousands. The cricket league had long since replaced the Chapel as the focus of organisation of cricket but it too declined at the same time as the chapels did. The loss of the tennis courts, both within the cricket club and in Hare Hill Park, signalled the end of local tennis. This said, the Littleborough Cricket Club, as well as being successful in the Central Lancashire League, is also a major social centre in the town with a active membership. They provide facilities for celebrations and parties and also host other events of many kinds.

Pennine Winemakers Guild

At the Church Street end of Hare Hill Road for many years the Parry family had retail interests including shoes, cycles, radio and television. In the early 1960s Mr Fred Parry was unwell and the doctor recommended two glasses of wine daily to combat some of his problems. Faced with the daunting cost of commercial wine at the time, he decided to brew his own. His first move was to join the Rochdale Wine Circle as did his wife Ethel.

By 1966, with diligent effort, they had 'absorbed' the main principles of the art so in that year with a number of fellow spirits they established a guild in Littleborough. Mrs Ethel Parry was the first President and in February 1966 the Littleborough winemaking circle was was floated.

The initial focus was and remains wine making and beer brewing but the guild has

The Wheatsheaf Buildings.

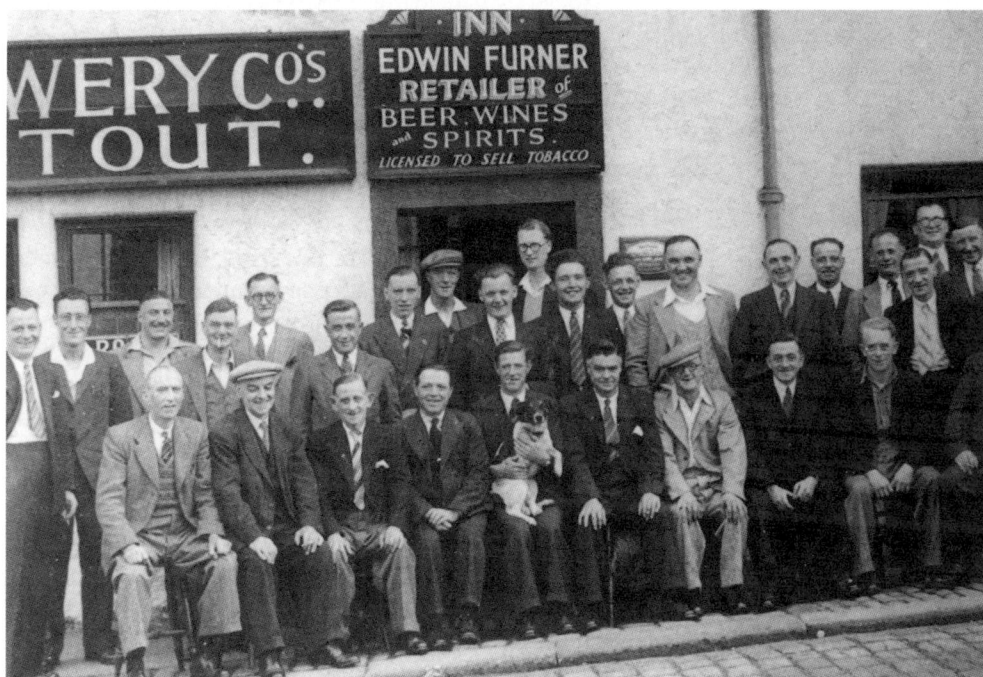

The Blue Ball at Smithy Bridge, men's trip about the late 1940s.

expanded its scope to include many other sociable and charitable aspects. It has raised more than £6000 since it was formed which has been donated to local charities.

There are some 60 members who meet monthly at the Littleborough Coach house and every meeting has a wine-tasting competition. The guild has entered, with success, into the many local competitions and shows. The popularity of wine drinking has increased dramatically and the guild has expanded its activities to include talks on and tasting of commercially produced wine. This has widened its appeal; membership now includes anyone who is interested in making or drinking wine.

Littleborough Lions

No great hint is given in this title about what they do, but many would say 'raise money for good causes'. They are in fact part of a national and international organisation claiming 1.4 million members in 42,000 clubs in 180 countries. In 1949 the first club was set up in Britain and today the Lions offer a humanitarian and caring service, country-wide.

All Lions clubs are autonomous and are responsible for their own community service and local fund raising activities. They do have some special interests such as the welfare of the blind and they claim that it was the Lions who introduced the idea of a white cane for identification of the blind. Another focus is youth activities especially for teenagers. The core objective of their activities is to give something back to their local community.

The Littleborough club started in 1984 because a member of the Heywood club came to live here. By 1985 it had advanced enough to tell Littleborough it existed and in the tradition of 'friendly societies' since the 18th century found its initial hospitality in the local pubs, notably the 'Queens' and the 'Fish'. By 1986 it had qualified for its Charter and like so many voluntary societies it may be short on numbers but at any time it is driven by a group of dedicated volunteers, who can be identified by their red sweaters at many of our community events. They have a president and their motto is 'we serve' which perhaps says everything.

Townswomen's Guild

In 1968 councillor Alice Holden organised a public meeting for local women interested in forming a Littleborough branch of this national organisation. There was strong support and she was elected president, to be followed some years later by councillor Rosemary Giffin. Both were elected during the period when Littleborough was an Urban District Council. Meetings were weekly and well attended despite the lack of any settled place to meet. A prefabricated building in the grounds of the local primary school was used until the Coach House was completed, when the group transferred there.

The brief of the guild covers a broad spectrum of issues with special concern for women but memorable highlights include the mini-pageant 'Women through the Ages' to celebrate H.M. the Queen's Silver Jubilee which was performed in several local venues and the guild's 30th Birthday Party in May 1998. This took the form of an Edwardian Music Hall, attended by members of other guilds. Over 90 members were present including twelve founder members and all wore Edwardian dress

Littleborough Historical and Archaeological Society

This society was formed from two existing local societies in 1972 and under the leadership of one of its founder members, the late Alan Luke BSc. Grad IMA, became a registered charity, a member of the North West Museums Service and achieved the accolade of provisional registration with the Museums and Galleries Commission. It has over 70 members who carry out its remit to extend education opportunities to the public by collecting, preserving and presenting for viewing and research, documentary and photographic archives, archaeological artefacts and reports. Its prized possessions include the comprehensive documentary collection, some of which dates back to the 12th century, the Littleborough Hoard of Roman coins found in Ealees valley and the archaeological collection which is reputed to be one of the best catalogued, in private hands, in the country. The society has produced a variety of publications and has many acknowledgements for providing information and co-operating in the production of many others.

The Society has two millennium objectives. Firstly they plan to establish a Local History Workshop and Archaeological Interpretation Centre where historians, local schools and the public at large can research the archives. Secondly they plan to extend the Society's archaeological investigation of the area, particularly of the Bronze Age settlement in the Piethorn valley which has already yielded fascinating evidence and may well prove to have national importance.

On a wider scale in Littleborough, the canal and Hollingworth Lake offer exciting possibilities in the leisure area.

Canal Development

It was the canal that first brought cheap coal and raw materials into Littleborough followed by the railway and road improvements. Linked to these developments we have traced the history of the industry and housing which came to fill our valleys and lowland areas with industry and people. As the railways and roads developed the canal finally closed. Recently a £12 million grant has been offered from Lottery Funds to reopen the Canal between Lancashire and Yorkshire. The rationale is primarily to support a drive to revitalise the South Pennine area with the re-introduction of active barge traffic for profit but mainly leisure, to offer a fine facility for fisherman and walkers and to create an area for nature observation and conservation. It would also lend support to many activities such as the development of bridleways, Hollingworth Lake Country Park and various leisure projects that can exploit the existence of a working canal facility locally.

In 1996-7 the Rochdale Canal Trust finally secured a commitment to funding from the Millennium Commission and English Partnerships for the full restoration of the canal. A total of £22.7 million was made available to complete the project by the year 2001. The agreement was for a phased restoration. The first phase required designs and bills of quantities for removing all the blockages on the canal. That phase was due to finish in March 1999 and involved Oldham, Rochdale and Manchester authorities. It was designed to demonstrate that the original bid was realistic and that it could finish on time. Phase Two demanded the rapid removal of eight blockages on the canal in 1999. Locally the major and visible blockage is behind the railway station, at the end

On the Rochdale Canal.

of Canal Street, where the road veers left over a bridge crossing the line of the canal (which runs through an large pipe underneath). In the Trust structure, Oldham is the lead Authority. It was started with two full-time employees, two co-ordinators and secondees from the Rochdale and Oldham authorities who work with project teams in their own areas.

As with other major millennium schemes there have been many concerns about the delays and difficulties which seem characteristic of this kind of funding. The wider scheme, when achieved, will result in a fully working canal and a major regeneration scheme at the Failsworth centre near Oldham.

Hollingworth Lake

This is a reservoir, built initially to supply water to the lower section of the Rochdale Canal, and would do so again if the canal is re-opened.

Earlier we traced the growth of leisure activities and holidays based on the area which prospered for sixty years but died in the early 20th century. Many years later a licence was issued allowing development of the area. The popularity of Hollingworth Lake grew steadily until in 1971, prompted by Littleborough Civic Trust, a working party was set up to consider the future. The working party included Lancashire County Council, Rochdale MBC, Littleborough and Milnrow UDC's and the West Pennine Water Board. After anxious negotiations they found a way to designate the area as a Country Park. From a combination of Greater Manchester council, Rochdale council and various other agencies and local sources enough money was realised to create an appropriate environment. This included adequate accommodation for cars, managing traffic, providing services, clearing and sterilising a domestic rubbish dump, creating

336

good fencing and providing an information centre with full facilities. Today there is an information centre, car parks, display areas, catering facilities, a conference and film room and many other services such as a water activity centre.

The lake continues to support fishing, sailing, rowing, wind surfing and boat trips; around the edges are toilet facilities, cafes, pubs, shops, camping grounds, rural walks and direct access to the Pennines. The important nature reserve at the marshy eastern end of the lake is notable. There is a bird hide to allow observation of the many species of bird which make either permanent use of the area, or visit, during annual migrations. Higher up, the Pennine Way comes down from Scotland on its way to Edale, hang gliders swoop and rise, people ride their horses along the bridle-ways and old pack horse routes and lower down canoes can be seen next to barges on the Rochdale Canal.

Parks need care and supervision and from modest beginnings in 1974 the staff rapidly escalated to five and has grown further as more facilities are made available. At the outset there were some 30,000 visitors annually which has grown to 130,000 or more today.

In 1988 the local people were surprised to be reminded that Hollingworth is a reservoir not a lake and by law must be inspected and repaired. Some looked at the cost and contemplated leaving it empty but happily other logic prevailed; a consortium of authorities backed by European and local money covered the costs. The restored lake is a metre lower which allowed the construction of the promenade between the Fisherman's Inn and the boat houses and re-organisation of sluices so that the eastern end bird reserve never dries out. The water activity centre is an initiative developed by Rochdale M.B.C. and it continues to develop courses in sailing, canoeing, rowing and sailboarding.

There are people everywhere in the Country Park, on mountain bikes, in boats and cars or on foot. The whole area is a magnet for people and their pleasure is obvious; it also represents a growing problem in terms of access, which will be a challenge needing a solution early in the 21st century. It is often forgotten that it was only at the creation of the country park that people were prohibited from driving all round the lake and another challenge, not yet solved, is to complete a satisfactory foot path to allow pedestrians to avoid the traffic hazards of the road to Rakewood.

The potential for all these leisure activities is partly due to the opening of the M62 motorway which relieved Littleborough of what had become a choking degree of through traffic, which frequently caused gridlock at peak traffic hours in the 1950s. An evening return to Littleborough from Manchester in winter could routinely take 1½ hours or more depending on the weather. If the Hollingworth Lake Park is to grow and service more and more people, there will be a real challenge to adequately handle the traffic problems that further growth will create.

Art and Culture

Littleborough lies in an area of considerable natural beauty, set on the edge of a major urban complex. In an era of modest prosperity it is perhaps not surprising that there is a renewed interest in the arts. The Coach House provides a pleasant setting for regular exhibitions ranging from crafts to formal paintings and sculpture.

We are fortunate to have a few able artists working in the area, leading the way and encouraging everyone. These include Walter Kershaw, Stuart Dawson and Geoff Butterworth.

On the canal looking toward Lightowlers.

Summary

A picture emerges of restored loom houses, rescued 17th and 18th century cottages, highly technical industries in spruced up mills, and practical uses emerging for the remaining large houses in the area. Stubley Hall is a restaurant, the New Hall is divided into dwellings, Town House is divided into flats. There is also an increasing respect for the values represented by our peat-covered upland areas. In addition there is the identification and preservation of the remaining buildings and areas that have real historical interest.

When the clean air acts freed us from the pervading pollution, plants began to grow again, mosses and lichens to re-establish themselves, and when we cleaned 150 years of grime off the local gritstone we found it was often 'golden' in colour. Suddenly nature seemed to be acting on our side and as site after site has been cleaned up, we can start to appreciate how attractive and interesting the area, in which we are lucky enough to live, actually is.

Epilogue to the Littleborough Story

The area does not qualify to be classified as 'rural' nor does it fit easily into any concept of urban regeneration. From the 1970s onwards there has been a conscious attempt to redefine a Pennine Identity and find a collective word to describe people who live in Littleborough. Local societies, environmental groups and individuals have all described the undeniable feeling of community and difference from other areas, but it is a complex topic. One factor was so keenly felt that it is worthy of a special mention.

There was a local feeling of being ignored by 'the powers that be' in the Rochdale Town Hall, a feeling heightened following the local government reorganisation in 1974. The Urban District Council structure was replaced and the new decision making process was perceived as distant and not taking much account of local needs. To address this problem four structures called 'townships' were created within the Rochdale Metropolitan Borough Council and each was given significant authority and some budget. Littleborough along with Wardle and Milnrow became the Pennine township. A later decision was made to appoint a Town Manager to each area with a remit to increase local decision making and make Council processes more accessible.

It will take years to establish whether or not the new township structure is robust enough to survive but some signs are good. The meetings are lively and well attended when there is a real issue. The allocation of modest sums of money for local distribution has had total acceptance. It may need further modification, but certainly has made a real reduction in the feeling that 'they don't care about us'.

Regeneration of the Littleborough area

An early initiative by the new Township Manager in Littleborough was the organisation of a consultation day, which was a valuable oppportunity to get comment from Littleborough people in a forum called 'Pennines, Past, Present, and Future'. The level of interest is shown by the fact that some 100 people attended on a sunny Saturday and worked all day.

The first part of the day was designed to share history and experience together, by chronicling changes both good and bad. The 'past' started from 1950 and the 'future' looked to perhaps 2010. The objective was to find common ground and suggest priorities for a regeneration strategy - the words suggest the need for improvement and very likely a current decline from some earlier standards. In practice, a theme that ran through much of the reminiscence was the loss of local provision. A summary of this exercise follows:

Generally, few questioned that Littleborough was a good place to live.

The 1950s emerged as a time which was remembered as one of richness of local facilities such as a market, a local newspaper, good public transport, active church and community based events, local administration, local job opportunities together with available apprenticeships in cotton and wool, engineering, mining and service industries. There were senior schools controlled locally, police were visible and effective and public facilities generally were well maintained. There was a variety of sport and leisure activity to cover most tastes. (*In each of the periods considered after this time, it saves space to say, few, if any, thought there had been anything but a decline in all these categories.*)

The 1960s there was still a village character in the 1960s, new house building was mainly under authority control and local administration was split between the U.D.C. and the Lancashire County Council. Some jobs still existed in agriculture and a variety of apprenticeships were still available for young people.

The 1970s were characterised as relatively traffic free with wide provision for children, adequate space, more local shops and common areas and a cleaner environment.

The 1980s highlighted the continued existence of a local High School, the positive development of the Hollingworth Lake Country Park and the good quality of the local libraries. Council houses were being sold to private buyers, new houses were springing up in every open space and there was a growth in numbers of children and (retrospectively?) no one seemed to be preparing for their future needs. The medical and transport structures were still in place and satisfactory.

In the 1990s they were aware of many problems. More people, more cars and lorries, more houses, more dogs, fewer local jobs, poor leisure facilities, loss of shops, schools and churches. Loss of policing, decline in hospital care, loss of many of our old local buildings such as the Central School and a loss of a sense of community. Some modest positive areas were identified.

An analysis of the general 'strengths and weaknesses' of our area was drawn up, as a basis for suggesting improvements followed by a lively session where everyone had the chance to state their preference, rating for projects in short, medium and long term brackets.

The most important issues for immediate attention in the view of the attenders at the forum were:

1. Provision of a leisure centre and swimming pool
2. Improved public transport
3. More provision for young people
4. Generation of more employment opportunities locally with an accent on leisure and tourism.
5. Restriction on any further house building.

The exercise was very successful, but it was agreed at the beginning that it was not a suitable forum to discuss key issues such as: how could change be achieved and what are the political or social weaknesses that might prevent it ?

The results of the day were turned into a report and submitted to an Officer Regeneration Panel for the Pennine Township. This group was given the brief to consider and locally implement, within the overall strategy of the Authority, suggestions from the community.

The outcome of this part of our story cannot be forecast in this book. If the original material has been retained and filed, despite all its limitations, it remains an interesting summary by Littleborough people of their life over the last sixty to seventy years and a marvellous platform from which someone might pick up the Littleborough story and bring it up to date say, one hundred years from now.

Whatever the outcome of the future consultations and plans, once again the wheel turns and nearly every remaining farm and barn in the upland areas is being converted into a desirable home for someone, a situation that last existed some 200 years ago. All eyes are turned to the development of the facilities in the township with a growing concern that we build in new concepts like 'sustainability' in everything we do.

You might even imagine Gordon Harvey and Fred Jackson chuckling to each other in old age (they did end up friends) as they look down on Littleborough where they went along our roads sticking in acorns in every spare plot of land. They might well say to each other:

'it is good that these present people still care about much the same things as we did, but if they find our title of 'The Beautiful Littleborough Society' rather quaint, what will the people 200 years on think about long words like environmental sustainability!'

Royal Oak
Inn

Old
Quarry

Air Shaft

HOLME HOUSE ST.

553
12·284

Summit

(555
·674

554
574
578

556
7·155

Old Clay

Mount Gilead
Church
U. Meth.

552
5·496

Spring

578

538
1·380

Reservoir

BM.701·5

Old Quarry

868

548
1·005

Moor Road
547
·211

546
1·860

Sunday School
B.M.636·7

542
634

Rosr.

540
·512

539
1·852

B.M.574·7

537
2·092

536
5·298

B.M.577·8

534
6·212

545
·999

Stansfield Hall
School

·587

Sladen
Wood
Ho.

569

569

Summit
Sanitary Ware Works

543
·294

Paul Row
541
·503

F.P.

Sladen
Wood
Mill
(Cotton)

Chy.

535
1·402

Tank

rook

Old Quarries
494
2·293

563

Chy.

498
5·431

Reservoir

Punchbowl
Bridge
Basin
Wharf

558

Summit
Quarries
499
6·808

493
12·427

Rock Nook

495
3·065

Cranes

496
·661

555

497
1·386

*From the Ordnance
Survey, 1910.*

S.P.

548

549

Weir

500
4·030

School

Sladen Terrace

Calderbrook
Terrace

492
2·169

484
1·130

541

482
5·029

483
·899

Rock Nook Mill
(Cotton)

475
2·696

BIBLIOGRAPHY

and Further Reading List

Introduction
Bagley, J. (1976), *A History of Lancashire*, Phillimore & Co Ltd, London & Chichester.
Fishwick, H. *A History of Lancashire,* Elliot Stock, 62 Paternoster Row, London.

Chapter One
Stephens, W.B. (1977), *Teaching Local History*, Manchester University Press.

Chapter Two
Barnes, Bernard. *Men and the Changing Landscape,* Liverpool University Press.
Collier. (1985), *Collier's Field Archaeology of Great Britain.*
Heywood & Jennings. (1996), *A History of Todmorden*, Smith Settle.
Pitts and Roberts. (1997), *Fairweather Eden*, Century.
Thornber, Titus. *The History of the Parish of Cliviger.*

Chapter Three
Beresford, Ellis. (1993), *Celt and Saxon*, Constable, London.
Hartley and Fitts. (1988), *The Brigantes,* Alan Sutton.
James, Simon. (1999), *Celts*, British Museum Press.

Chapter Four
Fishwick, H. (1889), *The History of the Parish of Rochdale*, James Clegg, London.
Hartley and Fitts. (1988), *The Brigantes,* Alan Sutton.
Maxim, James L. (1965), *A Lancashire Lion*, Authors Estate, Leeds.
  (a history of transport lines developed to cross Blackstone Edge and an assessment
  of the claim that the earliest is a Roman road)
Clayton, Peter. (1980), *A Companion to Roman Britain*, Omega Books.
Rivet & Smith. (1981),*The Place Names of Roman Britain,* Batsford.
Travis, John. (1890), *Historical & Personal Notes upon the Village of Littleborough,*
  R Chambers, Cheapside.

Chapter Five
Higham, Nick. (1992), *Rome, Britain and the Anglo Saxons,* Seaby.

Chapter Six
Collier, J. (1746), *A View of the Lancashire Dialect.*, Rochdale.
Ekwall, E. (1922), *Place Names of Lancashire.*
Fothergill, Jessie. (1900), *Healey,* Macmillan and Co, London.
March, H. C. (1880), *East Lancashire Nomenclature.*
McArthur, T. (1992), The Oxford Companion to the English Language,
  Oxford University Press.

Chapter Seven
Belloc, Hilaire. *Warfare in England.*
Colligan, A.W. (1974), *The Village Church*, Upjohn and Bottomley, Littleborough.
Fishwick, H. (1889), *The History of the Parish of Rochdale*, James Clegg, London.
Heape, Richard. (1926), *Inscribed and Dated Stones and Sundials in and adjoining the ancient Parish of Rochdale*, Cambridge University Press, privately printed.
Heywood & Jennings. (1996), *A History of Todmorden*, Smith Settle.
Hinde, T.(ed) *The Domesday Book - England's Heritage, Then and Now*, Tiger Books International, London.
Milne, Bury & Lewis, Solicitors. (1945),*The Pyke House Estate, Littleborough & Milnrow*, Auctioneers, Morley Street, Manchester.
Oakley, Rev. G. R. (1923), *In Olden Days, Lancashire Legends: Rochdale and Neighbourhood,* 2nd Ed. Edwards & Bryning Ltd, Rochdale.
The Palatine Notebook.
(1911-12) *Proceedings of Chetham Society*, Detail of Hundersfeld, Rochdale Library, Local Study Department, (No. 841) R80-73326.
Rochdale Observer. (1920s), *Old Buildings Round Rochdale*, Local Studies Library, (Scrap Book of Rochdale. Fine photographs of many of the old houses around Littleborough. The text is written with the pseudonym 'the Pilgrim' and is romantic rather than informative).
(1626), *Survey of the Manor of Rochdale*, Rochdale Library, Local studies.

Chapter Eight
Colligan, A.W. (1975), *Living Still (R.C.Church)*, Privately published.
Colligan, A.W. (1974), *The Village Church,* Upjohn and Bottomley, Littleborough.
Heywood & Jennings. (1996), *A History of Todmorden*, Smith Settle.
Wright, C. (1986), *Britain and Ireland (A Children's History)*, Kingfisher Books, London.

Chapter Nine
Aiken, John, (1878-1880), *Discovery of an ancient iron mine in Cliviger,* Trans. Manchester Geo. Soc.
Colligan, A.W. (1974), *The Village Church,* Upjohn & Bottomley, Littleborough.
Heape, Richard, (1926), *Inscribed & Dated Stones and Sundials, in and adjoining the ancient Parish of Rochdale,* Cambridge University Press, Private publication.
Heywood & Jennings. (1996), *A History of Todmorden*, Smith Settle.
Prince, W. F. *Inscribed and Dated Stones of some old Lancashire Houses,* Private Booklet.
Thornber, Titus, (1993), *A pre-industrial blast furnace,* The Rieve Edge Press, Burnley.

Chapter Ten
Colligan, A.W. (1974), *The Village Church,* Upjohn and Bottomley, Littleborough.
Colligan, A.W. (1977), *Non-conformist Chapels in Littleborough,* Private printing, G. Kelsall.
Colligan, A.W. (1977), *The Weighver's Seaport,* G. Kelsall, Littleborough.
Heywood & Jennings. (1996), *A History of Todmorden*, Smith Settle.
Heape, Richard, (1926), *Inscribed and Dated Stones and Sundials in and adjoining the ancient Parish of Rochdale*, Cambridge University Press, privately printed.
Parry, Keith. (1980), *Trans-Pennine Heritage*, David & Charles, London.

Rose, M. B. (1996), *The Lancashire Cotton Industry*, Lancashire County Books, Preston.
Wright, C. (1986), *Britain and Ireland (A Children's History)*, Kingfisher Books, London.

Chapter 11
Kershaw, J. (Oct 97 & Mar 98), *A history of the water supply to the Rochdale Canal,*
  Rochdale Canal Soc. Newsletters, Private publication.
Macdonald, M. (1974), *World from Rough Stones*, Hodder & Stoughton.
Travis, John. (1890), *Historical and Personal notes upon the Village of Littleborough*,
  R Chambers, Cheapside.

Chapter 12
Colligan, A.W. (1977), *The Weighver's Seaport*, G Kelsall, Littleborough.
Fothergill, Jessie. (1900), *Healey*, Macmillan and Co, London.
Parry, Keith. (1985), *Survivor! The Summit Tunnel*, privately printed, Littleborough.
Ware, Michael, E. *Britain's Lost Waterways Vol 1*, Moorland Publishing.

Chapter 13
(Friday, 29 August, 1997), *150 Years of Fothergill's*, Express, Rochdale, p14. Local
  Studies Library.
Law, B.R. (1995), *Fielden Brothers, Todmorden: The rise to Prominence 1782 - 1832* Trans.
  Halifax Antiqu. Soc. Vol.3.
Law, B.R. (1995), *Fieldens of Todmorden, A Nineteenth Century Business Dynasty,*
  G Kelsall, Littleborough.

Chapter 14
Cryer & Pearson. (1998), *May Newsletter, Brookfield & Albion mills,* Littleborough Hist.
  & Arch. Society, Private publication.
Rose, M.B. (1996), *The Lancashire Cotton Industry*, Lancashire County Books, Preston.

Chapter 15
Colligan, A.W. (1974), *The Village Church*, Upjohn and Bottomley, Littleborough.
Colligan, A.W. (1977), *The Weighvers Seaport*, G Kelsall, Littleborough.
Colligan, A.W. (1980), *Littleborough Cricket Club*, privately printed.
Fishwick, H. (1889), *The History of the Parish of Rochdale*, James Clegg, London.
Fothergill, Jessie. (1900), *Healey*, Macmillan and Co, London.
Heywood and Jennings, (1996), *A History of Todmorden*, Smith Settle.
Luke, Alan. (1984), *A History of Littleborough Pubs*, privately published, Littleborough.
Macdonald, M. (1974), *World from Rough Stones*, Hodder and Stoughton, London.
Newman, R. (1996), *The Archaeology of Lancashire*, Kent Valley Colour Printers, Kendal.
Waugh, E. *Poems*.
Travis, John. (1890), *Historical and Personal Notes upon the Village of Littleborough*,
  R Chambers, Cheapside.

Chapter 16
Church Members. (1970), *Calderbrook St James* (Centenary Book), Bilford Publications
  & Co Ltd, Chorley.

Colligan, A.W. (1977), *Non-Conformist Chapels in Littleborough, Lancashire,* Private printing, G Kelsall.

Colligan, A.W. (1974), *The Village Church,* Upjohn and Bottomley, Littleborough.

Colligan, A.W. (1975), *Living Still (R.C.Church),* privately published.

Gowland, D.A. (1979), *Methodist Secessions.* Chethams Society.

Hall, G. (1995), *The Parish Church of Dearnley, St Andrew. The first 100 years,* private publication, St Andrew's Church, Dearnley.

Heywood and Jennings. (1996), *A History of Todmorden,* Smith Settle.

Jackson, Joanne. (1997), *The effect of immigration on Littleborough 1850 - 1900,* Privately published.

Lindsey, J. (circa 1980), *A History of Fothergill and Harvey,* Private Publication.

Oakley, Rev. G. R. (1923), *In Olden Days, Lancashire Legends: Rochdale and Neighbourhood,* 2nd Ed. Edwards & Bryning Ltd. Rochdale.

Chapter 17

Colligan, A.W. (1977), *The Weighver's Seaport,* G Kelsall, Littleborough.

Colligan, A.W. (1980), *Littleborough Cricket Club,* privately published.

Directory of 1879, Rochdale Radcliffe & District, Macdonald.

Glasier, K.B. (1924), *Enid Stacy,* A commemorative service programme.

Greenhill Trustees. (1950), *Greenhill Centenary Celebrations,* Edwards & Bryning Ltd, Rochdale.

Kelsall, G. & Parry, K. (1981), *Looking back at Littleborough,* G. Kelsall, Littleborough.

Lancashire Education Committee. (1953), *Littleborough Central School, 1903-1953,* Observer Office, Rochdale.

Rochdale M.B.C. (1986), *Davenports 1872 Illustrated Holllingworth Lake Guide (facsimile).*

Tuckett, A. (1980-8), *Enid Stacy,* Bulletin issue 7. North West Labour History Society.

Turnbull, J. & Southern, J. (1955), *More than Just a Shop; Co-op History,* Lancashire County Books.

Chapter 18

Church Trustees. (1950), *Greenhill Centenary Celebrations,* Edwards & Bryning, Rochdale.

Colligan, A.W. (1974), *The Village Church,* Upjohn and Bottomley Ltd, Littleborough.

Littleborough Traders Association, (1932 1933 1934), *Littleborough Shopping Week Guide.*

Chapter 19

Lancashire Education Committee. (1953), *Littleborough Central School (1903 - 1953),* Observer Office, Rochdale.

Lord, C. (1997), *Old Postcards of Littleborough & Hollingworth Lake,* Christopher Lord Design.

Chapter 20

Cole, J. (1988), *Rochdale Revisited - A Town and its People.* G Kelsall, Littleborough.

Colligan, A.W. (1977), *Non-Conformist Chapels in Littleborough: Lancashire,* Private printing, G Kelsall.

Colligan, A.W. (1975), *Living Still,* (R.C. Church), Privately published.

Littleborough Urban District Council. (circa 1956), *Littleborough, Official Guide and Industrial Handbook,,* Burrow & Co.Ltd., Cheltenham and London.

Chapter 21

Pennines Township, R.M.B.C. (1997), *Pennines Past, Present & Future,* Pennines Township.

Parry, Keith. (1980), *Trans Pennine Heritage,* David & Charles, London.

Turnbull, J. & Southern, J. (1995), *More than Just a Shop, Co-op History,*
    Lancashire County Books.

Colligan, A.W. (1998), *The Weighver's Seaport,* G Kelsall, Littleborough.

Luke, Alan. (1984), *A History of Littleborough Pubs,* Privately published, Littleborough.

Gardiner, J. & Wenborn, N. (1995), *The History Today, Companion to British History,*
    The Bath Press.

The Co-operative Footware Department, Hare Hill Road, around 1920. Shopping habits have changed and Littleborough no longer has a shoe shop. The two men in the photograph are standing in front of what is now the entrance to the Co-op 'Late Shop'.

Mrs Iris Ahmad
Marilyn & Jeff Aldred
Mrs G. Allely
Erica & Roy Allen
Peter Alletson
Alltex Limited
Mrs Joan Angus
Joseph & Monica Angus
T. R. Armistead
D.B. Armistead
Gary Ashton
Raymond Ashton
Mrs M Ashworth
Jennie D. Ashworth
Peter Aspinall
Mr & Mrs G Backhouse
Mrs Mavis Backhouse
Archie Slater Bamford
Anthony Bancroft & Wendy Jackson
Ron & Jean Bannister
John P. Barker
Mr E Barnes
M.R.Barrow
A.S.Barrow
Mr & Mrs A Basnett and
    Mr & Mrs M Bywater
Mr. Gordon Batty
Keith Paul Bell, Angela Bell &
    Sophie Victoria Bell
Mai Bentley & Mick Chatham
Lynn & David Beswick
Mark & Paula Billington
Esme Booth
Norton & Margaret Booth
Mr & Mrs G. Bouchier
Annie Bracken
A.C. Bradley
Rosamund Brett
John Mark Brierley
Marie Briggs
Bernard Briggs
Audrey & William Briggs
Jeff Brookes
Rod Broome
William C Burrill
A. M. Burrill
Martin Burrill
David Burrill
Barbara Bush
Miss Anne Butterworth
Mrs Sadie Butterworth
John & Lynn Butterworth
Gladys Butterworth

Geoff Butterworth
Jack Izat Butterworth
Alan, Deirdre & Amanda Butterworth
Stan & Ann Butterworth
Mary Cairns
Vivienne and Ray Calderbank
Alex & Enid Calvert
Mr J Campbell
Elizabeth Canavan
N. Chadwick
Pat Chadwick
Mrs M.P. Chadwick
Bryan Chidgey
The Chippendales
Mrs. R.D. Chun
Cindy
Pauline Clark
Sebastian J.B. Clegg
Norman and Molly Clegg
Mr A.M. Clegg
Malcolm Clegg
Richard N B Clegg
Bernice Clifton
David and Dorothy Clough
Mrs G Cockayne
John & Sue Cole
Lucianne Collier
Gloria & Bill Collin
Hartley Keith Collins
Mr. D.J. Cork
Patrick Corrigan
Rachel Costello
L. M. Coulston
Graham & Susan Coward
Tony Cox
Rachael Debra Cox & Mark Robert Cox
Christina K. Cranston B.A. (Hons)
Stuart Cronshaw
Matthew Jon Cropper
Rachel Elizabeth Cropper
Barry Cropper JP
Val Crossley
Ronald William Cryer
Trevor Cryer
John & Marjorie Cummings
Clive H. Cunnah
Paul Davenport
Mr C Davenport
Dr & Mrs J.M. Dawson
Alfred M Day
Sheila Dearden
S & L Devereux
Frances Done

Russell Dixon, Martin J. Flanagan &
   Joseph P. Flanagan
David & Barbara Dop
K.T. and C. Douglas
P & P.M. Dunwell
Nora & Billy Durham
Peter J. Eddison
Ruth Edwards
Charlotte Edwards
Mr P G Elgey
Brian G Emerson
Councillor Peter Evans
J Fielden
Peter Hugh Fisher
Mrs B. Fletcher
Donald & Susan Fletcher
Richard A. Fletcher
Mr R. Foizey
Frank Ford
Mrs R.E. Foster
David Foster & Christine Mills
Marc R. & Georgina C. Foster
Austin Freeman
David M. Frost & M. Mary Frost
Ron & Rhona Fuller
Marjorie Gabbott
Miss M Gadsby
Christine & Bryan Garvey
Leo Garvey
Kevin Garvin
Frank Garvin
Philip Gibson
Rosemary Giffin
Mr M. Giles
Mrs J Gill
Donald Gillyett
Mr Andrew Gornall
Alan & Anne Gorton
Kevin Green
Bernard Green
Kenneth and Beryl Greenwood
Joan and Arthur Greenwood
Carole Greenwood
John Griffiths
Derek & Heather Gudgeon
Derek Guest
George and Cath Hallsworth
Dave and Sacha Halstead
Terry Halstead
Kevin & Madeleine Hardman
Geraldine Harkness
Margaret & John Harlow
Mrs Connie Harman (née Bolam)
Jim and Peggy Harrison
Liz & Norman Harrison

B.S. Hartley
M & C Haughton
Jean Hawkard
J. Martin Hawkard
John C Hawkins
Kevin,Kath, Catherine & David Hawkins
T. Hawkrigg
Harry & Norah Hawksworth
Neil S Hemingway
Margaret Hetherington
Richard Hetherington
Allan Hetherington
James Hey (The last Workhouse Master of
   Hollingworth 1823 - 1874)
Philip Heys
Norman Higham
Ms B. Highley
Joan and Leslie Higson
Henry Hiley
Dorothy Hinchliffe
Holy Trinity C.E. School
Mr J.H. Hollinrake & Mr R Wadsworth
Allen Holt
G.A. Hopcroft
Maurice & Margie Hopkins
   12th September 1953
Annie & Raymond Hopkinson
Maurice Hopkinson, Betty Manuell,
   Harriett & Derek Crabtree
Harry & Hazel Howard
George & Audrey Howarth
Pat & Arthur Howarth
Mrs B. Howe
Penelope & Theodore Hubbard
Anne Hudson
Michael Hughes & June Cropper
Miss B Hurrey
Peter Hurst
Dorothy Hurst
Arthur & Pat Hutchinson
Jean Iliff
Mollie Ireland & Sydney Knight
Mrs Sylvia Irvine
Rob & Sue Isherwood
Jackie & Steve
Bernard Jackson
C & L Jackson
Nicholas E. Jackson
Barbara, Peter and Joanne L. Jackson
Eric Jackson
Margaret Ann Jameson
Dorothy Jay
Rita & Eric Jefferson
Derek & Lyn Jefferson
Chris Jepson-Brown

Rita Kay
Emma Kay
Jennifer R. Kay
Cathryn E. Kay
John & Lis Kay
Janis Elizabeth Kelly
David John Kelly
Helen & Ben Kelsall
Lynne & George Kelsall
Dilys & Derek Kershaw
John & Jill Kershaw
Derrick Kershaw
To my Daughter Kirsty
Douglas Lahmers & Beatrice Lang
B.M. Lake
Roy and Agnes Latchem
Rory Patrick Lavin
Roz Lawson
Peter Lawson
Anne C. Lawson
Alan Lawson
Malcolm Leach
Michael Lilley
Littleborough Old Peoples Welfare Association
Littleborough Historical &
    Archaeological Society
Mary Livesey
Linda & Stephen Lockett
David & Veronica Logan
Mr & Mrs K. Longley
Annette Lord, Rochdale Observer
Doreen & Jack Lord
Pauline Lord
H & D Lord
Miss. Edith Lord
Thomas H. Lord
John Lord
Dorothy Lownds
A Lundy
Judith Anne Manock, née Holden,
    Peter Manock.
Allan Marshall
P. R. Marshall
B. Marshall
J. Marshall
Mrs N. Martin
Stanley Martin
Mary, Howard & Victoria Matthew
Mary,Cedric,Victoria & Howard Matthew
Christopher McGawley, Helen McGawley &
    Ellie-Morgan McGawley
Mr & Mrs J McGeoch
David & Sylvia McNamee
Thelma & Donald McNamee
Mr & Mrs J. Melia

Brian Middleton
Mrs E. A. Miller
Jame Thomas Mills
Marjorie J Mitchell
Mrs E Morrey
Gerry Morriss
Jenny Moss
Colin Moss
Christopher Moss
Brian & Velma Mottershead
Maggie Muir
T.C. Mumford
Michael & Brenda Murphy
Joan Murray née Fletcher
To a very special Nan
Patricia & James Nedderman
A J Nicholls
L & B Nield
Nuttall Family
Mr John O'Brien & Mrs Brenda O'Brien
Shannon Sky O'Callaghan
J & P O'Connell
David O'Neill
Mrs Sandra Owen
Geoffrey Palmer
Susan Park & Graham Park
Mr John S. Parker
Mr J Parker & Mrs M A Parker
J.P. Partington
John, Pamela & Matthew Paterson
Howard Pearson
Mark Pearson
Miss R Pearson
Pennine Winemakers Guild
Pennines Township Manager
Jack & Jessie Percival
Franklin Pickering
Richard J Pickis
Donald & Betty Pickis
Clive, Katryna, Richard & Jennifer Piggott
Sheila & Nigel Pilling
Stephen Pinnington & Yvonne Mynett
Jack & Christina Pollard
Graham Pollard
A. Anne Pomfret
Helen Powis
Douglas Pride
Mrs H Priest
Michael & Lynne Priestley
Desmond & Doreen Pugh
Thomas Quine
To my Daughter: Rachel
Vicky & Bill Radburn
L. Ratcliffe
Ian Ratcliffe

Derick & Maureen Rawlinson
Michelle L. Reckless
Albert & Jack Renfrey
Trevor James Rigby
James Rigby
Mr & Mrs R. Rigg
Edna Rigg
Mrs S Rigg
Hilda Riley
Margaret and Darren Ripley
Mr S E Rosbotham
Sheila Roebuck
Mr K Rosbotham
Mr & Mrs K Rose
Ben Rothwell
B & G Rothwell
C.B. Rowell
Pat Sanchez
Caroline & Andy Schlegel
Judith Schofield
S.A. & M. Schofield
James T Schofield
Mr & Mrs F Scholes
John Schoor
Hannah Jane Scott
John Shackleton
Mr David M Sharp
P. G. Sharrocks
Colin Shaw
Peter M. Shrigley
Fred Simpson
Mr & Mrs E. Smith
Gloria Smith
Ellen Smith
Michael A. Smith
Iain Spencer Gerrard & Elaine Gerrard
Mrs A.E. Spencer
Brian & Eileen Stafford
Miss B Stamp
Zelda M. Stanway - née Parker (Smithy Nook)
Elaine & Glenn Stott
Arthur Stott 1920-1981
Kathleen Stott
Neville and Doreen Stott
Rae Street
Alan & Betty Street
Mr & Mrs J. Sutcliffe
Alan Swain
Brian & Nella Tattersall
Mrs Jill Tattersall
Kathryn & Ian Taylor
R Taylor
Kenneth Taylor
Maureen Taylor
A.G. & F.A. Taylor

Geoffrey L. Taylor
Hilary L. Taylor
Antony W. Taylor
Keith & Margaret Thompson
Harry & Janet Townsend
Robert Toy
James Trainor & Robert Kennedy Trainor
Jim Trainor & April Kennedy
Jack Trickett
Malcolm & Sylvia Trickett
Mark Tweddle & Justina Tweddle
William Hugh Tweddle &
    Norma Annie Tweddle
Jeffrey & Paulette Nicole Varnom
Tom & Gloria Warburton
Eric Ward
John Wareing
Lynda Wass
Martin & Irene Watts
Ray Wellens
Mollie Whitaker
Sylvia White
Mrs Barbara Whittaker
Mrs Olive Whittall
Olive Whittall
Melvyn Wight
Keith & Pauline Wilbraham
Sylvia Wild
Mrs Joan Wild
Mavis Wilkinson
Chris Wilkinson
Jeremy Wilkinson
Peter Wilkinson
Brian Wilkinson
Mrs B Wilkinson
Polly & David Williams
Mrs Mary E. Williams
Mr & Mrs G.N. Williamson
Joyce F. Wilson
G Wilson
Rodney Wilson
Peter Wood
Andrew Wood
Frank Wood
Betty Wood
Max and Anitra Woolfenden
John and Susan Worthy
David & Jean Wright
M. Susan Wright
Edward and Pauline Wroe
Helen & David Wyatt
Mrs E Yearsley

ALLTEX LTD
Textile Dyers & Finishers

Sladen Mill, Halifax Road
Littleborough OL15 0LB

Tel: 01706 377374
Fax: 01706 377256

DEL LAGO RISTORANTE
(Italian Restaurant)

43 Lake Bank, Hollingworth Lake
Littleborough

Tel: 01706 376587

Established 1986

BARCLAYS BANK PLC
Littleborough Branch

Church Street, Littleborough

Tel: 01706 702400

Many years of Banking Services to the
Littleborough community

EDGE LEIGH CARE CENTRE

Halifax Road, Littleborough

Tel: 01706 378938

The quality, homely care centre
catering for your individual needs

RODNEY BARROW
Chartered Secretary

Tel: 01706 379858

Advice and Services to Business

THE FALCON INN

18-20 Church Street, Littleborough
OL15 9AA

Tel: 01706 378640

Over 300 years of service to
Littleborough since 1657

JOHN COLLIER
Consultancy Services

Tel/Fax: 01706 376807

Health & Safety Advice
to small/medium businesses

FOTHERGILL
ENGINEERED FABRICS LTD
Advanced Technical Fabrics

PO Box 1, Summit, Littleborough, OL15 0LU

Tel: 01706 372414

Established 1847

CUT N' DRIED
Hairdressers

42 Victoria Street, Littleborough

Tel: 01706 378984

GREEN BROS
Commercial Vehicle Dismantlers

Frankfort Mill Yard, Halifax Road,
Littleborough, Lancs, OL15 0HL

Tel: 01706 378784

Buyers of all types of vehicles, tractors and plant

DAVID HAUGHTON & SONS
Plastering, Tiling and Property Repairs

Tel: 01706 377990

Zero VAT rated.
Established 1978

ANDREW KELLY & ASSOCIATES
Estate Agents/Financial Advisors

24/26 Hare Hill Road, Littleborough

Tel: 01706 372225

Established 1995

HILTON DOCKER MOULDINGS LTD
Glass Fibre Laminators

Fredo Mill, Foxcroft Street, Littleborough

Tel: 01706 379358

Established 1969

GEORGE KELSALL
Antiquarian and Second Hand Bookseller

22 Church Street, Littleborough

Tel: 01706 370244

Established 1979

MR FRANK MILLS

Hollingworth Lake Caravan Park,
Rakewood, Littleborough, OL15 0AT

Tel: 01706 378661

Established 1961

KING WILLIAM IV INN ("THE KING BILL")
Good food, Ales & Hospitality

Shore Fold, Littleborough

Tel: 01706 372265

HOLLINGWORTH LAKE COUNTRY PARK
Visitor Centre

Rakewood Road, Littleborough, OL15 0AQ

Tel: 01706 373421

Established 1974

LITTLEBOROUGH COACH HOUSE TRUST LTD
Visitor Centre, Coffee Shop & Function Rooms

Lodge Street, Littleborough

Tel: 01706 378481
Established 1979

HOOSON & STUTTARD
Opticians

46 Victoria Street, Littleborough

Patricia M Hooson BSc (Hons) FBCO
Elaine M Stuttard FBDO

Tel: 01706 379783
Established 1985

LITTLEBOROUGH CRICKET CLUB
Mens Cricket, Football & Rugby
Ladies Cricket, Hockey & Rounders
Plus All Indoor Sports

Tel: 01706 374475
Established 1839

SUMMIT POST OFFICE
**Cards, Stationery,
Hardware, Confectionery**

88 Summit, Littleborough

Tel: 01706 378200

Established c1888
In the Firth Family for 88 Years (1911 to date)

UPSTAIRS DOWNSTAIRS
Café - Bistro

32 Church Street (On the Square), Littleborough

Tel: 01706 376844

Established 1991

SWING COTTAGE
**Craftshop, Guesthouse,
Singing Kettle Tea Rooms**

31 Lake Bank, Hollingworth Lake, Littleborough

Tel: 01706 379094

Established 1993

WEST PENNINE INSURANCE GROUP
Insurance Consultants

84 & 109 Church Street, Littleborough

Tel: 01706 377539 & 378990

Established 1961

TINKERBELL
Childrens Day Nursery

William Street, Littleborough

Tel: 01706 377800

Established 1989

The First Private Purpose-built Nursery in Littleborough

WONG HO
Chinese Restaurant

78-80 Church Street,
Littleborough, Lancashire

Tel: 01706 371828

Established 1992 - Michael P L Wong

KEITH UNDERWOOD B.D.S. Edin
Dental Surgeon

33 Hare Hill Road,
Littleborough, OL15 9AD

Tel: 01706 370058

Established 1984

LITTLEBOROUGH HISTORICAL & ARCHEOLOGICAL SOCIETY
**Researching & Preserving
the History of Littleborough**

Established 1972

J. Clegg & Bros (Rakewood) Ltd

RAKEWOOD MILL, LITTLEBOROUGH

Two Hundred Years of Service in the Textile Industry

Millennium Congratulations

Telephone 01706 378342

357

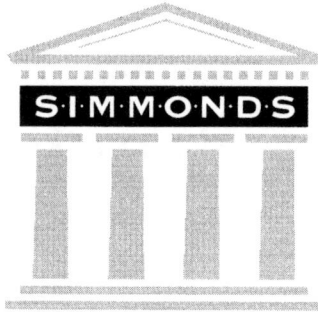

Pennines Township Commitee is pleased to support the production of this volume with a small financial contribution from the Township Fund. Local ward councillors are happy to take the opportunity of joining local people in marking the coming new Millennium. Pennines Township, which includes not only Littleborough, Smithy Bridge & Wardle but additionally Milnrow & Newhey, is characterised by a strong, varied and expert community and voluntary sector. Volunteer effort considerably enhances the quality of life here and this volume is one of the ways in which this valuable contribution is demonstrated.

Pennines Township Committee works alongside local people consulting with them and helping to provide the means through which their views can be heard. Making Council decision making more responsive to local need will lead to greater efficiency in delivery of local services.

The Township office located in Hare Hill House, Littleborough is staffed by the Pennine Township Manager and an Assistant Township Manager. Their work has included compiling a database of all voluntary and community groups so that contact with local people can be regularly and effectively established. The information is available to all Council departments for the purpose of consultation and in support of partnership working. Work in the first years of the Millennium will centre on the establishment of more accessible democratic structures in the Township.

e.r.Williams
(painting contractors) Ltd

Moorfield House, Shore Road, Littleborough, Lancashire, OL15 9LG

Tel: 01706 656966 Fax: 01706 642585

Sainsburys Superstore, Moor Allerton, Leeds (a recently completed contract)

E.R. Williams (Painting Contractors) Limited was established in 1970 by Mr Ray Williams, who had worked in the painting business all his life. He originated from Bala in North Wales and moved to the local area in his twenties, following a spell in National Service. He worked as a painter for Arthur Lords, a well known Rochdale company, for many years before setting up his own business. The company started with only three employees, two have since retired but one is still with the company, which now employs over fifty staff. Ray has taken a back seat in recent years and his son Bill now manages the business, his daughter Ruth is Company Secretary and his other son Peter is a Contracts Manager. As well as family, the company is lucky to have a long serving core workforce in the office and on site, which allows the business to survive (and grow) in the highly competitive construction industry.

Its clients include Bovis Construction plc., TNT (UK) Limted, UMIST, AMEX plc., Trafford M.B.C., McDonalds, Manchester Airport and J Sainsbury plc. The company has carried out many prestigious painting contracts ranging from The Trafford Centre, Manchester and the New Lowry Centre, Salford Quays to the internal redecoration of the Coach House Heritage Centre in Littleborough. The registered office of the company remains Moorfield House, but the business operates from Premier Works, 48-52 Toad Lane in Rochdale. We are looking forward to joining in the celebrations with Littleborough Civic Trust and to continued trading into the new Millennium.

Painting and Decorating Federation

British Decorators Association

A member of the CONSTRUCTION CONFEDERATION

Tygaflor Ltd

Tygaflor Ltd are pleased to support Littleborough Civic Trust in the publication of The Story of Littleborough.

Tygaflor are the world leaders in the manufacturing of P.T.F.E. (Polytetrofluoroethylene) coated fabrics, tapes and conveyor belts and have been in the old Fothergill & Harvey factory for approximately 40 years.

Since Thomas FOTHERGILL & Alexander HARVEY formed the original company over a 150 years ago, the company has been through many changes leading to the Tygaflor company of today.

In 1847 its business was in merchanting cotton yarns and cloths which by 1858 had grown and developed into a textile weaving company which was one of the first companies to produce "Khaki drill" for servicemens uniforms.

Over the next 40 years the company had expanded so much, that it then had 3 mills in the locallity all producing similar textile products. This "Group" became the foundation for development into new generation products resulting in the high technology business of today.

By the mid 1890's, Mr Fothergill and Mr Harvey had the foresight to indentify a need to diversify from the traditional cotton and woollen fabrics and in 1945 established a research unit to investigate and develop alternative high-tech materials.

This unit led the company to PTFE (teflon) and in 1959 the first TYGAFLOR coated fabrics were produced here in Littleborough. The TYGA-FLOR was originally adapted from the Bengal Tiger, because of its links with the army in India through its Khaki drill and "FLOR" because of the "fluor" in Polytetrafluoroethylene.

Such fabrics find themselves in use in a very diverse range of demanding applications and industries ranging from aerospace, automotive, textile, packaging, food processing and electrical. Sales have increased most years since 1959, with the majority being exported to over 60 countries worldwide.

Over recent years the company has had two new owners, a major international company called Courtaulds acquired the business during the late 1980's and after seven years in 1995 they sold the business to our current owners, and former major competitors, the **Chemfab Corporation of America**.

Despite all these changes, the company has maintained its commitment to employing an excellent local workforce to whom we are sincerely grateful for ensuring the continued success of the Tygaflor business. The company remains in good shape, will continue to develop and change along with the worlds' marketplaces and should continue to employ good local people for many years to come.

P.O. Box 2, Summit, Littleborough

INDEX

Notes

1. Page numbers in **bold** refer to main entries
2. An entry followed by *ety* denotes a root Old English Word with examples

LITTLEBOROUGH CIVIC TRUST...

is a voluntary body affiliated to the National Civic Trust. It was established in September 1971 to conserve and enhance the environment of Littleborough and has performed this role consistently throughout the last twenty-five years.

Among its many achievements are:

- an active role in the formation of the Littleborough Local Historical Society and the Coach House Project.
- a continuous review of planning applications, footpath diversions and local authority documents.
- extensive research towards the establishment of Hollingworth Lake Country Park.
- organised fortnightly walks since 1972 to safeguard and enjoy local footpaths.
- numerous tree planting and other environmental improvement operations both alone and in conjunction with other organisations.

The Trust is always happy to welcome new members wishing to participate in its activities.